HAMPSHIRE TREASURES

Published by
HAMPSHIRE COUNTY COUNCIL

MCMLXXXII

IBSN 0·900 908 7·26

12th Century All Saints Church, EAST MEON

HAMPSHIRE TREASURES SURVEY

Volume 6

East Hampshire

CONTENTS

FOREWORD

THE PARISH LISTS: Page   Page

The introductory notes on the title page of each parish list have been contributed by the County Library Department.

Footnote:
From the 1st April 1982 the new parish of Lindford will be formed.
Other minor adjustments to parish boundaries within the East Hampshire District, will also take effect from this date.

FOREWORD

I feel greatly honoured to be invited to write the Foreword to Volume VI of Hampshire Treasures — East Hampshire, outstanding both for its scenery and its variety. William Cobbett in 1825, refers to The Beauties, the matchless beauties of the scene when describing the Beech Hanger which runs for nearly twenty miles from Selborne to Butser, the spine of the District.

Alton and Petersfield, as shown by their many inns, were both "posting centres"; before becoming market places they grew with the advent of the railways and are the only towns in the District. Each has much of interest.

Alton has St. Lawrence Church whose doors were damaged in the Civil War. The Butts, where archers may have trained for Crecy, the Lord Mayor Treloar Hospital, famous for its orthopaedic work, and the Curtis Museum, which houses agricultural relics, are amongst other places of interest.

Petersfield, famous in Tudor times for its cloth manufacture and leather industry, has many fine buildings; an equestrian statue of William of Orange 'avenger of liberty' stands in the market place; the Heath reclaimed from swamp in 1867 and the large attractive Pond, constructed in 1750, are other features of interest.

There are some thirty four parishes abounding in charming churches, houses, cottages and inns; an oast house at Headley and a windmill at Chalton are unusual. At Chawton we find the home and museum of Jane Austen, whilst nearby Selborne houses both the Gilbert White and Oates Museums at the Wakes.

Incidentally, Gilbert White in 1770 refers to "Nore Hill", a noble chalk promontory sending two streams to different seas. The Rother joins the Arun in Sussex and the Wey finally reaches the Thames.

William Cobbett, describing the source of the River Itchen at Ropley Dene writes "This Vale of Meadows — few spots in England more fertile or more pleasant and none, I believe, more healthy". Of East Meon, he writes "Here is a fine valley" and of the magnificent twelfth century All Saint's Church with its Norman tower he asked "Where did the hands come from to make it"? Here also is the Court House where the Bishops of Winchester held Manorial Courts.

What would Cobbett write today? The soil in its wide variety has not changed; he "quitted flint and chalk and downs and took to sand, clay, hedges and coppice" journeying south of Petersfield. He would still find woods and pastures, even hops. Nature created the hills and valleys; man has clad them mostly for better but sometimes for worse!

Archaeology reveals evidence of thousands of years of man's habitation, with records of Bronze and Iron Age occupation. A Roman coin hoard found at Blackmoor confirms Roman occupation in the area.

The Saxons built their hill top village at Chalton, and evidence of their work is still found in some churches.

Of particular interest is the church at Colemore with its leper peephole, and the lovely church at Hartley Mauditt, isolated in a field since the surrounding village was deserted, due to emparkment of the surrounding land.

Both the Royal Navy and the Army are based in the area, and whilst the RAF has left Lasham, whence fighters flew in the war, the airfield has become widely known as a glider centre.

The County Council has established the Queen Elizabeth Country Park beneath Butser Hill (at 889ft the highest in Hampshire) and where Rudyard Kipling in his "Run of the Downs" concludes:—

> "And when you end on the Hampshire side,
> Butsers' old as Time and Tide"

Incidentally, when Cobbett rode from Hawkley to Greatham he commented "I am thinking whether I ever did see worst roads" (memories of the merit of the high road over the low road). We are reminded of these ancient routes by pictures of the Travellers Way at Grayshott and the open track at West Tisted.

In this volume there are many splendid photographs which I hope will encourage people to explore the District. They can also seek out the Sites of Special Scientific Interest which abound, especially in the north east, as well as some of the forty Scheduled Ancient Monuments.

This volume, like the others, is, of course, a "combined operation". Volunteer field correspondents have given many hours both outside and inside their homes, compiling these records for the Planning Department of the County Council. Their work will ensure that these treasures are neither forgotten nor, we trust, damaged, and will open the eyes of many to the beauty and the history around them.

We thank these volunteers, of three generations, most sincerely and I am sure that this volume will be widely studied and enjoyed.

James Scott

Lt. Col. Sir James Scott, B.T.., D.L.

INTRODUCTION

Origin of Survey

The survey springs out of the two "Countryside in 1970" conferences called on the Duke of Edinburgh's initiative in November 1963 and 1965. It became clear in the course of these conferences that many organisations were studying various aspects of human impact on the countryside without any form of liaison between them. One way of improving this liaison was seen to be the creation of a single record of all the "Treasures", county by county, so that the effects both of time and of development could be known and assessed. The second conference defined a Countryside Treasure as:—

> "Those natural or man-made features of the countryside which are of public interest by reason of their aesthetic, archaeological, historic, scenic, scientific, sociological or traditional interest, and whose deterioration or destruction would represent a serious loss to our heritage".

The Survey in Hampshire

The Hampshire County Council decided to begin a Treasures Survey and during 1967—68 a pilot survey was started in the Petersfield Urban and Rural Districts. Subsequently, the work has been developed as a joint project between the County Planning Department and the Hampshire Council of Community Service. The survey work has been carried out by volunteer Field Correspondents, recruited in the rural districts through the parish councils; through its contacts with the parish councils the Council of Community Service has been particularly helpful in ensuring co-operation. The survey material was transferred, in the Planning Department, onto draft lists, which were used to prepare the draft reports. It is the revision of these draft reports which has led to the publication of the "Hampshire Volumes", containing definitive lists of treasures within each of the county Districts.

This is the sixth volume of the series, and covers the whole of the area administered by the East Hampshire District Council.

Future Volumes	**Published Volumes**
Havant Borough	1. Winchester City District May 1979
Portsmouth City	2. Basingstoke & Deane Borough
Southampton City	1979
Eastleigh Borough	3. Hart District & Rushmoor Borough
Test Valley Borough	April 1980
Fareham Borough	4. Winchester City June 1980
Gosport Borough	5. New Forest District February 1981

Status of "Treasures"

The lists of Treasures include sites, features and buildings which already have some form of protection by law; the following is a summary of the main categories protected and the legislation protecting them.

What is protected	Legislation	Section
Areas of Outstanding Natural Beauty (AONB) County Open Spaces (COS)	) National Parks Act) 1949 supplemented) by Countryside Act 1968	37 1
Sites of Special Scientific Interest (SSSI), Nature Reserves	) National Parks Act) 1949 and Country-) side Act 1968	15,16,17
Tree Preservation Orders (TPOs) Buildings of Special Architectural of Historic Interest, Conservation Areas (CA)	)) Town and Country) Planning Act 1972)	60 54 277
Ancient Monuments	Historic Buildings and Ancient Monuments Act 1953	

The degree of protection afforded under these acts varies; in few cases can it be assumed that statutory protection means that the site will remain unchanged in its existing use. Protection can be taken away, sometimes (e.g. Ancient Monuments) without any public notice being given although, of course, the owner and the local authorities are informed. Generally, however, the intention to develop sites or buildings that fall into the classes listed will be advertised under the planning acts in local newspapers. The public have the right to object and the local planning authority must take account of their comments.

In addition to these protected items, the survey now lists for the first time those items judged by local people to be of special interest in the locality. It not only gives to the County and District Councils a record of this local judgment, but it makes available to everyone in Hampshire a guide, by local people, to their own parishes.

However, the inclusion of an item in this list as a Treasure confers no protection per se except that of recognition and recorded knowledge. The lists inform the local authority that the Treasure is valued locally and the reason why.

CLASSIFICATION

Group A   Natural Features; such as trees, fine views and Nature Reserves, ponds, etc.

Group B   Archaeological; Sites and Remains including:

              Ancient Monuments
              Stone Age
              Bronze Age
              Iron Age
              Roman
              Dark Age

Group C   Footpaths and Bridleways; including Old Travel Ways

Group D   Buildings, Monuments and Engineering Works

Group E   Street Patterns, Street Furniture and Open Spaces

Group F   Historical or Literary Associations

Notes on Classification

(i)   Treasures are listed parish by parish.

(ii)   Within each parish, Treasures are classified according to the list set out above.

(iii)   Treasures are listed in chronological order where the age is known, the exceptions being the towns of Alton and Petersfield, where for ease of reference entries in Group D have been placed in street order.

(iv)   Location is given, usually by the name of the property or feature; always by O.S. grid reference.

(v)   Grid references are generally six figure and may be read off all O.S. scales down to 1" = 1 mile.

(vi)   Many of the archaeological entries are taken from the records of the Ordnance Survey and will, as a rule, be recorded on the 6" to 1 mile series (1:12,500).

ABBREVIATIONS

A.O.N.B.:	Areas of Outstanding Natural Beauty
C:	Century
C.A.:	Conservation Area
C.O.S.:	County Open Space
E.H.D.C.:	East Hampshire District Council
N.P. Act:	National Parks Act, 1949
O.S.A.:	Ordnance Survey Antiquity
P.H.F.C.:	Proceedings of the Hampshire Field Club
S.A.M.:	Scheduled Ancient Monument
S.S.S.I.:	Sites of Special Scientific Interest
T. & C.P. Act:	Town and Country Planning Act, 1972
T.P.O.:	Tree Preservation Order
V.C.H.:	Victoria County History Hampshire
Vol.:	Volume

ACKNOWLEDGEMENTS

Without a great deal of help, both from private individuals voluntarily given, or from public authorities freely made available, preparation of these volumes would not have been possible. The Hampshire County Council and Hampshire Council of Community Service wish to acknowledge particulary the help and valuable advice of:

The East Hampshire District Council

The Parish Councils

The Field Correspondents

The Ordnance Survey

The Royal Commission on Historic Monuments

The Department of the Environment

The Local Societies

The Panel of Experts:

        Dr. D. P. S. Peacock
        Dr. E. A. Course, BSc (Econ), PhD
        R. Page Esq.
        P. H. Shelford Esq., BSc, DipEd, SGS
        J. Arlott Esq.
        D. W. Lloyd Esq.
        V. W. Emery, Esq.

Photographs by E. N. Lane, Hampshire County Planning Department.

The Local Planning Authority for the area covered by this volume is the East Hampshire District Council.

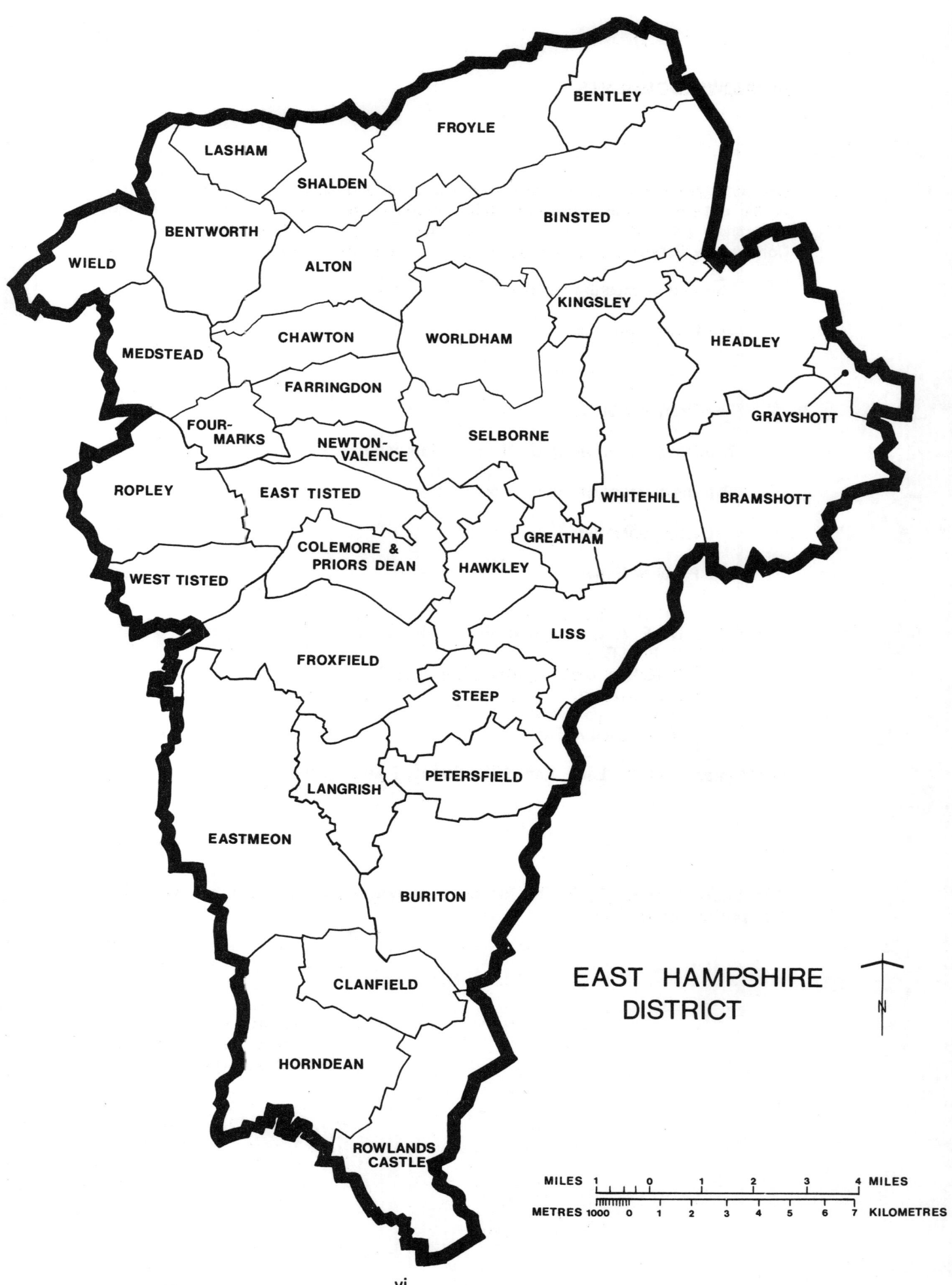

EAST HAMPSHIRE
DISTRICT

ALTON

The market town of Alton lies eighteen miles north-east of Winchester and for a long time was famous for its hops and breweries.

Edmund Spenser lived here circa 1590, as did Cardinal Newman from 1816 — 1819. Eggars Grammar School was founded in 1641. The town includes several fine Georgian buildings.

William Curtis, the botanist, was born here in 1746 and the Curtis Museum was founded in 1855. The Lord Mayor Treloar Hospital was opened here and has become world famous as a great orthopaedic hospital. The church, which is mainly Perpendicular but with a fine Norman tower, was the scene of the death of the Royalist, Colonel Boles, during a fierce fight with Parliamentary forces in 1643.

1

Description and Date	Remarks	Protection	Grid Ref. and Punchcard No.

Group A — Natural Features

Trees	Whitedown Lane. Scots pines, elms and beech standing in the area. Centred on grid reference.	T.P.O. No. 248	SU 704 389 0201 09
Trees	All Saints Vicarage. Horse chestnuts, hornbeam, beech and yew standing in the grounds.	T.P.O. No. 252	SU 714 387 0206 10
Trees	West Bank, Basingstoke Road. Several species including silver firs, maple, birch and horse chestnut.	T.P.O. No. 379	SU 711 387 0206 09A
Trees	Several species in the area of Well House Road, Beech.	T.P.O. No. 491	SU 695 389 0201 08
Trees	Holybourne Cottage, Holybourne. Species include copper beech, sycamore, cedar and maple.	T.P.O. No. 529 C.A.	SU 733 407 0202 25
Trees	On land bordering River Wey. Several trees of differing species.	T.P.O. No. 19 E.H.D.C.	SU 714 394 0204 101
Trees	On land between Lenten Street and River Wey. Several trees of differing species.	T.P.O. No. 19 E.H.D.C. C.A.	SU 713 394 0204 100
Trees	The Butts. Several trees of differing species standing in the area centred on grid reference.	T.P.O. No. 18 E.H.D.C. C.A.	SU 710 385 0206 23
Tree	No. 4, Railway Terrace, Papermill Lane. A single small-leafed lime.	T.P.O. No. 25	SU 722 397 0205 63
Trees	Chawton Park Road. Several trees of differing species standing in the area. Centred on grid reference.	T.P.O. No. 30 E.H.D.C.	SU 708 381 0201 25
Tree	No. 11, Fantails, Wooteys Estate. A pendunculate oak standing in the front garden.	T.P.O. No. 31 E.H.D.C.	SU 716 405 0203 07
Trees	Cramptons, Wellhouse Road, Beech. Several trees of differing species standing in this area.	T.P.O. No. 32 E.H.D.C.	SU 692 387 0201 26
Trees	Bartons End, Lenten Street. Several trees of differing species standing in the area.	T.P.O. No. 55 E.H.D.C.	SU 714 393 0204 102
Trees	Land at Wykeham House, Kings Road. Several species of trees standing in the area. Centred on grid reference.	T.P.O. No. 64 E.H.D.C.	SU 707 389 0204 24
Trees	Within the curtilage of the town centre there are many trees, some of which are the subject of this 'Blanket' order, which is centred on the grid reference given. The trees include two hornbeams at the Vicarage, and a mulberry and two Lawson's cypress' at the rear of buildings in the High Street. Other species include sycamore, copper beech, yew, lime and ash.	T.P.O. No. 453 C.A.	SU 718 393 0204 103

Group A — (cont.)

Description and Date	Remarks	Protection	Grid Ref. and Punchcard No.
Trees	Holybourne Lodge, London Road. A group of trees consisting of limes and a single beech.	T.P.O. No. 708 C.A.	SU 734 408 0202 44
Trees	Mount Dassell, Kings Road. Several trees of various species standing in the area centred on grid reference.	T.P.O. No. 643	SU 709 390 0206 25
Trees	West Dene, Medstead Road, Beech. Several species of different varieties.	T.P.O. No. 535	SU 683 387 0201 27
Trees	Will Hall Farm, Basingstoke Road. Area of beech trees of various types, centred on grid reference.	T.P.O. No. 16 E.H.D.C.	SU 706 391 0201 28
Trees	No. 50, Kings Road. Eight beech trees, one purple sycamore, three limes and a variegated sycamore standing along the north east boundary.	T.P.O. No. 83 E.H.D.C.	SU 707 389 0201 26
Trees	Ashdell Road. Trees of various species within the curtilage of Ashdell Estate.	T.P.O. No. 289	SU 723 391 0205 22

Group B — Archaeological

Bronze Age

Description and Date	Remarks	Protection	Grid Ref. and Punchcard No.
Implement	Great Wood. Well-preserved, lightly patinated bronze, looped palstave with 'trident ribbing' and deep stop ridge, found in heap of worked flints. Now in Winchester Museum. O.S.A. No. SU64 SE15. Ref: P.H.F.C., Vol. 9, 1920—4, p.p. 403—4.		SU 698 401 0201 05
Potsherds	The Butts. Two sherds from cinerary urns, found in the C.19. Now stored in Alton Museum. O.S.A. No. SU73 NW11.	C.A.	SU 711 385 0206 07

Roman

Description and Date	Remarks	Protection	Grid Ref. and Punchcard No.
Pottery	Lenten House. Approximately twenty five sherds, including one or two of New Forest ware, found in 1946. Now in Alton Museum. O.S.A. No. SU73 NW12.	C.A.	SU 715 393 0204 12
Settlement Site	Cuckoo Corner, Neatham. A considerable amount of material, including coins, has been excavated from this site, and is now in Alton Museum. Evidence would point to either a mansion or fortlet of C.1—4. being located on this site. O.S.A. No. SU74 SW14.	S.A.M. No. 420	SU 739 413 020230A
Remains	Mosaic pavement and coins found in the C.18. Exact find spots not known. O.S.A. No. SU73 NW4. Ref: 1. V.C.H., Vol. 1, p. 306. 2. V.C.H., Vol. 3, p. 308.	C.A.	SU 710 390 0204 20

Description and Date	Remarks	Protection	Grid Ref. and Punchcard No.

Group B — (cont.)

Description and Date	Remarks	Protection	Grid Ref. and Punchcard No.
Burials	High Street. Graves with pottery, including two complete jugs, a lamp and an onyx ring etc. Found circa 1840. Now in Alton Museum. O.S.A. No. SU73 NW17. Ref: 1. Natural History and Antiquities of Selborne, (White). 2. V.C.H., Vol. 1, p. 306.		SU 716 390 0205 21
Coins	Truncheaunts Farm. Bronze coin, a dupondius of Claudius, found in a field and presented to Alton Museum in 1932. O.S.A. No. SU73 NW18. Ref: County Museum Service, (Index No. 401. 33/58).		SU 726 389 0206 08
Building (Site)	Will Hall. Finds include hypocaust tiles, fragments of flanged pie dish and other sherds. O.S.A. No. SU73 NW21. Ref: P.H.F.C., Vol. 18, 1951—3, p.p. 125—138.		SU 704 389 0201 04
Coin	Halterworthy, Kings Road. Commemorative coin of Claudius II, found in 1955. Now in Alton Museum. O.S.A. No. SU73 NW23. Ref: Alton Museum (Access No. 1956/41).		SU 709 391 0206 09
Coin	Nether Street. Coin of Constantine the Great, found in 1940. Now in Alton Museum. O.S.A. No. SU73 NW25. Ref: Alton Museum (Access No. 401 33/78).		SU 719 395 0205 20
Coin, Tiles and Flints	Field at Wyards Farm. Coin of Vespasian, pieces of tile and large flints found in 1956. Site under pasture. O.S.A. No. SU63 NE5.		SU 698 388 0201 06
Remains	Pottery, glass, tiles and Iron Age brooches found in March 1891 in the grounds of Westbrook House (now a public park). O.S.A. No. SU73 NW26. Ref: P.H.F.C., Vol. 16, 1944—6, p. 310.		SU 714 392 0204 15
Coin	Barton End, Lenten Street. Coin of Constantine II found in 1938, now in Alton Museum. O.S.A. No. SU73 NW2.		SU 713 393 0204 13
Remains	Florence Treloar School. Roughly paved floor, fragments of coarse grey pottery and nails found in 1963. O.S.A. No. SU74 SW10. Ref: Letter (24.6.64) and diary note in Alton Museum.		SU 730 410 0202 27
Coin	Holybourne Churchyard. Coin of Constantine the Great (London Mint) found in 1936. O.S.A. No. SU74 SW13. Ref: Alton Museum (Access No. 401 33/59).	C.A.	SU 732 412 0202 28

Group B — (cont.)

Description and Date	Remarks	Protection	Grid Ref. and Punchcard No.
Pottery and Glass	Rim of small glass bottle and approximately twenty sherds found 1937 in grounds of house known as Cobbers. O.S.A. No. SU73 NW9.		SU 714 393 0204 14
Roman Town (Site)	Small unplanned town covering approximately 13 ha discovered 1969 during construction of Alton by-pass. Remains of buildings of crude chalk block construction found, several apparently used as bronze smelting workshops. O.S.A. No. SU74 SW14. Ref: 1. Hants Field Club Newsletter, No. 3, 1972, (Graham). p. 10. 2. D.O.E. Archaeological Excavation, 1970, (Graham), p. 64.		SU 740 411 0202 26

Saxon

Description and Date	Remarks	Protection	Grid Ref. and Punchcard No.
Potsherd	Sherd of a skillet found at Queens Park Nurseries, now in Alton Museum. O.S.A. No. SU73 NW20.		SU 706 390 0206 06
Burial Ground	Mount Pleasant Road. Forty-nine burials, (the majority, cremations) discovered during excavations in 1959, 1960—3. Grave goods include beads, spear-heads, shield bosses and a Roman urn. Majority of finds with the D.O.E.; remainder in possession of the County Museum Service. O.S.A. No. SU73 NW1. Ref: Mediaeval Archaeology, Vol. 14, 1960, p. 134.		SU 718 388 0206 05

Group D — Buildings, Monuments and Engineering Works

Amery Hill

Description and Date	Remarks	Protection	Grid Ref. and Punchcard No.
Farmhouse C.18	Amery Farm House. 2 storeys plus attic; three bays, the central one advanced a little. Red brick structure, tiled mansard roof with three dormers. Ground floor with central recessed door set in simple pilastered doorcase and flanked by flush sash windows. Brick band at first floor level. Sash windows. Brick dentil eaves cornice. Later addition at back.	T. & C.P. Act C.A.	SU 715 396 0204 18
Barn C.18	To east of Amery Farm House. Four bays long. Timber frame with brick infilling and old tile hipped roof.	T. & C.P. Act C.A.	SU 715 396 0204 18A
Cottage C.18	Amery Cottage. Wholly irregular composition, partly 1-storey plus attic and partly of 2 storeys. Partly of mediaeval masonry and flint, partly of brick and partly tile-hung. Tiled roof. Irregular fenestration by casements, mostly with leaded lights but one tall window with glazing bars.	T. & C.P. Act C.A.	SU 716 395 0204 05

Description and Date	Remarks	Protection	Grid Ref. and Punchcard No.

Group D — (cont.)

Amery Street

House C.16	No. 1. 2 storeys and attic. Colourwashed brick. Tiled roof. Seven bays. Ground floor with flush windows. In second bay a simple timber door. In fifth bay, a modern door set in slightly projecting brick surround with moulded stone pediment over. Broad band at first floor level. First floor flush windows with glazing bars. Moulded wood eaves cornice with irregular brackets. Three pedimented dormers.	T. & C.P. Act C.A.	SU 715 393 0204 01A
House C.16	Nos. 2 and 3. 2 storeys. Single tiled roof. No. 2, three bays. Colourwashed brick. Ground floor with central door flanked by two wide casement windows. Broad band at first floor level. First floor with central narrow casement window flanked by two wide casements. No. 3, two irregular bays. Timber-framed with some herringbone brickwork. Ground floor with door and wide casement window on right. First floor with one narrow and one wide casement.	T. & C.P. Act C.A.	SU 715 393 0204 01B
Building C.18	No. 16. Ye Olde Leathern Bottle House. 2 storeys. Two irregular bays plus a lower single storeyed C.19 addition on right. Timber-framed. Cement rendered. Tiled roof half hipped at one end. All windows metal casements except those in later addition.	T. & C.P. Act C.A.	SU 716 393 0204 50
Cottages (2) C.19	Nos. 23, 25. 2 storeys. Brick, partly chequered. Slate roof. Three bays wide. Ground floor has three windows and two simple doors beneath slated gable hoods. First floor has 3-segment-headed windows. Brick dentil eaves cornice. Formerly three cottages.	T. & C.P. Act C.A.	SU 716 394 0204 03

Anstey Mill Lane

Mill C.19	Anstey Mill. Coursed stone with brick dressings. Almost completely in ruins although it still retains its large iron water-wheel.	T. & C.P. Act C.A.	SU 721 399 0205 30
House C.19	No. 1. 2 storeys. Brick structure with pantile roof. Single bay. Ground floor with a door within a wooden tiled porch and a single window. Modern casement windows.	T. & C.P. Act	SU 729 400 0205 31
House C.19	No. 2. 2 storeys. Brick structure. Slate roof. Three bays. Ground floor with central door beneath a simple hood on brackets and two recessed sash windows with glazing bars. First floor with three recessed sash windows with glazing bars. On the right a single storey lean-to addition.	T. & C.P. Act	SU 729 400 0205 32

Description and Date	Remarks	Protection	Grid Ref. and Punchcard No.
Group D — (cont.)			
Cottage C.18	Anstey Cottage. 2 storeys plus attic. Three bays. Colourwashed stucco. Old tile roof with tile-hung gable ends. Ground floor with central 6-panel door in architrave surround within a modern porch. Single window either side. First floor with three windows.	T. & C.P. Act	SU 727 403 020224A
Anstey Road			
Building C.18	Alton General Hospital (Stores Block). 2 storeys and attic. Red brick. Slate mansard roof. Thirteen bays wide, the central one advanced and pedimented. Formerly the Alton Work-house. Erected 1793.	T. & C.P. Act	SU 724 399 0205 16
Building C.17	Amery Hill School. Formerly Eggar's Grammar School, founded in 1642 by John Eggar whose initials, in iron, are in the left hand gable. 2 storeys plus attic, three bays wide. Red brick, tiled roof with central stack of four chimneys. Ground floor with central ledged oak door, with original knocker, in heavy moulded oak frame within later porch flanked on either side by two 5-light, mullioned and transomed casement windows. Moulded band at first floor level. Mullioned first floor and attic windows. A plain band at foot of gables is carried down over windows to form a drip mould. Later additions at rear and left-hand side. O.S.A. No. SU74 SW11. Ref: 1. V.C.H., Vol. 2, p.p. 367, 387, 482. 2. History of Alton, (Curtis) p.p. 130—131, 300—1.	T. & C.P. Act	SU 724 400 0205 17
Houses (6) C.19	Nos. 69—79 (odd). 2 storeys. Colourwashed brick. Slate roof. Two bays wide. Ground floor with, on the left, a recessed sash window beneath a blank tympanum, on the right a simple door, also with blank tympanum. First floor with two square recessed sash windows. No. 69, has contemporary shop window with pilasters left and right and entablature over, replacing ground floor sash.	T. & C.P. Act	SU 726 401 0202 30
House C.19	No. 93. Thorn Cottage. 2 storeys. Stucco. Slate roof with flanking chimneys. Original house three bays wide. Ground floor with two tall windows and a central door with depressed arched head and radiating fanlight set within a frame of quadrant doric columns. Tuscan porch. First floor with three square windows. Later single bay extension.	T. & C.P. Act	SU 727 413 0202 23
House C.18	No. 95, Anstey Close. 2 storeys. Pebble-dashed walls. Tiled roof, hipped at one end. Central door in deep reveal, within Tuscan porch.	T. & C.P. Act	SU 727 403 0202 22

Description and Date	Remarks	Protection	Grid Ref. and Punchcard No.
Group D — (cont.)			
House C.19	No. 97, Anstey House. 2 storeys. Four bays wide. Stuccoed. Slate roof. Facade to the road with four tall recessed sash windows on ground floor, four similar but square windows on first floor. Central door with later lean-to porch, within a conservatory. Single bay extension on right.	T. & C.P. Act	SU 726 402 0202 31
Houses (2) C.18	Nos. 101, 101A. 2 storeys. Colourwashed brick. Old tile roof with flanking chimneys. Ground floor with central ledged door with modern porch. Two 2-light segment headed casement windows.	T. & C.P. Act	SU 726 402 0202 32
House C.18	No. 103, Mayfield School. 2 storeys. Pebble-dash walls. Hipped old tile roof. Later additions.		SU 727 403 0202 24B
Houses (6) C.19	Nos. 105—115. 2 storeys. Each house two bays wide and gabled. Colourwashed brick. Tile roof. Ground floor with a simple door on the left and a square sash window on the right. First floor with a single central sash window. No. 115 has a contemporary shop front and lean-to extension on left.	T. & C.P. Act	SU 727 403 0202 33
House C.19	No. 82, Anstey Gate. 2 storeys. Colour-washed brick walls. Tiled roof. Casement windows. Lean-to extension.		SU 727 403 0202 24
House C.19	Chandos Lodge. 2 storeys. Colourwashed brick structure. Slate roof. Diamond-shafted chimney. 1-storey extension.	T. & C.P. Act	SU 727 403 0202 21
Basingstoke Road			
Farmhouse and Outbuildings C.18	Will Hall Farm House. 2 storeys plus attic. Five bays wide, the central one pedimented. Brick structure, tiled hipped roof. Ground floor with central door under moulded and pedimented hood. Sash windows. 2-storey extension to left. Extensive C.17 to C.19 outbuildings in rectangular group to left.	T. & C.P. Act	SU 706 392 0201 01
Farmhouse C.17	Wyards Farm House. Dated 1691 in black headers. 3 storeys plus attic. Six bays wide, the third from the left advanced a little. Brick structure, tiled hipped roof. Mid C.18 doorcase with fluted pilasters and triglyph frieze. Brick band at first floor level. Mullioned and transomed 4-light casement windows.	T. & C.P. Act	SU 698 388 0201 02
Granary C.18	Wyards Farm. Small, weatherboarded, with half-hipped old tile roof.	T. & C.P. Act	SU 698 388 0201 02A

Description and Date	Remarks	Protection	Grid Ref. and Punchcard No.

Group D — (cont.)

Butts Road

Description and Date	Remarks	Protection	Grid Ref. and Punchcard No.
Inn C.19	The Dukes Head. 2 storeys. Colourwashed brick. Slate roof. Main entrance with Tuscan porch. Sash windows. James Burt, noted cricketer, who apparently weighed twenty two stones, lived here.	T. & C.P. Act	SU 714 389 0206 03
House C.18	No. 64, Butts House. 2 storeys. Three bays. Brick structure. Tile roof with flanking chimneys. Ground floor with central door within modern porch. Left and right single flush window with segmented heads. Extension to the right.	T. & C.P. Act	SU 711 386 0206 20
Cottages (3) C.18	Nos. 1—3, French Horn Cottages, (The Butts). 1-storey and attic. Brick structure. Casement windows. Tiled roof. Modernised.	C.A.	SU 711 385 0206 01

Church Lane, Holybourne

Description and Date	Remarks	Protection	Grid Ref. and Punchcard No.
Houses (2) C.18	Nos. 2 and 4. 2 storeys. Painted brick. Tile roof. Central chimney astride the ridge. First floor has single casement window. Ground floor has simple door and single broad segment-headed casement window.	T. & C.P. Act C.A.	SU 735 410 0202 34
House C.18	No. 8. 1-storey and attic. Timber-framed with colourwashed brick infilling. Thatched roof, with two eyebrow dormers. Ground floor has three casement windows. Simple door. To the right a single storey 1-bay weather boarded lean-to extension.	T. & C.P. Act C.A.	SU 735 410 0202 35
House C.19	No. 20. Manor House. 2 storeys. Red brick structure. Hipped slate roof. Sash windows. Modern extension to the right.	T. & C.P. Act C.A.	SU 731 411 0202 20
House C.18	No. 22. The Bourne. 2 storeys. Colourwashed brick. Old tile roof. Sash windows. Central modern glazed door. Simplified Tuscan porch. Single-storey modern extension to the right.	T. & C.P. Act C.A.	SU 733 411 0202 15
Church C.12	Holy Rood Church. Norman Nave and tower, C.13 chancel. Extensively restored in 1879 when the north aisle was also rebuilt. O.S.A. No. SU74 SW12. Ref: 1. Buildings of England, Hants and I.O.W. (Pevsner & Lloyd), p. 295. 2. V.C.H., Vol. 2, p.p. 514—5.	T. & C.P. Act C.A.	SU 732 412 0202 17
Farmhouse C.17/18	Manor Farm House, 2 storeys. Five bays. Brick structure. Old tile hipped roof. Ground floor has plain central door with rectangular fanlight over. Sash windows. Modern extension at rear.	T. & C.P. Act C.A.	SU 732 413 0202 13

Description and Date	Remarks	Protection	Grid Ref. and Punchcard No.

Group D — (cont.)

Description and Date	Remarks	Protection	Grid Ref. and Punchcard No.
Cottage C.18	Church Cottage. 2 storeys. Three bays. Colourwashed brick. Old tile roof. Casement windows. Door with small trellis porch to left.	T. & C.P. Act C.A.	SU 733 412 0202 14
House C.17	Holybourne House. 2 storeys. Five bays. Timber-framed, brick, old tile roof. Ground floor has central modern porch. Mullioned and transomed leaded casement windows. Brick band at first floor level. To the right a projecting gable wing with tile hanging. Single rectangular window running through ground and first floors.	T. & C.P. Act C.A.	SU 734 411 0202 19

Church Street

Description and Date	Remarks	Protection	Grid Ref. and Punchcard No.
Almshouses (4) C.17	Nos. 1, 2, 3, 4, Geales Almshouses. 2 storeys. Brick, tiled roof. On ground floor in each half of the block there is a central pair of oak doors with heavy wrought iron strap hinges. Mullioned and lattice-paned windows. All windows have stuccoed coverings to mullions and frames. Founded 1653. Ref: V.C.H., Vol. 2, p. 483. 2. History of Alton 1896 (Curtis) p. 104.	T. & C.P. Act C.A.	SU 718 395 0203 03
House C.18	No. 10. 2 storeys. Three bays. Brick structure with tiled roof. Ground floor with modern door on left and two windows. First floor has two windows complete with their Gothic glazing bars.	T. & C.P. Act	SU 718 395 0204 60
Houses (2) C.19	Nos. 15 and 15A. Early C.19. Perhaps originally one dwelling. 2 storeys, three gabled and barge-boarded bays. Rendered. Slate roof. Square windows in moulded surrounds with original glazing bars. No. 15, ground floor with door under simple hood and flanked by windows. No. 15A, ground floor with modern door to left and carriage door to right.	T. & C.P. Act C.A.	SU 717 395 0203 04
Cottage C.19	No. 16. Bell Cottage. Altered. 2 storeys, two bays. In addition a single-storeyed gabled and barge-boarded wing to the left, and a little advanced from the front of the house. Tile hung, slate roof. Ground floor with door in arched opening to the right and a window to the left. First floor with window on left. Both windows with original glazing bars.	T. & C.P. Act C.A.	SU 717 395 0203 05
Church C.15	St. Lawrence. Perpendicular church built round a Norman crossing tower. All four Norman arches still there. Jacobean pulpit. Bullet holes in south door from Parliamentary troops who attacked Royalist troops taking refuge in church. O.S.A. No. SU73 NW28. Ref: Buildings of England, Hants and I.O.W., (Pevsner & Lloyd), p. 76.	T. & C.P. Act C.A.	SU 717 396 0204 02

Description and Date	Remarks	Protection	Grid Ref. and Punchcard No.

Group D — (cont.)

Description and Date	Remarks	Protection	Grid Ref. and Punchcard No.
Inn C.18	The Eight Bells. 2 storeys. Painted brick, tiled roof. Canted front with irregular fenestration. Casement windows, some with segmental heads. Brick dentil eaves cornice.	T. & C.P. Act C.A.	SU 717 396 0203 06
Building C.17/18	Friends' House. 1-storey, with cottage of 1-storey and attic under same roof. Stuccoed walls. Tile roof. 2-storey, tile-hung projecting wing to right with entrance to hall which has large sash windows. Red brick wall to road has date 1672 in black headers. O.S.A. No. SU73 NW37. Ref: History of Alton, (Curtis), p. 134.	T. & C.P. Act C.A.	SU 717 396 0203 01

Cross and Pillory Lane

Description and Date	Remarks	Protection	Grid Ref. and Punchcard No.
House C.17/18	No. 7. C.17 with front altered in C.18. 2 storeys. Timber-framed, stuccoed plinth, colour washed brick. Tiled roof. Central door flanked by single bay windows rising through 2 storeys. Stone stringcourse at first floor level. Central small stone mullioned casement window with leaded lights.	T. & C.P. Act	SU 715 392 0204 27
Building C.17	No. 8. Shoestring. 2 storeys. Timber-framed with brick infilling. Tiled roof. Ground floor with central doorway flanked by pilasters and with a modern shop front on the left and a tripartite window on the right. First floor with sash windows, coving and tile-hung gable towards market square.	T. & C.P. Act	SU 716 392 0204 28

High Street

Description and Date	Remarks	Protection	Grid Ref. and Punchcard No.
House C.17	No. 1. 2 storeys plus attic, five bays wide. Rendered front, brick sidewalls. Tile hung gables. Tile roof. Late C.18 asymmetrical porch. Sash windows, complete with glazing bars. Moulded stringcourse at first floor level.	T. & C.P. Act C.A.	SU 719 394 0205 12
Buildings (2) C.18	Nos. 3 and 5. 2 storeys. Painted brick. Tiled roof. No. 3 two bays wide. Modern shop front. No. 5 one bay wide. Doorway flanked by pilasters supporting entablature on left, modern shop front on right.	T. & C.P. Act C.A.	SU 718 394 0205 33
Building C.18	No. 15. 2 storeys. Stucco. Tiled roof. Three bays wide. Modern shop front.	T. & C.P. Act C.A.	SU 718 394 0205 34
Building C.18	Nos. 19 and 19A. 2 storeys. Painted brick. Tiled roof. Four bays. C.19 shop front with door on left.	T. & C.P. Act C.A.	SU 718 393 0205 35
Barn C.17	At rear of No. 23. 2 storeys. Timber-framed with some brick infilling. Tiled roof of Queen-post construction. Four bays long.	T. & C.P. Act C.A.	SU 718 393 0205 36

Description and Date	Remarks	Protection	Grid Ref. and Punchcard No.
Group D — (cont.)			
Building C.18	The Swan Hotel. 2 storeys plus attic. Eight bays wide, painted brick. Tiled roof. Tuscan pedimented porch surmounted by a wrought iron inn sign.	T. & C.P. Act C.A.	SU 717 393 0205 11
Building C.18	No. 31. 3 storeys. Two bays. Stuccoed. Ground floor with C.19 shop front. Door within pedimented doorcase. Later single bay window on first floor, two sash windows on second floor. Parapet and blocking course.	T. & C.P. Act C.A.	SU 717 393 0205 37
Building C.18	No. 33. 3 storeys. Two bays. Stuccoed. Ground floor with modern shop front. Later single bay window on first floor. Two sash windows on second floor. Parapet and blocking course.	T. & C.P. Act C.A.	SU 717 393 0205 38
Building C.18	No. 35. 2 storeys plus attic. Two bays. Painted brick, tiled roof. Ground floor with modern shop front. Two sash windows on second floor. Single dormer window in roof.	T. & C.P. Act C.A.	SU 717 393 0205 39
Building C.18	No. 45. 2 storeys plus attic. Four bays. Colourwashed brick. Slate roof. Ground floor with modern shop front. Four flush framed windows with glazing bars. Two dormer windows in roof.	T. & C.P. Act C.A.	SU 717 392 0205 40
Building C.19	No. 49. 3 storeys. Two bays. Stuccoed. Shop front on ground floor with door to upstairs residence on right. Windows in moulded surrounds. Moulded band at second floor level.	T. & C.P. Act C.A.	SU 717 392 0205 41
Building C.17	No. 55. 2 storeys. Two bays. Timber-framed. Stuccoed. Old tile roof. Modern shop front. First floor has two sash windows with moulded surrounds. At the rear, exposed timber framing and a tile-hung gable.	T. & C.P. Act C.A.	SU 716 392 0205 42
House C.18	No. 59. 2 storeys plus attic. Six bays, stuccoed. Tiled mansard roof. Ground floor with door in panelled reveal and Tuscan surround. Five flush sash windows. Six similar windows on first floor. Three dormer windows in roof.	T. & C.P. Act C.A.	SU 716 392 0205 06
House C.18	No. 61. 2 storeys. Four bays. Brick structure and tiled roof. Ground floor rebuilt with modern central door and two tripartite windows.	T. & C.P. Act C.A.	SU 716 392 0205 07
Building C.18	No. 63. 2 storeys plus attic. Four bays. Brick, tiled roof. Ground floor with single tripartite window. Door with moulded surround and flat hood. Modern shop front and carriage way. Four sash windows on first floor.	T. & C.P. Act C.A.	SU 716 392 0205 08

Description and Date	Remarks	Protection	Grid Ref. and Punchcard No.

Group D — (cont.)

Description and Date	Remarks	Protection	Grid Ref. and Punchcard No.
Building C.18	Nos. 75, 77 and 79. 2 storeys plus attic. Brick structure, tiled roof. Ground floor shop fronts.		SU 716 391 0205 03
House C.18	No. 89. Original block 2 storeys. Three bays. Stuccoed, slate roof. Ground floor with central door and single tripartite window either side. First floor with central mullioned window and single tripartite window either side. Eaves cornice of Gothic arches. Altered in early C.19 and later.	T. & C.P. Act	SU 715 390 0205 01
Cottage C.19	No. 91. Fern Cottage. 2 storeys. Three bays. Attached to, and a little advanced from, No. 93. Red and yellow brick, slate roof. Sash windows.	T. & C.P. Act	SU 715 390 0205 44
Building C.18	Nos. 93 and 95, including No. 1, Mount Pleasant Road. 2 storeys, four bays wide. Originally one house. Colourwashed brick. Tiled roof. Sash windows. Original entrance is now that of No. 93. Fourth bay is No. 1 Mount Pleasant Road, with its entrance on the return.	T. & C.P. Act	SU 715 390 0205 02
Building C.19	The Crown Hotel. 2 storeys, four bays wide. Stuccoed, tiled roof. C.19 central door. Windows mainly sash, though some have been altered.	T. & C.P. Act C.A.	SU 718 394 0204 06
Building	No. 4. 2 storeys, six bays wide. Brick structure tiled roof. Central recessed door approached up four stone steps with wrought-iron rails. Flush windows, segment headed. Moulded cornice, parapet.	T. & C.P. Act C.A.	SU 718 394 0204 45
Building	No. 6. 3 storeys, six bays wide. Mid C.18 facade to earlier building. Vitreous and red brick structure. Central recessed door with fanlight of unusual pattern, approached by four stone steps with wrought-iron rails. Palladian style windows on ground floor. Six flush segment headed windows on first floor. Parapet.	T. & C.P. Act C.A.	SU 718 394 0204 63
House C.18	No. 8. 2 storeys plus attic. Four bays wide. Brick structure and tiled roof. Central recessed door within pedimented doorcase approached by three stone steps. Modern shop window on left. Sash windows. Parapet.	T. & C.P. Act C.A.	SU 718 394 0204 64
House C.18	No. 10. 2 storeys. Three bays wide. Stuccoed. 4-panel door with moulded surround and moulded hood on iron brackets. Sash windows. Parapet.	T. & C.P. Act C.A.	SU 717 394 0204 65

Description and Date	Remarks	Protection	Grid Ref. and Punchcard No.

Group D — (cont.)

Description and Date	Remarks	Protection	Grid Ref. and Punchcard No.
Inn C.16/18	The Baker's Arms. 2 storeys, three bays wide. C.18 timber-framed facade. Colourwashed brick. Slate roof. To the left of asymmetrically placed door a flush sash window, to right broad casement window. On first floor central blank window is flanked by single flush windows.	T. & C.P. Act C.A.	SU 717 394 0204 66
Buildings (2) C.19	Nos. 54 and 56. 2 storeys, brick. Modern shop fronts. No. 54, two bays wide, sash windows on first floor. No. 56, three bays wide. Canted bay window, blank window and recessed sash window on first floor.	T. & C.P. Act	SU 717 392 0204 67
House C.18	No. 74. Landsdowne House. 2 storeys plus attic. Five bays wide. Vitreous and red brick structure. Tiled, hipped roof. Central entrance with Tuscan pedimented doorcase, with two windows each side. Five sash windows. Single dormer window either side of roof.	T. & C.P. Act	SU 716 392 0204 23
Building C.18	No. 76. Westbrooke House. 3 storeys. Five bays wide, central one advanced. Brick structure and slate roof. Central door in pedimented stone doorcase. Modern steps. Sash windows.	T. & C.P. Act	SU 716 392 0204 24
Inn C.16/18	The White Horse. 2 storeys. Three bays. Colourwashed brick structure, old tile roof. Casement windows. Pilasters left and right support entablature across the facade at first floor level. Timber-framed C.18 facade to an earlier building.	T. & C.P. Act	SU 715 391 0204 25
Buildings (2) C.19	Nos. 96 and 98. 2 storeys. Colourwashed brick structure and old tile roof. No. 96, ground floor with door on left and C.19 shop front on right, with pilasters supporting entablature over it, single casement window on first floor. No. 98, altered C.19 shop window and casement window. Gabled dormer window. Extension on left.	T. & C.P. Act	SU 715 391 0204 68
Houses (2) C.18	Nos. 102 and 104. Originally one house. 2 storeys. Brick structure and tiled roof. No. 102, modern casement windows, door on left. No. 104, sash windows and central projecting painted brick porch.	T. & C.P. Act	SU 715 391 0204 69
Buildings C.18	Nos. 106—112. 2-storey row of shops. Old tile roof. Modern shop fronts. No. 106, pebbledashed with mid C.18 doorcase.	T. & C.P. Act	SU 715 390 0204 26

Description and Date	Remarks	Protection	Grid Ref. and Punchcard No.

Group D — (cont.)

Howards Lane, Holybourne

Description and Date	Remarks	Protection	Grid Ref. and Punchcard No.
House C.16/17	The Priory. 2 storeys plus attic. Three bays wide, the one on the right advanced a little and gabled. Constructed mainly of flint and stone with some brick, old tile roof. Irregular stone mullioned casement windows. Door in C.19 porch in gabled bay, to the right another C.19 gabled bay.	T. & C.P. Act C.A.	SU 733 409 0202 01
Farmhouse C.16/17	Howards. L-shaped in plan, 2 storeys. Facade has exposed timber framing with colour-washed brick infilling. Old tile roof. Irregular casements of various dates. Plain doors.	T. & C.P. Act C.A.	SU 731 411 0202 16
Barn C.17	To south-east of Howard's Farm House. 10-bay double entry weather-boarded barn with corrugated iron roof.	T. & C.P. Act C.A.	SU 731 411 0202 16A

Lenten Street

Description and Date	Remarks	Protection	Grid Ref. and Punchcard No.
Houses C.19	Nos. 6—14, 2 storeys, each house two bays wide. Houses marked off from one another by broad pilaster strips. Simple doors and sash windows set in grid formed by broad bands at first floor and eaves. Nos. 6 to 10. Tiled roofs. Nos. 12, and 14, slate roofs.	T. & C.P. Act C.A.	SU 715 393 0204 70
House C.19	No. 16, Lenten House. 2 storeys, three bays. Stuccoed, slate roof. Sash windows, blank window on first floor. Doorcase with dentilled cornice on heavy consoles.	T. & C.P. Act C.A.	SU 715 393 0204 71
House C.17	No. 16A. Stuccoed, tiled roof. Modern entrance. Modern weatherboarding at rear. Four hipped dormer windows in roof, other windows recessed sash and C.19 bay.	T. & C.P. Act C.A.	SU 715 393 0204 72
Cottages C.19	Nos. 1—7. Whitedown Cottages. 2 storey row of cottages. All two bays wide, except No. 3 which has three bays. Broad flat pilasters mark off individual cottages. Colourwashed brick. Slate roof. Each has single door with tiled hood, sash windows.	T. & C.P. Act	SU 712 393 0204 16
Building C.19	Nos. 11 and 13. 2 storeys, three bays wide. Stuccoed, slate roof. Modern shop front.	T. & C.P. Act C.A.	SU 715 393 0204 73
Buildings (4) C.19	Nos. 13A, 15, 15A and 17. 2 storeys. Two bays each, under single old tile roof. No. 13, with entrance under arch between Nos. 13 and 15A. Brick construction, colourwashed. Ground floor with modern shop front. No. 15A, red brick, sash windows, simple door. No. 17, stuccoed, door under 4-centred arch, modern shop window.	T. & C.P. Act C.A.	SU 715 393 0204 74

Description and Date	Remarks	Protection	Grid Ref. and Punchcard No.

Group D — (cont.)

Description and Date	Remarks	Protection	Grid Ref. and Punchcard No.
House C.19	No. 21. 2 storeys plus attic, four bays. Stuccoed. Slate roof with gabled dormer. Door has elaborately sculpted pilasters and bold volutes supporting a dentilled cornice. Windows in moulded surrounds with sculpted keystones. Boldly sculpted eaves brackets.	T. & C.P. Act C.A.	SU 715 393 0204 75
Building C.18	No. 23. Weybourne House. 2 storeys plus attic. Five bays. Stuccoed walls, tile and slate roof. Two doors with panelled reveals and doric pilaster surrounds. Two dormer windows in roof. Sash windows. C.19 addition to right.	T. & C.P. Act C.A.	SU 715 393 0204 08
House C.17/18	No. 25. William Curtis House. 2 storeys plus attic. Brick structure. Tiled roof hipped at one end. Central entrance with pedimented door-case. Flush windows. Two hipped dormer windows in roof. C.19 extension to left. Modern projection in right return. Birthplace of William Curtis, Botanist, in 1746.	T. & C.P. Act C.A.	SU 714 393 0204 11
House C.17/18	No. 31. The Old House and Roselle. 2 storeys. Five bays. Rendered brick walls, old tile roof. Modern glazed porch. C.19 mullioned windows. Early C.19 extension to the left now known as "Roselle", 2 storeys, two bays. Colourwashed brick walls, tiled roof.	T. & C.P. Act C.A.	SU 714 393 0204 10
Cottage C.18	No. 33. Lenten Cottage. 2 storeys. Two bays. Stucco with tile-hung upper part and gable end. Half hipped tile roof. 6-panel door. Casement windows.	T. & C.P. Act C.A.	SU 714 393 0204 09
Cottage	Flood Meadow Cottage. One storey and attic. Rendered brick walls. Tiled roof with gable ends.		SU 711 393 0204 17

London Road, Holybourne

Description and Date	Remarks	Protection	Grid Ref. and Punchcard No.
Building C.19	No. 97. Vineries Cottage. C.19 facade to earlier building. Brick construction, pantile roof. Shop door and window. Central simple door. Square casement windows with shutters. On the left another shop window, on the right a lower extension partly brick and flint, partly weatherboarded.	T. & C.P. Act C.A.	SU 733 408 020235A
Building C.18	Nos. 109 and 111. 2 storeys, four bays. Colourwashed brick. Half hipped tiled roof with central chimney. Ground floor with bay window running through two storeys. 6-panel door with surround. Moulded hood supported by plain console brackets. Sash windows.	T. & C.P. Act C.A.	SU 734 408 0202 02
House C.19	The Lawn. 2 storeys. Three bays wide. Colourwashed brick. Hipped slate roof. Original glazed door, later porch. On either side of door single canted bay window running through 2 storeys. Modern additions.	T. & C.P. Act C.A.	SU 735 408 0202 10

Description and Date	Remarks	Protection	Grid Ref. and Punchcard No.

Group D — (cont.)

Description and Date	Remarks	Protection	Grid Ref. and Punchcard No.
House C.18	Nos. 123 and 125. 2 storeys plus attic, three bays. Colourwashed brick with tiled roof. Central 6-panelled door with moulded cantilever hood. Casement windows. Two gabled dormers. To the left a single storey extension.	T. & C.P. Act C.A.	SU 735 409 0202 06
Cottages C.19	Nos. 127, 129, 131 and 133. 2 storeys. Limestone blocks, slate roof. 2 cottages at centre each 2 bays wide. Shops either side, within gabled and bargeboarded single bay wings.	T. & C.P. Act C.A.	SU 735 409 0202 07
Cottages C.16/17	Nos. 143 to 153. 2 storeys. Timber-framed construction with colourwashed brick infilling, Old tile roof. Irregular casements. No. 145 has rectangular bay windows with small panes.	T. & C.P. Act C.A.	SU 736 409 0202 03
Houses C.18	Nos. 155 and 157. Including Nos. 1 and 3 Lower Neatham Lane. 2 storeys and attic. Painted brick. Tile roof. Three dormer windows in roof. Two square mullioned and transomed windows, remainder sash. Door under moulded hood.	T. & C.P. Act C.A.	SU 737 410 0202 36
Cottage C.17	No. 159. Mapeys. Single storey and attic. Timber-framed with white painted brick infilling and some tile hanging. Tile roof. Irregular composition. Many of the windows with leaded lights. Modern door. To the right a C.19 white painted 2-storey brick addition with a tiled roof.	T. & C.P. Act C.A.	SU 737 410 0202 37
Building C.18	Andrews Endowed C. of E. Primary School. 2 storeys and attic. Purple brick with red dressings. Tiled roof with central chimney. Small engraved pane over door with inscription, 'Holybourn Free School. Endowed by Mr. Thomas Andrews, Anno Domini 1719'.	T. & C.P. Act	SU 732 408 0202 11
Cottage C.18	No. 104. Yew Tree. 2 storeys. Brick structure. Tile roof. Three bays. Sash windows. Central door beneath dentilled and pedimented hood.	T. & C.P. Act C.A.	SU 733 408 0202 38
Cottage C.17	No. 108. Tudor Cottage. Single storey and attic. Timber-framed with colourwashed brick infilling. Thatched roof. Ground floor has two casement windows, and central door within simple lattice porch with tiled roof. Three eyebrow dormer windows.	T. & C.P. Act C.A.	SU 733 408 0202 39
House C.18/19	Holybourne Lodge. 2 storeys with 3-storey central block. Colourwashed brick. Slate roof. Three bays. Sash windows. Modern door beneath Ionic pedimented porch.	T. & C.P. Act C.A.	SU 734 409 0202 09
House C.18/19	No. 114. The Beeches. 2 storeys. Colourwashed brick. Tiled roof. Porch with slender Tuscan columns. Sash windows.	T. & C.P. Act C.A.	SU 735 409 0202 08

Description and Date	Remarks	Protection	Grid Ref. and Punchcard No.

Group D — (cont.)

Description and Date	Remarks	Protection	Grid Ref. and Punchcard No.
Houses C.17/18	Nos. 116 and 118. Yeoman Cottage. Single storey plus attic. Timber-framed, exposed in the facade of No. 116, which has colourwashed brick infilling. Tiled roof. Modern casements. Dormer windows in roof. Colourwashed brick.	T. & C.P. Act C.A.	SU 735 409 0202 05
House C.18	No. 120. 2 storeys. Stone blocks with brick quoins. Thatched roof. Flanking chimney stacks. Casement windows.	T. & C.P. Act C.A.	SU 735 409 0202 04
House C.16	Nos. 124 and 126. 2 storeys. Timber-framed with colourwashed brick infill. Plastered on first floor. Tiled roof. Irregular modern leaded casements.	T. & C.P. Act C.A.	SU 736 410 0202 12
House C.18	Anne's Cottage. 2 storeys, three bays. Colourwashed brick. Tiled roof. Sash windows.	T. & C.P. Act C.A.	SU 736 410 0202 18
Cottage C.17/18	Oak Cottage. 2 storeys. Painted brick structure. Tiled half-hipped roof. Ground floor, four tripartite segment-headed windows. First floor four casement windows. All windows with leaded lights. Dentilled eaves cornice. Exposed timber-framing on the right return which is weatherboarded in its upper part. Modern single-storey extension to left.	T. & C.P. Act C.A.	SU 739 410 0202 40
Building C.18	Holybourne Forge. 2 storeys. Brick structure. Tiled roof. Tripartite windows with moulded cornices. Door with moulded hood and a broad entrance converted into a large glazed window. Dated 1722 in black headers.	T. & C.P. Act C.A.	SU 738 410 0202 41
Farmhouse C.17	Bonhams Farm. 2 storeys and attic. Timber-framed with brick infilling. Old tile roof. Six bays. Sash windows. Two hipped dormer windows in the roof. Panelled interior and original staircase with balusters. C.18 pedimented porch with fluted Tuscan pilasters.	T. & C.P. Act	SU 741 418 0202 42

Lower Turk Street

Description and Date	Remarks	Protection	Grid Ref. and Punchcard No.
Dwelling C.19	Culverton House. 2 storeys and attic. Stuccoed. Slate roof. Ground floor with central 6-panelled door with modern radial fanlight and within a deeply projecting broad porch. Porch with unfluted doric columns carrying bold arches and a balcony with early C.19 iron railings of an uncommon design with adorsed wings. Modern sash and casement windows all with shutters. At rear a range of offices terminating in an C.18 pedimented front piece.	T. & C.P. Act	SU 719 392 0205 45

Market Square

Description and Date	Remarks	Protection	Grid Ref. and Punchcard No.
Inn C.19	The Wheatsheaf. 2 storeys. Red brick. Slate roof. Six bays, the centre two advanced. Ground floor with asymmetrically placed porch on slender columns. Sash windows.	T. & C.P. Act C.A.	SU 715 392 0204 76

Description and Date	Remarks	Protection	Grid Ref. and Punchcard No.

Group D — (cont.)

Description and Date	Remarks	Protection	Grid Ref. and Punchcard No.
Building C.19	Town Hall. Erected by public subscription 1813, enlarged 1840, and subsequently. 2 storeys. Colourwashed brick. Slate roof. Five bays. Ground floor with, on the north, some segment-headed blank arches and modern shop fronts. Sash windows. On south a doorcase with scrolly brackets and irregular fenestration. Ref: V.C.H., Vol. 2, p. 473.	T. & C.P. Act C.A.	SU 716 393 0204 77

Market Street

Description and Date	Remarks	Protection	Grid Ref. and Punchcard No.
Buildings (2) C.19	Nos. 19 and 21. 2 storeys. Stuccoed. Tile roof. Sash windows. Three bays, that on left recessed slightly. Central doorway with pilasters and entablature and flanked on each side by a single contemporary shop front.	T. & C.P. Act C.A.	SU 716 393 0204 78
Building	No. 23. Altered C.18 facade to an earlier timber-framed building. 2 storeys and attic. Stuccoed. Old tile roof. Sash windows. Two bays. Gable with coping stones. Modern shop front.	T. & C.P. Act C.A.	SU 716 393 0204 79
Buildings (3) C.19	Nos. 25, 25A and 27. 2 storeys. Yellow stock brick. Old tiled roof. Four bays. Sash windows all with whitened heads and keystones. Ground floor with door to upper floor on left and modern shop front.	T. & C.P. Act C.A.	SU 716 393 0204 80
Inn C.18	The King's Head. 2 storeys. Colourwashed brick. Old tile roof. Sash windows all with segmental heads. Dentilled eaves cornice. Four bays. Doorway with simple pilasters and single entablature.	T. & C.P. Act C.A.	SU 716 393 0204 81
Building C.18	No. 29. 2 storeys. Stuccoed. Old tile roof. One bay wide with canted corner bay. First floor one broad flush casement window. Dentilled eaves cornice. The return in Amery Street has lower 2-bay extension of colourwashed brick with old tile roof. Sash windows.	T. & C.P. Act C.A.	SU 716 393 0204 82
Building C.19	No. 16. 2 storeys and a glazed and slated polygonal cupola. Stucco. Slate roof. First floor with two canted bay windows with blank panels and lions masks in cornice above. Mid C.19 shop front.	T. & C.P. Act C.A.	SU 716 393 0204 83
Buildings (2) C.19	Nos. 18 and 20. 3-storey. Stucco. Modern pantile roof. Sash windows with glazing bars. Three bays. Mid C.19 shop front with pilasters, volutes and entablature left and right of a central entrance.	T. & C.P. Act C.A.	SU 716 393 0204 84
Building C.19	No. 22. 2 storeys. Two recessed sash windows. C.19 shop front.	T. & C.P. Act C.A.	SU 716 393 0204 85

Description and Date	Remarks	Protection	Grid Ref. and Punchcard No.

Group D — (cont.)

Medstead Road, Beech

Buildings C.20	Beech Abbey. Flint gatehouse built circa. 1901, Monastery and church mainly of flint and stone built 1929 with modern additions in 1956 and 1970. A guest house was added to the Gatehouse in 1936. The church is not yet complete. The monastery is based on monastic pattern modelled on Tintern Abbey. Architect: Sir Chas. Nicholson.		SU 675 370 0201 07

Mill Lane

Building C.16	H.R.H. House. Much rebuilt in C.19. 2 storeys. Brick, upper part tile-hung with shaped tiles. Old tile roof. Irregular casement windows. On left single gabled dormer window at eaves level. All windows with iron diamond lattice. Some original timber-frame work exposed at back. On left a modern single storey addition.	T. & C.P. Act	SU 728 399 0205 86
Cottage C.19	Wey Cottage. 2 storeys. Brick with upper part hung with shaped tiles. Ground floor iron diamond lattice casement window. First floor windows modern. Doorway with modest porch.	T. & C.P. Act	SU 728 399 0205 87

Mount Pleasant Road

Inn C.19	The Hop Poles. 2 storeys. Colourwashed Ashlar. Slate roof. Sash windows. Two plain doors.	T. & C.P. Act	SU 715 390 0206 04

Normandy Street

Building C.18	No. 2. 2 storeys. Colourwashed brick. Tiled roof. Sash window. Modern shop front.	T. & C.P. Act C.A.	SU 718 395 0203 07
Building C.17/18	Nos. 4 and 6. Timber-framed with C.18 facade. 2 storeys plus attic. Stucco. Tiled roof. Sash windows. Three dormer windows in roof. Modern shop front.	T. & C.P. Act C.A.	SU 718 395 0203 08
Building C.18	No. 12. 2 storeys and attic. Colourwashed brick. Tiled mansard roof. Casement windows. Pedimented dormer window. Central pedimented late C.18 doorcase with modern door. Modern shop windows.	T. & C.P. Act C.A.	SU 719 395 0203 08
Buildings C.17/18	Nos. 24 and 24A. 2 storeys and attic. Timber-framed with C.18 facade. Colourwashed brick. Tiled roof. C.19 shop fronts.	T. & C.P. Act C.A.	SU 719 395 0203 02
Inn C.17	No. 72, The Barley Mow. 2 storeys. Timber-framed and altered. Ground floor peble-dashed. First floor tile-hung. Tiled roof. Sash windows. Three gabled windows. Simple door.	T. & C.P. Act	SU 720 396 0203 09

Description and Date	Remarks	Protection	Grid Ref. and Punchcard No.

Group D — (cont.)

Building C.17	No. 3. 2 storeys and attic. Painted brick. Old tile roof, half-hipped at rear. Moulded eaves cornice. First floor five blocked windows. Two dormer windows in roof. Lower block at rear. Timber-framed with brick infilling, half-hipped tile roof. Casement window.	T. & C.P. Act C.A.	SU 719 394 0205 46
Building C.19	No. 5. 3 storey. Stucco. Slate roof. Two bays with quoins left and right. Windows in moulded surrounds. Contemporary shop front.	T. & C.P. Act C.A.	SU 719 395 0205 47
Building C.17	No. 15. 2 storeys. Timber-framed but altered. Rendered. Tile roof. Casement windows. Modern shop fronts and doors.	T. & C.P. Act C.A.	SU 719 395 0205 48
Cottage C.19	No. 17. Normandy. 2 storeys. Red brick with some black diaperwork. Tiled roof. Gabled with elaborate chimney stacks. Three bays. Doorway with hood mould on foliage stops. Door with good iron work.	T. & C.P. Act	SU 719 395 0205 49
Buildings (2) C.17	Nos. 19 and 21. 2 storeys and attic. Timber-framed. Tiled roofs. No. 21 has modern black and white work with pebbledash infilling. Casement windows. Single dormer in roof. Central doorway flanked by modern shop fronts.	T. & C.P. Act C.A.	SU 719 395 0205 50
Church C.19	United Reformed Church. 2 storeys. Stuccoed. Slate roof. Minimum Gothic style Gabled elevation. Three bays wide with two narrow canted bays. Ground floor windows square. First floor pointed with either Y or intersecting Y-tracery. All windows with drip moulds. Parapet.	T. & C.P. Act	SU 720 396 0205 51
Buildings C.17	Nos. 43 and 45. 2 storeys and attic. Timber-framed with brick facade dated 1704 in black headers. Tiled roof. Sash windows. Two broad gabled dormer windows. Modern shop front.	T. & C.P. Act	SU 720 396 0205 52
Building C.19	No. 47. Circa 1800. 2 storeys. Painted brick. Tile roof. Sash window. 6-panelled door beneath simple hood.	T. & C.P. Act	SU 720 396 0205 53
Building C.19	Alton House Hotel. 2 storeys. Colourwashed stucco walls. Hipped slate roof. Large bow windows. Verandah on four slender columns.	T. & C.P. Act	SU 721 396 0205 15

Orchard Lane

Houses (12) C.19	Nos. 1—12. Orchard Terrace. 2 storeys. Red brick, rat-trap bond. Nos. 1—6 with a little polychrome. Slate roofs. Panelled doors. Sash windows.	T. & C.P. Act	SU 720 395 0205 54

Village Sign, BENTLEY

Description and Date	Remarks	Protection	Grid Ref. and Punchcard No.

Group D — (cont.)

Papermill Lane

Mill and Millhouse	Papermill. Both 2-storey stone buildings. Slate roofs. Mill seven bays. Red brick surround to windows. Mill house has casement windows. No machinery remains.		SU 723 395 0205 93
Cottage C.19	The Rock, Single storeyed rustic cottage. T-shaped in plan and of rough boulder construction. Slate roof with decorated ridge tiles. Mostly lattice windows.	T. & C.P. Act	SU 722 396 0205 60

Truncheaunts Lane

Building C.19	Kiln House. 2 storeys. Coursed stone painted white. Slate roof with two centrally placed pyramidal kiln heads. Ground floor with an open arcade of square piers carrying depressed arches with bold key stones. Outer two arches now blocked with metal casement windows. C.19 5-bay cast iron verandah as a covered way to principal door.	T. & C.P. Act	SU 727 381 0206 21

Turk Street

Houses (2) C.18	Nos. 8 and 10. Single storey and attic, stucco. Old tile roof, half-hipped, gabled at one end. No. 8, ground floor with asymmetrically placed segment-headed doorway. No. 10, one window and a simple door. Single dormer in roof. Exposed timber-framing in the gable.	T. & C.P. Act C.A.	SU 717 392 0205 61

Vicarage Hill

House C.18	No. 6. 2 storeys. Brick structure. Tiled mansard roof with flanking chimneys. Ground floor has two broad modern casement windows. First floor has sash windows. Dentil eaves cornice. Central door with broad porch.	T. & C.P. Act C.A.	SU 717 394 0204 90

Wellhouse Road, Beech

Cottages C.17	Nos. 24 — 30 (even). Well House Cottages. 2 storeys. Timber framed with brick infilling. Thatched roof. No. 24, modern iron casement windows. Thatched porch. Eyebrow eaves. Single-bay modern extension on right. Nos. 26 — 30 under a single roof. Casement windows. Nos. 26, 30 door under eaves. No. 28, thatched porch.	T & C.P. Act	SU 693 389 0201 20
House C.17	The Old Farm, formerly Beech Place. 2 storeys. L-shaped brick structure. Old tiled roof. Casement windows.	T. & C.P. Act	SU 687 385 0201 03

Description and Date	Remarks	Protection	Grid Ref. and Punchcard No.

Group D — (cont.)

Description and Date	Remarks	Protection	Grid Ref. and Punchcard No.
Donkey Wheelhouse C.18	No. 61, Beech Barns. Timber construction approximately 10ft. in diameter, with extended spindle carrying the well rope. Contained in heavy size timber-framed building with slate roof and tiled ridge.	T. & C.P. Act	SU 687 385 0201 10

Westbrooke Road

Statues (2) C.18	Public gardens. White marble, very weathered. Male and female head and shoulders with baroque draperies. Set on modern pedestals circa. 1934/35.	T. & C.P. Act	SU 714 392 — 715 391 0204 91

Whitedown Lane

Inn C.18	The French Horn. 2 storeys. Painted brick. Tiled roof with flanking chimneys. Casement windows. Central simple door.	T. & C.P. Act C.A.	SU 710 385 0206 22

Windmill Hill

House C.18/19	Stillions. 2 storeys. Pebble dash. Slate roof. Casement windows. Central simple door within segment-headed arch and beneath moulded wooden hood. On right a single-storeyed stable block.	T. & C.P. Act	SU 721 390 0205 62

Group E — Street Patterns, Street Furniture and Open Spaces

Sundial C.18	Churchyard of St. Lawrence to south of east end. Baluster of stone. Dial and gnomon of copper. Signed 'Dolland London'.	T. & C.P. Act C.A.	SU 717 395 0204 61
Milestone C.18/19	London Road. A quadrant in plan and with a pyramidal top. Inscribed 'Holybourn (sic). London 45. Alton 1. Farnham 8'.	T. & C.P. Act	SU 732 407 0202 34A
Milestone C.18/19	Bonhams, London Road, Holybourne. A quadrant in plan and with a pyramidal top. Inscribed 'London 45. Alton 2. Farnham 7'. Resited when the A31 bypass was built.	T. & C.P. Act	SU 744 415 0202 43

Group F — Historical or Literary Associations

House C.16	No. 1, Amery Street. Home in 1590, of Edmund Spenser, the Elizabethan poet and author of "The Faerie Queen".	T. & C.P. Act C.A.	SU 715 393 0204 01
House C.17/18	No. 25, Lenten Street, William Curtis House. Birthplace of William Curtis, C.18 botanist. Founder of Botanical Gardens at Lambeth Marsh, Bermondsey and Brompton.	T. & C.P. Act C.A.	SU 714 393 0204 11

Group E — (cont.)

Description and Date	Remarks	Protection	Grid Ref. and Punchcard No.
Buildings C.20	Beech Abbey, Medstead Road, Beech. Between 1890 and 1895 monks of the Anglican Order of St. Paul lived in wattle huts and tents until the Gatehouse was completed. This is the only "House" left in the Order of St. Paul and its object is to offer sanctuary to retired seamen of all classes. An old settle in the cloisters is reputed to have come from the 'Mayflower'.		SU 675 378 0201 07

BENTLEY

Bentley is five miles north-east of Alton on the main Farnham Road and attractively set in the meadows of the river Wey. The church, built between 1130 and 1140, has much thirteenth century work to show, as well as a finely carved Norman arch which separates the chancel from the north chapel. An unusual feature, the chancel clerestory, was added in the fifteenth century at the same time as the lower part of the tower was built. The early Jacobean altar rails and a priest's seat are also of interest.

Description and Date	Remarks	Protection	Grid Ref. and Punchcard No.

Group A — Natural Features

Description and Date	Remarks	Protection	Grid Ref. and Punchcard No.
Trees	Avenue of approximately sixty lime trees, forming a fine skyline from St. Mary's Church to Bury Court.		SU 784 447 — 782 451 1601 42
Trees	Station Road. Of the two oaks planted in 1953 to commemorate the Coronation only one remains, now protected by palings. A plaque recording the event has been provided by the Parish Council.		SU 784 437 1601 54
Trees	St. Mary's Church. An avenue of ten yews, three of which have been recently replanted. The originals reputed to be 500-600 years old. The branches of two of the trees on the south-east, having a spread of over 60ft., are supported by oak beams.		SU 784 446 1601 53

Group B — Archaeological

Roman

Description and Date	Remarks	Protection	Grid Ref. and Punchcard No.
Cremation	Bury Court Farm. Twelve keel-shaped and flat shouldered urns containing burnt burials and pottery, found in oval grave. Now in Basingstoke Museum. O.S.A. No. SU74 SE1.		SU 777 446 1601 43
Potsherds	Crocks Farm. Fragments of pottery found many years ago in area of a carriage drive. O.S.A. No. SU74 SE3. Ref: 1. A History of Bentley, (Lang). 2. Alice Holt Forest. Its history and its Roman/British potteries, (Wade).	C.A.	SU 778 437 1601 44
Building (Site)	Glade Farm. Tiles, pottery etc. found. Probable site of villa. O.S.A. No. SU74 NE6.		SU 779 458 1601 45

Post Norman

Description and Date	Remarks	Protection	Grid Ref. and Punchcard No.
Motte and Bailey	West of Steers Copse. Ploughed over motte with surrounding ditch and remains of a bank. Several fragments of Roman tiles found in the area. Excavated in 1979 and 1980. O.S.A. No. SU74 NE9. Ref. A.P. (R.A.F.) 1066/UK/1710/3001.		SU 793 462 1601 46

Group D — Buildings, Monuments and Engineering Works

Description and Date	Remarks	Protection	Grid Ref. and Punchcard No.
Church C.12	St. Mary the Virgin. C.13 and C.15 alterations. Upper tower early C.18. North and south aisles and porch C.19. Large Purbeck marble font. O.S.A. No. SU74 SE2. Ref: 1. Bentley in Hampshire, (Lang) 2. Church and Village of Bentley St. Mary in Hampshire, (Eggar). 3. Buildings of England; Hants and I.O.W., (Pevsner & Lloyd), p.100.	T. & C.P. Act	SU 784 447 1601 01

Description and Date	Remarks	Protection	Grid Ref. and Punchcard No.

Group D — (cont.)

Description and Date	Remarks	Protection	Grid Ref. and Punchcard No.
Building C.16/17	The Red Lion. Stucco and pebbledash structure, originally two or three timber-framed and brick cottages. Ridge tiled roof, double hipped. Wall decoration of C.16/17 recently revealed on interior wall. An inn from the early C.18 until 1975.		SU 785 440 1601 41
Farmhouse C.16/17	Coldrey House, Lower Froyle. 2 storeys. Red brick structure. Long ridge tiled roof, half hipped either end. Fine Georgian elevations. Rear wing timber-framed.	T. & C.P. Act	SU 771 437 1601 04
House C.17	Ganwells, Alton Road. 2 storeys. Roughcast facade masking older structure. Old ridge tiled roof. Sash windows. Panelled porch with ornamental fretwork and modillioned cornice.	T. & C.P. Act C.A.	SU 781 439 1601 02
House C.17	Jenkyn Place, formerly Bentley House. Large restored Queen Anne house, much enlarged and altered in the C.20. 2 storeys. Red brick. Wide plinth of coursed stone blocks. Hipped tiled roof. Fine gardens and good C.19 ancillary buildings.		SU 782 444 1601 08
Cottages (2) C.17	Somerset Cottages. One cottage, single storey with two gabled dormers, and the other 2 storeys with tiled gable. High ridge tiled roof.		SU 783 439 1601 14
Cottage C.17	Marelands Cottage, London Road. Single storey. Limewashed brick, one end partly timber-framed. Half-hipped ridge tiled roof.		SU 790 441 1601 25
House C.17	Marelands. 2 storeys. Red brick structure. Ridge tiled roof. Three sets of widely, spaced lattice casement windows. C.18 and C.19 additions. Fine site, proportion and detail. Associations with Gilbert White. Ref: 1. A Hampshire Manor, (Dutton). 2. Country Life Magazine, 15.5.42.	T. & C.P. Act	SU 793 438 1601 06
Inn C.17	The Bull, London Road. 2 storeys. Creamwashed brick with wide plinth abutting the road. Old hipped tiled roof. Core of building timber-framed.		SU 803 444 1601 32
Cottage C.17/18	Ash Cottage, Alton Road. 2 storeys. Limewashed brick. Hipped tiled roof. Sash windows. Centre pedimented doorway with fluted Doric pilasters.	C.A.	SU 779 438 1601 17
House C.17/18	Prestons, The Drift. 2 storeys. Timber-framed with brick infilling. Partially tile hung. Steep hipped tiled roof. Originally three cottages.		SU 781 434 1601 22
Building C.17/18	The Coach-House at Ganwells, Alton Road. Brick and stone structure. Steep ridge tiled roof, with half-hipped ends. Now partially converted into private residence.	C.A.	SU 781 438 1601 15

Description and Date	Remarks	Protection	Grid Ref. and Punchcard No.
Group D — (cont.)			
Cottage C.17/18	Clements Cottage. Timber framed with brick infilling. Ground floor plain C.18 brick. Ridge tiled roof. Plain centre chimney with coupled stacks. L-shape plan.	T. & C.P. Act	SU 783 435 1601 05
Cottage C.17/18	John O'Pease, Church Lane. 2 storeys. Coursed stone and brick. The property enlarged and the roof raised in about 1800. Restored in 1980.		SU 784 445 1601 56
Cottage C.17/18	Gardeners Cottage, Marsh House. Timber-framed with herring bone brickwork and plaster in-filling on ground floor, tile hung above. Ridge tiled roof with centre chimney. C.18 wing to left. Two dwellings.		SU 797 445 1601 31
Farmhouse C.17/18	Hill Farm. 2 storeys. Red brick walls, ridge tiled roof. Large centre brick chimney. Mullioned lattice casement windows. C.18 elevations.		SU 802 453 1601 36
Building C.18	Greystones, Alton Road. Stone built barn, converted into private residence.	C.A.	SU 780 438 1601 40
House C.18	Tanners, Alton Road. 2 storeys. Limewashed brick, plinth and band. Tiled roof, hipped to left. Tile hung wing to right.	C.A.	SU 781 438 1601 16
Farmhouse C.18	Glade Farm. 2 storeys. Red brick walls. Long ridge tiled roof. The house and its associated farm buildings, oast houses etc., make a fine group.		SU 781 460 1601 34
Farmhouse C.18	Bury Court Farm. 2 storeys. Red brick walls. Long ridge tiled roof. Sash windows.		SU 782 451 1601 35
Farmhouse C.18	Bentley Green Farm. 2 storeys. Stuccoed walls. Half-hipped ridge tiled roof. Sash windows. Centre door and light columned porch.		SU 782 435 1601 23
Cottage C.18	The Old Forge, Alton Road. 2 storeys. Brick and tile-hung. Lattice casement windows. Tiled roof. Single storey wing.	C.A.	SU 779 438 1601 19
Farmhouse C.18	Crocks Farm, Alton Road. 2 storeys. Red brick structure. Ridge tiled roof. Sash windows. Fine brick walling.	T. & C.P. Act C.A.	SU 778 437 1601 03
Cottages (3) C.18	Alleyne's Cottages, Carters Green. 2 storeys. Limewashed brick walls. Ridge tiled roof. Casement windows. Recently renovated.		SU 786 441 1601 10
Farmhouse C.18	Baileys Cottage, School Lane. 2 storeys. Stone blocks with red brick dressings. Tiled roof, half-hipped to left. Lattice casement windows.		SU 786 445 1601 09
House C.18	Fox Hall, Carters Green. 2 storeys. Stuccoed walls. High pitched slate roof. Sash windows. Gabled dormers with ornamental bargeboards. Light columned porch.		SU 786 441 1601 11

Description and Date	Remarks	Protection	Grid Ref. and Punchcard No.

Group D — (cont.)

Description and Date	Remarks	Protection	Grid Ref. and Punchcard No.
House C.18	Grafton Cottage, Carters Green. 2 storeys. Limewashed brick walls. Two hipped tiled gables with lead ridges. Exceptionally attractive and unaltered.		SU 786 441 1601 12
Cottages (2) C.18	The Cage, London Road. 2 storeys. Red brick walls. Long ridge tiled roof with half-hipped ends. Six small wooden casement windows. Name derived from village lockup which stood nearby in the C.19.		SU 786 440 1601 13
Farmhouse C.18	South Green, formerly Hawkins Farm, Rectory Lane. 2 storeys. Limewashed brick. Sash windows. Short ridge tiled roof.		SU 786 437 1601 24
House and Barn C.18/19	Pamplins. 2 storeys. Red brick with occasional blue headers. Ridge tiled roof. Thatched and weatherboarded barn adjoining.		SU 788 445 1601 26
Farmhouse C.19	Perryland, East Green. 2 storeys. Coursed stone blocks with red brick dressings. Hipped slate roof. Sash windows.		SU 794 449 1601 27
House C.19	Northbrook. Large Regency house standing in small park. 3 storeys. Yellow rendered walls. Slate roof. Sash windows. Columned porch. Good associated outbuildings and cottages.		SU 808 447 1601 33
Cottages (2) C.19	Nos. 8 and 9, East Green. 2 storeys. Lime-washed brick and tilehung. Half-hipped ridge tiled roof. Forms pleasant group with nearby cottages.		SU 799 448 1601 28
House C.19	The Old Rectory, London Road. 2 storeys. Limewashed brick. Victorian low pitched slate roof. Sash windows. Probably occupied 1823–1838 by Rev. Henry Austen, brother of Jane Austen.		SU 786 440 1601 55
Obelisk C.19	London Road. Tapering, square granite obelisk. 5 ft. high. Dated 1897.		SU 786 440 1601 52
Cottages (3)	Crocks Cottages, Alton Road. 2 storeys. Timber-framed with brick infilling. Ridge tiled roof. Possibly C.17.		SU 778 437 1601 29
Building	Antique Shop, Alton Road. Restored single storey structure. Timber-framed with brick infilling. Half-hipped tiled roof. Large contemporary bread oven incorporated in central stack. Probably C.17.	C.A.	SU 780 438 1601 18
Cottages (2)	Nos. 12 and 13, East Green. Single storey with gabled dormer. Coursed stone blocks, partly random stone, and partly exposed timber-framing with brick nogging. Forms pleasant group with nearby cottages.		SU 799 447 1601 30

Description and Date	Remarks	Protection	Grid Ref. and Punchcard No.

Group D — (cont.)

Barn	The Great Barn, Marelands. Large brick structure. Tiled roof brought down as pentice in front and to rear. Centre projected hipped wagon entrances. Fine interior timbered roof, Queen-post construction.	T. & C.P. Act	SU 793 438 1601 07

Group E — Street Patterns, Street Furniture and Open Spaces

Village Sign	The 'Bentley Book', Alton Road. Designed by Lord Baden-Powell for the Daily Mail competition for village signs 1923. Forms open book showing map of Bentley and a resume of points of historic interest. Surmounted by a 'Lych gate' construction in oak, formerly thatched, now shingled and capped by a carved figure of Will the Archer, made by Mrs. R. Eggar.	C.A.	SU 783 439 1601 39
Milestone	London Road. Stone of good form, with cut letters inlaid and painted, reading 'Bentley. London 42, Alton 5, Farnham 4.'		SU 786 440 1601 51
Boundary Stone	South side of A.31 on the Hampshire/Surrey border, located at given grid reference.		SU 812 447 1601 50

BENTWORTH

Bentworth is a scattered settlement some four miles north-west of Alton. It includes several hamlets within its bounds and buildings of interest such as Bentworth Hall, Gaston Grange and Burkham House. The church is of interest having the chancel arch and nave arcades dating from the twelfth century, illustrating well the transition from the Norman to the Early English style. A thirteenth century font, a Jacobean chest and an altar from the time of Charles II are also worthy of note. In this church was christened George Wittes — poet and author. A fervent Parliamentarian, George Wittes sold all his lands at Bentworth to raise a troop of horse for Cromwell.

Description and Date	Remarks	Protection	Grid Ref. and Punchcard No.

Group A — Natural Features

Description and Date	Remarks	Protection	Grid Ref. and Punchcard No.
Tree	Village green. Oak planted 1919 in centre, in thanksgiving for end of First World War.		SU 664 401 1602 32
Woodland	Bentworth Lodge. Area to the north of the Lodge with interesting flora.		SU 683 403 1602 50

Group B — Archaeological

Stone Age

Implement	Mesolithic Thames pick found in Woodmans Field. Now in Newbury Museum. O.S.A. No. SU63 NE4.		SU 680 399 1602 45

Bronze Age

Cremation	North of Nancole Copse. Tripartite cinerary urn found in 1955 containing cremation of an adult. Urn is exhibited in Alton Museum. O.S.A. No. SU64 SE8. Ref: Alton Museum, (Access No. 1956.9.)		SU 663 421 1602 42

Iron Age

Rubbish Pit	Holt End. Belgic pottery and animal bones found in face of Quarry 1954. O.S.A. No. SU63 NE3.		SU 658 391 1602 44

Roman

Coin	Tinkers Lane. Bronze coin of Valentinian I found in garden. Now stored in Alton Museum. O.S.A. No. SU63 NE2.		SU 664 399 1602 43
Rubbish Pit	Wivelrod. Finds include pottery, bone objects, spindle-whorls and fragments of roofing tiles. C.1/4. O.S.A. No. SU63 NE9. Ref: P.H.F.C. Vol. 15, 1941-3, p.p. 246—7.		SU 675 383 1602 46

Group C — Footpaths and Bridleways

Old Travel Way	Public Footpath No. 24 from Rushmoor to Ashley, continued as Path No. 23 Dirty Lane to Jenny Green Lane and through New Copse to Path No. 28 Chawton boundary. Appears to have been in use from at least the C.13.		SU 648 409 — 669 375 1602 34
Old Travel Way	Wadgetts Lane, formerly Wadstreet. Public footpath No. 25.		SU 668 406 — 684 410 1602 35
Old Travel Way	Tinkers Lane. Public Footpath No. 26. Old road from centre of village and the church, through the common fields to the hamlet of Wivelrod, possibly the earliest settlement in the parish.	C.A.	SU 664 401 — 676 384 1602 36

Description and Date	Remarks	Protection	Grid Ref. and Punchcard No.

Group D — Buildings, Monuments and Engineering Works

Description and Date	Remarks	Protection	Grid Ref. and Punchcard No.
Church C.12/13	St. Mary. Flint with stone dressing. West tower with wooden belfry and broached shingle spire added 1890. Flint and stone C.14 south porch. Chancel C.13. Square stone font, panelled, on four short pillars. Wooden pyramid font cover 1605. O.S.A. No. SU64 SE12. Ref: 1. V.C.H., Vol. 4, p.p. 70—1. 2. Buildings of England; Hants and I.O.W., (Pevsner & Lloyd), p.p. 100—1	T. & C.P. Act C.A.	SU 665 403 1602 01
House and Chapel C.14	Hall Farm. Mediaeval hall house with gabled crosswings. 2-3 ft. thick flint walls, rendered. 2 storeys. Porch with upper room and gable. Immense chimney stack containing fireplace and ovens of squared chalk in place of screen. Solar wing C.15, with C.16 staircase. Chapel, now part of farm building, built of coursed knapped flints with stone quoins. O.S.A. No. SU 63 NE1. Ref: 1. Buildings of England; Hants & I.O.W., (Pevsner & Lloyd), p. 101. 2. V.C.H., Vol. 4, p.p. 68—70.	T. & C.P. Act C.A.	SU 663 399 1602 05
House C.17	Ashley Cottage. Based on central back to back plan. Enlarged C.19, with brick and flint additions. Reconstructed in recent years.		SU 651 401 1602 40
House C.17	Medstead Grange. Core of this much enlarged house is a C.17 farmhouse of 2-storey central back to back fireplace plan.		SU 656 381 1602 37
House C.17	Holt Cottage. 1½ storeys. Timber-framed with brick infilling, brick and flint gable end wall. White painted. Thatched half-hipped roof. Typical central back to back chimney style.		SU 659 391 1602 15
House C.17	The Old Bungalow, Holt Lane End. Single storey. Painted brick walls. Slate roof. Visible timber corner post suggests house may have been timber-framed originally.		SU 660 392 1602 25
House C.17	Tilborans, Holt Lane End. 2 storeys. Brick and flint, painted and part rendered. Slate gabled roof. Modern windows. Extensions of both C.19 and more recent date.		SU 660 391 1602 24
House C.17	Holt Green. 2 storeys. Reconstructed gable roof, modern tiles. Wooden casement windows. C.18 extensions in brick and flint. Original interior plan, central back to back fireplaces. Restored and enlarged in recent years.		SU 660 392 1602 23
House C.17	St. Andrews Cottage, Holt Lane. 2-storey, painted brick and flint, pebble dash and tile-hung. Central back to back fireplace plan. Enlarged.		SU 661 397 1602 26

Description and Date	Remarks	Protection	Grid Ref. and Punchcard No.
	Group D — (cont.)		
House C.17	Ivalls Cottage, formerly Blundells. 2 storey. Red brick with blue headers. Hipped thatched roof continued over modern extension. Modern leaded casement windows. In C.18 and C.19 blacksmith's house with adjoining forge and hayloft over, now converted for use as garage.	C.A.	SU 664 401 1602 08
House C.17	Hunts Cottage. 2-storey. Timber-framed with brick infilling. Thatched roof. Modern leaded casement windows. 1-storey brick and flint extension with thatched roof. Modern half-hipped projecting wing, tile-hung.	C.A.	SU 664 402 1602 12
House C.17	Ivalls Farm Cottage. Timber-framed with white painted brick infilling. Tiled gabled roof with three dormer windows. Later brick and flint extension.	T. & C.P. Act C.A.	SU 665 401 1602 04
House C.17	Hookers Place. 2 storeys. Painted brick walls. Tiled roof, half-hipped at north end. Plinth and string course. Window replacements of various styles.	C.A.	SU 666 401 1602 06
House C.17	Greensleeves. 1½ storeys. Timber-framed with painted brick infilling, some herringbone pattern. Thatched roof with ridge, half-hipped to right. South wall and gable, roughcast. C.18/19 brick and flint extension with hipped slate roof.	T. & C.P. Act C.A.	SU 668 403 1602 02
Inn C.17	The Sun. 2 storeys. Painted brick and flint, part rendered. Slated gabled roof. Chimneys on gable ends. May have been built as a single unit to which a second was added soon after.	C.A.	SU 670 402 1602 28
Farmhouse C.17	Wivelrod Old Farm. 2½ storeys. Brick plinth and string course. Thatched roof. Interior plan, central back-to-back fireplaces. Restored 1969.		SU 675 384 1602 19
House C.17	No. 2, Gadwick Cottages, Thedden. 1½ storeys. White painted brick. Slated roof, gabled, with two dormer windows. Wooden casement windows elsewhere.		SU 680 389 1602 22
House C.18	The Cottage, Holt Lane End. 2 storeys. Painted brick walls. Gabled slated roof. Originally two cottages. Restored and enlarged.		SU 659 391 1602 27
House C.18	Burkham House. 2½ storeys. Constructed of light rose bricks made on site. Tiled gabled roof with tall chimney stack each end. Sash windows. Parapet with stone edge. C.19 extensions.		SU 650 426 1602 18

Group D — (cont.)

Description and Date	Remarks	Protection	Grid Ref. and Punchcard No.
House C.18	Ivy Cottage, Wardies. 2 storeys. White painted brick. Slate hipped roof. Some visible internal timbers at rear of Ivy Cottage, suggest house was originally timber-framed. Remainder C.18 and C.19. Now two dwellings.	C.A.	SU 662 400 1602 09
House C.18	Hop Bine Cottage, former Winters Farm. 1½ storeys. Brick walls. Corrugated iron roof. Centre panel door, triple casements each side. To the left a C.19 2-storey addition for hop-drying. Slated gabled roof.		SU 662 404 1602 29
House C.18	Ivalls House. 2 storeys. White painted brick and flint. Hipped tiled roof with dentil course at eaves. Mainly sash windows.	C.A.	SU 664 401 1602 07
House C.18	Penton Cottage, Church Street. 2 storeys. Pebble dash front. Gabled slated roof with tiled ridge. Chimney each end with timber-framing and white painted brick infilling. Only remaining example in village of symmetrical C.18 style small house.	C.A.	SU 664 402 1602 20
House C.18	No. 1, Drury Lane Cottages. 1½ storeys. Brick walls. Wrapped round thatched gable roof with long slope at rear. Casement windows. C.19 porch.		SU 664 404 1602 30
Farmhouse C.18	Parsonage Farm, L-shaped. 2 storeys. Painted brick walls, half-hipped slate roof. Casement windows. Much enlarged and modernised in recent years.	C.A.	SU 668 402 1602 31
House C.19	Rose Cottage, Holt Lane. 2 storeys. Brick and flint, painted. Slated gabled roof. Modern windows. Originally two cottages, enlarged and converted into single dwelling.		SU 661 397 1602 38
Farmhouse C.19	Manor Lodge, Wellers Place Farm. 2 storeys and cellar. White painted brick. Hipped tiled roof. Sash windows. Square centre porch with two fluted columns. Part of earlier house, together with brick and flint outbuildings, incorporated into wing to right. High brick and flint boundary wall.	C.A.	SU 662 400 1602 10
Building C.19	St. Mary's C. of E. Primary School and School Cottage. Built 1848 as integrated building under gabled tiled roof. Flint walls with red and blue brick quoins. School room high single storey. Large modern windows. School cottage at east end.	C.A.	SU 664 402 1602 21

Description and Date	Remarks	Protection	Grid Ref. and Punchcard No.
Group D — (cont.)			
House C.19	Mulberry House, formerly the Rectory. 2 storeys, attic and basement. Stuccoed walls. Parapet. Hipped slate roof with flat dormer. Sash windows. Centre square porch with frieze and two columns. Linked buildings may include remains of earlier Rectory built circa 1680. Ref: Buildings of England; Hants & I.O.W., (Pevsner & Lloyd), p. 101.	T. & C.P. Act C.A.	SU 667 402 1602 03
House	Paddock Bend, Holt Lane. 1½ storeys. Brick and flint, painted. Slated half-hipped roof. Hearth Tax 1674 records house on this site.		SU 661 395 1602 39
House	Lindzey (or Lindsay) Cottage. Flemish-bond brick walls. Thatched hipped roof. Two swept dormers. Brick plinth showing original position of door. Small extensions.	C.A.	SU 664 402 1602 13
House	Strawtop, Drury Lane, formerly Post Office. Long narrow structure of red brick with thatched half-hipped roof. C.18 timber-framing in gable ends. Post Office extension built circa 1930. Whole now converted to domestic use.		SU 667 406 1602 14
Farmhouse and Barns	East End Farm. 2 storeys. Rendered and painted east front. Rear elevation, brick and flint with original fenestration, important as last unpainted example of vernacular in village. Slated roof. Believed largely rebuilt in C.18 using old materials. Timber-framed barns, one of which may be C.16.	C.A.	SU 669 402 1602 17
Farm Buildings	Wellers Place Farm. Two timber-framed barns with hipped wagon entrances. Granary on staddle stones. Barn built of red and blue bricks, hipped tiled roof and dentil course at eaves. Centre barn tie-beam and an entrance post marked "T. King 1767". Timbers repaired and reroofed 1975.	C.A.	SU 662 400 1602 11
Group E — Street Patterns, Street Furniture and Open Spaces			
Village Green	Bentworth Holt Green. Registered with Commons Commissioners. Ref: C.R.O. Manor of Bentworth Hall Court Roll 85 M70/1 & 2.		SU 660 392 1602 33
Group F — Historical or Literary Associations			
Farmhouse	East End Farm. According to Manor Roll, house leased by George Wither, Senior, in 1580 and as such, likely birthplace of George Wither the poet, in 1588.	C.A.	SU 669 402 1602 17

Description and Date	Remarks	Protection	Grid Ref. and Punchcard No.

Group F — (cont.)

House	Hunts Cottage. Documentary evidence that house belonged to family of George Wither the poet and was probably home of his father, who died 1629.	C.A.	SU 664 402 1602 12
House	No. 2, Gadwick Cottages. Built circa 1667 by Elizabeth Wither. The house to which she retired after the death of her husband George Wither, the poet.		SU 680 389 1602 22
Village Green	Once the site of the village pound, where stray animals were kept penned until claimed by their owners. The village green was extended as part of the Lord of the Manor's waste-land. It now forms a wide verge along the side of the high street. In 1919 an oak was planted on the green in thanksgiving for the end of the First World War.	C.A.	SU 664 401 1602 32

Binsted is situated on the banks of the Wey some four miles north-east of Alton. Included in the parish is the Alice Holt Forest, home of the Forestry Commissioner's Research Station. This area has been a noted source of timber since mediaeval times. The attractive twelfth century church commands fine views over the surrounding countryside and contains an effigy of Richard de la Bere in the chapel. The body of Field Marshal Viscount Montgomery lies buried in the churchyard. The village itself contains many attractive examples of brick and timbered cottages. The Admiralty built a semaphore station at Binsted circa 1826, as one of a chain of such stations linking London and Portsmouth.

Description and Date	Remarks	Protection	Grid Ref. and Punchcard No.

Group A — Natural Features

Description and Date	Remarks	Protection	Grid Ref. and Punchcard No.
Viewpoint	From Binsted churchyard looking towards Monkswood, with Roxford farmbuildings in the foreground.	C.A.	SU 771 409 1603 66
Viewpoint	From Camp View, Wyck to south. Over gate, before "private" notice.		SU 761 395 1603 67
Viewpoint	From Isington Road to Mill Court. View from Monkswood to south west all round to north and to Alice Holt Forest on the east — including Froyle and Bentley.		SU 768 418 1603 68
Trees	Millers House, Isington. Very tall yew hedge by the River Wey.		SU 773 427 1603 78
Tree	Mill Court. Beautiful, old and very unusual weeping beech on the south bank of the River Wey.		SU 756 417 1603 77
Trees	Binsted churchyard. Very old yew trees, one said to be over eight hundred years old.	C.A.	SU 771 409 1603 75
Tree	Neatham Manor. Ancient oak tree of enormous girth.		SU 740 406 1603 71
Wooded Hill	Stephenfield Copse, Wheatley Road. Interesting woodland, mixed — Scots pine, yew, cherry, beech and others.		SU 755 395 1603 70
Trees	Birdworld, Holt Pound. Several species including Scots pine, hornbeam, lime and Lawson cypress.	T.P.O. No. 472	SU 811 432 1603 99
Forest	Alice Holt. Large area of attractive woodland. Extensively used for informal countryside recreation. Picnic areas, bridle paths, etc. Ref: The Royal Forests of England, (Cox), p.p. 79, 85, 309.		SU 810 420 1603 96
Trees	Bentley Station. Two oaks on adjoining land on north side.	T.P.O. No. 12 E.H.D.	SU 792 430 1603 100
Woodland	Monks Wood. An area of typical chalk woodland with varied flora.		SU 742 393 1603 101

Group B — Archaeological

Roman

Description and Date	Remarks	Protection	Grid Ref. and Punchcard No.
Pottery	Steen Farm. Pot found 1951. Present location not known. O.S.A. No. SU74 SE8.		SU 755 411 1603 51
Coin	Manor Cottages. Sestertius of Hadrian, C.2 A.D. Found in garden on line of Roman road from Silchester to Chichester. O.S.A. No. SU74 SW18.		SU 742 407 1603 55

Description and Date	Remarks	Protection	Grid Ref. and Punchcard No.

Group B — (cont.)

Inhumation	Hay Place Farm. C.4 inhumation burial, stone coffin and pottery found some years ago. Sarcophagus containing skeleton presented to British Museum. O.S.A. No. SU73 NE1. Ref: Archaeological Journal, Vol. 9, 1852, p.12.		SU 780 394 1603 47
Building (Site)	Wyck. Remains of villa discovered 1818. Large quantity of tiles and mortared flints found in the area. O.S.A. No. SU73 NE2. Ref: Journal of Roman Studies, Vol. 33, 1943, p. 75.	S.A.M. No. 429	SU 758 393 1603 48
Building (Site)	Neatham Manor Orchard. Remains found 1860. Coins from site in Alton Museum. O.S.A. No. SU74 SW17. Ref: V.C.H., Vol. 1, p. 306.		SU 749 411 1603 54
Pottery and Tiles	West of Malms Farm. Heavy scatter of pottery (including Samian ware) and tiles found in oil pipeline trench 1963. Finds in Haslemere Museum. O.S.A. No. SU74 SW8.		SU 749 411 1603 53

Romano-British

Pottery Kiln (Site)	Alice Holt Forest. Main area of kiln mounds lies in south end of forest. Two distinct features visible in the area. (a) Large irregular mounds of black earth and pottery, probably covering site of kiln. (b) Scatter of pottery associated in some cases with slight mounds of "natural soil", possible dumps or storage sites. O.S.A. No. SU84 SW23. Ref: 1. Archaeology, Vol. 28, 1840, p.p. 453—4.	S.A.M. No. 199	SU 809 401 1603 44

Post Norman

Earthworks	Monkswood. Occupying ridge and slopes on top of hill. Three continuous enclosures contained within larger enclosure. Probable site of a mediaeval establishment. O.S.A. No. SU73 NW22. Ref: Field Archaeology as Illustrated by Hampshire (Williams-Freeman), p. 386.		SU 742 393 1603 45
Pottery Kiln	West of Bentley Station. Kiln constructed of sawn blocks of local limestone. Finds include potsherds, charcoal, ashes, lumps of clay, and animal bones. O.S.A. No. SU74 SE4. Ref: Country Life. April 7th, 1944, p.p. 594—5.		SU 788 430 1603 50

Description and Date	Remarks	Protection	Grid Ref. and Punchcard No.

Group B — (cont.)

Description and Date	Remarks	Protection	Grid Ref. and Punchcard No.
Mediaeval Village (Site)	South Hay. Formerly in Alice Holt Forest. Clearly marked site with bank, well, and some house platforms sited on well drained slope. Ref: 1. V.C.H, Vol. 2, p.p. 488. 2. Deserted Mediaeval Villages (Beresford and Hurst).		SU 773 398 1603 97
Mediaeval Village (Site)	Neatham, Waverley Abbey. Population 96 in Domesday Survey. Grange, oratory and mill. Ref: 1. V.C.H, Vol. 2, p. 512. 2. V.C.H, Vol. 1, p. 510.		SU 742 405 1603 95
Ancient Site	Westcourt (or Westcote). Deserted mediaeval village. Ref: V.C.H, Vol. 2, p. 486.		SU 765 412 1603 98
Possible Earthworks	Neatham Down. Depressions and possible earthworks cut by oil pipeline. Pits containing flints and black, burnt or decayed organic matter. O.S.A. No. SU73 NW35. Ref: Alton Museum File No. A/C 3 (Sketch plan and section drawing).		SU 735 392 1603 46

Group C — Footpaths and Bridleways

Description and Date	Remarks	Protection	Grid Ref. and Punchcard No.
Ancient Travelway	The Straits, Kingsley. Possible Roman causeway and track which may run to Roman kiln site.		SU 781 390 — 787 391 1603 91

Group D — Buildings, Monuments and Engineering Works

Description and Date	Remarks	Protection	Grid Ref. and Punchcard No.
Church C.12	Holy Cross. Consists of a chancel with a south aisle, north chapel, and north vestry, a nave and aisles with western tower and south porch. The walls appear to be constructed of chalk rubble with clunch dressings, plastered on the interior and roughcast on the outside. The church was restored in 1863 but still retains some C.12—C.15 work. On the north side of the chancel is a C.14 chapel containing a good stone effigy of Richard de Westcote, who is portrayed as a knight in mail armour. The nave and west tower date from the late C.12. The altar is a Jacobean oak table. The vestry contains a mural brass dated 1595. The albaster font is dated 1896. In 1972 a glass panelled belfry screen was added. The churchyard contains the grave of Field Marshal the Viscount Montgomery of Alamein. O.S.A. No. SU74 SE7. Ref: V.C.H, Vol. 2, p. 488.	T. & C.P. Act C.A.	SU 771 409 1603 01
Farmhouse C.16	West Court. Coursed stone and random brick structure. Ridge tiled roof. Much altered and restored. Interior contains old timber, an original heavy moulded bressummer and some good inserted Elizabethan panelling.	T. & C.P. Act	SU 765 410 1603 06

Description and Date	Remarks	Protection	Grid Ref. and Punchcard No.
Group D — (cont.)			
Cottage C.16/17	Church Cottage. Timber-framed with brick and plaster infilling. Plinth of random rubble and brick. First floor over-hang on exposed joist ends.	T. & C.P. Act C.A.	SU 771 408 1603 04
Tithe Barn C.16/17	Mill Court. Coursed stone blocks. Ridge tiled roof. 'Priests house' at one end. Believed to have been a monastic building under Waverley Abbey.	T. & C.P. Act	SU 758 417 1603 07
Dovecote C.16/17	Neatham Manor. Rectangular coursed stone and brick structure. Tiled roof with wooden cupola. O.S.A. No. SU74 SW16.		SU 741 406 1603 34
House C.17	Binsted Wyck. Former farmhouse considerably enlarged and altered in the C.19 and incorporated into Victorian mansion. Brick and stone structure. Probably the last time 'Binsted Rock' was used for building.		SU 759 394 1603 85
Farmhouse C.17	Bumbles Farm, Wyck. 2 storeys. Coursed stone blocks with red brick quoins. Red tiled roof. Modern casements.		SU 760 395 1603 43
Farmhouse C.17	Stubbs Farm. 2 storeys. Coursed and random stone, patched in places with red brick. Ridge tiled roof.	T. & C.P. Act	SU 769 398 1603 09
Farmhouse C.17	Camices Farm. Timber-framed structure in centre, random stonework to left, plain C.19 brickwork to right. Red tiled roof.		SU 785 411 1603 17
Cottages (2) C.17	Groveland Cottages, formerly a farmhouse. 2 storeys. Red brick plinth and rusticated band. Gable with exposed timber-framing on upper floor. Ornamental square panel with date 1687 and initials "IK" on gable near road.		SU 799 441 1603 20
Farmhouse C.17/18	Kings Farm. Part single storey, part 2-storey. Coursed stone blocks. Red tiled roof. Plain wooden casement windows.	C.A.	SU 771 411 1603 11
Dovecote C.18	Neatham Mill. Coursed stone structure. Hipped red tiled roof. Forms interesting group with mill, grange and barn.		SU 739 407 1603 84
Cottage C.18	Roxford Cottage. Brick and stonework masking earlier timber-framed structure. Red tiled roof. Single storey. Small gabled dormer.	T. & C.P. Act C.A.	SU 771 408 1603 03
House C.18	The Millers House, formerly Isington Mill House. Coursed and random stone with lime-washed brick dressings. Slate roof. Sash windows.		SU 774 427 1603 23
House C.18	Valenders, Isington. 2 storeys. Red brick structure. Red tiled roof. Splayed 2-storey bay windows to left and right, probably modern.		SU 776 425 1603 26

Description and Date	Remarks	Protection	Grid Ref. and Punchcard No.

Group D — (cont.)

Description and Date	Remarks	Protection	Grid Ref. and Punchcard No.
Farmhouse C.18	River Hill Farm. 2 storeys. Red brick structure. Sash windows. Centre doorway and light columned porch. Ridge tiled roof.		SU 788 411 1603 18
Mill House and Barns (2) C.18/19	Turks Farm. Formerly Groveland Mill. 2 storeys. Hipped tiled roof. Early C.19 wing with three sash windows, slate roof with spreading eaves and modern half-timber porch. Timber-framed and red brick barn adjoining, and weatherboarded barn to extreme right.		SU 802 442 1603 21
Mill House C.19	Neatham Grange. 3-storey stuccoed structure. Sash windows. Lower 2-storey wing to right, partly limewashed brick with tiled roof. Pleasantly sited by the mill stream.		SU 731 407 1603 31
Manor House C.19	Mill Court. 2 storeys. Coursed stone blocks. Slate roof with wide spreading eaves. Sash windows in wide stone frames. Ionic columned porch. Flanking wings are late Victorian additions. History of the Manor dates back to 1367. Ref: Binsted, A Picture of its Past and Present, (Binsted Women's Institute).		SU 757 417 1603 29
House C.19	Telegraph House. 3 storeys and basement. Square whitewashed stuccoed structure. Flat roof. Mostly double hung sash windows with glazing bars.	T. & C.P. Act	SU 785 414 1603 58
House C.19	Alice Holt Lodge. 2 storeys. Brick structure. Tiled roof. Parapet. Sash windows and large bay window. Centre double door with arched fanlight. Ref: Journal of Forestry Commission, No. 27, 1958.		SU 803 427 1603 83
Mill House	Upper Neatham Mill. 2 storeys. Limewashed brick. Gable end has tile hung attic and exposed timber-framing on first floor. Ridge tiled roof. Possible C.18 or earlier.		SU 733 404 1603 35
Farmhouse	Roxford Farm. Possibly C.17. North facade at side towards churchyard has exposed timber-framing with limewashed brick infilling, and wide plinth. 2 storeys. Ridge tiled roof. East facade towards road has gables covered with fishscale tile-hanging on first floor. Plain door.	T. & C.P. Act C.A.	SU 771 408 1603 02
Barn	Upper Neatham Mill. Large weatherboarded structure with red tiled roof. Limewashed brick addition.		SU 733 404 1603 36
Mill and Barn	Neatham Mill. Mostly C.19. Limewashed brick and stone. Slate roof. 2 storeys. High painted boarded portion at back as oversailing gabled hoist. Weatherboarded barn with mansard slate roof.		SU 739 407 1603 32

Description and Date	Remarks	Protection	Grid Ref. and Punchcard No.

Group D — (cont.)

Description and Date	Remarks	Protection	Grid Ref. and Punchcard No.
Manor House	Neatham Manor. 2 storeys. Red brick front, possible C.18. Character of gabled elevation at rear suggests core is an Elizabethan manor. Probable site of a monastic grange. Much restored and altered. O.S.A. No. SU74 SW16. Ref: 1. V.C.H, Vol. 2, p.p. 512—4. 2. O.S. Map of Monastic Britain, 1954.		SU 740 406 1603 33
Mill House	The Fulling Mill House. 2 storeys. Timber-framed with red brick infilling, some modern herringbone brickwork at side. Remains of the Old Mill can be seen on island at the back. Ref: Binsted, A Picture of its Past and Present, (Women's Institute).		SU 755 417 1603 30
Barn	Wyck Farm. Stone and brick structure. Tiled roof.		SU 756 395 1603 87
Farm Buildings	Wyck Farm. Fine group including hopkilns, brick and stone barns and stables.		SU 759 397 1603 64
Cottages (2)	The Thatched Cottage, Wyck. Single storey. Thatched roof and eaves. Left part, coursed stone blocks. Red brick to the right. Modern lattice casement windows. Restored.		SU 757 396 1603 42
Barn	West Court Farm. Weatherboarded with corrugated iron roof. Good structural timberwork. Six bays with double wagon entrances. Ref: Binsted, A Picture of its Past and Present, (Women's Institute).		SU 765 411 1603 72
Hop Kilns (2)	West Court. Round structures. Brick with stone base.		SU 766 411 1603 63
Barns (2)	Roxford. Stone and brick structures. One slate roof, one tiled.	C.A.	SU 771 408 1603 73
Granary	Roxford Farm. Small square weatherboarded structure, on staddle stones. Hipped tiled roof.	C.A.	SU 771 408 1603 10
Hop Kilns	Roxford Farm. Stone kilns, partial intact, partial ruins. Slate roofs. Fine stone and brick barn wall beside road.	C.A.	SU 771 408 1603 74
Cottages (2)	Welford Cottages. Single storey and dormers. Timber-framed and limewashed brick. Modern half-hipped ridge tiled roof. Modern additions.	T. & C.P. Act C.A.	SU 771 410 1603 05
Barns	Kings Farm. Weatherboard with stone and brick. Partly tiled roof.	C.A.	SU 771 401 1603 88
Hopkilns and Barn	Kings Farm. Red brick structures. Tiled roof. Barn with inscription "D. Inwood, 1857".	C.A.	SU 771 411 1603 60
Cottages (2)	Nos. 2, and 3, The Street. 2 storeys. Timber-framed with brick and plaster infilling. Ridge tiled roof. Centre chimney stack.	C.A.	SU 772 410 1603 12

Description and Date	Remarks	Protection	Grid Ref. and Punchcard No.

Group D — (cont.)

Description and Date	Remarks	Protection	Grid Ref. and Punchcard No.
House	White Hart. Former Inn converted to private house 1963. Limewashed, C.18 brick exterior masking earlier timber-framed structure. Thatched roof. Old bread oven.		SU 773 411 1603 13
Barn	Eggars Farm. Weatherboarded structure with red tiled roof.		SU 774 425 1603 79
House	South Hay House. An attractive restored and extended property of 2 storeys with red tile roof. The eastern part is C.20 timber framing with brick infilling, the centre part probably C.15/16 timber framed with red brick infilling. The extension to the west is of Bargate stone with brick dressings probably of C.17 date.	T. & C.P. Act	SU 775 397 1603 08
Building	South Hay House. Former wagon store converted to garage and stables. Stone blocks with brick dressings. Red tiled roof.		SU 775 397 1603 40
Barn	South Hay House. Mainly stone structure with some weatherboarding. Once formed part of a hopkiln.		SU 775 397 1603 39
Cottage	Colesons, South Hay. Part timberframed with brick infilling, part plaster and part stone. Limewashed. Originally two cottages.		SU 775 398 1603 82
Farmhouse	Hay Place Farm. Present house built 1955 incorporating smaller red brick structure, possibly C.17. Possibly on site of a much earlier building.		SU 775 407 1603 23
Hopkilns	Hay Place. Three round brick and stone structures.		SU 775 408 1603 62
House	Cobdens, formerly The Elms. Partly timber-framed and partly plain C.19 brick. Old ridge tiled roof. Formerly a school and Almshouses. Converted to one house in the 1950's.		SU 777 411 1603 15
Cottage	Wheatley Lane End Cottage. 2 storeys. Brick on ground floor, Victorian tile-hanging above. Thatched roof. Interior exposed beams. Recently restored.		SU 782 411 1603 16
Cottage	Hoggatts, Wheatley Lane. 2 storeys. Part timber-framed with brick and plaster infilling, part lime-washed plaster. Ridge tiled roof.		SU 783 395 1603 37
Farm Buildings	Hoggatts, Wheatley Lane. Barn, part weather-board and timber-framed. Hopkiln, limewashed and red brick.		SU 783 395 1603 38
House and Barn	Binsted Place. Red brick structure, part circa 1680, part circa 1800. Fine old interior beams and bread oven in open fireplace. Nearby C.17 barn built of Selborne stone. Fine stone walls in garden.		SU 784 411 1603 92

Description and Date	Remarks	Protection	Grid Ref. and Punchcard No.

Group D — (cont.)

Description and Date	Remarks	Protection	Grid Ref. and Punchcard No.
Barn and Hopkilns (4)	Wheatley Farm. Stone kilns with slate roofs. Fine weatherboarded barn with tiled roof.		SU 785 400 1603 61
Farmhouse and Stables	Wheatley House. 2 storeys. Coursed and random stone with brick dressing, south front limewashed. Red tiled roof. Stone stable block with arches and slate roof.		SU 785 460 1603 41
House	Barnfield House, Wheatley. Part timber-framed with brick and plaster infilling, part stone and part hanging tiles. Limewashed. Magnificent view over Alice Holt Forest.		SU 787 415 1603 57
Cottage	Peppercorn Cottage, Blacknest. Limewashed brick structure. Part said to date from the C.17.		SU 797 415 1603 93
Cottage	"At the Crossways", Blacknest. L-shaped with projecting pentice to rear. Part timber-framed, part plain brickwork. Thatched roof.		SU 798 414 1603 19
Hopkiln	Cobdens Farm, Holt Pound. Limewashed structure. Slate roof. Now converted to house.		SU 814 441 1603 81
Hopkilns (2)	Old Kiln Farm, Holt Pound. Round limewashed structure with red tiled roof. Now converted to house.		SU 817 437 1603 80
Cottages (2)	Eggars Cottages, Isington. 2 storeys. Limewashed brick with exposed timber-framing. Hipped red tiled roofs.		SU 775 425 1603 25
Mill	Isington Mill. Picturesque restored property incorporating round hop kilns with steep slate roofs. 2 storeys. Red brick wing may be C.18. Modern limewashed brick addition to rear.		SU 774 428 1603 24
Cottage	The Thatched Cottage, Isington. Exposed light timber-framing with limewashed brick infilling. Thatched roof. Formerly two cottages.	T. & C.P. Act	SU 780 426 1603 27
Farmhouse	Isington Close. Old part possibly C.17/18. 2 storeys. Limewashed brick. Steep hipped tiled roof. C.19 addition has two gables with ornamental bargeboards. Restored in recent years.		SU 783 427 1603 28

Group E — Street Patterns, Street Furniture and Open Spaces

Description and Date	Remarks	Protection	Grid Ref. and Punchcard No.
Mounting Block	Stone mounting block sited at Kings Farm.		SU 771 411 1603 65
Well	By the River Wey near Mill Court Lodge. Holy or Wishing Well, covered by beehive shaped stone cover. Deep and clear. Believed to be very ancient.		SU 755 417 1603 76

Group F — Historical or Literary Association

Description and Date	Remarks	Protection	Grid Ref. and Punchcard No.
Manor Farmhouse C.16	West Court. In 1330 Robert and Nicola de la Bere owned the Manor of Binsted St. Clare. After adding the Westcote Chapel to Binsted Church in 1331, Richard de la Bere applied to the King for a Royal Warrant to endow a chaplain who would celebrate Mass daily in the Chapel. Ref: Binsted, A Picture of its Past and Present, (Women's Institute).	T. & C.P. Act	SU 765 410 1603 06
Farmhouse C.17/18	Kings Farm. In 1849 the owner, Mr. Daniel Inwood, directed in his will that farm and property should be sold and the proceeds to be used to found a hospital in Alton, known as the Inwood Cottage Hospital. The sale took place in 1874.		SU 771 411 1603 11
House C.19	Telegraph House. Built in the Napoleonic Wars to form part of the proposed visual signal line from London to Plymouth, which was to branch from the existing Admiralty Semaphore System from London to Portsmouth. Ref: Binsted, A Picture of its Past and Present (Women's Institute).	T. & C.P. Act	SU 785 414 1603 58
Mill	Isington Mill. Post war home of Field Marshal, the Viscount Montgomery of Alamein until his death in 1976. Long wooden building between house and river contained his wartime caravans, which are now in the Imperial War Museum, London.		SU 774 428 1603 24

BRAMSHOTT

The manor of Bramshott was held by two unnamed freemen in the reign of Edward the Confessor, and at the time of the Domesday Survey it was held by Edward of Salisbury. The manor was split in the fifteenth century but by 1550 the entire manor was held by the Mervyn family. In 1610 the manor of Bramshott was conveyed to John Hooke and later passed to the Whitehead and Dennis families. The manor house has remained largely unaltered since the fifteenth century and parts may be even earlier. It is believed to be the oldest continuously inhabited house in Hampshire and was taken over by the War Office in 1917.

The industrial history of the parish can be traced back to the Romans who worked iron here. Henry Hooke, lord of the manor between 1616 and 1625, was responsible for developing the iron industry in the seventeenth century, but by the mid eighteenth century it had died out again. The association of the parish with the ironworks is recorded in the name Hammer Bottom. The other industries which have been carried on in the parish have included paper-making, milling, forestry and broom-making, the last two connected with Woolmer Forest and the adjacent heath-lands.

The church of St. Mary dates back to the thirteenth century, though it was much restored in the Victorian period. It contains some remains of mediaeval stained glass as well as some late nineteenth century examples.

The parish has associations with Sydney and Beatrice Webb, founders of the Fabian Society, who built Passfield Corners. In 1929 Sydney Webb was created Lord Passfield, and on their deaths the house was left to the London School of Economics.

Description and Date	Remarks	Protection	Grid Ref. and Punchcard No.
Group A — Natural Features			
Fenland	Conford Fen. An area ½ mile long and 300 yds. wide astride Hollywater Stream. Fen and bog vegetation in close proximity, resulting from the moor soil being acid and the stream carrying alkaline salts. Lime loving flora encouraged.	N.P. Act S.S.S.I.	SU 820 330 2301 26
Tree	Linchborough Lodge, Woolmer Forest. Known as Queen Victoria's oak. Reputed to be the tree under which Queen Victoria picnicked in 1859, when she visited the troops camped at Woolmer, accompanied by the Prince Consort, Princess Royal, and Prince of Wales. Tablet recording the details erected in 1902, and now in the custody of the Parish Council.		SU 815 332 2301 71
Trees	No. 60, Haslemere Road, Liphook. Two large horse chestnuts on the land to the rear and within the grounds of the above property.	T.P.O. No. 4 E.H.D.	SU 844 315 2301 100
Trees	Southern boundary Fletchers Field, between Midhurst Road and Portsmouth Road, Liphook.	T.P.O. No. 26 E.H.D.	SU 840 311 2301 101
Woodland	Waggoners Wells. Surrounding the three pools made by damming the river, possibly in connection with the iron industry.	N.P. Act S.S.S.I.	SU 859 342 2301 46
Trees	North Lodge, Woolmer. A belt of beautiful beeches, five or six deep, which sweep round northern edge of open fields from North Lodge west towards Dog Kennel Firs.		SU 844 346 2301 41
Trees	Rectory Lane. A mature beech at junction with Woolmer Lane. Several attractive birch and beech trees along upper part of lane.		SU 843 333 2301 47
Trees	Chiltlee Manor, Liphook. Several trees of various species standing within the curtilage of the above property.	T.P.O. No. 74 E.H.D.	SU 842 314 2301 103
Trees	Chiltley Place, Liphook. Most of the trees are within the gardens and roadsides of an estate, formerly the grounds of Chiltley Place.	T.P.O. No. 119	SU 845 310 2301 55
Trees	Attractive trees mainly on the perimeter of the filling station at Bramshott Chase. Centred on grid reference.	T.P.O. No. 307	SU 871 337 2301 56
Trees	A variety of species of trees within the grounds of Claremont, London Road, Liphook.	T.P.O. No. 504	SU 840 321 2301 88
Trees	Various trees growing between the railway line and Goldenfields, Chiltley Lane, Liphook. Centred on grid reference.	T.P.O. No. 702	SU 847 312 2301 89

Group A — (cont.)

Description and Date	Remarks	Protection	Grid Ref. and Punchcard No.
Pond	Wheatsheaf Pond, Wheatsheaf Common, Liphook. Recently cleaned by volunteers. Mentioned in C.18 as a fishpond belonging to Rogate-Bohunt Manor. Ref: 1. A Hampshire Parish, (Newman), p. 34. 　　　2. Liphook Community Magazine, Summer 1976, p. 3.		SU 837 305 2301　76
Pond	Hollywater Pond, Woolmer Forest. Pond about 300 yds. long, on Hollywater flowing from Conford Moor. Dam and sluices remain. Sizeable trees now cover area. Ref: A Hampshire Parish, (Newman) p.p. 3, 111.		SU 810 334 2301　72
Area of Ecological Importance	Bramshott and Ludshott Commons. Area as a whole represents one of the best examples of open heathland and has a wide variety of flora and fauna.	N.P. Act S.S.S.I.	SU 858 345 2301 102

Group B — Archaeological

Bronze Age

Description and Date	Remarks	Protection	Grid Ref. and Punchcard No.
Bowl Barrow (Probable)	Golf Course, Liphook. Mound 30 m. in diameter and 1.8 m. high with a ditch. Planted with conifers. Golf tee cut into south side. O.S.A. No. SU83 SW5.		SU 832 303 2301　29
Barrow (Possible)	200 yds. south of Bramshott Court. Mound 14.0 m. in diameter and 1.7 m. high. No trace of ditch, situated close to River Wey. May be part of lay-out of formal garden. Locally known as "Druids Mound" and surmounted by old yew trees. O.S.A. No. SU83 SW2.		SU 832 335 2301　27

Roman

Description and Date	Remarks	Protection	Grid Ref. and Punchcard No.
Pottery	Pieces of New Forest type pottery found when digging a trench at Hurnlands near Passfield. O.S.A. No. SU83 SW9. Ref: P.H.F.C. Vol. 19, 1955, (Rolston), p.p. 12—19.		SU 831 348 2301　91

Group D — Buildings, Monuments and Engineering Works

Description and Date	Remarks	Protection	Grid Ref. and Punchcard No.
Church C.13	Church of St. Mary, Bramshott. Cruciform plan, present nave and aisles date from 1872. North and south transepts with early perpendicular windows. Two squints from transepts into chancel. Shingled broach spire. Fine C.15 brass of John Weston and his wife. O.S.A. No. SU83 SW10. Ref: 1. Buildings of England; Hants. and I.O.W., (Pevsner and Lloyd) p.p. 140—1. 　　　2. V.C.H. Vol. 2, p. 494. 　　　3. Rural Life in Hants, (Capes), p.p. 217, 296—7.	T. & C.P. Act	SU 842 328 2301　01

Description and Date	Remarks	Protection	Grid Ref. and Punchcard No.

Group D — (cont.)

Description and Date	Remarks	Protection	Grid Ref. and Punchcard No.
House C.14/15	Bramshott Manor. Parts may be of earlier date. Originally a hall and solar. Stone ground floor with C.14/15 windows with cusped arches. Upper storey tile-hung with tiled roof. Oak timbers of original upper hall in roof. Elizabethan oak staircase, and stone fireplace of about 1530 with initials 'E.M.'. O.S.A. No. SU83 SW8. Ref: 1. Buildings of England; Hants. and I.O.W., (Pevsner and Lloyd), p. 141. 2. V.C.H., Vol. 2, p. 492.	T. & C.P. Act	SU 842 328 2301 03
Farmhouse C.16	Passfield Farm. 2 storeys. L-shaped plan. Timber-framed with rubble filling, except for south wing. Hipped, tiled roof with old chimney. Casement windows with glazing bars. Ref: A Hampshire Parish, (Newman), p. 110.	T. & C.P. Act	SU 823 342 2301 07
Cottage C.16	Adams Cottage, Rectory Lane. 2 storeys. North wall timber-framed with brick and rubble filling. South wall of whitewashed ironstone. Tiled roof, Victorian extension with square bay window. Originally built for keepers in the Royal Forest of Woolmer. Ref: A Hampshire Parish, (Newman), p. 65.	T. & C.P. Act	SU 842 329 2301 04
Gatehouse C.16	Bramshott Place. Small square 2-storey building circa. 1575. Brick structure with moulded brick columns at corners, ending in stone finials. Roof obscured by ogee gables with brick coping and finials. Two brick doorways of 4-centred arches. Oriel windows with diamond leaded glazing. Located in the grounds of C.19 Bramshott Place, now part of King George's Hospital, which replaced a C.16 manor house. O.S.A. No. SU83 SW12. Ref: 1. V.C.H. Vol. 2, p.p. 491—2. 2. Buildings of England; Hants. and I.O.W. (Pevsner and Lloyd), p. 141.	T. & C.P. Act	SU 843 322 2301 31
House C.16	Conford House, Conford Park, Nr. Liphook. 2 storeys and dormers. Timber-framed, with stone and brick facing except on west end. Tiled hipped roof with windbraces and dropped ties. Sash windows of later date. Outshots on north and west sides. Possibly built on site of hall house, re-using some building materials. Ref: A Hampshire Parish, (Newman). p. 120.	T. & C.P. Act	SU 825 329 2301 05
House C.16	Passfield House. Tiled roof with central chimney. Tile-hung gables. Some half-timbering with brick infilling and signs of earlier timber work. Partly herringbone ironstone infilling on south face. Pink rough cast east front. Rustic timber porch with tiled roof. House refronted in late C.18. Recent additions.		SU 823 342 2301 22

Group D — (cont.)

Description and Date	Remarks	Protection	Grid Ref. and Punchcard No.
House C.16	Tap House, The Square, Liphook. Single storey and dormers. Tiled roof with three gabled dormers. Part timber-framed with rubble infilling, part plaster rendered. Casement windows with glazing bars. Once the tap of the Crown Inn, now called Ship House.	C.A.	SU 840 315 2301 20
Cow Byre C.16/17	In grounds of Blue Vines. Single storey, timber-framed with herringbone infilling visible inside and out. Tiled roof. Leaded casement windows inserted.		SU 836 327 2301 13
House C.16/17	Covers Farm, Church Lane. 2 storeys. L-shaped plan. Stone structure, some timber-framing visible inside. Squared and coursed stone with galleting. Casement windows. Small central porch. Barn with slate roof, and stone and weatherboard walls. Ref: 1. Rural Life in Hampshire, (Capes), p.p. 248, 345. 2. A Hampshire Parish, (Newman), p.p. 41, 79, 92, 109.		SU 840 329 2301 35
Stables and Garden Walls C.16/17	Ludshott Manor. Stables of ironstone with stone quoins and a tiled roof. Arched entrance with gable and stone coping. Garden walls with stone door openings and 4-centred arches. Two similar doorways in dairy. O.S.A. No. SU83 SW7.		SU 842 340 2301 12A
Cottage C.16/17	Quarry Cottage. 2 storeys. Brick structure. Tiled roof with barn end, and some timber-framing. Old central chimney. Casement windows with glazing bars.		SU 824 343 2301 25
House C.17	The Forge, Passfield. 2 storeys. Coursed rubble with brick dressings. Tiled roof with barn end hip. Later casement windows. South west end may be older with dressed stone quoins and rubble wall. Date 1602 or 1603 on front. Sun Insurance sign.		SU 823 343 2301 24
Building C.17	Links Hotel, formerly the Wheatsheaf Inn. 2 storeys. Overhanging bays on upper storey. Tiled roof and walls partly tile hung. Part may be of earlier date. Some timber-framing inside. Door with hood. Casement windows.		SU 837 306 2301 11
House C.17	Waterside House. Rear central portion circa. 1638, a fine yeoman's house. Much enlarged in Jacobean style stone in 1921. Materials brought from a Northumbrian castle. Old barn coverted into drawing room. Arms and motto on wall. Additions with leaded casement windows and drip courses.		SU 828 336 2301 73

Description and Date	Remarks	Protection	Grid Ref. and Punchcard No.

Group D — (cont.)

Description and Date	Remarks	Protection	Grid Ref. and Punchcard No.
Building C.17	No. 10, The Square, Liphook. Located on the corner. Jettied 2-storey building. Tiled roof with brick chimney. South side and gables tile-hung. Modern shop front. Interior beams. Ref: A Hampshire Parish, (Newman), p. 106.	C.A.	SU 839 315 2301 52
Building C.17	No. 12, The Square, Liphook. 1½ storeys. Tiled roof with sag in ridge. Three tiled dormers sprung above eaves with casement windows below. White plastered front. 2-storey tiled wing at rear now part of No. 14.	C.A.	SU 839 315 2301 52A
Building C.17	No. 6, The Square, Liphook. Timber-framed with rubble and a little brick infilling. Casement and dormer windows. Tiled roof with old external chimney. House and chimney part tile-hung. Later cement rendered wing.	C.A.	SU 839 315 2301 63
House and Barns C.17	Malthouse Farm, Haslemere Road, Liphook. Timber-framed and brick house with steep tile roof. Early staircase. Mullioned window discovered in kitchen. At one time belonged to Winchester College and tenants paid rent in grain. Wood and stone barns. Main barn carries College Arms.		SU 843 316 2301 65
Inn C.17	Royal Anchor Hotel, Liphook. Originally 2 storeys with a third added under a mansard tiled roof. Whitewashed brick with a heavy cornice and egg and dart moulding below. Sash, and half hexagonal bay windows on two floors. Doorcase with pediment and fanlight obscured by Royal arms. Gable of 3 storeys on west side. Interior has oak panelling, and an Elizabethan door presented by Queen Victoria, located in the bar. Ref: Buildings of England, Hants. and I.O.W., (Pevsner and Lloyd), p. 319.	T. & C.P. Act C.A.	SU 839 315 2301 06
Cottage C.17/18	Wheatsheaf Pond Cottage. Tiled roof with tile hung dormers. White plastered stone or brick structure. Modern brick extension. Deeds date from 1701. Timber-framing visible inside.		SU 837 306 2301 77
House C.18	Bramshott Vale. Brick structure of 2 storeys and attics. Wooden cornice, hipped tiled roof with three dormers. Fanlight and panelled door beneath classical porch with pediment and Ionic columns. Interior has C.18 oak staircase, panelling and fireplaces. Old garden wall. Part dated 'H.B. 1700'. Ref: 1. Buildings of England; Hants and I.O.W., (Pevsner and Lloyd), p. 141. 2. A Hampshire Parish, (Newman), p. 31.	T. & C.P. Act	SU 837 328 2301 02

Description and Date	Remarks	Protection	Grid Ref. and Punchcard No.

Group D — (cont.)

Description and Date	Remarks	Protection	Grid Ref. and Punchcard No.
Toll House C.18	Old Toll House, Cold Ash Hill. Rendered structure with hipped, tiled roof. Metal windows, fairly modern shutters and porch with ridged hood. Addition at rear. Home of Charles Cover, turnpike keeper in 1830. Ref: A Hampshire Parish, (Newman), p. 105.		SU 842 323 2301 86
House C.18	Chiltlee Manor, Liphook. 2 storeys. Plaster faced with slate roof. Sash windows. Porch supported on columns approached up three steps. Door with reeded surround. Coursed stone addition of about 1830 on south side with two octagonal 2-storey bay windows. Interior modernised to accomodate offices in 1980. Ref: 1. Rural Life in Hampshire, (Capes), p. 274. 2. A Hampshire Parish, (Newman), p.p. 46, 47, 50.	T. & C.P. Act	SU 842 314 2301 15
House C.18	Downlands. 3 storeys. Brick with stone quoins. Slate roof with wide eaves. Porch supported on Ionic columns. Sash windows and Victorian bay windows. Kitchen quarters of sandstone with brick dressings. Stone vase as garden feature.		SU 851 336 2301 08
House C.18	Old Mill, Bramshott. Formerly a corn mill on the River Wey. Roughly coursed sandstone with tiled roof. Main part 3 storeys and dormers, with 2-storey and dormer section. Datestone by door 1750. Mill modified in early C.20 as house. Some machinery remains, but waterwheel gone. Sluices and half the millpond remain.	C.A.	SU 837 332 2301 44
House C.18	Glebe House, Rectory Lane. Built about 1702. Brick structure. Additions of 1834 and 1870. Used as Rectory between 1702 and 1922. Monkhouse, a Rector, built the fine wood-beamed barn behind the house in 1815.		SU 846 332 2301 58
Building C.18/19	Holly Cottage, Woolmer Lane. 2 cottages combined, with later additions. 2 storeys and dormers. Rubble structure with brick dressings to doors and windows. Tiled roof. Dwelling recorded on site 1730.		SU 842 333 2301 79
Cottage C.18/19	Nut Tree Cottage, Weavers Down. 2 storeys. Coursed stone structure with white mortar. Extended in brick. Large modern extension in white-washed brick at rear. Tiled roofs. Brick dressings to windows and doors. Modern glazed door.		SU 820 312 2301 37

Description and Date	Remarks	Protection	Grid Ref. and Punchcard No.

Group D — (cont.)

Cottage C.18/19 — Old Forge, Conford. 2 storeys. Roughly coursed sandstone with brick quoins. Tiled roof with gable ends. External chimney on western gable. Modern additions including wing on north east corner. Diamond shaped leaded windows. Home of the head of the Moss family who were 'edge tool' makers in C.19. The 1851 census records that there were four households of Moss' involved in the tool-making work, but the business closed in 1916.

SU 825 329
2301 51

House C.18/19 — Ship House, No. 3, The Square, Liphook. White plaster-faced brick. Slate roof. Sash windows and glazing bars. Earlier remains at rear. Formerly the Old Ship Inn.

C.A.

SU 839 314
2301 19

Cottage and Outbuildings C.19 — Bramshott Cottage. Rebuilt 1826 on site of earlier cottage. Stone structure with tiled roof. Stable used as garage. Barn converted to studio.
Ref: A Hampshire Parish, (Newman), p. 45.

SU 842 332
2301 36

Hopkilns (4) C.19 — Near Passfield House Farm. Two circular oast houses together, and a circular and a square oast house separated by barn. Sandstone and rubble structures with tiled roofs cemented over. Square oast house and barn with slate roofs. Used for storage only.

SU 824 345
2301 23

House C.19 — Ludshott Manor formerly known as Woolmer Lodge. Built 1827—8 in plain Tudor style. On site of earlier house. Some outbuildings of Elizabethan or Jacobean date.
O.S.A. No. SU83 SW7.
Ref: 1. Buildings of England; Hants and I.O.W., (Pevsner and Lloyd), p. 141.
2. A Hampshire Parish, (Newman), p.p. 42—45.
3. Rural Life in Hampshire, (Capes), p.p. 275—6, 281.

SU 842 340
2301 12

House C.19 — Osbornes, Portsmouth Road, Liphook. 2 storeys. Slate roof and plaster faced walls. Regency cast iron verandah on south side. Sash windows. Traces of earlier work, Queen Anne date. Panelled door with hood.

T. & C.P. Act
C.A.

SU 839 314
2301 17

Building C.19 — Formerly Liphook School, now a library. Begun in 1872 when Sir William Erle gave the site and a donation to build a National School for girls and small boys. Squared stone structure with tiled roofs. Many additions. Small shingle-hung tower with shingled roof.

SU 840 316
2301 85

Description and Date	Remarks	Protection	Grid Ref. and Punchcard No.

Group D — (cont.)

Description and Date	Remarks	Protection	Grid Ref. and Punchcard No.
Entrance Gates C.19	Downlands. Wrought iron gates, flanked by square piers topped by stone vases decorated with rams heads. Low curved wall and iron railing connects with taller brick piers also capped by stone vases.		SU 851 332 2301 09
House and Grounds C.19	Foley Manor, Liphook. Stone and stuccoed house with slate roof. Victorian rendered wing added to north west porch with Tuscan columns, pilasters and pediment over round-headed doorway. Victorian staircase. Extensive lawns with trees, gazebo, fountain, lake and bronze equestrian statue. Ref: A Hampshire Parish, (Newman), p.p. 48—50.		SU 827 307 2301 68
House C.19	Passfield Place. Large white rendered house, with tiled roof. Two shallow wings, and small protruding porch. Once owned by Sidney and Beatrice Webb, whose gravestones are in the woods nearby. Ref: A Hampshire Parish, (Newman), p. 128.		SU 824 338 2301 48
Shops (2) C.19	Nos. 1, and 2, Tweenways, The Square, Liphook. 2 storeys, cream, plaster faced walls. Double hipped slate roof with plaster cornice. Sash windows. Rear extension of sandstone and brick dressings. Originally a private house.	C.A.	SU 839 315 2301 21
Building C.19/20	Goldenfield and Lychgate, 53 and 51, Chitley Lane. 2 storeys. Stone and timber construcion. First floor partly tile-hung. Five gables in roof, all at different levels. To the rear is a tall gabled annexe. Chimney stacks of various styles. Weather boarded clock tower and cupola. The west wing gives the appearance of a separate house and is now used as such, known as Lychgate. Two plates on the timber and brick porch of the main house read 'Built by Mary Anne Robb 1891: Architect Philip Webb' and 'Built by M.A. Robb 1905: Architect Owen Little'.		SU 848 311 2301 106
House C.20	Bohunt Manor, Portsmouth Road, Liphook. Built about 1928 on site of an C.18 farm-house. Stones from the walls and barns re-used in present structure. Farm recorded on this site in 1597. Ref: Rural Life in Hampshire, (Capes), p.p. 141 and 340.		SU 835 310 2301 67
Building C.20	Church Centre, Portsmouth Road, Liphook. Opened 1969. Rectangular plan. Brown brick walls on low plinth. 4-gabled roof over main room, each gable of two triangular sheets of glass. Two well recessed doorways on front, and six tall metal windows. Part used as church on Sundays.		SU 838 312 2301 83

Description and Date	Remarks	Protection	Grid Ref. and Punchcard No.

Group D — (cont.)

Description and Date	Remarks	Protection	Grid Ref. and Punchcard No.
Rectory C.20	Portsmouth Road, Liphook. Built 1922, by H. Inigo Triggs. Pale, roughly coursed stone walls. Tiled roof with two brick chimneys. Left hand side of front, tile hung with two 'portholes'. Gabled projecting centre section containing front door.		SU 839 313 2301 82
House C.20	Tilburys, Passfield. Stone structure with brick dressings to windows. Tiled roof. Half-timbering at northern end. Rebuilt about 1920.		SU 824 346 2301 54
House C.20	Clerks, Rectory Lane. Built 1911 on old site in Elizabethan/Jacobean style. 2 storeys. M-shaped tiled roof with gabletted ends. Squared stone walls with brick quoins and dressings. 2-storey porch and casement windows. Old weatherboarded barn, on stone plinth. Timber-framed with tiled roof. Lower sections either side of weatherboarding and stone. Ref: Rural Life in Hampshire, (Capes), p.p. 122, 125, 144, 247.		SU 846 332 2301 38
House C.20	Coopers Bridge. 2 storeys. Brick structure. Hipped tiled roof descending in places to just above ground floor windows. Brick chimney stacks with over-sailing courses. Dormer windows in roof. All windows rectangular in shape with leaded lights. Designed in 1911 by local architect, H. Inigo Triggs.		SU 835 335 2301 109
House C.20	Bramshott Court. A stone built house on site of C.17 Fir Grove, most of which was demolished in 1832, leaving only one block of out-buildings which were incorporated into the present house. This has now been divided into six dwellings. The gardens designed by Gertrude Jekyll though long neglected, have now been partially restored.	C.A.	SU 831 337 2301 108
Monument C.20	In front of Liphook Post Office. The 'Flora Thompson Memorial'. A bust portraying the writer as a young woman, which is set on a brick plinth. The sculpture has a green bronze finish and is the work of a local artist, Philip Jackson. Flora Thompson well-known for her book 'Lark Rise To Candleford', lived for many years in the area, at one period working in the Old Post Office, where her husband was Postmaster.		SU 839 313 2301 107

Description and Date	Remarks	Protection	Grid Ref. and Punchcard No.

Group D — (cont.)

Building	The Cricketers, Passfield. Sandstone, part rendered, with some visible timber framing. Parts may be of C.16 date. 1½ storeys. Tiled roof with half hipped dormers. An inn between 1850 and 1902. Stone farm build- ing with tiled roof. Tie beam roof with angle braces.		SU 823 342 2301 40
Inn	The Deer's Hut, Longmoor Road, Liphook. Main section C.18 or earlier. Coursed stone structure, ground floor whitewashed, tile hung above. Tiled roof. Single storey extension to left and right, of colourwashed coursed stone. Casement windows. Faces onto Green.		SU 824 317 2301 49
Ice House	Foley Manor, Liphook. Underground circular bricked chamber, located in field behind stables, covered by grass. About 12 ft. across internally with dome supported by an iron pole. Steps down into it now filled by earth, what does remain of entrance is covered with wire.		SU 825 308 2301 92
Inn	The Green Dragon, London Road, Liphook. 2 storeys. Roughly coursed rubble with tiled roof. 2-storey extension at rear. Whitewashed front with tile hung dormers. Alehouse believed to have stood here before the Dissolution. Ref: A Hampshire Parish, (Newman), p. 109.	C.A.	SU 839 315 2301 87
Farmhouse	Holme Hills Farmhouse. 2 storeys. Squared stone walls with brick quoins and arches over lower windows. A stone lean-to at either end, with slate roofs. Chimneys serve bread ovens in each lean-to. Central double doors under a slate-roofed porch. Two stores with tiled roofs, one stone, and one wooden-planks.		SU 824 326 2301 42
House	Linchborough Lodge, Woolmer Forest. 2 storeys. Brick faced with tiled roof. Present building looks C.18/19, but traces of much older work. Old beams visible inside. Also signs of an earlier steeper roof. Cellar. Possible site of Edward I's Hunting Lodge. Ref: A Hampshire Parish, (Newman), p.p. 60, 61, 67, 68.		SU 815 333 2301 70
Houses	Nos. 2, and 3, Links Cottages, and The Old Club House, Liphook. Converted from the outbuildings of the Links Hotel. Stone walls with brick dressings to doors and windows. Tiled roofs. Visually important on entry to Liphook.		SU 837 307 2301 66

12th Century Church and Village Pond, BURITON

Description and Date	Remarks	Protection	Grid Ref. and Punchcard No.

Group D — (cont.)

Description and Date	Remarks	Protection	Grid Ref. and Punchcard No.
House	Old Forge, Griggs Green. Whitewashed coursed stone. 2 storeys. Tile roof. Tile hung extension at rear, possibly where blacksmith worked. Casement windows with glazing bars. Deeds go back to early C.18. Ref: A Hampshire Parish, (Newman), p. 61.		SU 823 316 2301 50
Cottages (2)	Primrose Cottages, Tunbridge Lane, Bramshott. 2 storeys. Irregularly coursed stone with two brick quoins. Gabled slate roof. Two pairs of brick chimneys astride ridge. Casement windows, some on ground floor with brick arched tops. Date stone on back 1844 W.H. 1749. C.20 extensions to both cottages.	C.A.	SU 838 329 2301 59
Barn	Priors Farm. Single storey. Timber-framed structure with tarred wood sides. Half boarded ends with stone infilling at lower level.		SU 851 346 2301 39
Cottages	Haslemere Road, Liphook. On south side Nos. 12–26 mainly C.19 of sandstone with tilehanging and steep gabled roofs. Buildings on north side, Nos. 1–17, more varied. Some originally labourers' cottages attached to Moss's Farm. Pleasant cottages important as a group.	C.A.	SU 840 315 2301 64
Oast Houses (2)	Quinces. One circular oast house of sandstone and brick with cement covered coned roof. The other, square with tiled roof and brick structure. Recent outbuildings. Chalcraft family bought house in 1758 to become centre of their hop industry.		SU 839 331 2301 14
Cottages (2)	Radstock and Green Brow Cottages, Hammer Vale. Close to a small green. Both built of stone with brick dressings to windows and doors. One slate, one tile roof.		SU 869 326 2301 61
Cottage	Roundabout Cottage, on corner of Church Lane and Tonbridge Lane. Brick on stone plinth with tiled roof. 2 storeys. Lower part with rendered brick walls, possibly added in C.18/19 as a hop kiln and drying room. Later porch of galleted stone with tiled roof. Ref: A Hampshire Parish, (Newman), p. 103.	C.A.	SU 839 329 2301 60
Building	No. 14, The Square, Liphook. 2 storeys. Roughly coursed stone with brick arched dressings to windows and door. Slate roof with chimney. Upper storey of north gable roughcast.	C.A.	SU 839 315 2301 52B
House	The Stone Place, Passfield. Stone structure with tiled roof. Curved brick headings to some windows on north side. End on to road. Old stone barn at rightangles to house.		SU 824 344 2301 53

Description and Date	Remarks	Protection	Grid Ref. and Punchcard No.

Group D — (cont.)

Description and Date	Remarks	Protection	Grid Ref. and Punchcard No.
House	White House, Passfield. Originally a 2-storey, stone walled cottage with brick quoins and dressings. West side whitewashed. Casement windows. Door under tiled hood. Modern 2-storey brick extension with tiled roof, at rear.		SU 818 339 2301 43
House and Barn	Yewcroft, Conford. Coursed stone with brick dressings. Tiled roof, casement windows. Brick porch. Recent rendered additions. Galleted stone barn with steep tiled roof. Converted to garage. Ref: A Hampshire Parish, (Newman), p. 57.		SU 825 329 2301 78
House	Beech Court, 127 Haslemere Road, Liphook. Formerly known as Collyers Farm. Stone walls with timber-framing, which have been covered externally with white roughcast. Modern windows. At one time converted into two cottages, but completely restored in 1970s to a single dwelling.		SU 849 317 2301 105
Building	Bramshott School and School House. Central section part timber-framed, formerly the old Bell Inn. Large stone hall built on west end dated 1843. Wooden vaulted ceiling similar to one in church. Schoolmasters quarters built on east end, constructed of stone with tile hanging above. Closed about 1974. Ref: A Hampshire Parish, (Newman), p.p. 99—101, 115, 119.		SU 843 331 2301 75
House	Bramshott Meadows. Four bays, timber-framed hall house, probably early C.15. Many C.19/20 additions including stone cladding on the oldest part of building. Modern windows. Tiled hipped roof with gablets. C.19 porch and east wing built of local brick, stone and timber. Riverside garden contains channels and sluices, part of the complex system of aqueducts in the area.	C.A.	SU 833 333 2301 110
Channels and Sluices	Water meadows of Bramshott and Ludshott Manors. A single arch stone bridge carries brick lined water channel, near Radford Bridge. At Passfield two arches of a stone 'aqueduct' with sluice slots survives. Large numbers of field channels cover wide area. Centred on grid reference. Ref: 1. Rural Life in Hampshire, (Capes), p. 220. 2. A Hampshire Parish, (Newman), p. 4.	S.A.M. No. 471	SU 842 323 2301 81
Aqueduct	Bramshott Court. Part of the River Wey water meadows system, of which the sluice gates and brick channels still survive.	S.A.M. No. 474 C.A.	SU 833 334 2301 111

Group D — (cont.)

Description and Date	Remarks	Protection	Grid Ref. and Punchcard No.
Sluices	Pophole. Masonry of large dressed stone blocks, with some repair in brick of two sets of sluices, which controlled flow of water from Hammer Pond to C.16/18 Iron Mill. The Mill stood on the stream just where the counties of Sussex, Surrey and Hampshire meet, and was established by Lord Montague. Ref: 1. Wealden Iron Industry, (Straker), p. 449. 2. The Priory and Manor of Lychmere and Shulbrede, (Ponsonby), p. 182.		SU 874 326 2301 62

Group E — Street Patterns, Street Furniture and Open Spaces

Description and Date	Remarks	Protection	Grid Ref. and Punchcard No.
Boundary Stone C.18	On eastern verge of B. 3004 near junction to Burgh Hill Lane. Circa 1790. Marks Manor boundaries. Oval headed stone about 2 ft. 6 ins. high. Inscribed "Sir. T.M. Manor of Ludshott and L + S Manor of Oakhanger".		SU 828 333 2301 69

Group F — Historical or Literary Associations

Description and Date	Remarks	Protection	Grid Ref. and Punchcard No.
House (Site) C.16	Bramshott Place. Built 1570/80 by a Godalming clothier. Balfour's headquarters before the Battle of Cheriton. In 1768 the owner, Sarah Whitehead married the Rector and went to live at Glebe House. House became a farm, then derelict. In 1850 the house was demolished, leaving the Tudor gatehouse, and a new house was built. O.S.A. No. SU83 SW12.		SU 843 322 2301 31
Ironworks (Possible Site)	Waggoners Wells, Bramshott. Site at zenith during C.16/17. Henry Hooke made three dams across the stream in 1615 to form three large ponds which still remain. These were possibly used in connection with the iron mill, though no slag has been found. O.S.A. No. SU83 SE18. Ref: Rural Life in Hampshire, (Capes), p.p. 170, 182.	N.P. Act S.S.S.I.	SU 859 342 2301 33
Burial Ground C.17/18	Bramshott Court. A plot near the road was used as a Quakers burial ground from 1661—1761, and was formally conveyed to them by Henry Streeter in 1718. Part of low surrounding wall still visible at foot of adjoining roadside wall.		SU 835 338 2301 112

Description and Date	Remarks	Protection	Grid Ref. and Punchcard No.

Group F — (cont.)

Description and Date	Remarks	Protection	Grid Ref. and Punchcard No.
Inn C.17	Royal Anchor Hotel, Liphook. Reputed to have been an inn on the site since 1416. Famous inn on the London—Portsmouth Road. One of the Georges, Queen Victoria, Pepys and Nelson are said to have slept there. An Elizabethan door presented by Queen Victoria bears the Royal Arms. Ref: 1. Rural Life in Hampshire, (Capes), p. 218. 2. A Hampshire Parish, (Newman), p.p. 303/4, 17, 86, 97, 103/4.	T. & C.P. Act C.A.	SU 839 315 2301 06
Building	Cottage adjoining Midland Bank, Liphook. Formerly The Post Office, where Flora Thompson, author of 'Lark Rise to Candleford' lived and worked from 1916—1927. Building bears a plaque to her memory.	C.A.	SU 839 316 2301 93
Mill House (Site)	Bramshott. 100 yds. downstream from the Old Mill. Burnt down by suffragettes Oct. 1913 as it was owned by the brother of McKenna, a Liberal Minister and later Chancellor of the Exchequer. Only steps and part of the garden wall remain.	C.A.	SU 836 332 2301 44A
Mill C.19	Passfield Mill, Passfield. Records show that this was originally the site of an iron mill, and was converted to a paper mill late in the C.17. The existing brick building with two blind arches incorporating a date-stone 1857—70, was probably erected on the site after a series of fires in the late C.18 and early C.19. The mill pond is now dry. Mill, Mill House and adjoining building have been converted to accommodate a modern industry.		SU 819 344 2301 94
House C.20	Little Boarhunt, 73 Portsmouth Road, Liphook. This house was rebuilt for himself by H. Inigo Triggs, an architect who worked locally and who also designed the New Rectory at Liphook, and Cooper's Bridge at Bramshott. He died in 1923 and there is a memorial tablet dedicated to him in Bramshott Church. H. Inigo Triggs wrote the standard work on 'Formal Gardens in England and Scotland' (1901—2) and his Elizabethan sunken garden is an interesting feature of Little Boarhunt. Ref: Buildings of England; Hants and I.O.W., (Pevsner and Lloyd), p. 829.		SU 839 307 2301 104

BURITON

The principal manor in the parish of Buriton was known as Mapledurham; other manors were West Mapledurham, Weston, Ditcham and Sunworth. For several centuries the manor was held by the Clare family, dukes of Hereford and Gloucester. In 1719 the land was bought by Edward Gibbon, grandfather of the historian, with money from the South Sea Company; the manor eventually descended to the historian himself.

The manor house is a fine specimen of early Georgian architecture of which Gibbon wrote in his autobiography: "An old mansion in a state of decay has been converted into the fashion and convenience of a modern house . . . and if strangers had nothing to see the inhabitants had little to desire". The principal industries in the parish have been farming and lime-burning.

The church of St. Mary has a very fine twelfth century interior although the exterior of the chancel is thirteenth century. The eminent seventeenth century botanist, John Goodyer, is buried here. His reputation was so great that during the Civil War a royalist general ordered his men " . . . on all occassions to defend and protect John Goodyer, his house, servants, family, goods, chattels and estates of all sorts from all damages, disturbances and oppressions whatever."

Group A — Natural Features

Description and Date	Remarks	Protection	Grid Ref. and Punchcard No.
Grassland	Butser Hill, part of the Queen Elizabeth Country Park. An area of chalk grassland, with a history of scientific recording. Yew woods in south east facing coombes. Fine views over surrounding countryside.	N.P. Act S.S.S.I. A.O.N.B. C.O.S.	SU 710 190 2302 06
Area of Ecological Importance	Coulters Dean. 13 acres of chalk grassland, where recordings have been made for almost half a century. Centred on grid reference.	N.P. Act S.S.S.I. A.O.N.B.	SU 747 191 2302 68
Pond	Bo-Peep Pond, Ramsdean Road. Used by fishermen.	N.P. Act A.O.N.B.	SU 722 214 2302 28
Trees	At the junction of High Street, North Lane and Bones Lane. Four horse chestnut trees standing on an area of grass. Also a plane tree planted April 1977 to mark the Silver Jubilee.	C.A. N.P. Act A.O.N.B.	SU 740 201 2302 29
Forest	Queen Elizabeth Forest, south west of Buriton Village, and part of the Country Park. Centred on grid reference.	N.P. Act A.O.N.B. C.O.S.	SU 720 180 2302 01
Pond	Buriton village pond, outside St. Mary's parish church.	C.A. N.P. Act A.O.N.B.	SU 739 200 2302 04
Sarsen Stone No. 12A	Bolinge Hill Cottages. The stone forms a footstep to one of the dwellings.	N.P. Act A.O.N.B.	SU 737 215 2302 91
Sarsen Stones (2) No. 12B	Possible part of Wayside Cross.	N.P. Act A.O.N.B.	SU 756 217 2302 90
Viewing Point	Fine views from the footpath across Headdown. Glimpses through the trees of the countryside surrounding Buriton and Petersfield, and eastwards over the farmland to West Sussex.	N.P. Act A.O.N.B.	SU 736 194 2302 86A
Viewing Point	Head Down. Magnificent view from the footpath of the countryside and the sea near Hayling Island.	N.P. Act A.O.N.B.	SU 736 187 2302 86B
Viewing Point	From the drive to Ditcham Park School, in front of the house, south to Hayling Island.	N.P. Act A.O.N.B.	SU 748 175 2302 87
Viewing Points	War Down, within the Queen Elizabeth Country Park. A variety of different views which open up along the forestry ride. Panoramas north to Petersfield and its countryside, west to Butser, and south to Isle of Wight and the sea when the weather is favourable. Centred on grid reference.	N.P. Act A.O.N.B. C.O.S.	SU 727 199 2302 88
Trees	Nurstead Estate. Several trees of differing species standing in the above estate. Centred on grid reference.	T.P.O. No. 21 E.H.D.C. N.P. Act A.O.N.B.	SU 750 215 2302 102

Description and Date	Remarks	Protection	Grid Ref. and Punchcard No.
Group A — (cont.)			
Trees	Buriton Village. Trees of differing species standing in the area centred on grid reference.	T.P.O. No. 27 E.H.D.C. C.A. N.P. Act A.O.N.B.	SU 740 220 2302 103
Trees	Buriton Village. Standing to the western side of South Lane. Centred on grid reference.	T.P.O. No. 27 E.H.D.C. N.P. Act A.O.N.B.	SU 738 199 2302 104
Group B — Archaeological			
Stone Age			
Mesolithic Finds	Microliths, axes and sharpening flakes found in fields on Butser Hill. Some finds in Portsmouth City Musem. O.S.A. No. SU72 SW20.	N.P.Act A.O.N.B. C.O.S.	SU 715 201 2302 73
Flint Axe	Lower Palaeolithic axe found on loamy part of clay with flints at 889 ft. Axe in Hampshire County Museum Service collection, Winchester. O.S.A. No. SU72 SW19.	N.P. Act A.O.N.B.	SU 725 205 2302 58
Bronze Age			
Bowl Barrow (Probable)	Low mount 10m. in diameter south west of Round Copse, on east facing slope of Butser Hill. O.S.A. No. SU72 SW8. Ref: P.H.F.C., Vol. 14, 1940, (Grinsell), p. 358.	N.P. Act S.S.S.I. A.O.N.B. C.O.S.	SU 719 207 2302 100
Bowl Barrows (5)	North end of Wardown. Barrows reduced by ploughing prior to planting with firs in 1936. O.S.A. No. SU71 NW2. Ref: P.H.F.C., Vol. 14, 1938–40, (Grinsell), p. 358.	N.P. Act A.O.N.B. C.O.S.	SU 728 198 2302 59
Palstave	Found in field half a mile north of Buriton, in 1967. Palstave has flanged sides and stopridge. O.S.A. No. SU72 SW23. Ref: Portsmouth Museum Card Index.	N.P. Act A.O.N.B.	SU 743 208 2302 74
Settlement Site	Hut and pit excavated in 1968. Site now beneath road. O.S.A. No. SU71 NW4. Ref: Antiquaries Journal, Vol. 1, Part 1, 1970.	N.P.Act A.O.N.B.	SU 717 181 2302 76
Iron Age			
Pits	Two small pits filled with wood and charcoal found. Each contained a single inverted pot. O.S.A. No. SU71 NW16. Ref: Antiquaries Journal, Vol. 37, 1957, (Frere), p.p. 218–220.	N.P. Act A.O.N.B. C.O.S.	SU 733 175 2302 10

Description and Date	Remarks	Protection	Grid Ref. and Punchcard No.

Group B — (cont.)

Description and Date	Remarks	Protection	Grid Ref. and Punchcard No.
Settlement Site	Coarse sherds, quern fragments and pot boilers found in this area. Site under pasture. O.S.A. No. SU72 SW12.	N.P. Act S.S.S.I. A.O.N.B. C.O.S.	SU 719 208 2302 57

Iron Age/Romano-British

Occupation Site	Hut site, pottery, two brooches and small items uncovered. A beaker, six bronze plates and a socketed blade of a knife found. Masonry building and ditched enclosure excavated 1964. Centred on grid reference. O.S.A. No. SU71 NW16. Ref: Antiquaries Journal, Vol. 37, 1957, (Frere), p.p. 218—220.	N.P. Act A.O.N.B. C.O.S.	SU 734 174 2302 12

Iron Age/Roman

Lynchets	Presumed lynchet system obscured by forest. O.S.A. No. SU71 NW5.	N.P. Act A.O.N.B. C.O.S.	SU 720 192 2302 66
Lynchets	South east of Butser Hill. Centred on grid reference. O.S.A. No. SU71 NW5.	N.P. Act S.S.S.I. A.O.N.B. C.O.S.	SU 719 196 2302 61

Roman

Pottery	Found among lynchets on Wardown. Whole area covered by forest. O.S.A. No. SU71 NW8.	N.P. Act A.O.N.B. C.O.S.	SU 728 192 2302 65
Occupation Site	Poor Peter field, Woolver Brow. Pottery and tile found during laying of gas main. O.S.A. No. SU71 NW11.	N.P. Act A.O.N.B.	SU 745 192 2302 13
Settlement Site	Probable Romano-British farming site in Holt Down Plantation. Excavations revealed a rectangular flint built room with painted plaster in geometric patterns. Roof of hexagonal sandstone shale tiles. Traces of two other buildings found. Rubbish pit contained New Forest, Castor, and Samian ware, coins, shells, keys and a statuette. Site overgrown. O.S.A. No. SU71 NW7.	S.A.M. No. 316 N.P. Act A.O.N.B. C.O.S.	SU 721 176 2302 09

Saxon

Spear Head	Found at foot of fire tower on Wardown in 1963. Now in Portsmouth Museum. O.S.A. No. SU71 NW2. Ref: P.H.F.C., Vol. 14, 1938—40, (Grinsell), p. 358.	N.P. Act A.O.N.B. C.O.S.	SU 726 198 2302 63

Description and Date	Remarks	Protection	Grid Ref. and Punchcard No.
Group B — (cont.)			
Font	At the Manor House, Buriton. Removed from East Meon Courthouse and brought to present site circa. 1922. Ref: P.H.F.C., Newsletter, Vol. 1, No. 8, 1968.	C.A. N.P. Act A.O.N.B.	SU 740 201 2302 05
Post Norman			
Deserted Village (Site)	Mapledurham. Hundred = Finchdean. Forty-nine heads of families recorded in 1086. Ref: V.C.H., Vol. 3, p. 88.	N.P. Act A.O.N.B.	SU 732 214 2302 89
Pillow Mound	Southwest of Round Copse. 13m. in length and 6.3m. in breadth. Surrounded on three sides by a ditch 2m. across. Site under pasture. O.S.A. No. SU72 SW3. Ref: Antiquity, Vol. 4, 1930, (Piggott), p. 199.	N.P. Act S.S.S.I. A.O.N.B. C.O.S.	SU 719 208 2302 53
Period Unknown			
Spur Dyke	Slight irregular bank and ditch on southeast spur of Butser Hill. Constructed in two sections with a gap of 27.4m. between. Mutilated by flint digging. O.S.A. No. SU71 NW3. Ref: Antiquity, Vol. 4, 1930, (Piggott), p. 192.	S.A.M. No. 15 N.P. Act S.S.S.I. A.O.N.B. C.O.S.	SU 714 199 2302 60
Cross Dyke	Earthwork on northeast spur of Butser Hill. Single bank and ditch. Also sunken trackway of later date. Probable that only excavation will prove relationship with adjoining earthworks. O.S.A. No. SU72 SW5. Ref: 1. Antiquity, Vol. 4, 1930 (Piggott), p. 192. 2. Aspects of Archaeology, 1951, "Cross Ridge Dykes in Sussex." (Curwen), p.p. 93, 107.	S.A.M. No. 15 N.P. Act S.S.S.I. A.O.N.B. C.O.S.	SU 719 204 2302 55
Flint Working Site	On edge of furze scrub. No trace remains. O.S.A. No. SU71 NW10.	N.P. Act A.O.N.B. C.O.S.	SU 723 193 2302 67
Group C — Footpaths and Bridleways			
Old Travel Way	Kiln Lane. Running south west from Buriton. Formerly called Bridge Lane and originally spelt Hill Lane. Centred on grid reference.	N.P. Act A.O.N.B.	SU 736 202 2302 56
Turnpike Road	The original Butser turnpike road. A contour road serving the limeworks, leading to summit of the pass.	N.P. Act A.O.N.B.	SU 726 205 — 724 201 2302 21

Description and Date	Remarks	Protection	Grid Ref. and Punchcard No.
Group C — (cont.)			
Ridgeway	South Hants Ridgeway, running east-west along the South Downs from Sunwood Farm to Butser Hill. In some places it becomes a track used as a bridle way and footpath. The track continues eastwards over the Hampshire Boundary to become the South Downs Way in Sussex.	N.P. Act A.O.N.B.	SU 715 200 — 757 194 2302 15
Crest Track	North-south track through Head Down and Camelsdown.	N.P. Act A.O.N.B.	SU 736 196 — 738 170 2302 16
Crest Track	Woolver Lane. Track leading southwest from the ridgeway.	N.P. Act A.O.N.B.	SU 742 195 — 740 191 2302 17
Crest Track	From Butser to Petersfield Heath, west of Whiteland Copse. Track probably of Mesolithic date, runs north/south. Ref: Archaeology, June 1930.	N.P. Act S.S.S.I. A.O.N.B. C.O.S.	SU 718 205 — 710 200 2302 19
Crest Track	Evanshall Lane. Ancient track south from the ridgeway.	N.P. Act A.O.N.B.	SU 744 195 — 744 192 2302 18
Travelway	Former London-Portsmouth Coach Road, which runs through Gravel Hill Bottom. War Down on the left and Holt Down on the right are within the Queen Elizabeth Country Park.	N.P. Act A.O.N.B. C.O.S.	SU 719 182 — 732 198 2302 20
Group D — Buildings, Monuments and Engineering Works			
Church C12	St. Mary's Church. Stone structure. C.13 chancel with wall painting. Inside, 4-bay arcades of late C.12 with round piers and multi-scalloped capitals. Tower rebuilt in 1714. Purbeck marble font. Two monuments of note. O.S.A. No. SU72 SW16. Ref: Buildings of England; Hants and I.O.W., (Pevsner and Lloyd), p. 154.	T. & C.P. Act C.A. N.P. Act A.O.N.B.	SU 740 200 2302 31
Building C.17	Nos. 26—28, High Street. Malmstone and brick with some timber work. Tiled roof with central chimney. At one time probably a yeoman's house, but greatly altered. Ref: Buriton and Its People, (Yates).	C.A. N.P. Act A.O.N.B.	SU 738 201 2302 08
Cottage C.17	Toads Alley, South Lane. Formerly two dwellings. Structure of malmstone with brick dressings. Tiled roof with four bedroom windows at eaves level. Small brick extension to south. Some timber-framing visible inside.	C.A. N.P. Act A.O.N.B.	SU 738 199 2302 51
Cottage C.17	Whistlers, South Lane. Formerly two cottages. Malmstone with brick dressings. Thatched roof with half dormer casement windows.	C.A. N.P. Act A.O.N.B.	SU 737 198 2302 52

Description and Date	Remarks	Protection	Grid Ref. and Punchcard No.
Group D — (cont.)			
Cottage C.17	Glebe Farm Cottage, Kiln Lane. 2 storeys. Malmrock with brick dressings. Thatched roof descending at back with tiled lean to. Small bedroom casement windows at eaves level. Slated single storey well house at north end, now incorporated into house.	N.P. Act A.O.N.B.	SU 737 202 2302 41
Cottage C.17	Lawn Cottage, North Lane. 2 storeys. Malmstone and brick structure. Some timber-framing on west side with brick filling. Thatched roof. Wooden casement windows. Lean to at southern end.	N.P. Act A.O.N.B.	SU 734 203 2302 49
Farmhouse C.17	Bolinge Hill Farm. Dated 'T.B. 1636'. L-shaped plan. 2 storeys. Malmstone with brick dressings. West and west end of south front tile-hung. Tiled roof with two hipped dormers. Casement windows. C.18 extension to north with lead roof and sash windows. Interior shows timber-framing and oak ceiling beams.	T. & C.P. Act N.P. Act A.O.N.B.	SU 735 212 2302 32
Farmhouse C.17	Old House Farm, Nursted Rocks. Malmstone walls with brick dressings. Some timber-framing with brick infill. Tiled roof half-hipped at south end, gabled at north end. South wall tile hung on upper part with galleting below. Later wooden porch. Casement windows.	N.P. Act A.O.N.B.	SU 758 212 2302 101
Cottage C.17	Rock Cottage, Nursted Rocks. Formerly Uphill Farm Cottage. Malmstone with brick dressings. Tiled roof. Single dormer with hipped gable. Some timber-framing. Casement windows, those on ground floor with cambered arches. Recent porch.	N.P. Act A.O.N.B.	SU 760 212 2302 40
Cottages C.17/18	Nos. 15, and 16, Bones Lane. Malmstone with brick dressings. Very irregular thatched roof. Sash windows with glazing bars. No. 15 has one diamond leaded window at eaves. Ref: Buriton and Its People, (Yates).	T. & C.P. Act C.A. N.P. Act A.O.N.B.	SU 739 201 2302 37
Cottage C.17/18	Dolphin Cottage, No. 20, Bones Lane. 2 storeys. Malmstone with a brick dressing of old thin bricks. Thatched roof with old chimney. Door and windows have cambered arches. Casement windows. Ref: Buriton and Its People, (Yates).	C.A. N.P. Act A.O.N.B.	SU 739 202 2302 42
Cottage C.17/18	Rock Cottage, Bones Lane. Originally two cottages. 2 storeys. Malmstone with brick dressings. Double hipped tiled roof. Casement windows with glazing bars. Doors with gabled tiled hoods. Ref: Buriton and Its People, (Yates).	C.A. N.P. Act A.O.N.B.	SU 739 202 2302 43

Description and Date	Remarks	Protection	Grid Ref. and Punchcard No.

Group D — (cont.)

Description and Date	Remarks	Protection	Grid Ref. and Punchcard No.
Cottage C.17/18	No. 27, Bones Lane. Malmstone with dressing of old bricks. 2 storeys. Tiled roof hipped at east end. Two chimneys. Cambered arch windows. South wing with tile-hung gable. Ref: Buriton and Its People, (Yates).	N.P. Act A.O.N.B.	SU 739 204 2302 44
House C.18	Bottom House, Gravel Hill Bottom. Colour-washed malmstone with brick dressings. Stuccoed at either end. 2 storeys. Tiled roof. Sash windows with glazing bars. Timber-framing visible inside. Formerly the Bottom Inn mentioned by Charles Dickens in 'Nicholas Nickleby'.	N.P. Act A.O.N.B. C.O.S.	SU 718 182 2302 23
Barn C.18	Newbarn, Finchdean Road. Tiled roof with gable ends. Lower part of stone, with wood above. Wood may once have been part of earlier barn, bears marks where cattle have rubbed. New oak doors. Large cast iron water tank outside. Brought from Pike Spicers Brewery, Portsmouth, by horse and wagon early this century.	N.P. Act A.O.N.B.	SU 732 181 2302 77
Farm Building C.18	Dean Barn Lane. Brick structure with tiled roof built on two sides of a yard. Wooden framework. Originally used to house cattle and farm implements, now used by the Forestry Commission.	N.P. Act A.O.N.B.	SU 737 195 2302 78
Barn C.18	Faggs Barn, New Barn Lane. Flint with brick facings. Tiled gabled roof. New oak doors. One of group of flint and brick farm buildings now used by Forestry Commission.	N.P. Act A.O.N.B.	SU 733 196 2302 79
Buildings C.18	Post Office and adjacent house, High Street. 3 storeys, with 2-storey cottage adjoining to east. Creamwashed brick with part tile, part slate roof. Square windows with glazing bars. Lean-to shop projects to road.	C.A. N.P. Act A.O.N.B.	SU 738 201 2302 45
Cottages (4) C.18	Nos. 38, 40, 42 and 46 High Street, south of Five Bells Inn. Formerly the poorhouse and dated 1791. Built round three sides of a central courtyard away from road. 2 storeys. Malmstone structure with brick dressings. Tiled roof. Casement windows with glazing bars and some remains of leaded lights.	T. & C.P. Act C.A. N.P. Act A.O.N.B.	SU 738 201 2302 47
House C.18	The White House, High Street. Double fronted house of 2 storeys. Rendered malmstone and brick. Slate roof. Sash windows with glazing bars. 6-panelled door with flat hood over.	C.A. N.P. Act A.O.N.B.	SU 738 201 2302 46
Inn C.18	Five Bells, High Street. Cream-washed stone and brick. 2 storeys. Tiled roof, sash windows with glazing bars, and sliding casements on upper floor. Mediaeval cellars. Barn of malmstone and brick adjoins the Inn. Hipped tiled roof. Sash windows.	C.A. N.P. Act A.O.N.B.	SU 740 205 2302 24

Description and Date	Remarks	Protection	Grid Ref. and Punchcard No.

Group D — (cont.)

Description and Date	Remarks	Protection	Grid Ref. and Punchcard No.
House C.18	Manor House, Buriton. Mainly early C.18 with some traces of C.16 structure. Central 2-storey portion of south front, malmstone with brick dressings. Tiled roof. Sash and casement windows. Two brick porches with tiled gabled roofs. C.16 timber-framing visible inside. Elizabethan chimney on west wall. Single storey range of malmstone and brick to west. To east, and round eastern front is a 3-storey Queen Anne building, of brick structure with cornice and parapet. Tiled roof. Stone keystones to windows. Sash windows with glazing bars. Interior has some C.17 panelling and an C.18 oak staircase. Once the home of Edward Gibbon, the historian.	T. & C.P. Act C.A. N.P. Act A.O.N.B.	SU 740 201 2302 36
Dovecot C.18	Manor House. Hexagonal brick building on malmstone and brick plinth. Tiled roof with simple wooden entrance for doves. Interior lined with dove holes. Wall of malmstone with brick coping connects dovecot to house.	T. & C.P. Act C.A. N.P. Act A.O.N.B.	SU 740 201 2302 36C
Orangery C.18	Manor House. Single storey brick building with hipped tiled roof. South front has partly glazed door with sash window either side. West side has square-paned leaded casement windows. Close by are gate and gate-posts of cast iron. The orangery forms the north west corner of a walled garden.	T. & C.P. Act N.P. Act A.O.N.B.	SU 740 201 2302 36D
Stables C.18	Manor House. 2 storeys. Malmstone with brick dressings. Tiled roof with projecting gable in centre portion. Round window of gauged brickwork in gable. Doors and windows have brick dressings. Now converted into dwellings.	T. & C.P. Act C.A. N.P. Act A.O.N.B.	SU 740 201 2302 36A
Barn C.18	Manor House. Tiled roof descends low on south side to form aisle. Malmstone structure with brick dressings. Two gabled doorways project into courtyard. Round opening of gauged brickwork in gable. Fine timbered interior of ten bays.	T. & C.P. Act C.A. N.P. Act A.O.N.B.	SU 740 201 2302 36B
Barn C.18	Old Ditcham Farm. Large barn of seven bays. Malmstone and brick dressings. South side of flint with brick band. Tiled roof. Massive gable and doorway for waggons. Round-headed windows and ventilators. Several outbuildings adjoining. Interior has massive pointed malmstone arches carrying roof. Date on arch 1757.	T. & C.P. Act N.P. Act A.O.N.B.	SU 760 203 2302 35

Description and Date	Remarks	Protection	Grid Ref. and Punchcard No.

Group D — (cont.)

House C.18	Nurstead House. East front of malmstone with rusticated brick quoins. 2 storeys and attics. Sash windows with stone surrounds. Slate roof with four flat dormers. Centre of front projects with pediment. Classical doorcase with pediment and four steps leading to it. West front has gothic glazed windows, and one Venetian window. Three dormers. Brick garden wall to north with coping and urn. Interior contains an Adam style fireplace and some C.17 panelling.	T. & C.P. Act N.P. Act A.O.N.B.	SU 749 213 2302 33
Outbuildings C.18	Nurstead House. 2 storeys. Malmstone and brick with a tiled roof. Brick gable end with a depressed arch in ground floor. Long round-headed window above. Brick pilasters with stone ball finial and coping. Weather vane on gable. Believed to have been a chapel, but now a stable with loft above.	T. & C.P. Act N.P. Act A.O.N.B.	SU 749 213 2302 33A
Farmhouse C.18	Nurstead Great Farm. Mainly C.18, but interior walls and cellars seem to be of James I date. 2-storey west front with plaster facing. Hipped tiled roof. Sash windows with glazing bars. Victorian porch. East side of 2 storeys. Grey headers with red brick dressings, and cornice. Sash windows. Single storey kitchen wing to south.	T. & C.P. Act N.P. Act A.O.N.B.	SU 753 213 2302 34
Stable C.18	West of Nurstead Great Farm. Malmstone and brick. Centre portion projects slightly. Double hipped tiled roof. Stable has loft above.	T. & C.P. Act N.P. Act A.O.N.B.	SU 753 213 2302 34B
Farmbuildings C.18	Enclosing farmyard at Nurstead Great Farm. Two large brick and timber barns with tiled roofs, and connecting cow sheds. Weatherboarded granary with double hipped tiled roof.	T. & C.P. Act N.P. Act A.O.N.B.	SU 753 213 2302 34A
Farmhouse C.18	Deans Farm, Weston. 2 storeys coursed malmstone with some brick infill, and dressings. Tile-hung upper storey. Tiled roof with hipped gable. Sash windows with glazing bars.	N.P. Act A.O.N.B.	SU 725 221 2302 30
Houses	Nos. 29, and 31, North Lane. Mainly C.18 but some traces of earlier hall house have been found. 2 storeys. Malmstone and brick dressings. Thatched roof, wooden casement windows. Brick steps to door.	C.A. N.P. Act A.O.N.B.	SU 741 203 2302 48
House	The Old Rectory, High Street. Mainly C.18 but interior has remains of hall buildings of C.13/14. 2 storeys with parapet. Plaster faced malmstone front faces east with slightly projecting wings north and south. Sash windows. Door with flat hood and simple fanlight over. Service wing to north west. Tiled roof. Roof facing small courtyard has three flatheaded dormers.	T. & C.P. Act C.A. N.P. Act A.O.N.B.	SU 739 200 2302 38

Description and Date	Remarks	Protection	Grid Ref. and Punchcard No.

Group D — (cont.)

Description and Date	Remarks	Protection	Grid Ref. and Punchcard No.
Fire Insurance Plaque	Rose Cottage, No. 23, North Lane.	C.A. N.P. Act A.O.N.B.	SU 742 203 2302 27
War Memorial	Outside St. Mary's Church.	C.A. N.P. Act A.O.N.B.	SU 740 200 2302 03

Group E — Street Patterns, Street Furniture and Open Spaces

Open Space	Butser Hill. 500 acres of downland on large chalk headland with steep sides. Fine views to Petersfield and Portsmouth. Part of the Queen Elizabeth Country Park and provided with footpaths, bridleways, picnic areas and car parks.	N.P. Act S.S.S.I. A.O.N.B. C.O.S.	SU 710 190 2302 06

Group F — Historical or Literary Association

Limeworks (Disused)	Buriton Limeworks. On both sides of Halls Hill. Begun about 1863 by Benjamin Forder. Horses were used until 1923 to pull trucks, then locomotives took over. Works employed up to 100 men. Lime mainly used in building industry.	N.P. Act A.O.N.B.	SU 735 197 2302 25
Limeworks (Disused)	Butser Limeworks. Probably earlier than Buriton works. In 1871 Samuel Seward described as farmer and limeburner. Lime used for agricultural purposes mainly on neighbouring farms. Works closed 1966/7.	N.P. Act A.O.N.B.	SU 726 204 2302 26
Manor House (Site)	Sunworth Manor House, Downley Bottom. Area has two modern buildings and remains of several older ones. Well 270 ft. deep. Engine operated pump in brick building, also drove a generator 1903. Slaughterhouse near wellhouse of C.19 or earlier date.	N.P. Act A.O.N.B.	SU 753 181 2302 22
Historical Association	Park Barn. There was formerly a school and laundry at this site which were used in connection with Ditcham House.	N.P. Act A.O.N.B.	SU 748 171 2302 92
Glassworks (Site)	One mile south-east of Queen Elizabeth Forest. Glass found on this site dated circa. 1600. Excavation in 1971 found evidence of a brick kiln. Similar sites discovered in vicinity in recent years.	N.P. Act A.O.N.B.	SU 739 169 2302 75

CHAWTON

Chawton is famous for its association with Jane Austen who came to live here in 1809, leaving for Winchester only shortly before her death in 1817. The Austen's house is now open to the public and contains many momentoes to Jane Austen. The Knight family have owned Chawton House since the beginning of the sixteenth century and it sits impressively amid the trees beside its neighbour the attractive nineteenth century Church of St. Nicholas.

Description and Date	Remarks	Protection	Grid Ref. and Punchcard No.

Group A — Natural Features

Description and Date	Remarks	Protection	Grid Ref. and Punchcard No.
Tree	Adjacent Jane Austen's House. Oak tree, planted as a sapling by Jane Austen.	C.A.	SU 708 375 1604 29
Trees	Chawton Glebe. Roadside trees and shelter belts on boundaries of former Glebe Farm extending on portion of old A32 Fareham Road. Centred on grid reference.	T.P.O. No. 2 E.H.D. C.A.	SU 706 370 1604 30
Tree	Adjacent Jane Austen's House. Horse chestnut planted 1967 to commemorate the 150th anniversary of Jane Austen's death.	C.A.	SU 708 375 1604 27
Tree	Copper beech planted to commemorate the coronation of King George VI and Queen Elizabeth in 1937.	C.A.	SU 708 374 1604 28
Trees	Imbrook Copse. An area of mixed hardwoods consisting mainly of oak, ash, beech and hazel. Centred on grid reference.	T.P.O. No. 70 E.H.D.	SU 696 369 1604 31

Group B — Archaeological

Iron Age/Romano-British

Description and Date	Remarks	Protection	Grid Ref. and Punchcard No.
Field System	Crocklands Copse. Lynchets and field banks on south-east slope, covering total area of 10 acres. O.S.A. No. SU63 NE6.		SU 696 365 1604 23

Post Norman

Description and Date	Remarks	Protection	Grid Ref. and Punchcard No.
Earthworks	South of Chawton House. Thought to be park pale but probably an old enclosure complex. Large bank and south facing ditch runs along Chawton/Farringdon parish boundary. O.S.A. No. SU73 NW15. Ref: P.H.F.C., Vol. 12, 1932–4, p. 85.		SU 697 364 — 716 364 1604 25
Gallows (Probable Site)	Gibbet Copse. Traditional site of gallows, mentioned in 1560. Exact position not known. O.S.A. No. SU63 NE7. Ref: V.C.H., Vol. 2, p. 498.		SU 678 362 1604 22
Parks (2)	Chawton Park Wood. Well preserved banks with ditches which apparently divided two ancient parks. Centred on grid references. O.S.A. No. SU63 NE8.		SU 683 367 — 689 377 1604 21
Dene Holes (2)	Holm Wood. Depressions thought to be dene holes but probably old chalk pits. O.S.A. No. SU73 NW11. Ref: Archaeology in the Field 1953, (Crawford) p. 234.		SU 712 364 1604 26
Dene Hole	South west of Southfield Farm. Circular depression in centre of old tree-covered trackway, probably a collapsed dene hole. O.S.A. No. SU73 NW33.		SU 701 362 1604 24

Description and Date	Remarks	Protection	Grid Ref. and Punchcard No.

Group D — Buildings, Monuments and Engineering Works

Description and Date	Remarks	Protection	Grid Ref. and Punchcard No.
Manor House C.16	Chawton House. Enlarged C.17/18. Entrance front, flint rubble mixed with stone blocks. Panelled red brick parapet. Tiled roof. South front, red brick gabled with many original stone mullioned windows. Internally rich in panelling and woodwork. O.S.A. No. SU73 NW29. Ref: 1. Country Life 2.2.45 and 27.6.03. 2. Jane Austen Correspondence. 3. Buildings of England; Hants and I.O.W., (Pevsner & Lloyd) p. 163.	T. & C.P. Act C.A.	SU 708 370 1604 13
Stables C.16	Chawton House. Dated 1593. Symmetrical range with projecting gables to right and left. 2 storeys and attic. Long ridge tiled roof.	T. & C.P. Act C.A.	SU 708 370 1604 15
Farmhouse C.17	Chawton Park Farm. Restored and enlarged. 2 storeys. Red brick with blue headers. Ridge tiled roof with three hipped dormers. Five mullioned transomed lattice casements.		SU 696 377 1604 19
House C.17/18	Baigens. 2 storeys. Brick structure. Ridge tiled roof. Four square-paned lattice casements on first floor. C.19 diamond-paned metal casements below. Elizabethan murals exposed by removal of old plaster. Projecting chimney in red Tudor brickwork.	T. & C.P. Act C.A.	SU 706 375 1604 06
Farmhouse C.18	Pounds Farm. 2 storeys. Red brick with occasional blue headers. Old hipped tiled roof. Sash windows. Centre door in plain plastered surround with flat projecting hood on ornamental brackets, carved to represent angels.	C.A.	SU 706 375 1604 07
Cottages (3) C.18	Nos. 1, 2, and 3, Malthouse Cottages. Part 2-storey, part single storey. Brown and red brick structure. Long ridge tiled roof, hipped to left, half-hipped to right. Victorian gabled porches have ornamental bargeboards.	C.A.	SU 707 372 1604 09
Farmhouse C.18	Home Farm. 2 storeys with single storey addition to left. Red brick structure. Ridge tiled roof. Extension of flint rubble with brick pilasters.	C.A.	SU 709 370 1604 14
House C.18	Chawton Lodge, Winchester Road. 2 storeys. Lime-washed brick structure. Tiled roof. Sash windows.	C.A.	SU 707 375 1604 05
Cottages (3) C.18	Nos. 1, 2, and 3, Pond Cottages. Single storey. Brick with brick plinth. Thatched roofs. No. 3 incorporates old timber-framed structure. Pair of well-preserved crucks visible internally, possibly C.15.	T. & C.P. Act. C.A.	SU 708 375 1604 11

Description and Date	Remarks	Protection	Grid Ref. and Punchcard No.

Group D — (cont.)

Description and Date	Remarks	Protection	Grid Ref. and Punchcard No.
House C.18	Jane Austen's House. Standing at junction of roads to Winchester and Alton. 2 storeys. Red brick with blue headers. Corbelled brick eaves. Hipped tiled roof. Sash windows. Memorial tablet in front of house. Now a small museum and open to the public at certain hours. O.S.A. No. SU73 NW(M)2. Ref: 1. The Clarke Lectures, (Chapman). 2. Buildings of England; Hants and I.O.W., (Pevsner & Lloyd), p. 163.	T. & C.P. Act C.A.	SU 708 375 1604 01
Church C.19	Saint Nicholas. Flint structure with large south west tower. Original church destroyed by fire 1871, rebuilt 1872. Monument with effigy of Sir Richard Knight (1679) rescued from old church. O.S.A. No. SU73 NW10. Ref: 1. Buildings of England; Hants and I.O.W., (Pevsner & Lloyd), p. 163. 2. V.C.H. Vol. 2, p.p. 500—1.	T. & C.P. Act	SU 707 370 1604 16
House C.19	Chawton Glebe. 2 storeys. Limewashed brick. Slate roof with wide spreading eaves. Sash windows. Earlier wing to rear.	C.A.	SU 706 371 1604 20
House	Prowtings. 2 storeys. Plain C.18 rendered facade over earlier structure. Hipped tiled roof. Single storey wing to right. Old walled garden adjoins to left.	C.A.	SU 707 377 1604 08
Cottage	Vincient Cottage. Limewashed brick with plinth. Thatched gable towards road. Modern tiled pentice addition. 5-light lattice casements.	C.A.	SU 709 378 1604 17
Cottages (2)	Thatch Cottage, Winchester Road. Single storey with eaves cut around three upper windows. Exposed timber-framing with red brick infilling on right, red brick with blue headers on left. Recently restored to a very high standard and converted to one dwelling.	T. & C.P. Act C.A.	SU 707 375 1604 18
Cottage	Orchard Cottage. L-shaped with short tiled gabled wing at rear. Brown brick with wide plinth of flint and attic string course. Thatched roof.	C.A.	SU 708 374 1604 12
Cottages (2)	Clinkers and Forge Cottage. 2 storeys. Brick with timber-framing partly exposed in centre. Thatched roofs. Two stout oak boarded doors.	T. & C.P. Act C.A.	SU 708 376 1604 10
Cottages (2)	Ivy Cottages. Brick structure. Thatched roof with eaves squarecut around two upper windows. Square-paned lattice casement windows. Gable on right has exposed timber-framing.	T. & C.P. Act C.A.	SU 708 376 1604 02
Cottage	Denmead Cottage, Wolf Lane. Single storey and two gabled dormers. Timber-framed with brick infilling. Thatched roof. Modern lattice casement windows.	T. & C.P. Act C.A.	SU 709 378 1604 04

Group D — (cont.)

Description and Date	Remarks	Protection	Grid Ref. and Punchcard No.
Cottages (4)	The Street. 2 storeys. Brick on ground floor, tile-hung above with band of fishscale tile hanging. Hipped tiled roof. Possibly C.18.	C.A.	SU 708 376 1604 03

Group F — Historical or Literary Associations

Description and Date	Remarks	Protection	Grid Ref. and Punchcard No.
House C.18	Jane Austen's House. Home of the famous authoress from 1809—1817. Inscription on front of house reads — "Jane Austen lived here from 1809—1817 and hence all her works were sent into the world. Her admirers in this country and in America have united to erect this tablet. Such art as hers can never grow old".	T. & C.P. Act C.A.	SU 708 375 1604 01

CLANFIELD

Clanfield and Chalton parishes were amalgamated in 1932, and were part of the Hundred of Finchdean at the time of the Domesday Survey.

The whole area is dominated by Windmill Hill and the windmill, recently restored, provides an outstanding focal point for the area. A mill is known to have stood here as early as 1289.

Chalton is a small village with many ancient sites in its area and several interesting buildings. The Church of St. Michael is a thirteenth century structure and the registers include burials in woollen cloth from 1678 — 1746. Parts of the 'Red Lion' public house, opposite the church, are said to be over 500 years old.

Clanfield began as a small village but in the last 50 years has spread over a large area. The village has some old thatched cottages and a thatched village well-head. The Church of St. James was rebuilt in 1875 and contains two ancient mediaeval bells.

Description and Date	Remarks	Protection	Grid Ref. and Punchcard No.

Group A — Natural Features

Description and Date	Remarks	Protection	Grid Ref. and Punchcard No.
Pond	West Lane. Beside bend in road near Old Farm. One of two ponds originally in village.	N.P. Act A.O.N.B.	SU 730 161 2303 36
Pond	Junction of Chalton Lane and Pond Lane. Attractive feature of the village.		SU 697 167 2303 17

Group B — Archaeological

Stone Age

Flint Working Sites	Large numbers of mesolithic flint implements found to south and east of Chalton windmill. Finds include cores, flakes, axes and microliths. Also the site of Neolithic flint axe factory. O.S.A. No. SU71 NW26.	N.P. Act A.O.N.B.	SU 717 159 2303 35

Bronze Age

Bowl barrow	Barrow almost ploughed out, but flint mound still visible. O.S.A. No. SU71 NW22. Ref: P.H.F.C., Vol. 14, 1938—40, (Grinsell), p. 359.	N.P. Act A.O.N.B.	SU 734 156 2303 23
Saucer Barrow	Southwest of Chalton Down. O.S.A. No. SU71 NW13. Ref: P.H.F.C., Vol. 14, 1938—40, (Grinsell), p. 359.	N.P. Act A.O.N.B.	SU 715 170 2303 12
Bowl Barrow	Barrow 22.0 m. in diameter. Stands in ploughed field surmounted by telegraph pole. O.S.A. No. SU71 NW14. Ref: P.H.F.C. Vol. 14, 1938—40, (Grinsell), p. 358.	N.P. Act A.O.N.B.	SU 716 166 2303 21

Iron Age

Pottery and Earthworks	Dense scatter of pottery. Traces of earthworks and hut hollows in unploughed land. O.S.A. No. SU71 NW45.	N.P. Act A.O.N.B.	SU 722 161 2303 37
Storage Pit	Pit contained pottery, a bronze ring and possible loom weights. Field under cultivation. O.S.A. No. SU71 NW15.	N.P. Act A.O.N.B.	SU 736 170 2303 22

Iron Age/Roman

Occupation Site	Finds of pottery, brooches and a coin dating from C.1/4 A.D. Two small pits contained charcoal and an iron age pot. Masonry building and late Roman hut excavated 1965. Romano-British beaker and six bronze plates found in a lynchet. O.S.A. No. SU71 NW16. Ref: Antiquities Journal, Vol. 37, 1957, (Frere), p.p. 218—20.	N.P. Act A.O.N.B.	SU 734 174 2303 38

Group B — (cont.)

Roman

Description and Date	Remarks	Protection	Grid Ref. and Punchcard No.
Building (Site)	Trench dug in 1966 cut through flint-packed post holes into which Roman tile had fallen. Possible site of a timber building. Traces of a flint wall also found. O.S.A. No. SU71 NW25.	N.P. Act A.O.N.B.	SU 724 155 2303 34

Romano-British

Description and Date	Remarks	Protection	Grid Ref. and Punchcard No.
Pottery	Romano-British pottery located in a possible flint lined well. Ref: South Hants Archaeological Research Group Records.		SU 705 165 2303 32
Village (Site)	Hill top early Saxon village. Excavations revealed traces of sixty timber structures dating from the C.6. Chalton was in the hundred of Finchdean. Centred on grid reference. Ref: 1. History of People and Places in Hampshire, (Jowett and Jowett), p. 136. 2. V.C.H., Vol. 1, p. 478. 3. V.C.H., Vol. 3, p.p. 107–110. 4. Deserted Mediaeval Village Research Group Reports, 1970, 1971, 1974.	S.A.M. No. 440 N.P. Act A.O.N.B.	SU 734 173 2303 14

Period Unknown

Description and Date	Remarks	Protection	Grid Ref. and Punchcard No.
Earthwork	Possibly the site of an early windmill or Chalton telegraph station. Centred on grid reference. O.S.A. No. SU71 NW24.	N.P. Act A.O.N.B.	SU 716 160 2303 25
Earthwork	Circular ringwork of platform type beside the London Portsmouth Road. O.S.A. No. SU71 NW13.	N.P. Act A.O.N.B.	SU 715 170 2303 20

Group C — Footpaths and Bridleways

Description and Date	Remarks	Protection	Grid Ref. and Punchcard No.
Bridleway No. 9	Runs northwest from Chalton Lane to a point near Gravel Hill on the edge of Holt Down.	N.P. Act A.O.N.B.	SU 717 180 — 721 166 2303 28

Group D — Buildings, Monuments and Engineering Works

Description and Date	Remarks	Protection	Grid Ref. and Punchcard No.
Church C.13	St. Michael's, Chalton. Mid C.13 chancel with tall slender lancet windows. Most of rest of church late C.14. Flint structure with quoins of red brick or stone. Renovated in C.19. Tower lit by lancet windows with battlements added in Georgian times. Tiled roof. Mass dial. Ref: Buildings of England; Hants and I.O.W., (Pevsner and Lloyd), p. 161.	T. & C.P. Act C.A. N.P. Act A.O.N.B.	SU 732 159 2303 01

18th Century Stone and Thatch Cottage, CLANFIELD

Description and Date	Remarks	Protection	Grid Ref. and Punchcard No.
Group D — (cont.)			
Inn C.16	Red Lion, Chalton. Possibly of earlier date. 2 storeys. Timber-framed with brick and rubble filling. Overhanging upper storey with recessed centre portion and connecting timber braces. Hipped thatched roof, low at the back. Casement windows with glazing bars. Rear extensions of colourwashed flint and brick. Ref: Buildings of England; Hants and I.O.W., (Pevsner and Lloyd), p. 162.	T. & C.P. Act C.A. N.P. Act A.O.N.B.	SU 731 160 2303 03
Cottages C.16	Nos. 132 and 133, North Lane. 2 storeys. Timber-framed with flint infilling. Central chimney. Double hipped thatched roof descending to door lintel at rear. Casement windows, those on ground floor with leaded panes.	N.P. Act A.O.N.B.	SU 698 168 2303 08
Cottage C.16/17	Rose Cottage, North Lane. 2 storeys. Thatched roof. Timber-framed with infilling whitewashed. Casement windows. Brick chimneys. Modern thatched extension.	N.P. Act A.O.N.B.	SU 698 169 2303 09
Cottage C.17	Sleepy Hollow, South Lane. 2 storeys. Half-timbered with brick infilling. Corrugated iron roof, once thatched. Ground floor casement windows with glazing bars. Dormer windows at eaves. Formerly two cottages.	C.A. N.P. Act A.O.N.B.	SU 732 160 2303 05
Farmhouse C.17/18	Old Manor Farm, North Lane. 2 storeys. Partly timber-framed with pebble-dash and brick facings. Irregular tiled roof with gables. C.19, 2-storey addition on south east side. Symmetrical 3-window front. Slate roof with projecting gables. Flint walls with galleted joins and red brick dressings. Gauged red brick arches to recessed sash windows with glazing bars. Gabled porch with round arched door-way and panelled door approached by steps.	T. & C.P. Act N.P. Act A.O.N.B.	SU 698 170 2303 40
Cottage C.18	Glebe Cottage, South Lane, Chalton. Malm-stone with brick dressings, on brick and flint plinth. Casement windows. Thatched roof. Additions of later date at each side.	N.P. Act A.O.N.B.	SU 730 157 2303 06
Windmill C.18/19	Chalton windmill. Fine site on Windmill Hill, clearly seen from A3 road. Site of mill recorded there 1289. Tower mill of brick, plaster rendered. Cap of wood and metal. Now renovated to form a dwelling. Ref: County Records Office (Clark-Jervoise Papers).	T. & C.P. Act N.P. Act A.O.N.B.	SU 716 160 2303 02
Church C.19	St. James. Built 1875. Flint walls and porch. Tiled roof. Prominent double open bellcote, a village landmark. Internal walls of red and yellow brick with black and red stripes at intervals. West window taken from old church. C.14 octagonal font. Mediaeval bells. Ref: Buildings of England; Hants and I.O.W., (Pevsner and Lloyd) p. 179.	N.P. Act A.O.N.B.	SU 697 168 2303 16

Description and Date	Remarks	Protection	Grid Ref. and Punchcard No.

Group D — (cont.)

Description and Date	Remarks	Protection	Grid Ref. and Punchcard No.
Farmhouse C.19	Woodcroft Farm, Chalton. Older part at rear. 2 storeys. Flint with brick dressings and brick dentil cornice. Slate roof and sash windows at front, tiled roof and casement windows with some diamond leaded lights at rear. Single storey lean-to addition.	N.P. Act A.O.N.B.	SU 738 161 2303 07
Farmhouse	Manor Farm, Chalton. Late C.17 front of flint with red brick dressings. Sash windows. C.19 gabled porch with decorative bargeboards. Some parts of house date from early Middle Ages. Excavations have revealed C.13 building near the farm. Replaced by timber-framed house in C.14 of which some timber posts survive. C.16 fireplace. House altered many times. Ref: 1. Chalton Conservation Area booklet. 2. South Hants Archaeological Research Group Records.	C.A. N.P. Act A.O.N.B.	SU 733 159 2303 13
Building	Chalton Priory. Irregular mediaeval building of stone with stone quoins. Mid C.18 front of flint with red brick dressings. Sash windows. Cornice obscures original roof line. House formerly known as The Rectory. C.19 alterations.	C.A. N.P. Act A.O.N.B.	SU 731 159 2303 15
Building	The Old School, South Lane. Originally St. James' Church Hall. Partly single storey, remainder 2 storeys. Flint structure with brick quoins. Tiled gabled roof with bargeboards and gabled dormer. Casement windows surmounted by cambered arch.		SU 697 167 2303 41
Cottages (3)	Rose Cottage, Mews Cottage and another, Pond Lane. L-shaped block. Rose Cottage of C.18/19 date. Flint with brick quoins and a slate roof. Mews Cottage and the other cottage probably of C.17 date. Close vertical timber framing with flint filling, asbestos slate roof. All of 2 storeys with casement windows.		SU 698 168 2303 24
Well	Village well. Thatched well head supported on timber posts. Open sides. Some original machinery remains, some has been accurately replaced by the local blacksmith.	N.P. Act A.O.N.B.	SU 697 168 2303 11
Forge	Flint with brick dressings. Tiled roof. Wooden stable door.		SU 698 168 2303 33

Group E — Street Patterns, Street Furniture and Open Spaces

Description and Date	Remarks	Protection	Grid Ref. and Punchcard No.
Open Space	The southernmost tip of Holt Down Plantation. This is part of the Butser Hill open space and the Queen Elizabeth Country Park including information centre and ancient farms project.	N.P. Act A.O.N.B. C.O.S.	SU 721 174 2303 39

Group E — (cont.)

Description and Date	Remarks	Grid Ref. and Punchcard No.
Dwellings (2)	2 Chapel Cottages and Westagon Lodge, little Hyden Lane. Formerly Nos. 1, 2 and 3 Chapel Cottages and Chapel adjacent to No. 1. 2 storeys. Flint structure. Hipped roof with intermediately placed chimney. No. 2 Chapel Cottages formed from the original Nos. 2 and 3, has a tiled roof and square-paned lattice windows. Westagon Lodge, the original No. 1, has a blue slate roof and casement windows, and utilises the chapel as a garage.	SU 695 175 2303 42
Dwellings (3)	Bethel Cottage and Bethel House, Little Hyden Lane. These dwellings have been formed from a group of buildings which originated as one cottage, which was enlarged by the addition of a house built onto one side and a chapel plus a detached Sunday School building on the other. Flint structure, partly clad and partly rendered. The slate roof is hipped at one end and partly 'M' shaped; it is gabled with bargeboards. The windows are gabled dormers and diamond shaped lattice-paned casements. The three dwellings have been formed from the original cottage and house, whilst the chapel and Sunday School serve as a studio and a garage.	SU 696 173 2303 43

COLEMORE AND PRIORS DEAN

Orginally Colemore and Priors Dean were two separate parishes but have always been closely associated. They were not united into one parish until 1932. The parish of Colemore, sometimes spelt Colmer, produced some distinguished men in the seventeenth and eighteenth centuries. The Rev. John Greaves, rector of Colemore, had three illustrious sons: John was born in 1602 and became a celebrated mathematician, Edward studied medicine and became a physician to Charles II, and Thomas followed oriental studies and had a distinguished career at Oxford. A later rector of Colemore, the Rev. Richard Pococke, was the father of the famous explorer, Richard Pococke, whose Eastern Travels were published in the 1740s.

The manor of Colemore was granted to Southwick Priory and confirmed by a charter of King Richard in 1198. At the dissolution of the monasteries in 1538 Henry VIII granted the manor first to Anne of Cleves and later to Katherine Howard in 1541. The manor was later held by the Compton family and passed by marriage into the famous Tichborne family.

The parish of Priors Dean is so called because the manor of Dean was included with Colemore in a charter of King John dated 1203, which confirmed the holdings of Southwick Priory. Since this date the two manors have followed the same descent; the old manor house at Priors Dean was once the seat of the Tichborne family, and memorials to members of the Compton and Tichborne families can be seen in Priors Dean church.

Description and Date	Remarks	Protection	Grid Ref. and Punchcard No.
Group A — Natural Features			
Viewing Point	Fine views from the Colemore to Slade Farm road, northwards over the countryside to East Tisted and Newton Valence.	N.P. Act A.O.N.B.	SU 712 304 2304 21
Trees	Quin Hay Farm. A line of trees formerly on eastern edge of an unnamed copse which has now disappeared. Mainly ash trees. Centred on grid reference.	T.P.O. No. 505 N.P. Act A.O.N.B.	SU 724 290 2304 20
Woodland	The Warren. A wooded chine of 62 acres, north of Warren Corner. Trees of various species. A nature reserve; managed by the Hampshire and I.O.W. Naturalist Trust.	N.P. Act S.S.S.I. A.O.N.B. C.O.S.	SU 730 285 2304 13
Woodland	Farrow Hill. A continuation of The Warren. Woodland provides attractive scenery. Centred on grid reference.	N.P. Act S.S.S.I. A.O.N.B.	SU 735 291 2304 14
Trees	Standing on a triangular green in front of Colemore Church, one beech and one weeping birch, in an an area of scenic beauty giving added dignity to the church.	N.P. Act A.O.N.B.	SU 706 307 2304 12
Area of Ecological Importance	Wealden Edge Hangers. Mainly wooded and easterly-facing escarpment of the Hampshire chalk plateau at the western extremity of the weald. Wide variety of woodland types on steep slopes, with small intervening areas of chalk grassland and scrub. Rich and diverse fauna and flora contribute to making this area one of the most interesting and important series of chalk woodlands in Britain.	N.P. Act S.S.S.I. A.O.N.B.	SU 737 312 — 735 259 2304 30
Group B — Archaeological			
Stone Age			
Neolithic Sherd	Fragment of yellowish brown Peterborough ware with rows of triangular bird bone impressions in furrows. Found close to Manor Farm. O.S.A. No. SU72 NW2. Ref: Archaeological Journal, Vol. 38, 1931, (Piggott), p. 151.	N.P. Act A.O.N.B.	SU 729 297 2304 22
Bronze Age			
Bowl Barrows (3)	Possible barrows in a field north east of Priors Dean. Centred on grid reference.	N.P. Act A.O.N.B.	SU 732 300 2304 17
Barrow (Remains)	On the crest of a hill just west of Hawkley Hanger. Barrow which is almost ploughed out is 25.0 m. in diameter. O.S.A. No. SU72 NW16.	N.P. Act A.O.N.B.	SU 735 299 2304 16

Description and Date	Remarks	Protection	Grid Ref. and Punchcard No.

Group B — (cont.)

Post Norman

Description and Date	Remarks	Protection	Grid Ref. and Punchcard No.
Windmill Mound	Steep-sided circular mound 25.0 m. in diameter, surrounded by a ditch crossed by three causeways. Top of mound has cruciform depression. Located close to Windmill Copse and Windmill Farm. O.S.A. No. SU72 NW1.	N.P. Act A.O.N.B.	SU 713 294 2304 18
Deserted Village (Site)	Prior's Dean Hundred = East Meon. Centred on grid reference. Ref: 1. V.C.H., Vol. 1, p.p. 415, 423, 436—7. 2. Deserted Mediaeval Villages (Beresford and Hurst).	N.P. Act A.O.N.B.	SU 728 296 2304 26
Deserted Village (Site)	Colemore Hundred = East Meon. Centred on grid reference. Ref: 1. V.C.H., Vol. 1, p. 500. 2. V.C.H., Vol. 4, p.p. 415, 423—5. 3. Deserted Mediaeval Villages (Beresford and Hurst).	S.A.M. No. 456 N.P. Act A.O.N.B.	SU 706 307 2304 25

Period Unknown

Description and Date	Remarks	Protection	Grid Ref. and Punchcard No.
Crop Marks	Traces of four or five enclosures on Becksteddle Farm. Site on slope of a dry valley, and under crop. Possible site of Iron Age/Romano-British farmstead. O.S.A. No. SU63 SE14.	N.P. Act A.O.N.B.	SU 700 306 2304 27

Group C — Footpaths and Bridleways

Description and Date	Remarks	Protection	Grid Ref. and Punchcard No.
Footpaths	Runs north—south through Hawkley Hanger. ½ mile west of Hawkley village.	N.P. Act S.S.S.I. A.O.N.B.	SU 737 290 — 737 300 2304 15
Footpath	Runs through wooded chine of Farrow Hill, west of Hawkley village.	N.P. Act S.S.S.I. A.O.N.B.	SU 738 293 — 739 290 2304 28

Group D — Buildings, Monuments and Engineering Works

Description and Date	Remarks	Protection	Grid Ref. and Punchcard No.
Church C.12	Priors Dean. Rendered nave and chancel with bell turret. Norman north doorway. Early English chancel. Alabaster monuments to Compton, Tichborne and Stoughton. Very large yew tree in churchyard, regarded as one of the finest in Hampshire. O.S.A. No. SU72 NW3. Ref: Buildings of England; Hants and I.O.W., (Pevsner and Lloyd), p. 471.	T. & C.P. Act N.P. Act A.O.N.B.	SU 727 296 2304 02

Description and Date	Remarks	Protection	Grid Ref. and Punchcard No.

Group D — (cont.)

Description and Date	Remarks	Protection	Grid Ref. and Punchcard No.
Church C.12/13	St. Peter Ad Vincula, Colemore, Nave of C.12/13. Chancel rebuilt 1874. Victorian bell turret with spire replaces west tower. Norman Purbeck marble font. Reroofed and restored by Redundant Churches Fund. O.S.A. No. SU73 SW14. Ref: Buildings of England; Hants and I.O.W., (Pevsner and Lloyd), p. 181.	T. & C.P. Act N.P. Act A.O.N.B.	SU 705 307 2304 01
Farmhouse C.15	Goleigh Farm, Priors Dean. 2 storeys, ironstone with stone quoins on ground floor. Upper storey timber, close studding with ironstone and plaster filling. Tile-hung gables and tiled roof. North face of malmstone and brick, south face of malmstone. Casement windows with some diamond-leaded lights. One blocked stone mullion window. Later extensions at north end.	T. & C.P. Act N.P. Act A.O.N.B.	SU 746 312 2304 03
Building C.16	Slade Farm, Priors Dean. 2 storeys. Brick with timber work at each end. South side with tile hung upper storey. Hipped tiled roof. Tudor chimney. Casement windows.	T. & C.P. Act N.P. Act A.O.N.B.	SU 717 302 2304 04
Farmhouse C.17	Manor Farm, Colemore. Parts may be of earlier date. Brick structure stuccoed on south and west sides. North side with brick pilasters. Double hipped tiled roof with one hipped dormer. Flint porch with malmstone dressings. Sash windows. East side with three hipped gables and older casement windows.	T. & C.P. Act N.P. Act A.O.N.B.	SU 706 307 2304 05
Farmhouse C.17	Manor Farm, Priors Dean. Late C.17 and earlier. South front of 3 storeys, brick on flint plinth. Double hipped tiled roof with half dormers. East end of malmstone with brick dressings and large exterior chimney. Timber-framed interior with panelling and C.16 fireplace. Old brick garden wall.	T. & C.P. Act N.P. Act A.O.N.B.	SU 728 296 2304 06
Farmhouse C.18	Church Farm, Priors Dean. 2-storey brick building with tiled roof. Sash windows. Wing at rear with casement windows. Farm buildings of same date.	N.P. Act A.O.N.B.	SU 725 300 2304 07
Farmhouse C.18	Field Farm, Priors Dean. 2 storeys. Brick, with upper storey tile hung. Gabled roof. Casement and sash windows with glazing bars.	N.P. Act A.O.N.B.	SU 710 298 2304 08
House C.19	Formerly the Rectory at Colemore, close to the church. Rendered facade with shallow projecting wings. Slate roof. Central door with pedimented doorcase. Sash windows with delicate glazing bars.	N.P. Act A.O.N.B.	SU 706 307 2304 10
Building C.19	Old School House, Colemore. Single storey mid C.19 school. Creamwashed brick and flint. Half-hipped tiled roof. Porch with brick arch. Addition at rear, and upper storey inserted in roof on south side.	N.P. Act A.O.N.B.	SU 704 305 2304 11

Description and Date	Remarks	Protection	Grid Ref. and Punchcard No.

Group D — (cont.)

Description and Date	Remarks	Protection	Grid Ref. and Punchcard No.
Cottages (2)	Nos. 1, and 2, Common Cottages, Becksteddle Farm. No. 2 facing road to farm, flint and brick, thatched roof, casement windows. Possibly of C.17 date. No. 1 joined to the back of No. 2, brick with tiled roof.	N.P. Act A.O.N.B.	SU 695 299 2304 19
Cottages (2)	Nos. 1, and 2, Knapp Cottages. 2 storeys. Flint with brick dressings. Hipped tiled roof, with dormers at back. Casement windows with glazing bars. Brick and tile lean-to additions.	N.P. Act A.O.N.B.	SU 703 306 2304 09
Inn	The White Horse. A pleasant example of vernacular architecture. A halting place for travellers. The lounge bar was originally a smithy. The inn is the subject of Edward Thomas' longest poem, 'Up in the Wind'. In the lounge bar is a carved wooden plaque, erected in 1978 to mark the poet's birth centenary. Ref: Edward Thomas Country, 1978, (Whiteman), p.p. 32—33.	N.P. Act A.O.N.B.	SU 714 290 2304 29

EAST MEON

The boundaries of the present parish of East Meon date back to 1894 when the parish lost a number of its tithings to neighbouring parishes.

Until the Norman Conquest no distinction was made between East and West Meon. The first recorded mention of East Meon occurs in the mid-eleventh century, when the manor was granted to the monks at Winchester. It remained almost continuously with the bishops of Winchester until, as a result of the Root and Branch Bill, it was sold in 1648—9; however, at the restoration of the monarchy the bishops of Winchester once again found themselves lords of the manor.

The Church of All Saints is the oldest building in the parish and dates from about 1150. A stone marked "Amens Plenty" is thought to cover the grave of roundhead soldiers killed in a fight preceeding the Battle of Cheriton (1644) during the Civil War. Also of note is the black Tournai marble font of circa 1130 — 40, which is one of four such fonts in Hampshire.

The bishops of Winchester held their memorial courts in the mediaeval Court House which is the second oldest building in East Meon. At the beginning of the twentieth century it was used to house farm workers and the Great Hall was a cow byre, but in 1927 the building was restored and is occasionally used for theatrical performances.

Description and Date	Remarks	Protection	Grid Ref. and Punchcard No.

Group A — Natural Features

Description and Date	Remarks	Protection	Grid Ref. and Punchcard No.
Butser Hill	500 acres of downland in a prominent position with fine views to Petersfield and Portsmouth. An area of chalk grassland with a history of scientific recording. Fairly level summit with spurs running out in every direction. Part of The Queen Elizabeth Country Park.	N.P. Act S.S.S.I. A.O.N.B. C.O.S.	SU 710 200 2305 63
Landscape Feature	Vineyard Hole, north east of East Meon. About 30 m. deep, but only rough grass and bushes grow there now. Partially surrounded by a wire fence, and occasional hawthorn and elm trees, there are also sycamore, an oak tree, and a prominent evergreen oak.	N.P. Act A.O.N.B.	SU 684 221 2305 82
Attractive River Reach	The River Meon meanders through the parish from its source near South Farm. It runs beside the High Street of East Meon crossed by several bridges.	N.P. Act A.O.N.B.	SU 676 222 2305 89
Downland	Oxenbourne Down, Hilhampton Down and Wascoombe Bottom, south west of Butser Hill. 168 acres of mixed yew woodlands, chalk scrub and chalk grass land. Managed by the Hants. and I.O.W. Naturalists Trust as a reserve.	N.P. Act S.S.S.I. A.O.N.B.	SU 710 190 2305 140
Woodland	Oxenbourne Lythe. A wooded slope between East Meon and Butser Hill. An area of scenic beauty.	N.P. Act A.O.N.B.	SU 704 210 2305 83
River Source	Source of River Meon, south of South Farm and East Meon village.	N.P. Act A.O.N.B.	SU 685 203 2305 156
Viewing Point	Southwest from Privett Road. Views over Drayton Down, Emmet's Down and Henwood Down.	N.P. Act A.O.N.B.	SU 673 233 2305 84
Parkland	At Westbury House. Extensive ornamental grounds on the lower slopes of Henwood Down. The River Meon passes through the estate. There are some fine specimen trees.	N.P. Act A.O.N.B.	SU 657 239 2305 139
Trees	All Saints Church. Various species standing in the area centred on grid reference.	T.P.O. No. 37 E.H.D. N.P. Act A.O.N.B.	SU 680 223 2305 155
Trees	Across entrance to Glenthorne Meadow. An oak, chestnut, and three limes, all in good condition, backed by a row of a further nine limes.	C.A. N.P. Act A.O.N.B.	SU 680 221 2305 91
Tree	Recreation Ground. An oak tree planted to commemorate the Silver Jubilee of King George V in 1935. It now stands about 30 ft. in height.		SU 683 220 2305 162

Description and Date	Remarks	Protection	Grid Ref. and Punchcard No.

Group A — (cont.)

Description and Date	Remarks	Protection	Grid Ref. and Punchcard No.
Trees	Recreation Ground. A group of five chestnut trees plus two copper beeches, planted in the early 1960s.		SU 683 220 2305 161
Tree	Mistletoe Cottage, High Street. A walnut tree stands in the garden. Possibly the finest tree in the parish, it may have survived from an orchard recorded in the 1851 Tithe Terrier.		SU 682 219 2305 160
Trees	Hyden Hill. A curved belt of mixed species forming a pleasant focal point for a panoramic view of the surrounding farmland and downs. Viewed from the main road on Hyden Hill.	N.P. Act A.O.N.B.	SU 682 192 2305 157
Trees	Fishpond Cottages, Oxenbourne. An impressive group of white poplar stands beside the cottages.		SU 694 211 2305 164
Trees	Five lime trees in East Meon Churchyard. Approximately 20 m. apart, on the edge of the churchyard, running alongside the road. Attractive trees approximately 18—30 m. high.	C.A. N.P. Act A.O.N.B.	SU 680 220 2305 90
Sarsen Stones (4) No. 22B	Collected from War Hill early in the 1900s by a former owner of Bereleigh House, and relocated as part of a water garden in the grounds.	N.P. Act A.O.N.B.	SU 678 235 2305 144
Sarsen Stone No. 22C	At the junction of High Street and Frogmore Lane.	N.P. Act A.O.N.B.	SU 682 220 2305 145
Sarsen Stone No. 22E	Located at pedestrian entrance to Westbury House, near ruined chapel of St. Nicholas. Probably parish boundary marker.	N.P. Act A.O.N.B.	SU 657 239 2305 147
Sarsen Stone No. 22A	Ridlington Farm. Possibly a boundary stone.	N.P. Act A.O.N.B.	SU 664 236 2305 143

Group B — Archaeological

Stone Age

Description and Date	Remarks	Protection	Grid Ref. and Punchcard No.
Flint Site	A Mesolithic site on the summit of Salt Hill, and Neolithic artifacts on the lower slopes. Important neolithic finds include re-chipped axes and leaf shape arrowheads. O.S.A. No. SU62 SE11. Ref: Archaeological Newsletter, No. 5, 1955, (Draper), p. 199.	N.P. Act A.O.N.B.	SU 673 202 2305 130
Axe	Polished axe of Neolithic date found on Oxenbourne Farm, 1919. 9¾ ins. by 2½ ins. wide. O.S.A. No. SU62 SE14.	N.P. Act A.O.N.B.	SU 690 210 2305 133

Description and Date	Remarks	Protection	Grid Ref. and Punchcard No.

Group B — (cont.)

Description and Date	Remarks	Protection	Grid Ref. and Punchcard No.
Ancient Site	A secondary Neolithic site on Oxenbourne Down. Considered to be an implement factory site.	N.P. Act A.O.N.B.	SU 715 185 2305 150
Long Barrow	Salt Hill. Half mile north of South Hants Ridgeway. Normal barrow of Wessex type with flanking ditches, orientated north east to south west. O.S.A. No. SU62 SE12.	S.A.M. No. 404 N.P. Act A.O.N.B.	SU 672 201 2305 131
Dyke	A cross-ridge dyke at the top of Harvesting Lane, comprising a ditch with side banks extending from above very steep natural slopes. Part has been under plough for many years and can only be traced on air-photographs. One of a series set across ridges that give access to Butser Hill. O.S.A. No. SU71 NW1.	N.P. Act S.S.S.I. A.O.N.B.	SU 708 195 2305 134
Bowl Barrow	Barrow north east of Drayton House, under crop. 40 m. across with a maximum height of 1 m. O.S.A. No. SU62 SE7.	N.P. Act A.O.N.B.	SU 673 239 2305 127
Bowl Barrow	West of a spur of Long Down. Under pasture in fair condition. Ditch not apparent. 25 m. in diameter and 0.6 m. high. O.S.A. No. SU61 NE3.	N.P. Act A.O.N.B.	SU 669 197 2305 137
Bowl Barrow	Large barrow in Hyden Wood. Tree covered, with faint traces of a ditch. O.S.A. No. SU61 NE7.	N.P. Act A.O.N.B.	SU 692 189 2305 113
Bowl Barrow	In copse near Hyden Cross. 11 m. in diameter, grass and tree covered. Site only of another barrow. O.S.A. No. SU61 NE8. Ref: P.H.F.C., Vol. 14, 1938—40, Hampshire Barrows (Grinsell), p. 358.	N.P. Act A.O.N.B.	SU 682 189 2305 114
Bowl Barrow (4)	On north-east slopes of Hyden Hill. No trace of surrounding ditches. O.S.A. No. SU61 NE9. Ref: P.H.F.C., Vol. 14, 1938—40, (Grinsell), p. 358.	N.P. Act A.O.N.B.	SU 689 192 2305 115
Bowl Barrow (Probable)	Ploughed down mound 20 m. by 0.5 m. north of Martin's Down. Scattered with large flints. O.S.A. No. SU62 NE19.	N.P. Act A.O.N.B.	SU 660 261 2305 120
Cross Dykes	Ditches in the grounds of H.M.S. Mercury (formerly Leydene House). Multiple earth-work about 850 m. in length astride South Hampshire Ridgeway. Series of two banks and three ditches, centred on grid reference. There is a barrow on the east side. O.S.A. No. SU61 NE6. O.S.A. No. SU61 NE5.	S.A.M. No. 135 N.P. Act A.O.N.B.	SU 679 193 2305 112

Description and Date	Remarks	Protection	Grid Ref. and Punchcard No.

Group B — (cont.)

Description and Date	Remarks	Protection	Grid Ref. and Punchcard No.
Bowl Barrow	In the grounds of H.M.S. Mercury. 135 m. in diameter with no visible ditch. Tree covered but otherwise in good condition. O.S.A. No. SU61 NE5.	S.A.M. No. 120 N.P. Act A.O.N.B.	SU 680 193 2305 60
Bowl Barrows (2)	Two mounds and traces of a third on War Hill. All are tree covered. O.S.A. No. SU62 SE1. Ref: P.H.F.C., Vol. 14, 1938—40, (Grinsell), p. 355.	S.A.M. No. 109 N.P. Act A.O.N.B.	SU 682 257 2305 61
Bowl Barrow	Large spread mound, probable barrow, under crops. West of Tigwell Farm. O.S.A. No. SU62 SE6.	N.P. Act A.O.N.B.	SU 675 243 2305 126

Iron Age

Description and Date	Remarks	Protection	Grid Ref. and Punchcard No.
Field System	Contour lynchets average 2 m. in height with cross banks up to 0.5 m. Centred on grid reference. O.S.A. No. SU62 SE1.	N.P. Act A.O.N.B.	SU 655 222 2305 124
Field System	Contour lynchets 1 m. in height on western slopes of Salt Hill. Cross banks up to 0.5 m. survive. O.S.A. No. SU62 SE1.	N.P. Act A.O.N.B.	SU 667 203 2305 129
Field System	North of War Hill on a west facing slope. Lynchets under pasture and woodland on average 2 m. high. O.S.A. No. SU62 NE14.	N.P. Act A.O.N.B.	SU 682 258 2305 117

Roman

Description and Date	Remarks	Protection	Grid Ref. and Punchcard No.
Sculpture	Head of a woman carved in soft limestone 6½ ins. high. Found at back of Redwood Cottage. Probably of second half of C.2. A.D. Now in possession of the British Museum. O.S.A. No. SU62 NE21.	N.P. Act A.O.N.B.	SU 664 256 2305 122

Post Roman

Description and Date	Remarks	Protection	Grid Ref. and Punchcard No.
Boundary Earthwork	Immediately west of Peak Farm. A ditch between two banks of a defensive nature facing north. Centred on grid reference. O.S.A. No. SU62 NE7. Ref: Field Archaeology as Illustrated by Hampshire, 1915, (Williams-Freeman), p.p. 292—3.	N.P. Act A.O.N.B.	SU 663 253 2305 116
Jutish Buckle Plate	Found east of West Meon Hut on A272 road to Petersfield. Rectangle of bronze-gilt with a central garnet setting. Border of animal pattern. Possibly found in a barrow or mound alongside the road. Find in Winchester Museum. O.S.A. No. SU62 NE15. Ref: Antiquities Journal, Vol. 17, 1937, (Hooley), p.p. 199—200.	N.P. Act A.O.N.B.	SU 669 262 2305 119

Description and Date	Remarks	Protection	Grid Ref. and Punchcard No.

Group B — (cont.)

Post Norman

Description and Date	Remarks	Protection	Grid Ref. and Punchcard No.
Mediaeval Village (Site)	Westbury, in the grounds of Westbury House. On river level near the ruined Chapel of St. Nicholas or on the hillside above. Ref: 1. V.C.H., Vol. 1, p. 481. 2. V.C.H., Vol. 3, p.p. 63, 68, 245–6. 3. Deserted Mediaeval Villages, (Beresford and Hurst).	S.A.M. No. 268 N.P. Act A.O.N.B.	SU 657 239 2305 148
Park (Site) C.13	Mascoombe Bottom. No trace of the park remains but the name is preserved in Park Farm and Park Down. O.S.A. No. SU62 SE8. Ref: V.C.H., Vol. 1, p.p. 61, 67.	N.P. Act A.O.N.B.	SU 680 230 2305 128
Chapel (Site)	Site of St. Mary in the Fields Chapel, at Chapel Field, South Farm. Mentioned in records as early as 1318. A Chapel-of-ease annexed to the parish church. No trace of a building survives.	N.P. Act A.O.N.B.	SU 680 230 2305 128
Mediaeval Village (Site)	Located in a field much ploughed south of Stock's Farm. Not possible to plot the earthworks. Hundred = East Meon. O.S.A. No. SU62 NE10. Ref: Deserted Mediaeval Villages, (Beresford and Hurst).	N.P. Act A.O.N.B.	SU 666 266 2305 149

Period Unknown

Description and Date	Remarks	Protection	Grid Ref. and Punchcard No.
Earthwork	Southwest end of Butser Hill, across approach to summit. Probable cross dyke bank and ditch separated by a berm. The main Ridgeway crossed Butser Hill at this point. O.S.A. No. SU72 SW11.	S.A.M. No. 15 N.P. Act A.O.N.B. C.O.S.	SU 712 200 2305 136
Earthwork	Cross ridge dyke of two parallel banks with ditch. Cut in two places by tracks and densely covered with furze. Probably of Iron Age date. O.S.A. No. SU72 SW10. Ref: Antiquities, No. 4, 1930, (Piggott), p. 138.	S.A.M. No. 15 N.P. Act A.O.N.B. C.O.S.	SU 711 199 2305 135
Enclosure	Rectangular plan, north-west of Great Copyhold Copse, Peak Farm. O.S.A. No. SU62 NE20.	N.P. Act A.O.N.B.	SU 670 258 2305 121

Group C — Footpaths and Bridleways

Description and Date	Remarks	Protection	Grid Ref. and Punchcard No.
Bridleway	Path runs from H.M.S. Mercury to Butser. Centred on grid reference.	N.P. Act A.O.N.B.	SU 699 191 2305 85
Old Travel Way	Alternative routes on Hyden Hill, Clanfield Road centred on grid reference.	N.P. Act A.O.N.B.	SU 682 191 2305 92

Description and Date	Remarks	Protection	Grid Ref. and Punchcard No.

Group C — (cont.)

Description and Date	Remarks	Protection	Grid Ref. and Punchcard No.
Ancient Lane	Halmaker Lane. Runs alongside Westbury Forest where it formed a boundary of the Tithing of Riplington, and is marked as such on the tithe map dated 1636. South of Coombe Cross Lane the lane continues southward, unnamed, until it joins the South Hants Ridgeway.	N.P. Act A.O.N.B.	SU 668 232 — 675 192 2305 165

Group D — Buildings, Monuments and Engineering Works

Description and Date	Remarks	Protection	Grid Ref. and Punchcard No.
Church C.12	All Saints. Cruciform plan with ashlar faced Norman tower of circa 1150. Lead covered broach spire with small cockerel weathervane added later. West doorway and several windows of Norman date. C.13 south aisles of nave and chancel Tournai marble font circa 1130–40. Fine vigorous carving on the sides and top. Church clock with four faces and gold hands. O.S.A. No. SU62 SE15. Ref: Buildings of England; Hants and I.O.W., (Pevsner and Lloyd), p.p. 199–200.	T. & C.P. Act C.A. N.P. Act A.O.N.B.	SU 680 222 2305 01
Chapel C.13	Ruins of the Chapel of St. Nicholas, in the grounds of Westbury House. Part of east wall and most of west wall still standing, also large part of north and minimal part of south walls. Plain circular font removed to East Meon Church. Restoration to ruins carried out in 1981. O.S.A. No. SU62 SE3. Ref: 1. V.C.H. Vol. 3, p.p. 74–5. 2. P.H.F.C. Vol. 2, 1890–3, (Nisbett), p.p. 1–14.	T. & C.P. Act S.A.M. No. 268 N.P. Act A.O.N.B.	SU 657 239 2305 04
Building C.14	The Court House. A manorial court house whose origins date from Norman Conquest, or earlier. Malmstone and flint fabric with dressings and plinth of Langrish stone. Two C.14 windows. South wall rebuilt C.17 and gable tile-hung. Rafter roof with King-posts and tie beams. Corbels carved with heads of kings and bishops. 2-storey extension of similar fabric, now a library. Original staircase of oak leads to an outside door. C.16 farmhouse at rightangles to court house. Timber-framed with brick infill and tiled roof. O.S.A. No. SU62 SE9.	T. & C.P. Act C.A. N.P. Act A.O.N.B.	SU 681 222 2305 06
Cottage C.14	Forge Sound, formerly 1 and 2, Hockley Cottages. Timber-framed with brick infill. Tiled roof. Hipped gable ends with scalloped tile bands. Casement windows. Sun Insurance sign and Farmers Fire and Life Insurance sign on gable ends. Originally an open hall house.	C.A. N.P. Act A.O.N.B.	SU 681 221 2305 45

Description and Date	Remarks	Protection	Grid Ref. and Punchcard No.

Group D — (cont.)

Description and Date	Remarks	Protection	Grid Ref. and Punchcard No.
Cottages C.14/15	Riverside. Two connected cottages of cream-washed brick, partly timber-framed. Thatched roof. The more southerly cottage includes a wooden shuttered shop front, formerly a butcher's shop, with latticed wood-work for ventilation, it also has a slate roof porch. The cottage to the north has been provisionally assessed as a one-aisled open hall house of the second half of C.14, or possibly early C.15.	C.A. N.P. Act A.O.N.B.	SU 681 221 2305 46
House C.14/16	The Tudor House, The Square. 3 storeys. First and second storey jettied on north and east elevations. Timber-framed with malmstone and flint filling, brick infill above. Casement windows, original mullioned and transomed window on ground floor. Tiled roof descends to ground floor level on west side. Interior has some oak panelling. South side plaster faced. Western wing of the building is thought to be C.14. The house is believed to have been built for the bailiff of the manor of East Meon.	T. & C.P. Act C.A. N.P. Act A.O.N.B.	SU 679 221 2305 19
Mill C.16	Drayton Mill. L-shaped plan. Timber-framed with tiled roof and five dormers on south side. Diamond-leaded pane windows. Mill race now diverted. Site reputed to be in Domesday Book.	N.P. Act A.O.N.B.	SU 671 230 2305 77
Cottages (2) C.16	Sebastopol Cottages. Timber-framed with brick and flint infilling. Thatched roof. Gable end towards road of flint and rubble. Casement windows.	N.P. Act A.O.N.B.	SU 679 219 2305 38
Cottages (3) C.16	Nos. 1, 2, and 3, Cross Cottages. 2 storeys. Timber-framed with brick and flint infilling. Colour washed. Thatched roof descending to door level at back. Lattice porches on brick foundations. Casement windows. Formerly the Angel Inn.	T. & C.P. Act C.A. N.P. Act A.O.N.B.	SU 680 221 2305 13
Cottage C.16/17	Forge Cottage. Timber-framed with part brick and part lath and plaster whitewashed infilling. East end gable is tile-hung. Thatched roof with bedroom windows at eaves level. C.18 extension at east end, partly tile-hung. Substantial single storey extension on south side.	C.A. N.P. Act A.O.N.B.	SU 682 219 2305 34
House C.16/17	Heycroft House. Situated on south west corner of the square. 3-storey timber-framed house, with brick infilling. Four bays, of which the two more easterly are late C.16, the others are early C.17. Most of the eastern elevation infilling consists of herringbone brickwork. The west elevation is jettied.	C.A. N.P. Act A.O.N.B.	SU 687 221 2305 54

Description and Date	Remarks	Protection	Grid Ref. and Punchcard No.

Group D — (cont.)

Description and Date	Remarks	Protection	Grid Ref. and Punchcard No.
House and Gate Posts C.17	Glenthorne, High Street. Brick with purple headers and brick plinth. Rusticated quoins. Tiled roof with wooden eaves and cornice. Sash windows. Doorway with brick pediment and moulded surround. C.19 cast-iron railings. Farmers' General Life Assurance sign. Recent additions. Timber-framed back with tiled roof. Round headed staircase window. C.18 gate-posts of flint and brick with stone ball finials.	T. & C.P. Act C.A. N.P. Act A.O.N.B.	SU 680 221 2305 15
Barn C.17	West of the Court House. Timber-framed with brick and flint structure. Thatched roof with weathervane. Converted for use as a garage.	T. & C.P. Act C.A. N.P. Act A.O.N.B.	SU 680 222 2305 07
Cottage C.17	Hookley Cottage, formerly two cottages. Joined to Brook Cottages by a thatched roof over a public footpath. Brick with some timber work. Whitewashed front. Mainly casement windows with glazing bars.	C.A. N.P. Act A.O.N.B.	SU 681 221 2305 43
Cottages (2) C.17	Brook Cottages, High Street. Plaster faced brick with tile-hung upper storey. Thatched roof with dormers at rear. Casement windows.	C.A. N.P. Act A.O.N.B.	SU 681 221 2305 44
Cottage C.17	Mill Cottage, Frogmore. 2 storeys. Timber-framed with brick infill. Tiled roof with four dormers. Hipped gable end to road. Recent porches. Sash windows on ground floor, casements above.	T. & C.P. Act N.P. Act A.O.N.B.	SU 684 221 2305 20
Cottages C.17	3, and 4, Church Road. Timber-framed with whitewashed brick infilling. Tiled roof, hipped at west end. Casement windows with glazing bars.	C.A. N.P. Act A.O.N.B.	SU 679 222 2305 39
Cottage C.17	Hebberdens, Lower Bordean. Possibly of earlier date. 2 storeys. Timber-framed with brick infilling. Tiled roof. Diamond-paned leaded casement windows. Bay window on upper storey of south elevation.	T. & C.P. Act N.P. Act A.O.N.B.	SU 691 247 2305 03
Cottages (2) C.17	Fishpond Cottages. 2 storeys. Timber-framed, with mainly herringbone brick infilling at front, some malmstone at the sides, which are partly tile-hung. Double hipped tiled roof. Modern extension at east end.	N.P. Act A.O.N.B.	SU 694 211 2305 26
House C.17	Oxenbourne House. 2 storeys. T-shaped plan. Malmstone with brick dressings. Tiled roof with tile-hung dormers. Timber-framed extension to south with brick infill. Later additions of flint and random rubble. Verandah supported on four pillars. Leaded windows. Farmers Life and Fire Insurance plaque on wall.	N.P. Act A.O.N.B.	SU 691 213 2305 67
Barn C.17	Oxenbourne House. Timber-framed and weather-boarded. Single storey. Thatched roof. Large modern doors at front.	N.P. Act A.O.N.B.	SU 692 213 2305 98

Description and Date	Remarks	Protection	Grid Ref. and Punchcard No.

Group D — (cont.)

Description and Date	Remarks	Protection	Grid Ref. and Punchcard No.
Cottages (4) C.17	Nos. 1, 2, 3, and 4, Kew Cottages. 2 storeys. Thatched roof with hipped gable ends. Nos. 1 and 2 of flint with brick dressings. Simple hood porches. Nos. 3 and 4 of brick with some timber work.	C.A. N.P. Act A.O.N.B.	SU 678 221 2305 36
Cottages (2) C.17	Nos. 1, and 2, Old Bell Cottages. 2 storeys. Whitewashed brick with tiled roof and old chimneys. No. 1 has some timber work on western wall. Hood over door. No. 2 recessed behind front garden with gabled dormer and Elizabethan half dormer window. Formerly The Old Bell Public House.	C.A. N.P. Act A.O.N.B.	SU 680 221 2305 50
Cottage C.17	The White Cottage, High Street. Timber-framed with brick and plaster filling. Thatched roof with central chimney. Restored with modern window frames and doors.	T. & C.P. Act C.A. N.P. Act A.O.N.B.	SU 680 221 2305 17
House C.17/18	Upper Bordean. Georgian style with Victorian additions. Flemish bond brickwork at front, and coursed flint at sides. Slate hung parapet. Tiled roof. Part tile hanging on west side. C.19 porch. Bay, sash and casement windows.	N.P. Act A.O.N.B.	SU 689 250 2305 78
Farmhouse C.17/18	Peak Farm. 2 storeys. 1728 Georgian front elevation consisting of brickwork using purple headers. Moulded brick cornice and parapet. Tiled roof. Sash windows surmounted by flat arches. Plaster faced stone door surround approached by three semi-circular stone steps. Older portion to north and west.	T. & C.P. Act N.P. Act A.O.N.B.	SU 666 254 2305 02
Cottage C.17/18	Wheelwright Cottage. Formerly two cottages. Brick structure using purple headers. Tiled roof, once thatched. Casement windows. Farmers Fire Insurance sign. The western part of the building dates from C.17, whilst the bay to the east dates from C.18, added when the front brick elevation was constructed.	C.A. N.P. Act A.O.N.B.	SU 681 220 2805 48
Farmhouse C.18	Hyden Farm. 2 storeys and attic and semi-basement. Brick with purple headers. Tiled roof with two gabled dormers. Casement windows on ground floor with arches and shutters. South side tile hung. Wooden porch with hipped tiled roof.	N.P. Act A.O.N.B.	SU 679 175 2305 28
Farmhouse and Cottages (2) C.18	Coombe Farmhouse. 2 storeys. Brick and flint structure with scribed plaster covering at front. Brick extension on south side, built in same style. Modern brick porch on north side. Casement windows. Three brick chimney stacks, roof re-tiled in modern grey tiles. Plaster covered brick porch with tile hood. The cottages consist of one building, formerly four dwellings. Random flint walls at front, brick at back. Casement windows. Clay tile roof. Brick porch.	N.P. Act A.O.N.B.	SU 662 206 2305 73

Group D — (cont.)

Description and Date	Remarks	Protection	Grid Ref. and Punchcard No.
House C.18	Coombe Cross. Formerly a farmhouse. Brick with hipped tiled roof. Large Regency porch with barrel shaped roof. Sash windows with glazing bars. Addition of later date with wooden verandah.	N.P. Act A.O.N.B.	SU 667 210 2305 24
Farmhouse C.18	Stoneylands Farm. 2 storeys. Flint structure with pebbledash covering. Slate roof. Casement windows. Originally two cottages. Very old brick roundhouse in the garden, believed to be one of only four left in Hampshire.	N.P. Act A.O.N.B.	SU 692 203 2305 71
Cottage C.18	At South Farm. Adjoining the former Mill. Single storey plus dormers. Roughcast brick structure. Tiled roof. Tiled, gabled dormers with tile-hanging. Casement windows with cambered arches. The oldest part of the building is the south east section. Red brick extension to the north with slate roof and round headed casement windows.	N.P. Act A.O.N.B.	SU 684 207 2305 33
Barn C.18	Upper Barn. Single storey. Coursed flint with brick dressings. Unusual brick dentilled ventilation apertures in walls.	N.P. Act A.O.N.B.	SU 696 207 2305 99
Farmhouse C.18	Lower Farm. West front of malmstone and brick. C.19 brick and tile porch. Tiled roof. South side of brick, and extension pebble-dashed. Sash windows.	N.P. Act A.O.N.B.	SU 685 209 2305 31
Cottage C.18	Giant's Cottage, Oxenbourne. Unusually large random flints with brick dressings. Thatched roof with central chimney. A large flint giant's face is a feature in the front wall. Bedroom windows inset in thatch which over-hangs on struts. Outshots each end. Originally two cottages.	N.P. Act A.O.N.B.	SU 692 211 2305 27
Farmhouse C.18	Oxenbourne Farm. Brick and flint, with timber-framing visible inside. Front pebbledashed and whitewashed. Hipped gables, tiled roof. Porch supported on two large pebbledashed pillars. Casement windows.	N.P. Act A.O.N.B.	SU 693 213 2305 66
Cottage C.18	Pond Cottage, Oxenbourne. Coursed flint walls with brick dressings. Tiled roof. Casement windows. Later brick extensions.	N.P. Act A.O.N.B.	SU 690 216 2305 69
Farmhouse C.18	Hilhampton Farm. Malmstone with brick dressings. Slate roof with four chimneys. Casement windows. Brick porch with slate roof. Extension on east side.	N.P. Act A.O.N.B.	SU 699 217 2305 70
Farmhouse C.18	Lower House Farm. 2 storeys. Malmstone and brick. Double hipped tiled roof. Sash windows. C.19 brick tiled porch. On the south side the brick extension to the east is pebble-dashed. In places rebuilt in 1942.	T. & C.P. Act N.P. Act A.O.N.B.	SU 689 217 2305 65

Village Street and River Meon, EAST MEON

Description and Date	Remarks	Protection	Grid Ref. and Punchcard No.
Group D — (cont.)			
Cottages (2) C.18	Templar's Brow, south of the Smithy. Flint with brick dressings. Thatched roof. Casement windows at eaves level.	N.P. Act A.O.N.B.	SU 682 218 2305 35
Building C.18	Blacksmith's shop. Single storey. Almost C-shaped in plan. Brick with tiled roof. Casement windows with glazing bars.	C.A. N.P. Act A.O.N.B.	SU 683 219 2305 100
Cottage C.18	Farriers, High Street. Rendered facade of brick quoins and malmstone. Modern tiled roof. Doorway with fanlight, pilasters and pediment. Casement windows.	C.A. N.P. Act A.O.N.B.	SU 682 220 2305 154
House C.18	Ivy House. Double-fronted. Brick with tiled roof. Sash windows with cambered arches and glazing bars. Simple latticed porch.	C.A. N.P. Act A.O.N.B.	SU 682 220 2305 153
Cottage C.18	Fern Cottage. Double fronted. Coursed flint with brick dressings. Slate roof. Sash windows with cambered arches. Latticed porch. Later brick extension on south side.	C.A. N.P. Act A.O.N.B.	SU 682 220 2305 47
Cottage C.18	Barnards. Formerly No. 1, Barnards Cottages. Double fronted, whitewashed brick. Tiled roof. Sash windows with glazing bars.	T. & C.P. Act C.A. N.P. Act A.O.N.B.	SU 680 221 2305 18
Cottage C.18	Middle Barnards. Formerly Nos. 2, and 3 Barnards Cottages. Colour-washed brick, tiled roof. Sash windows, with the exception of one casement.	C.A. N.P. Act A.O.N.B.	SU 680 221 2305 51
Cottage C.18	Barnards Corner. Formerly Nos. 4, 5 and 6, Barnard's Cottages. White washed brick. Casement windows some with leaded lights.	C.A. N.P. Act A.O.N.B.	SU 680 221 2305 52
Building C.18	Goddard's Garage, High Street. Formerly the coachhouse of 'Glenthorne'. Coursed knapped flint structure, with flint flake galleting on south wall and glass galleting on east elevation.		SU 680 221 2305 163
Cottages (2) C.18	Clare cottage and No. 11, High Street. 2 storeys. Brick structure consisting of purple headers, with flat band between the storeys. Tiled roof. Casement windows.	C.A. N.P. Act A.O.N.B.	SU 681 221 2305 42
House C.18	Brooklyn House, High Street. 2 storeys. Brick with flat band between storeys. Tiled roof. Door with porch. Sash windows with glazing bars. Two bay windows to right of door.	T. & C.P. Act C.A. N.P. Act A.O.N.B.	SU 681 221 2305 16
Inn C.18	The George, Church Street. Colourwashed brick. Tiled roof with gabled ends. Sash windows and two gabled dormers. Sign of St. George and Dragon with wrought iron bracket and bunch of grapes.	T. & C.P. Act C.A. N.P. Act A.O.N.B.	SU 680 221 2305 10

Description and Date	Remarks	Protection	Grid Ref. and Punchcard No.

Group D — (cont.)

Description and Date	Remarks	Protection	Grid Ref. and Punchcard No.
Building C.18	The Post Office, Church Street. Single storey. Colour washed brick. Gabled dormers in tiled roof. Lower windows sash, upper casements. Central door with simple hood, shop window.	T. & C.P. Act C.A. N.P. Act A.O.N.B.	SU 680 221 2305 11
House C.18	The Vicarage, formerly The White House, Church Street. 2 storeys. Flint with brick dressings, white plastered facade. Slate roof with wide eaves. Rear flint and brick extension.	T. & C.P. Act C.A. N.P. Act A.O.N.B.	SU 680 222 2305 09
Cottage C.18	Church Cottage, Church Street. Queen Anne building of brick with grey headers. Tiled roof with three gabled dormers. Leaded casement windows with flat arches. Flint garden wall one section in brick with rounded brick coping.	T. & C.P. Act C.A. N.P. Act A.O.N.B.	SU 680 222 2305 12
Building C.18	Cross Keys, The Cross. Brick with purple headers. South side tile hung. Slate roof. Modern latticed windows with flat arches over. Later additions in flint and brick.	T. & C.P. Act C.A. N.P. Act A.O.N.B.	SU 679 222 2305 14
House C.18	Vicarage Lodge, The Cross. Double-fronted. Colourwashed and plastered flint and brick. Tiled roof. Pent hood to door. Projecting section near road suggests a former toll house.	C.A. N.P. Act A.O.N.B.	SU 679 222 2305 40
Cottage C.18	Court House Cottage. 2 storeys. Brick walls. Thatched roof with central chimney. Casement windows. Built about 1770.	T. & C.P. Act C.A. N.P. Act A.O.N.B.	SU 681 222 2305 08
Building C.18	Mill House, Frogmore. 2 storeys. Brick structure covered with scribed and colour-washed plaster. Rear of property constructed of flint and brick. Windows have plaster mullioned surround. Sash windows. Regency porch. At boundary of garden to south there is a cast iron railing and a gate, both of regency period.	N.P. Act A.O.N.B.	SU 684 220 2305 59
Cottage C.18	Bridge Cottage, Frogmore. Coloured-washed brick structure. Thatched roof with barn ends. Central chimney. Casement windows.	N.P. Act A.O.N.B.	SU 684 221 2305 56
Cottage C.18	Compton Cottage. 2 storeys. Whitewashed malmstone and brick on north and east elevations. Tile-hung on south and west elevations. Double hipped tiled roof with gabled dormer. Casement windows with glazing bars. Door with simple porch.	N.P. Act A.O.N.B.	SU 684 222 2305 58
Building C.18	Park Lodge. 2 storeys. Random flint walls with brick dressings. Casement windows with gothic arches in dentilled brick. Clay tile roof with hipped gable ends. Roof extends down to first storey on west side. Single brick chimney stack with decorative chimney pots.	N.P. Act A.O.N.B.	SU 687 225 2305 81

Description and Date	Remarks	Protection	Grid Ref. and Punchcard No.

Group D — (cont.)

Description and Date	Remarks	Protection	Grid Ref. and Punchcard No.
Cottage C.18	Drayton Cottage. Coursed flint with brick dressings. Slate roof with four gabled dormers, and large chimney. Tile hung east wall. Casement windows with glazing bars. Originally two cottages.	N.P. Act A.O.N.B.	SU 668 232 2305 76
Farmhouse C.18	Drayton Farm. 2 storeys. Coursed flint with brick dressings. Slate roof, with hipped gable ends, and brick chimney stack. Casement windows.	N.P. Act A.O.N.B.	SU 670 232 2305 75
Farmhouse C.18	Riplington Farm. 2 storeys. Plaster faced brick. Slate roof with two lead covered dormers, and hipped gable ends. Sash windows. Central brick porch.	N.P. Act A.O.N.B.	SU 664 237 2305 74
Stables C.18	Westbury House. Seven bays of recessed brickwork with semi-circular heads and sash windows. Central entrance. Tiled roof. Flanked by 2-storey brick towers with tiled roofs. Each has an arched entrance for carriages. Wrought iron weathervane and C.18 clock on north tower. The building includes former living accommodation for grooms.	T. & C.P. Act N.P. Act A.O.N.B.	SU 657 238 2305 05
Ice Houses C.18 (2)	In the grounds of Westbury House. The icehouses are in good condition, recently cleared and found to be approximately 15—20 ft. deep. Brick lined and cylindrical in shape under grass covered domes. They are approached by brick-lined passages in which the doors were originally situated.	N.P. Act A.O.N.B.	SU 658 238 2305 158
Lodge C.18	Bereleigh Estate. L-shaped plan. 2 storeys. Coursed flint with brick dressings. Slate roof. Verandah supported on four brick pillars also has slate roof. C.19 brick bay window added to front.	N.P. Act A.O.N.B.	SU 686 242 2305 80
Farmhouse C.18	Tigwell Farm. Plaster-faced brick. Tiled roof with two chimneys. Casement windows. Small porch on east side.	N.P. Act A.O.N.B.	SU 681 245 2305 79
Cottages (2) C.18/19	Bottle Ale Cottages, Frogmore. Flint with brick dressings. Middle section projects, thatched roof. Casement windows, some with leaded panes. New verandah, and brick southern elevation.	N.P. Act A.O.N.B.	SU 684 221 2305 57
Cottage C.18/19	Hyde Cottage. 2 storeys. Coursed knapped flint, brick quoins. Hipped slate roof, brick chimneys. C.19 and modern casements. Panelled door in modern surround.	T. & C.P. Act A.O.N.B.	SU 683 228 2305 159

Description and Date	Remarks	Protection	Grid Ref. and Punchcard No.

Group D — (cont.)

Description and Date	Remarks	Protection	Grid Ref. and Punchcard No.
Farmhouse C.18/19	Park Farm. 2 storeys. East side plaster-faced brick. Double hipped tiled roof, sash windows. North wing has casement windows, and two gabled tiled dormers in inner roof, with some original leaded panes. South wing added in 1810, plaster-faced, with slate roof. Sash windows and projecting porch.	N.P. Act A.O.N.B.	SU 685 232 2305 29
House C.19	Drayton House. Plaster-faced flint. Slate roof. Sash windows with shutters to upper storey south windows. Slate roofed verandah on south side supported by five columns. Whitewashed brick north face, with sash windows. Long staircase window in same wall as hooded door.	N.P. Act A.O.N.B.	SU 672 236 2305 25
Almshouses C.19	Forbes Almshouses, Nos. 1, 2, 3, 4 and 5, Church Street. 2 storeys. Flint with stone dressings. Malmstone band between the storeys. Tiled roof with gable ends. 2- and 3-light sash windows. Stone chimney stacks. Lead covered dormers in roof. Two double door-ways in ashlar. Forbes coat-of-arms and dedication over doorway. Dedicated by Mrs. Forbes as a memorial to her husband. On the opposite side of the road two further single-storey Almshouses, also of flint with stone dressings, were built in 1906, financed by the trustees of the original Forbes Almshouses.	C.A. N.P. Act A.O.N.B.	SU 680 222 2305 64
House C.19	Lythe House. 3 storeys. Colour washed plaster-faced brick. Tiled roof with gabled dormers. Sash windows, glass roofed verandah.	N.P. Act A.O.N.B.	SU 700 215 2305 72
Building C.19	Windwhistle and The Old School House, The Hyde. One building which formerly housed both the school and the master's house. Built circa. 1845, of coursed knapped flints with a slate roof. Now converted into two dwellings. Windwhistle part 1-storey and part 2 storeys was East Meon School. The Old School House of 2 storeys, was formerly the master's house.		SU 683 223 2305 151
House C.19	Samuel Kille House, The Square. 2 storeys. Part of front elevation consists of purple headers with red brick dressings. Moulded brick band between the storeys. West side of knapped flint galleted with bottle-glass, with an occasional brick string course. The letters 'S.K.' are outlined in flint work. East side of the building has one cut-brick moulded window arch blocked. Sash windows, tiled roof. Dated 1825. The whole house now colour-washed.	C.A. N.P. Act A.O.N.B.	SU 679 221 2305 53

Description and Date	Remarks	Protection	Grid Ref. and Punchcard No.

Group D — (cont.)

Description and Date	Remarks	Protection	Grid Ref. and Punchcard No.
Shop C.19	South side of High Street, adjacent to Fern Cottage. 3-bay shop front with connecting wooden cornice and fascia board. Three sash windows with glazing bars above. Slate roof. Later projecting wing to east.	C.A. N.P. Act A.O.N.B.	SU 681 220 2305 49
War Memorial C.20	Centre of East Meon. Erected 1922 but bronze plaque added to commemorate 1939-45 war dead. Ashlar stone in form of pillar with cross on top. Built on terraced stone platform.	C.A. N.P. Act A.O.N.B.	SU 680 221 2305 103
Cottage	Orchard Cottage, High Street. Front appears to be C.19 but timber framing visible on south side. Rendered walls with slate roof. Central doorway with pediment.	C.A. N.P. Act A.O.N.B.	SU 682 220 2305 152
Farmhouse	South Farm. Brick, flint, greensand stone blocks and mixed stone structure. South facing wing was the original timber-framed house, being an open-hall house of two bays, probably dating to C.15. Upper floor, chimney and east end added C.16. Also added at this time the west wing with jettied front facing west. Substantial alterations in C.18.	N.P. Act A.O.N.B.	SU 684 207 2305 32

Group E — Street Patterns, Street Furniture and Open Spaces

Description and Date	Remarks	Protection	Grid Ref. and Punchcard No.
Mounting Block	Oxenbourne House.	N.P. Act A.O.N.B.	SU 691 213 2305 109
Lych Gate	Church of All Saints. Wooden framework supported on brick and flint blocks. Roof with hipped gable ends. Wooden gates.	C.A. N.P. Act A.O.N.B.	SU 680 222 2305 108
Well Head	Forbes' Almshouses. Built 1858. Coursed flint with brick quoins. Tiled roof. South side of structure left open for access. Well now filled in.	C.A. N.P. Act A.O.N.B.	SU 680 221 2305 104
Green	Washer's Triangle. Two seats placed on a small triangle of mown grass planted with young trees. Located in the centre of the village beside the river. A pleasant resting place for residents and visitors alike. The former site of three old thatched cottages.	C.A. N.P. Act A.O.N.B.	SU 681 221 2305 102

Group F — Historical or Literary Associations

Description and Date	Remarks	Protection	Grid Ref. and Punchcard No.
House C.20	Westbury House. Following a disastrous fire in November 1904 which completely gutted the original Palladian style house, the owner Col. Le Roy Lewis completely rebuilt the house. The new house incorporated many improvements new to the C.20 such as electric lighting, internal telephones and a hot water system. Ref: West Meon (Collins & Hurst), p.p. 56—63.	A.O.N.B.	SU 657 238 2305 160

EAST TISTED

The village lies four miles south of Alton on the A32 amid extensive woodlands. Rotherfield Park is a large mansion standing on high ground in large parklands and is built in a mixture of castellated Italian and Gothic styles. The Church of St. James was largely rebuilt in 1846 and is noteworthy for the exceptionally fine monuments to the Norton family.

Description and Date	Remarks	Protection	Grid Ref. and Punchcard No.
Group A — Natural Features			
Woodland	Stony Brow plantation. Forming a natural extension to the parkland and woodland which farms a large proportion of the parish.	N.P. Act A.O.N.B.	SU 684 307 1605 11
Trees	Anchor Corner. Several species standing in the area centred on grid reference.	T.P.O. No. 45 E.H.D. N.P. Act A.O.N.B.	SU 696 315 1605 20
Sarsen Stone No. 23A	Road junction below St. James' Church.	C.A. N.P. Act A.O.N.B.	SU 700 322 1605 21
Group B — Archaeological			
Bronze Age			
Bowl Barrow	Alongside the A32, north of the village. Oval mound. No visible ditch. Probably a much reduced bowl barrow. O.S.A. No. SU73 SW3. Ref: P.H.F.C., Vol. 14, (1938–40), p. 354.	N.P. Act A.O.N.B.	SU 702 328 1605 16
Post Roman			
Earthwork	2 miles long. Running from the northern edge of Winchester Wood, across the main Fareham/Alton road to Colemore. Consists of single bank and ditch of considerable proportions. O.S.A. No. SU63 SE8. Ref: P.H.F.C., Vol. 12, 1932–4, p. 85.	S.A.M. No. 466 N.P. Act A.O.N.B.	SU 685 327 — 702 306 1605 10
Cross Valley Dyke	Crossing the A32 road near the southern boundary line of the parish. An iron age sherd was picked out of the bank to the east of the road. O.S.A. No. SU63 SE9. Ref: P.H.F.C., Vol. 13, (1935–7), p.p. 55–7.	N.P. Act A.O.N.B.	SU 692 311 1605 13
Post Norman			
Ancient Site	Site of a deserted mediaeval village. Hundred = Selborne. Ref: V.C.H., Vol. 3, p. 30.	S.A.M. No. 455 N.P. Act A.O.N.B.	SU 707 323 1605 15
Group D — Buildings, Monuments and Engineering Works			
Farmhouse C.18	Old Place. Incorporating C.16/17 structure, probably the manor house of East Tisted. 2 storeys. Brick structure. Long ridge tiled roof. Rustic porch. O.S.A. No. SU73 SW8. Ref: V.C.H., Vol. 3, p.p. 30–2.	N.P. Act A.O.N.B.	SU 709 323 1605 04

Description and Date	Remarks	Protection	Grid Ref. and Punchcard No.
Group D — (cont.)			
House C.19	Rotherfield Park. Built 1820 on site of Tudor mansion, of which only the cellars remain. Originally stuccoed and battlemented, now refaced in stone and recast. Surrounded by beautiful parkland. O.S.A. No. SU63 SE4. Ref: 1. Buildings of England; Hants and I.O.W., (Pevsner and Lloyd), p. 203. 2. V.C.H., Vol. 3., p.p. 30—4. 3. Country Life. 23, 30 April and 7 May 1948.	N.P. Act A.O.N.B.	SU 694 323 1605 05
House C.19	The Rectory. Built in Tudor style with steep gables. Ref: Buildings of England; Hants and I.O.W., (Pevsner & Lloyd), p. 204.	C.A. N.P. Act A.O.N.B.	SU 701 323 1605 01
Cottage C.19	The Lodge, Rotherfield Park. Single storey. Octagonal shaped. Pointed Gothic windows. Curved screen walls with piers topped by stone ball finials.	C.A. N.P. Act A.O.N.B.	SU 700 322 1605 09
Church C.19	St. James. Built 1846 incorporating remains of C.13/14 church. Tall western tower with staircase turret, open parapet and pinnacles. Interesting C.16 and C.17 table tombs of the Norton family. O.S.A. No. SU73 SW4. Ref: Buildings of England; Hants and I.O.W., (Pevsner & Lloyd), p. 203.	T. & C.P. Act C.A. N.P. Act A.O.N.B.	SU 701 322 1605 03
Cottage	Ivy Cottage. Restored and enlarged. 2 storeys. Timber-framed with herringbone brick infilling. Lattice casements. Ridge tiled roof. Part to right may be C.17. Exposed timber-framing with limewashed brick and plaster. Thatched roof.	N.P. Act A.O.N.B.	SU 705 322 1605 07
Cottage	The Almshouses. Part to left timber-framed with brick infilling. Thatched roof. Part to extreme right flint rubble with short ridge tiled roof.	C.A. N.P. Act A.O.N.B.	SU 701 327 1605 08
Cottages (2)	Home Farm Cottages. Ground floor brick patched with flint. Exposed timber-framing on first floor with herringbone brick nogging. Thatched roof.	T. & C.P. Act N.P. Act A.O.N.B.	SU 705 322 1605 06
Group E — Street Patterns, Street Furniture and Open Spaces			
Milestone	Sited on A32, marked 'London 52 miles'.	N.P. Act A.O.N.B.	SU 700 321 1605 12

View Across Rotherfield Park, EAST TISTED

Description and Date	Remarks	Protection	Grid Ref. and Punchcard No.

Group E — (cont.)

Description and Date	Remarks	Protection	Grid Ref. and Punchcard No.
Pond	Southeast of Ivy Cottage. Now a 'classic' English village pond, with grass verges, shrubs and willow trees around it. A seat completes this pleasant village amenity which was created from the once overgrown pond by voluntary effort on the part of the residents.	N.P. Act A.O.N.B.	SU 706 322 1605 02

FARRINGDON

Farringdon lies some three miles south of Alton, the main village being half a mile to the east of the A32. The church is Norman and is associated with Gilbert White, who was curate here for 25 years. A large ornamental brick building known as Massey's Folly is used as a school and parish hall.

Description and Date	Remarks	Protection	Grid Ref. and Punchcard No.
Group A — Natural Features			
Trees	Farringdon Place. Variety of species including yew, ash, oak, cedars and limes.	T.P.O. No. 23 E.H.D.	SU 712 352 1606 40
Trees	Manor Farm. Over one hundred beech and larch trees known as Jubilee Clump.		SU 705 358 1606 44
Group B — Archaeological			
Bronze Age			
Beaker	Gravel Pit, Lower Farringdon. Beaker found September 1938. Cruciform design on the base, of which only two examples are known. Now in Alton Museum. O.S.A. No. SU73 NW5.		SU 704 354 1606 38
Roman			
Coin	Cruck Cottage. Sestertius of Trajan found 1936. Now in Alton Museum. O.S.A. No. SU73 NW32.	C.A.	SU 711 353 1606 37
Post Norman			
Park Pale	Encloses area centred around Park Cottage. Best preserved along, and to the north side of Woodside Lane. Interior now arable land. Centred on grid reference.		SU 701 360 1606 01
Manor	Manor House. Present structure built on site of old Manor House. Chapel of the Bishops of Exeter reputed to have stood at east end of 'Chapel Orchard'.		SU 711 355 1606 39
Group D — Buildings, Monuments and Engineering Works.			
Church C.12/13	All Saints. Enlarged and restored in 1858. West Tower C.13 with lancets below and unusual bell openings in the form of small pointed quatrefoils. Two good perpendicular windows in nave separated by brick porch. Gilbert White, the naturalist, was curate here from 1760—1785, and one of the parish registers contains entries in his handwriting. O.S.A. No. SU73 NW8. Ref: 1. V.C.H., Vol. 3, p.p. 21—2. 2. Buildings of England; Hants and I.O.W., (Pevsner & Lloyd), p.p. 230—1.	T. & C.P. Act C.A.	SU 712 354 1606 02
Farmhouse C.17/18	Street House Farm. 2 storeys. Red brick with two bands of blue brick. Long ridge tiled roof. Plain sash windows. Core probably a timber-framed structure.	T. & C.P. Act	SU 705 349 1606 36

Description and Date	Remarks	Protection	Grid Ref. and Punchcard No.

Group D — (cont.)

Description and Date	Remarks	Protection	Grid Ref. and Punchcard No.
House C.17/18	The Forge. 2 storeys. Random stone with red brick quoins and dressings. Attic with exposed timber-work and herringbone brick nogging. Wing to right of limewashed brick. Ridge tiled roof.		SU 705 350 1606 29
Farmhouse C.18	Upper Woodside Farm. 2 storeys. Limewashed brick, with plinth and band. Hipped tiled roof. Plain mullioned and transomed windows under segmental lintels on ground floor. Victorian porch.		SU 691 357 1606 35
Cottage C.18	Farringdon Cottage. Recast C.19. 2 storeys. Limewashed brick walls. Ridge slate roof. Transomed casements with triple 'Gothic' pointed toplights and square-headed dripmoulds.		SU 704 354 1606 30
Farmhouse C.18	Farm Cove. 2 storeys. Brick on ground floor. Victorian tilehanging above. Ridge tiled roof, brought down as part pentice to rear. Modern lattice casement windows.		SU 704 345 1606 32
Farmhouse C.18	Annett's Farm. Stuccoed in C.19. 2 storeys. Ridge tiled roof brought down as pentice to rear. Double and triple sash windows. Centre door.	N.P. Act A.O.N.B.	SU 706 346 1606 33
House C.18	Manor House. 2 storeys. Front recast C.19. Part stone, part brick structure with some timber-framing. Ridge tiled roof. Sash windows. Single storey wing. Victorian gabled porch. Parts of the house older than date shown. Built on site of Old Manor House. O.S.A. No. SU73 NW7.		SU 711 355 1606 03
Cottage C.18	Beloms. 2 storeys. Stuccoed, with wide plinth and band. Hipped tiled roof. Sash windows. Centre panelled door under columned porch.	C.A.	SU 713 353 1606 13
Cottages (2) C.18/19	Gilberts Cottages. 2 storeys. Colour-washed brick with plinth and band, and exposed timber-work in attic. C.19 wing to left, partly brick on edge. Ridge tiled roof.	C.A.	SU 712 353 1606 06
Cottages (3) C.18/19	Old School Cottages and Fern Cottage. Interesting group with C.19 gabled projecting school building in centre. Fern Cottage, 2 storeys with ridge tiled roof. Cottages to right, partly timber-framed and partly thatched.	C.A.	SU 714 350 1606 23
Building C.19	Village Hall and School. Red brick and terracotta structure. Two towers, the taller with shaped gable saddle back roof. All windows with french basket arches. See also Group 'F'.	C.A.	SU 711 353 1606 41

Description and Date	Remarks	Protection	Grid Ref. and Punchcard No.

Group D — (cont.)

Description and Date	Remarks	Protection	Grid Ref. and Punchcard No.
Farmhouse	Lower Woodside Farm. 2 storeys. Red brick with occasional blue brick and Victorian fishscale tile hanging above. Steep pitched ridge tiled roof. Possibly C.17. Now two dwellings.		SU 694 358 1606 34
House	Farringdon Villa. Georgian house refronted in stucco with Regency-Gothic facade. Ridge tiled roof with plain parapet. Pedimented columned porch.		SU 704 353 1606 31
Cottage	Copelands. Restored. Limewashed brick walls. Thatched roof, with eaves square cut around single upper window. Panelled door and rustic thatched porch. Thatched pentice to rear.		SU 705 350 1606 26
House	Malt House. 2 storeys. Red brick walls. Ridge tiled roof. Sash windows. Modern projecting porch.		SU 705 351 1606 27
Building	The Old Barn Cafe. Restored. Colourwashed brick and plaster. Thatched roof brought down as pentice to left. Lattice casement windows. Thatched and weatherboarded barn projects at side to right.		SU 705 351 1606 28
Cottage	The Cross. 2 storeys. Brick walls. Thatched roof. Two casement windows. Thatched porch. Tiled pentice additions to rear.	C.A.	SU 714 350 1606 24
Cottage	The Thatched Cottage. Red brick, partly patched with flint to right. Thatched roof with eaves square cut around four upper windows.	C.A.	SU 715 350 1606 25
Cottage	Bunkers Cottage. Restored. Colourwashed brick walls. Thatched roof with eaves square cut around three upper windows. Pentice to rear.	C.A.	SU 712 350 1606 22
Cottage	Beloms Cottage. Restored. Single storey and two half dormers. Colourwashed brick walls. Modern pantiled roof, brought down as pentice to rear.	C.A.	SU 713 354 1606 14
Farmhouse	Jordans. Restored and enlarged. Timber-framed with herringbone brick infilling on first floor. Brick and tilehung wing to right, possibly incorporates old structure. Modern lattice casement windows. Paved courtyard in front and old flint wall lining road.	C.A.	SU 710 351 1606 15
Cottage	Hawthorn Cottage. Enlarged and recast. Single storey and two gabled dormers. Timber-framed and brick walls. Ridge pantiled roof. Centre gabled porch.	C.A.	SU 710 350 1606 16

Description and Date	Remarks	Protection	Grid Ref. and Punchcard No.

Description and Date	Remarks	Protection	Grid Ref. and Punchcard No.
Cottages (2)	Street House Farm Cottages. Single storey. Limewashed brick walls. Long thatched roof with eaves square cut around two upper windows. Pentice to rear. Lattice casement windows.	C.A.	SU 710 350 1606 17
Cottage	Holly Cottage. Restored and altered. Single storey and three gabled half-dormers. Flint rubble with stone quoins. Hipped tiled roof.	C.A.	SU 711 351 1606 18
House	West Cross. 2 storeys. Front covered with hanging slates in C.19. Modern ridge pantiled roof. 2-storey projection at rear with exposed timber-framing. Possibly C.18.	C.A.	SU 711 351 1606 19
Cottage	The Croft. Restored, enlarged and recast. Single storey and four gabled half-dormers. Brick walls. Ridge tiled roof.	C.A.	SU 711 351 1606 20
Cottages (2)	Forming part of The Croft property. Exposed timber-framing and red brickwork. Thatched roof with eaves square cut around four upper windows.	C.A.	SU 711 352 1606 21
House	Manor House Farm, west of Farringdon Church. 2 storeys. Rendered front elevation, part stone and part brick with timber-framing on first floor on rear elevation. Lead light casement windows. Tiled roof. Large porch on front with steep pitched tile roof with pilastered brick side walls.		SU 711 354 1606 43
Cottage	Thatch Cottage. Restored. Limewashed back walls, with small portion of red brick herringbone filling. Thatched roof. Modern lattice casement windows.	T. & C.P. Act C.A.	SU 712 353 1606 04
Cottage	Berry Cottage. Single storey. Limewashed brick with partly exposed timberwork. Ridge tiled roof. Three half dormers with flat pentice roofs.	C.A.	SU 712 354 1606 05
Cottage	Hardings. Single storey and three gabled half dormers. Limewashed brick with exposed light timberwork to right. Modern ridge tiled roof. Restored and enlarged.	C.A.	SU 713 353 1606 07
Cottage	Rose Cottage. Interesting fragment of old timber-framed structure forming part of modern brick cottage. 2 storeys. Hipped gable to right has stout corner posts and corner bracketing on first floor.	C.A.	SU 711 353 1606 08
Cottage	The Tylers. 2 storeys. Front faced with cement rendering in C.19. Steep hipped tiled roof with oversailing boarded eaves. Exposed timber-framing in half-hipped gable. Plain centre door.	C.A.	SU 711 353 1606 09

Description and Date	Remarks	Protection	Grid Ref. and Punchcard No.

Group D — (cont.)

Cottage	Angerton. Single storey. Colourwashed brick and plaster infilling. Exposed light timber-framing. Tiled roof with eaves waved over three upper windows. Single storey additions to left and to rear.	C.A.	SU 711 353 1606 10
Cottage	Cruck Cottage. Single storey with three gabled attic windows in centre. Exposed light timber-work with brick infilling. Long ridge thatched roof.	C.A.	SU 711 353 1606 11
Cottage	Old Timbers. Single storey and two gabled dormers. Timber-framed with modern red brick herringbone infilling. Ridge tiled roof.	C.A.	SU 713 353 1606 12

Group F — Historical or Literary Association

| Building | Village Hall and School. Designed and built over a period of 30 years, by the then Rector T.H. Massey, with the assistance of one labourer and one carpenter. He died in 1919 having been Rector of All Saints Church for 62 years. The building is known as "Masseys Folly".
Ref: Buildings of England; Hants and I.O.W., (Pevsner & Lloyd), p. 231. | C.A. | SU 711 353
1606 41 |

FOUR MARKS

Situated some four miles south-west of Alton on the main Winchester road, Four Marks lies astride the main coaching road from London to Winchester. At the highest point in the parish — Telegraph Lane — the Admiralty erected a semaphore post as one of a chain of signal stations between London and Plymouth.

Description and Date	Remarks	Protection	Grid Ref. and Punchcard No.
Group A — Natural Features			
Trees	Windmill Inn. Three firs standing on land fronting the Winchester Road and forming part of the curtilage of the property.	T.P.O. No. 44 E.H.D.	SU 671 352 1607 13
Trees	Lymington House, Lymington Bottom Road. Many species within the grounds of the property.	T.P.O. No. 90 E.H.D.	SU 666 343 1607 15
Trees	Winstone Rise. Nine beech, six oaks, and two ash, on the land to the south east of the property.	T.P.O. No. 745	SU 667 351 1607 14
Group B — Archaeological			
Stone Age			
Implement	Brislands Lane. Neolithic polished flint axe found 1957. Now in Alton Museum. O.S.A. No. SU63 SE3. Ref: Alton Musem (Access No. 1957/100).		SU 664 341 1607 11
Group D — Buildings, Monuments and Engineering Works			
Farmhouse C.16	Headmoor Farm, Headmoor Lane. Attractive low brick and timber structure. Thatched roof. Leaded window panes. Original beams. Built 1580.		SU 685 339 1607 07
Farmhouse C.17	Cobb Farm, Hawthorn Road. Flint, brick and cob structure. Believed built in 1620.		SU 671 337 1607 04
Cottage C.17	Hawthorn Cottage Farm. Brick and flint structure. Thatched roof. Built 1690.		SU 680 341 1607 06
Cottage C.17	Beech Farm, Hawthorn Road. Flint and brick structure. Thatched roof. Modern tiled extension. Believed to have been one of the verderer's cottages, situated as it is close to Hawthorn Wood and Kitwood. Has the date 1697 over the fireplace.		SU 675 337 1607 08
Cottage C.17	Jayswood Cottage, Hawthorn Lane. Half-brick, half-timbered and flint structure. Thatched roof. Victorian extension. Built 1660.		SU 679 336 1607 09
Farmhouse C.19	Kitfield Farm, Kitwood Lane. Flint and brick structure. Slate roof. Central chimney. Small extension each end. Typical small farmhouse. Built 1869.		SU 667 336 1607 03
Cottage C.19	Budgett Cottage, Lymington Bottom. Built 1817. Front elevation flint and brick, with brick each end. Small sash windows. Tin roof.		SU 667 341 1607 02

Group D — (cont.)

Cottage	Keepsake Cottage, formerly Pilgrims Way, Lymington Bottom. Beautiful old building of chalk block and flint with original timber beams throughout.		SU 666 343 1607 01

Group E — Street Patterns, Street Furniture and Open Spaces

Ponds	Swelling Hill Ponds. Natural ponds, one time drinking water supply. Duck houses in centre, with various types of duck and water fowl frequenting the pond. Landscaped banks, with seats provided. A pleasant spot as the result of voluntary work by residents and Parish Council.		SU 662 328 1607 12

Group F — Historical or Literary Association

Building C.18	Semaphore Farm, Telegraph Lane. Once part of the proposed visual signal line from London to Plymouth, which was a branch from the existing Admiralty Semaphore system from London to Portsmouth. Living quarters of men who manned the telegraph. Built 1794.		SU 681 374 1607 05

Swelling Hill Ponds, FOUR MARKS

FROXFIELD

The modern civil parish of Froxfield was enlarged by the addition of Privett parish in 1932. Froxfield is situated on high ground with magnificent views of the dramatic hangers which are so typical of this part of East Hampshire. The early inhabitants of Froxfield include the Romans, who have left traces of an encampment in the south of the parish. Fragments of an earthwork running across the parish are supposed to have formed part of the boundary between the ancient kingdoms of Wessex and Sussex.

Froxfield is first recorded in a grant of land of the tenth century; it is not mentioned by name in the Domesday Book as it was included in the great episcopal manor of East Meon. The estate of Basing Park in the parish of Froxfield was held by the Love family for over 200 years from 1567. Robert Love left £1,000 to establish a free school in 1733. Another long-established local family were the Silvesters, who lived in Froxfield for 300 years.

Privett was included in the manor of West Meon until the seventeenth century when it was first recorded as a separate manor. The earliest mention of a chapel in Privett occurs in 1391, when reference is made to the fabric of Holy Trinity chapel. The present church dates from 1876 — 78 and was built on the site of the old church, of which nothing now remains.

Description and Date	Remarks	Protection	Grid Ref. and Punchcard No.

Group A — Natural Features

Description and Date	Remarks	Protection	Grid Ref. and Punchcard No.
Area of Ecological Importance	Hangers to the north-east of parish near Oakshott. Dramatic scenery of hills, woods and beechhangers known locally as Little Switzerland. One of the most interesting and important series of chalk woodlands in Britain. Magnificent views over surrounding countryside from many footpaths. Reston, Roundhills and Happersnapper hangers form only part of a County Open Space and informal nature reserve. Centred on grid reference.	N.P. Act S.S.S.I. A.O.N.B. C.O.S.	SU 736 273 2306 22
Sarsen Stone No. 28A	In the farmyard of Bydean Farm.	N.P. Act A.O.N.B.	SU 704 262 2306 69
Sarsen Stone No. 28B	Beside the gateway of Bydean Farm.	N.P. Act A.O.N.B.	SU 704 262 2306 68
Sarsen Stone No. 28C	Opposite the gateway of Bydean Farm.	N.P. Act A.O.N.B.	SU 704 262 2306 65
Sarsen Stone No. 28D	Beside ditch of Froxfield entrenchment, south-west of Ventom's Farm.	N.P. Act A.O.N.B.	SU 703 252 2306 67
Sarsen Stone No. 28E	Beside long entrenchment, Bydean Farm.	N.P. Act A.O.N.B.	SU 702 265 2306 66
Sarsen Stone No. 28F	On the road verge opposite Bydean Farm entrance.	N.P. Act A.O.N.B.	SU 704 262 2306 64
Sarsen Stone No. 28G	In the garden of Broad Hanger, north of Broad Way.	N.P. Act A.O.N.B.	SU 712 258 2306 63
Sarsen Stone No. 28H	Large buried stone in field east of Staple Ash Lane.	N.P. Act A.O.N.B.	SU 704 252 2306 62
Sarsen Stone No. 28I	Located in garden of Ventom's Farm.	N.P. Act A.O.N.B.	SU 703 252 2306 71
Sarsen Stone No. 28J	In the wall fabric of Ventom's Farm.	N.P. Act A.O.N.B.	SU 703 252 2306 70
Sarsen Stone No. 73B	Concentration in high clay.	N.P. Act A.O.N.B.	SU 700 250 2306 61

Group B — Archaeological

Stone Age

Description and Date	Remarks	Protection	Grid Ref. and Punchcard No.
Flint Axes (2)	Polished axes of Neolithic date. Both found in a field west of Ventom's Farm one on surface, one during construction of pylon. O.S.A. No. SU62 NE16.	N.P. Act A.O.N.B.	SU 697 253 2306 43

Description and Date	Remarks	Protection	Grid Ref. and Punchcard No.

Group B — (cont.)

Bronze Age

Description and Date	Remarks	Protection	Grid Ref. and Punchcard No.
Bowl Barrows (4)	Located in a copse west of Fawley Lane. Known as The Devil's Jumps or The Jumps. Alleged to be the site of a battle between the Danes and Saxons, and near site of a Civil War skirmish. Traces of three other barrows and a bank. O.S.A. No. SU62 NE8. Ref: 1. P.H.F.C., Vol. 14, 1938—40, (Grinsell), p.p. 28—29, 355. 2. Civil War in Hants, 1904, (Godwin), p. 177.	S.A.M. No. 41 N.P. Act A.O.N.B.	SU 667 281 2306 42
Barrow	Site of a possible bowl barrow, south east of Laydean Farm. Mound 20 m. in diameter and 0.3 m. high. Land under crop, no other visible evidence remains. O.S.A. No. SU62 NE12.	N.P. Act A.O.N.B.	SU 695 260 2306 46
Bowl Barrow	Wheatham Hill. Tree planted barrow 26.0 m. in diameter, with traces of ditch. Stands on crest of prominent ridge. Hollow at centre. O.S.A. No. SU72 NW8.	N.P. Act S.S.S.I. A.O.N.B.	SU 745 271 2306 31
Bowl Barrow	Mutilated barrow, north east of Crabtree Cottage. Part destroyed by road, part reduced by ploughing. Originally measured 18.0 m. in diameter by 2.0 m. in height. O.S.A. No. SU72 NW6. Ref: 1. P.H.F.C., Vol. 9, 1920—4, p.p. 399—400. 2. Archaeological Review, Vol. 1, 1888, p. 281.	N.P. Act A.O.N.B.	SU 725 267 2306 30
Bowl Barrow	Grass covered and tree planted. 24.0 m. in diameter and a maximum 2.8 m. height. Large hollow at centre. Centred on grid reference. O.S.A. No. SU72 NW12.	N.P. Act A.O.N.B.	SU 703 273 2306 35
Bowl Barrow	Irregular shaped mound north east of Crabtree Cottage with no trace of ditch. Excavation revealed a cremation, bronze knife/dagger and chisel. Finds in Winchester Museum. O.S.A. No. SU72 NW5. Ref: 1. P.H.F.C., Vol. 9, 1920, p. 399. 2. Archaeological Review, 1888, p. 281.	N.P. Act A.O.N.B.	SU 724 268 2306 24
Bowl Barrows (5)	South of King's Cottage. Features now ploughed out, not definitely identified as barrows. Centred on grid reference. O.S.A. No. SU72 NW10.	N.P. Act A.O.N.B.	SU 717 257 2306 33

Description and Date	Remarks	Protection	Grid Ref. and Punchcard No.

Group B — (cont.)

Roman

Description and Date	Remarks	Protection	Grid Ref. and Punchcard No.
Earthworks	Stand on summit of east to west ridge, north east of Ridge Farm. Main rectangular enclosure about 80 x 150 m. Rampart 2.0 m. high on north and west sides. Ditch on south side. Remains of another enclosure to north. O.S.A. No. SU72 NW11. Ref: 1. V.C.H., Vol. 1, p.p. 308—9. 2. Field Archaeology as Illustrated by Hampshire, (Williams-Freeman), p.p. 285—6, 398.	S.A.M. No. 83 N.P. Act A.O.N.B.	SU 715 250 2306 20
Building (Site)	Quantity of building material and pottery found on the surface of a field north of Limekiln Copse. O.S.A. No. SU72 SW13.	N.P. Act A.O.N.B.	SU 703 244 2306 23
Entrench- ments	Probably of Dark Age date, possibly Romano-British. Three short parallel dykes which run across a shallow valley and a fourth dyke 2—3 miles long to the west. Another entrenchment 300 yds. long is crossed by the Dean Road. All appear to be defensive works of rampart and ditch. Possibly a tribal boundary, clearly defined at north and south ends where it is covered with trees. Centred on grid reference. O.S.A. No. SU72 NW4. Ref: Field Archaeology as Illustrated by Hampshire, 1915, (Williams-Freeman), p.p. 33, 286—92, 374—6.	S.A.M. No. 33 N.P. Act A.O.N.B.	SU 702 256 2306 21
Dene Hole	North of Broadmore Copse. Sunk to obtain chalk to spread on the land, and improve the soil. The true dene hole descends vertically, opening into one or more chambers off the central shaft. Those listed are examples of many within the parish. O.S.A. No. SU62 NE9.	N.P. Act A.O.N.B.	SU 682 279 2306 47
Dene Hole	Located south east of Bydean Farm. Hole about 12.1 m. deep revealed when the brick vaulting collapsed in 1952. Now overgrown. O.S.A. No. SU72 NW7.	N.P. Act A.O.N.B.	SU 705 261 2306 60
Dene Hole	West of Green Farm. Shaft 40 ft. deep which opens into a bee-hive shaped chamber. O.S.A. No. SU72 NW7.	N.P. Act A.O.N.B.	SU 702 255 2306 25
Brick Works	Probable site of mediaeval brick works west of Privett. O.S.A. No. SU62 NE(M)3.	N.P. Act A.O.N.B.	SU 672 269 2306 49

Group C — Footpaths and Bridleways

Description and Date	Remarks	Protection	Grid Ref. and Punchcard No.
Ancient Lane	Ridge Top Lane, runs along woodland edge, bounded by large banks. This lane forms part of the network of lanes along the ridge of the Hangers.	N.P. Act A.O.N.B.	SU 718 251 — 728 257 2306 75

Description and Date	Remarks	Protection	Grid Ref. and Punchcard No.
Group D — Buildings, Monuments and Engineering Works			
Cottage C.16	No. 20, Bailey Green. Thatched roof with hipped gable. Flint with brick quoins and some timber-framing. Casement windows.	N.P. Act A.O.N.B.	SU 669 273 2306 59
Cottage C.16	Basing Dene. Tudor cottage of flint with brick dressings. Thatched roof with two dormers at eaves. Casement windows, some with moulded brick dripstones. Timber-framed interior.	T. & C.P. Act N.P. Act A.O.N.B.	SU 700 275 2306 02
Cottage C.16/17	Honeycritch Cottage, Honeycritch Lane. 2 storeys. Flint and brick walls extended at both ends 1975. Tiled roof formerly thatched. Casement windows with some leaded lights. 1841 Census reveals that the building was divided into three cottages occupied by twenty-two people.	N.P. Act A.O.N.B.	SU 731 273 2306 08
House C.17	Guiles, Froxfield Green. Timber-framed with brick filling visible at back. Flint west wall. Refronted in C.18 and now plaster faced. Sash windows with glazing bars. Simple Regency porch. Thatched roof.	T. & C.P. Act N.P. Act A.O.N.B.	SU 704 255 2306 03
Cottages (2) C.17	King's Cottage and a cottage numbered 49, west of Vinnell's Farm. 2 storeys. Timber-framed with flint and brick dressings. Thatched roof.	N.P. Act A.O.N.B.	SU 717 258 2306 09
Cottage C.17	No. 45, close to Bydean Farm. Dated 1660. Timber-framed with flint and brick dressings. Thatched roof with central chimney. Casement windows.	N.P. Act A.O.N.B.	SU 704 262 2306 11
Cottage C.17	Middle Oakshott, Oakshott. Possibly of earlier date. Country house of malmstone with brick dressings. Tiled roof with dormers. Casement windows. Interior has oak beams and C.17 oak panelling.	N.P. Act A.O.N.B.	SU 740 279 2306 14
Cottage C.17	Spencers Cottage. North east of Wyke Green Farm. Timber-framed with brick infilling partly herringbone. Tiled roof with old chimney at south end. Casement windows.	N.P. Act A.O.N.B.	SU 726 265 2306 19
Cottage C.17	Thatchers, Warren Corner. Formerly two dwellings. Timber-framed with tile hung walls. Thatched roof. Bedroom windows at eaves. Casement windows with restored leaded lights. Modern additions.	N.P. Act A.O.N.B.	SU 726 279 2306 17
Cottage C.17/18	Loves Charity, Froxfield Green. 2 storeys. Two hipped dormers. Brick structure with tiled roof. Casement windows with leaded glazing. Stone over door inscribed 'The gift of Robert Love Esq. 1733'. Modern additions.	T. & C.P. Act N.P. Act A.O.N.B.	SU 704 256 2306 04

Description and Date	Remarks	Protection	Grid Ref. and Punchcard No.
Group D — (cont.)			
Farmhouse C.18	Bower Farm. Flint with brick dressings, flat band between storeys. Double hipped slate roof. Sash windows with glazing bars.	N.P. Act A.O.N.B.	SU 697 265 2306 06
Farmhouse C.18	Cole's Farm. Date about 1760 or earlier. Brick front, the rest of flint with brick dressings. Tiled roof, formerly thatched. Timber-framing visible inside.	N.P. Act A.O.N.B.	SU 692 280 2306 07
Farmhouse C.18	Filmore Hill Farm. Brick 2-storey building steeply pitched tiled roof descending to door level at back. Casement windows, those on ground floor with cambered arch tops. Exterior chimney at north end.	N.P. Act A.O.N.B.	SU 661 273 2306 16
Cottages (2) C.18	Nos. 70, and 71, Froxfield Green. Flint walls with brick dressings. Thatched roof with upper storey windows at eaves level. Casement windows, those on ground floor with cambered arches.	N.P. Act A.O.N.B.	SU 704 255 2306 12
Farmhouse C.18	Higher Oakshott, Oakshott. 2 storeys. Malmstone with brick dressings. Tiled roof. Casement windows. Older wing at rear, with moulded brick plinth.	N.P. Act A.O.N.B.	SU 738 284 2306 15
Building C.18	Holly Lodge, Froxfield Green. Brick walls with purple headers. Slate roof. Door with semi-circular head and fanlight. Porch supported on slender columns. Back of flint with brick dressings.	N.P. Act A.O.N.B.	SU 704 256 2306 13
Farmhouse C.18	Ivy House Farm, Ivy House Lane. Formerly several cottages. Flint with decorative brick dressings. Thatched roof with hipped gable end. Blocked doorways visible. Casement windows with glazing bars.	N.P. Act A.O.N.B.	SU 712 273 2306 72
Building C.18	The Slade. 2 storeys of plaster-faced brick. Double hipped slate roof. Sash windows. Semi-circular porch with fluted columns. Rear of Queen Anne date with tiled roof. Parts of house date back to C.16. Now divided into three dwellings.	N.P. Act A.O.N.B.	SU 717 267 2306 10
Farmhouse C.18	Week Green Farm, Wyke Green. 2 storeys and attics. Brick and rubble with plaster faced front. Tiled roof with two hipped, tiled dormers. Projecting central portion with porch supported on four pillars. Sash windows.	T. & C.P. Act N.P. Act A.O.N.B.	SU 728 266 2306 05
Farmhouse C.18	Wyke Green Farm, Soalwood Lane. 3 storeys. C.18 plaster faced front with Victorian wing and porch. Tiled roof. Sash windows. Older part to south of brick with hipped gable and tiled roof. Casement windows with glazing bars and small panes.	N.P. Act A.O.N.B.	SU 726 264 2306 18

Description and Date	Remarks	Protection	Grid Ref. and Punchcard No.

Group D — (cont.)

Description and Date	Remarks	Protection	Grid Ref. and Punchcard No.
Church C.19	Church of St. Peter, High Cross. Built 1862 by Martineau. Nave and chancel with south west steeple. Contains Norman arcade of three bays removed from the old church. Round piers with trumpet-scallop capitals. Ref: Buildings of England; Hants and I.O.W., (Pevsner & Lloyd), p. 293.	T. & C.P. Act N.P. Act A.O.N.B.	SU 711 265 2306 01
Church C.19	Holy Trinity, Privett. Built 1876—8 by Blomfield on site of earlier church. Early English and decorated styles. Nave with aisles square chancel, and west tower with broach spire. Stone structure with tiled roof. Lancet windows to chancel, aisles and clerestory.	T. & C.P. Act N.P. Act A.O.N.B.	SU 676 269 2306 48
Lych Gate C.19	Holy Trinity Church, Privett. Built 1876—8 on north side of churchyard. Gabled, tiled roof supported on ballustraded arcades with arched openings.	T. & C.P. Act N.P. Act A.O.N.B.	SU 676 269 2306 73
House	The Red House, Cockshott Lane. Built by Geoffrey Lupton of local handmade bricks and tiles, with massive oak framing. Floors of oak planks, some are 2 ins. thick and up to 32 ins. wide.	N.P. Act A.O.N.B.	SU 732 267 2306 54
Cottage	The Thatched Cottage, Filmorehill Lane. Brick structure on flint plinth. Thatched roof. Ground floor served as cattle stalls and fodder store with living room and bedroom on first floor. Extensively restored.	N.P. Act A.O.N.B.	SU 661 274 2306 26
Farmhouse	Trees Farm. 2 storeys. Brick structure with tiled roof. Well timbered interior, possibly of cruck construction.	N.P. Act A.O.N.B.	SU 705 261 2306 58

FROYLE

Froyle is situated on the A31 some three miles north-east of Alton. The church is a mixture of eighteenth century brickwork and fourteenth century stone; it contains a monumental brass of 1575 and a stained glass east window that combines the arms of Edward the Confessor and of France. Since the introduction of the National Health Service the Lord Mayor Treloar College for crippled boys has been located at Froyle.

Description and Date	Remarks	Protection	Grid Ref. and Punchcard No.

Group B — Archaeological

Stone Age

Flint Implement	North east of Dickers Plantation. Finds include arrowheads, axes, scrapers and palaeolithic flakes. Area centred on grid reference. O.S.A. No. SU74 SW1.		SU 723 436 1608 45

Bronze Age

Bowl Barrow	North of Yarnhams Farm. 32 m. in diameter, 1.0 m. high. O.S.A. No. SU74 SW2. Ref: 1. P.H.F.C., Vol. 14, 1938—40, p. 350. 2. P.H.F.C., Vol. 10, 1926—30, p. 73.		SU 741 449 1608 46

Roman

Roofing Tiles and Sherds	Yarnhams Farm. Finds discovered on south eastern slope, approximately ¼ mile below crest of ridge. Absence of bricks or building stone suggests site of a timber building. O.S.A. No. SU74 SW6.		SU 773 438 1608 47
Building (Site)	South west of Coldrey House. Substantial remains of villa or homestead farm. Finds include pottery, bronze ring, iron implements and a coin. O.S.A. No. SU74 SE5. Ref: Roman Coldrey, (Wade), (small pamphlet).		SU 770 436 1608 41
Coin	Nedfield Hay. Coin of Constantine II found in garden. O.S.A. No. SU74 SE10. Ref: Alton Museum Access Register.		SU 759 442 1608 42

Post Norman

Rectangular Earthwork	Penley Copse. Possibly a mediaeval homestead and associated enclosure. Foundations of buildings consisting of low turf banks, with flints on and about them. O.S.A. No. SU74 NE5. Ref: 1. Field Archaeology as Illustrated in Hampshire, (Williams-Freeman), p.p. 308, 425. 2. P.H.F.C., Vol. 13, 1935—7, p. 229.	S.A.M. No. 34	SU 776 458 1608 50
Cross (Remains)	Froyle Cross, on south side of St. Mary's Church. Believed to be base of mediaeval cross to Nicholas De Ely Bishop of Winchester (1268—1280). Now forms base of memorial to the daughter of the then residents of Froyle Place, dated 1911. Ref: P.H.F.C., Vol. 22, 1961, p.p. 35—6.	C.A.	SU 775 428 1608 43

Description and Date	Remarks	Protection	Grid Ref. and Punchcard No.

Group B — (cont.)

Description and Date	Remarks	Protection	Grid Ref. and Punchcard No.
Dene Hole (Probable)	Yarnhams Farm. Pit, 1.82 m. in diameter and 6.08 m. deep, now filled in. Site visible as slight depression. O.S.A. No. SU74 SW20.		SU 743 436 1608 48

Period Unknown

Burial Places	Burrells Copse. "Heathen Burial Places" mentioned in charter of A.D. 973. O.S.A. No. SU74 NE4. Ref: Archaeological Journal, Vol. 81, 1927, (Grundy), p.p. 53—54.		SU 764 457 1608 49

Group D — Buildings, Monuments and Engineering Works

Church C.14	St. Mary of the Assumption. Consists of C.14 chancel, nave with north porch, vestry and tower. Rebuilt in brick 1722. Jacobean communion rail. Interesting original series of arms in upper tracery of the east window. O.S.A. No. SU74 SE6. Ref: 1. V.C.H., Vol. 4, p. 505. 2. Buildings of England; Hants and I.O.W., (Pevsner & Lloyd), p. 237.	T. & C.P. Act C.A.	SU 755 428 1608 01
House C.16	Husseys, Lower Froyle. Core an Elizabethan timber-framed structure, enlarged and altered in the C.18. 2 storeys. Red brick. Ridge tiled roof. Sash windows. Ref: Buildings of England; Hants and I.O.W., (Pevsner & Lloyd), p. 238.	T. & C.P. Act	SU 765 442 1608 11
House C.16	Froyle Place, Upper Froyle. Enlarged and altered 1865 — now Treloar's College. Core may be of early mediaeval date. Part 2 storeys, part 3 storeys. Coursed stone blocks. Ridge tiled roof. Tall brick chimneys. Modern additions. Ref: 1. Country Life, 19.12.41. 2. Buildings of England; Hants & I.O.W., (Pevsner & Lloyd), p. 237.	T. & C.P. Act C.A.	SU 755 428 1608 02
Farmhouse C.17	Silvesters Farm, Lower Froyle. 2 storeys. Part stone blocks with red brick dressings, part timber-framed with brick infilling. Tiled roof. Ornamental tile-hung gable on front elevation.	T. & C.P. Act	SU 762 441 1608 13
Farm-buildings C.17	Silvesters Farm, Lower Froyle. L-shaped group with single storey stable wing. Thatched and weatherboarded barn.		SU 761 441 1608 27
Farmhouse C.17	Blundens, Upper Froyle. 2 storeys. Timber-framed with red brick infilling. Uneven ridge tiled roof. Large gable to right, brought down as pentice.	T. & C.P. Act C.A.	SU 757 431 1608 09

Stone Stile, FROYLE

Group D — (cont.)

Description and Date	Remarks	Protection	Grid Ref. and Punchcard No.
Cottage C.18	Long Barlands, Lower Froyle. 2 storeys. Lime-washed brick. Thatched roof. Three casement windows. Rear extension with thatched roof. Dated 1773. Originally two cottages.		SU 755 445 1608 18
Cottage C.18	Oak Cottage, Lower Froyle. 2 storeys. Red brick with stone plinth and brick band. Short half-hipped ridge tiled roof. Rear portion partly timber-framed.		SU 757 444 1608 22
House C.18	Beech Cottage, Lower Froyle. 2 storeys. Lime-washed coursed stone blocks. Ridge tiled roof. Tile-hung gables at front and end. Recently renovated.		SU 757 444 1608 23
Farmhouse C.18	Hodges, Lower Froyle. 2 storeys. Red brick structure. Ridge tiled roof. Attic with single dormer.	T. & C.P. Act	SU 757 444 1608 14
Cottage C.18	Blue Cottage, Lower Froyle. 2 storeys. Lime-washed brick on older timber-framed structure. Tiled roof. Plaque with date '1737' and initials 'A.C. Alton'. Tithe Barn which recently stood in Kent Lane, Alton, was dismantled and re-erected as two floor extension to this cottage.		SU 758 443 1608 25
Building C.18	Froyles Stores, Lower Froyle. 2 storeys. Rendered and pebble dash. Tiled roof. Modern single storey shop to left.		SU 761 442 1608 29
Cottage C.18	Glebe Cottage, Lower Froyle. Limewashed rendered walls. Slate roof. Sash windows.		SU 761 442 1608 54
House C.18	Bridge House, Lower Froyle. Part rough-cast, part coursed stone blocks with brick dressings. Half-hipped ridge tiled roof. Tile-hung attic gable. A date stone is inscribed '1712 E.K.L.'.		SU 764 440 1608 31
House C.18	Brewery House, Lower Froyle. 2 storeys. Lime-washed brick with stone blocks to left. Side elevation, red brick. Ridge tiled roof.		SU 764 441 1608 33
House C.18	Thatched Cottage, Lower Froyle. 2 storeys. Red brick on ground floor, tile-hanging above. Thatched roof. Centre thatched porch. Parts of building believed to date back to 1588.		SU 765 443 1608 38
Farmhouse C.18	Brocas Farm, Lower Froyle. 2 storeys and attic. Red brick walls. Ridge tiled roof. Tile-hung gables. Dormer windows to attic.	T. & C.P. Act	SU 766 439 1608 12

Description and Date	Remarks	Protection	Grid Ref. and Punchcard No.

Group D — (cont.)

Description and Date	Remarks	Protection	Grid Ref. and Punchcard No.
Building C.18	Froyle Mill and Mill House, Lower Froyle. Recently renovated and wholly converted into private residence. Original house of limewashed brick with tiled roof. Adjoining mill of limewashed brick. 2 storeys and attic with dormer. Mansard truss tiled roof. Single storey addition has coursed stone walls with brick dressings.		SU 768 428 1608 40
House C.18	Highway House, Lower Froyle. 2 storeys. Grey cement rendered facade. Steep hipped tiled roof with modern dormers.		SU 769 435 1608 39
Inn C.18	Hen and Chicken, Upper Froyle. 3 storeys. Part red brick, part limewashed brick walls. Tile-hung gable. Ridge tiled roof. Sash windows. Large flat roofed porch with two pillar supports.		SU 756 422 1608 17
House C.18	The Vicarage, Upper Froyle. 2 storeys with single storey wing. Brick walls. Part tile-hung gable. Ridge tiled roof. Pentice additions to rear.	T. & C.P. Act C.A.	SU 755 429 1608 06
House C.18	The Manor House, Upper Froyle. Originally known as Froyle Manor. 2 storeys and attic with ornamental dormers. Red brick walls. Facade re-cast at later date. Tiled roof. Fine early Georgian staircase. Ref: Buildings of England; Hants and I.O.W., (Pevsner & Lloyd), p. 237.	T. & C.P. Act C.A.	SU 754 426 1608 05
Cottage C.18	Froyle Cottage, Upper Froyle. 2 storeys and attic. Red brick walls. Hipped tiled roof. Centre projecting porch. Brick and slate roofed annexe.	T. & C.P. Act C.A.	SU 754 427 1608 03
House C.18/19	Old Shrubbery House, Upper Froyle. 2 storeys. Red brick walls. Hipped tiled roof. Edwardian porch. Two octagonal projecting bays. Modern gable addition to rear.	T. & C.P. Act	SU 785 424 1608 10
House C.19	Froyle House, Upper Froyle. 3 storeys. Stuccoed walls. Slate roof partly screened by dwarf parapet. Large Victorian splayed bay at side to west.	T. & C.P. Act C.A.	SU 753 426 1608 04
Cottage C.19	The Thatched Cottage, White Ground, Upper Froyle. Exposed light timber-framing with limewashed brick infilling, part tile-hung. Thatched roof projects beyond wall on front elevation on rustic supports to form covered way.		SU 751 426 1608 16
Cottage	Little Barlands, Lower Froyle, formerly Rose Cottage. Exposed timber-framing with limewashed brick infilling. Thatched roof.		SU 755 445 1608 19

Description and Date	Remarks	Protection	Grid Ref. and Punchcard No.

Group D — (cont.)

Description and Date	Remarks	Protection	Grid Ref. and Punchcard No.
Cottages (2)	Nos. 1, and 2, Ewelme, Lower Froyle. 2 storeys. Timber-framed with red brick infilling on right. Coursed stone blocks with red brick dressings on left. Thatched roof.		SU 759 442 1608 28
House	Brecklands, Lower Froyle. 2 storeys. Red brick with brick cornice. Hipped tiled roof. Casement windows. Originally a workhouse until Alton Workhouse was built in 1793.		SU 760 441 1608 51
Cottage	Golden Cottage, Lower Froyle. Light timber-work exposed at one end. Limewashed brick. Small attic gable windows. Thatched roof.		SU 761 442 1608 30
Cottages	Pond Cottage and Appletree Cottage, Lower Froyle. Timber-framed with half-hipped tiled gable. Part thatched roof. Archway with first floor accommodation over. Renovated and altered in recent years but character retained.		SU 764 441 1608 32
Cottage	Brewery Cottage, Lower Froyle. Red brick walls with exposed timber-framing on first floor. Half-hipped ridge slate roof. Originally two cottages.		SU 765 441 1608 34
Granary	Husseys, Lower Froyle. Exposed light timber-work with brick infilling. Weatherboarded one side and one end. Tile-hung gable. On staddle stones.		SU 764 443 1608 37
Barn	Husseys, Lower Froyle. Large weatherboarded structure. Modern pantiled roof, half-hipped ridge.		SU 764 443 1608 36
Building	Husseys, Lower Froyle. Garage and stable block. Part brick and stone, part weatherboarded. Half-hipped ridge tiled roof.		SU 765 443 1608 35
House	Church Cottage, Lower Froyle. 2 storeys. Timber-framed with white plaster and brick infilling. Boarded gable. Thatched roof. Originally two cottages. Believed to be C.17.		SU 758 443 1608 26
Cottage	Fern Cottage, Upper Froyle. Exposed timber-framing with creamwashed brick and plaster infilling. Thatched roof.	T. & C.P. Act C.A.	SU 756 430 1608 07
Cottages (2)	The Post Office and Post Office Cottage, Upper Froyle. Timber-framed with brick infilling. Cottage to right — coursed stone blocks with bands of flint. Hipped tiled dormer. Thatched roof.	T. & C.P. Act C.A.	SU 756 431 1608 08
Cottage	Blundens Farm, Upper Froyle. Timber-framed with red brick infilling. Ridge tiled roof, part hipped, with bonnet hip tiles. Tiled dormers.	C.A.	SU 757 432 1608 09A

Description and Date	Remarks	Protection	Grid Ref. and Punchcard No.
Group D — (cont.)			
Cottage	Combe Field Cottage, Upper Froyle. Timber-framed with red brick infilling. Thatched roof with eaves squarecut around three upper windows. Modern porch. Lattice casements.	C.A.	SU 757 434 1608 15
Farm Buildings	Hodges Farm. Weatherboarded barn with hipped tiled wagon entrance. Thatched roof. Small granary on staddle stones.		SU 758 444 1608 24
Group E — Street Patterns, Street Furniture and Open Spaces			
Stile	Old stone stile set in boundary wall, entering public right of way footpath at its junction with layby, forming part of the old A31 road. Believed to have been constructed by French prisoners-of-war in the early C.19, but may be much older than this.		SU 760 427 1608 52
Group F — Historical or Literary Associations			
Fulling Mill	Mill Court. Mentioned in the C.14 and in 1600. "There was a Fulling Mill at Mill Court belonging to Henry Wheeler". Disused. O.S.A. No. SU74 SE12. Ref: 1. M.S. Notes "Historical Notes on Froyle" (Knight). 2. V.C.H., Vol. 2, p. 402.		SU 755 417 1608 44

GRAYSHOTT

Grayshott is situated right on the Hampshire/Surrey border ten and a half miles south-east of Alton, along the Bordon to Hindhead road and only half a mile from the main A3 London to Portsmouth road. St. Luke's parish church was built in 1901 of local stone in the Early English style. Grayshott is well known for its attractive situation among thickly wooded hills of the area.

Description and Date	Remarks	Protection	Grid Ref. and Punchcard No.

Group A — Natural Features

Trees	Hurstmere Close. One holly, an American arborvitae and a beech standing separately, also a group of three silver birch, and four areas containing trees of various species.	T.P.O. No. 378	SU 878 354 1609 01
Trees	Junction of Hammer Lane and Headley Road. Wellingtonia and one Norway spruce on roadside verge.		SU 856 358 1609 06
Trees	Field opposite Grayshott Hall, Headley Road. Mixed species mainly oak, rowan, beech and Scots pine, forming pleasing groups and shelter belt. Centred on grid reference.	T.P.O. No. 6 E.H.D.	SU 860 358 1609 11
Parkland	Grayshott Hall. 45 acres of parkland containing many fine trees including Japanese cedars, Douglas firs, wellingtonia, sequoias and tulip trees. The whole area one of scenic beauty.		SU 857 357 1609 05
Trees	St. Anne's, Headley Road. Several trees of various species standing in an area within the grounds of the property.	T.P.O. No. 5 E.H.D.	SU 866 353 1609 10
Natural Feature	Whitmore Hanger, bordering Whitmore Vale/ Sports Field. Steep sandstone hanger overlying Atherfield clay from which springs occur. Beautiful wooded area consisting mainly of beech and oak. Crest of hanger commands extensive views to north west. Area bordered by public footpaths.		SU 868 357 — 860 362 1609 09

Group C — Footpaths and Bridleways

Old Travelway	Stoney Bottom. From Haslemere to Waggoners Wells. Lane bordered by thickly wooded slopes. Western end runs into marshy land where several springs form stream feeding Waggoners Wells Lakes. Partly owned by the National Trust.		SU 863 345 — 879 348 1609 03
Bridleway No. 13	Whitmore Vale to Hammer Lane. Track from country lane up steep wooded hanger to ridge of hill, through extensive woodland of exceptional beauty.		SU 861 359 — 850 360 1609 40
Bridleway No. 6 to Footpath No. 10	Whitmore Vale, Hammer Lane to parish boundary. Path climbing wooded hanger and crossing high ridge to Hammer Lane, continuing into deep valley and up following the parish boundary.		SU 859 364 — 849 366 1609 39
Footpath No. 7	Beech Lane to Whitmore Vale. Scenic path commencing on ridge of beech hanger with extensive views. Skirts edge of fields and descends through woodland to country lane.		SU 867 356 — 859 363 1609 38

Description and Date	Remarks	Protection	Grid Ref. and Punchcard No.

Group C — (cont.)

Description and Date	Remarks	Protection	Grid Ref. and Punchcard No.
Bridleway No. 4	Junction of Headley Road/Waggoners Well Road to Ludshott Common. Path leading through woodland belt to open heath and commanding extensive views. Follows parish boundary.		SU 861 353 — 850 359 1609 37
Bridleways Nos. 14 and 15	Five Ways (Hill Road) to Waggoners Wells. Broad track commencing at village centre, descending by old cottages and turning right on to old travel-way to Waggoners Wells. Following valley of exceptional beauty.		SU 872 353 — 862 345 1609 36
Bridleway No. 2 and Footpath No. 1	Ruffits, Headley Road to Kingswood Lane. Scenic path traversing two steep densely wooded hills and valleys.		SU 867 353 — 869 347 1609 35

Group D — Buildings, Monuments and Engineering Works

Description and Date	Remarks	Protection	Grid Ref. and Punchcard No.
Cottages (6) C.18	Whitmore Vale. Originally squatters dwellings along ancient valley track known locally as a "bottom". Cottages and lane with adjacent stream and wooded hanger present a pleasant rural feature.		SU 865 359 — 853 371 1609 42
House C.18	Grayshott House, Headley Road. Stone structure built on older foundations. Well maintained in original style.		SU 862 353 1609 32
Building C.19	Grayshott Hall. Large brick structure with tower, built 1862 on site of old settlement, and standing in 45 acres of parkland bordering Ludshott Common. Alfred, Lord Tennyson, lived here in 1867. Ref: Buildings of England; Hants and I.O.W., (Pevsner & Lloyd), p. 260.		SU 857 357 1609 05
Buildings C.19	Nos. 1—7, Headley Road. Row of shops built circa 1890 when the village was first developed. Typical local design and structure; local stone and tile hung walls.		SU 874 353 1609 15
Cottages (3) C.19	The Pines, Headley Road. Terrace built circa 1890 when the village was first developed. Typical local design and structure; local stone and tile hung walls. Not altered appreciably since erection.		SU 874 353 1609 16
Building C.19	Crossways House, Crossways Road. Original village shop and post office. Built 1884 of local sandstone.		SU 873 352 1609 18
House C.19	Hunters Moon, Kingswood Firs. Large brick dwelling house with associated stables and out-buildings of a pleasing and well preserved design. Built 1887.		SU 868 349 1609 26

Description and Date	Remarks	Protection	Grid Ref. and Punchcard No.

Group D — (cont.)

Description and Date	Remarks	Protection	Grid Ref. and Punchcard No.
Cottages (2) C.19	Presidents Cottages, School Road. Terrace of two (originally three) brick cottages, built and owned by Edward I'Anson.		SU 869 354 1609 29
Building C.19	The Convent of the Cenacle, Headley Road. Brick structure, built as a mansion 1862. First of large houses in developing area and given to the Order of Our Lady of the Cenacle in 1913. Used as a military hospital 1914—1918.		SU 865 352 1609 30
Church C.19	St. Luke, Headley Road. Built 1899 on site of temporary church in Early English style. Tower and spire added 1910. Nave and east windows outstanding examples of early C.20 stained-glass. Ref: Buildings of England; Hants and I.O.W., (Pevsner & Lloyd), p. 260.		SU 872 353 1609 33
Building C.19	Grayshott Hall Lodge, Headley Road. Attractive stone lodge built circa 1884 adjacent main gate to Grayshott Hall. In mature wooded setting.		SU 856 358 1609 34
Cottage C.19	Bowes Cottage, Whitmore Vale Road. Stone built farm cottage dating from the early part of the C.19.		SU 870 357 1609 41
Church C.20	St. Joseph, Headley Road. Built 1911 in pleasing Gothic style with bell-turret over east end of nave. Crucifix erected in memory of Canadian soldiers who died in adjacent military hospital 1914—1918. Ref: Buildings of England; Hants and I.O.W., (Pevsner & Lloyd), p. 260.		SU 864 353 1609 31
Buildings C.20	Village Halls, Headley Road. Well appointed halls built as early village amenity in 1901 with socio-logical motives by enterprising and beneficent residents.		SU 878 353 1609 17
Memorial	Five Ways (Road Junction). War memorial, a replica of a C.13 Gloucestershire Cross. Wrought iron railings and gate on two sides of memorial garden.		SU 873 353 1609 13
Railings	Five Ways (Road Junction). Handmade, inscribed wrought iron railings surrounding specimen tree. Given by Girl Guides to commemorate Silver Jubilee of King George V, 1935.		SU 872 353 1609 12

Group E — Street Patterns, Street Furniture and Open Spaces

Description and Date	Remarks	Protection	Grid Ref. and Punchcard No.
Boundary Stone	Hampshire/Surrey border, Headley Road.		SU 878 353 1609 07
Boundary Stone	Grayshott/Headley Parish, Land of Nod.		SU 847 366 1609 08

Description and Date	Remarks	Protection	Grid Ref. and Punchcard No.

Group E — (cont.)

Historic Street Pattern	Victoria Terrace, Jubilee Terrace and Pendarvis, Crossways Road.		SU 874 352 1609 19
Historic Street Pattern	Crossways Road. Large dwelling houses of typical local structure and design in wooded setting, presenting a pleasant and characteristic street pattern of the late C.19.		SU 874 352 — 877 350 1609 20
Historic Street Pattern	Five Ways. Junction of Headley Road, Crossways Road, Whitmore Vale Road and Hill Road. Meeting place of five roads forming 'hub' of village; of exceptional open and pleasant character. Area includes village green, war memorial and garden and children's playing green.		SU 873 353 1609 14

Group F — Historical or Literary Associations

Cottage C.18	Plum Tree Cottage, Stoney Bottom. Stone structure; originally a squatters dwelling. Extensively altered but remains in character.		SU 872 352 1609 25
Cottage C.18	Well Cottage, Stoney Bottom. Stone structure; originally a squatters dwelling. Extensively altered but remains in character.		SU 871 351 1609 24
Cottage C.18	Silvae, Stoney Bottom. Stone structure; originally a squatters dwelling, with concealed cellar, probably used to store contraband.		SU 871 351 1609 23
Cottage C.18	Bramshott Cottage, Stoney Bottom. Stone structure; originally a squatters dwelling. Modernised but remains in character.		SU 877 349 1609 22
Cottage C.18	Yew Tree Cottage, Crossways Road. Stone structure; originally a squatters dwelling. Extensively altered but remains in character.		SU 878 349 1609 21
Cottage C.19	Broomsquires Cottage, Stoney Bottom. Remaining example of several cottages built circa 1820. Occupied until 1939 by makers of birch and heather brooms — a local industry. Ref: Hindhead, 1898, (Wright).		SU 871 350 1609 02
Building C.19	Grayshott C. of E. Primary School, School Road. Central part erected as school in 1871 under auspices of "The National Society for the Education of the Poor according to the principles of the Church of England". Original plaque and bell remains over doorway. Building used as first village Church from 1873 to 1891.		SU 869 355 1609 28

Group F — (cont.)

Description and Date	Remarks	Protection	Grid Ref. and Punchcard No.
Building C.19	Grayshott Pottery, School Road. Originally part of building contained laundry — an enterprise founded and sponsored by local benefactress Miss l'Anson to give employment to village girls.		SU 870 355 1609 27
Inn C.19	Fox and Pelican. Built and directed in 1899 by "Grayshott and District Refreshment Association", whose sponsors included Sir Frederick Pollock and George Bernard Shaw. Support given to the venture by the Archbishop of Canterbury and the Bishop of Chester. Name derived from connection with Bishop Fox of Winchester.		SU 873 353 1609 04

GREATHAM

The manor of Greatham was held by Queen Edith in the time of Edward the Confessor, but at the Domesday Survey (1086) it belonged to William the Conqueror. In later years the manor passed through many families by marriage and by purchase, including the Devenish, Marshall, Norton, Freeland and Love families.

A manor house was recorded as early as the year 1286 and the property comprising the manor included arable land, pastures, woodland and farm buildings. The ancient place name of Le Court was used when the manor house was rebuilt in 1866. In the 1940s Le Court House was bought by Group-Captain Leonard Cheshire, who in 1948 began to take in people suffering from incurable diseases. Le Court became the first home in a world-wide network of hospices for the incurably sick, now known as the Cheshire Homes.

An area of land near Woolmer Forest had been used for army training since the 1870s, and in 1903 Longmoor Camp was established as a permanent military station. Occupying over 40 acres, the camp included the garrison church of St. Martin, a Roman Catholic chapel, a military hospital, school and welfare centre. The Royal Engineers constructed a railway for the purposes of moving some huts from Longmoor Camp to the adjacent army depot at Bordon; the Longmoor railway survived until 1969.

Description and Date	Remarks	Protection	Grid Ref. and Punchcard No.

Group A — Natural Features

Description and Date	Remarks	Protection	Grid Ref. and Punchcard No.
Tree	Single tulip tree in front of the Rectory.		SU 774 305 2307 18

Group B — Archaeological

| Flint Flakes and Cores | A flint floor with numerous flakes and cores found whilst ploughing Greatham Moor. O.S.A. No. SU73 SE28. Ref: P.H.F.C., Vol. 9, 1920–4, (Williams-Freeman), p. 136. | | SU 782 302
2307 14 |

Group D — Buildings, Monuments and Engineering Works

Church C.13	Remains of old Church of St. John, on village green. Malmstone and ironstone structure with single lancet windows. Chancel plaster rendered with tiled roof. Tomb with recumbent figure of Dame Caryll, 1632. Nave roofless and in ruins. O.S.A. No. SU73 SE20. Ref: V.C.H., Vol. 2, p. 508.	T. & C.P. Act N.P. Act A.O.N.B.	SU 773 303 2307 01
Farmhouse C.15	Goleigh Farm, Liss Forest Road. 2 storeys. East end of ironstone with sandstone quoins, oldest part. Ironstone west end with brick dressings. Tiled roof with gable ends. Stone mullion windows with dripstones. Massive brick chimney. 2-storey gabled projection on north side of ironstone with brick dressing. Dated 1685.	T. & C.P. Act N.P. Act A.O.N.B.	SU 775 299 2307 03
Farmhouse C.17	Deal Farm, formerly Theale Farm, Farnham Road. 2 storeys. Ironstone structure with brick quoins. Upper storey tile hung. Timber-framed with ironstone infilling at rear. Tiled roof with hipped gables. Central chimney. Wooden casement windows. Ironstone garden wall with rounded top.	T. & C.P. Act N.P. Act A.O.N.B.	SU 776 308 2307 05
Mill C.17	Greatham Mill. 3 storeys. Colourwashed brick with two gables. Slate hung and slate roofed. Overshot mill wheel and machinery in working order. Last used for milling in 1926, but tested successfully in 1947/8. O.S.A. No. SU73 SE2. Ref: Buildings of England; Hants and I.O.W., (Pevsner and Lloyd), p. 260.	T. & C.P. Act N.P. Act A.O.N.B.	SU 765 304 2307 04A
House C.17	Greatham Mill House. Adjoins Mill. 2 storeys. Brick with brick dentilled cornice. Tiled roof with four gables at rear. Casement windows. Later extension connects the barn which is of ironstone structure with tiled roof. O.S.A. No. SU73 SE2. Ref: Buildings of England; Hants and I.O.W., (Pevsner and Lloyd), p. 260.	T. & C.P. Act N.P. Act A.O.N.B.	SU 765 304 2307 04B

Group D — (cont.)

Description and Date	Remarks	Protection	Grid Ref. and Punchcard No.
Cottage C.17	Pook Cottage, Church Lane. 2 storeys. Timber-framed with brick and ironstone infilling. Tiled roof with three gabled dormers. Casement windows with glazing bars. Later porch with tiled roof. Ironstone south wall galleted, with brick dressings. Upper storey tile hung.	N.P. Act A.O.N.B.	SU 771 308 2307 09
Farmhouse C.17	Rooks Farm, Farnham Road. 2 storeys. Timber-framed with ironstone infilling, and some later brickwork. Tiled roof with two gabled dormers. Old central chimney. Casement windows. Extension to south.	T. & C.P. Act N.P. Act A.O.N.B.	SU 774 306 2307 06
Cottages (2) C.17	Swains Cottages, Farnham Road. Structure of ironstone with brick dressings. Timber-framing at rear. Thatched roof with eaves dormers. Three in front, two at back. Wooden casement windows. Central chimney.	T. & C.P. Act N.P. Act A.O.N.B.	SU 773 304 2307 07
Barn C.18	Deal Farm. Abuts the road. Ironstone structure with brick dressings. Tiled roof.	N.P. Act A.O.N.B.	SU 776 308 2307 17
House and Stables C.18	Goulds House, Farnham Road. 2 storeys and attics. Ironstone with brick dressings. Tiled roof with two hipped tiled dormers. Casement windows in cambered arches. C.19 porch. Rear wing. 2-storey stables of ironstone with brick dressing and single storey extension to road.	T. & C.P. Act	SU 774 304 2307 08
Cottage C.19	Manor Cottage, Farnham Road. Stone structure, one end stucco with some repairs in brick. 2 storeys. Thatched roof with dormers, and two chimneys, small paned casement windows. Plain porch.	N.P. Act A.O.N.B.	SU 771 300 2307 13
Church C.19	St. John's, Farnham Road. Gothic revival style. Stone structure with tiled roof. Bell tower with spire. Pointed arch windows with leaded panes. Large open porch with gabled roof. 2-storey vestry in similar style with casement windows. Plain oak pews.	T. & C.P. Act N.P. Act A.O.N.B.	SU 773 304 2307 11
House	Cases House, Selborne Road. Mainly C.18, but remains of older cottage at south end. Ironstone with brick dressings and brick dentilled cornice. 2 storeys. Sash windows with cambered arches. Wooden doorcase with pediment and plain fanlight. C.20 wing. Ironstone garden wall with rounded brick coping.	T. & C.P. Act N.P. Act A.O.N.B.	SU 771 301 2307 02
Stables	Greatham Mill. 2 storeys. Brick structure with tiled roof. Gable at east end tile hung. Part converted to garage.	T. & C.P. Act N.P. Act A.O.N.B.	SU 765 304 2307 04C

Description and Date	Remarks	Protection	Grid Ref. and Punchcard No.

Group D — (cont.)

Description and Date	Remarks	Protection	Grid Ref. and Punchcard No.
Building	The Rectory. 2 storeys. Front circa 1810. Plaster rendered with cornice and parapet. Earlier structure behind, of ironstone with a tiled gabled roof. Sash windows. Later C.19 addition to east.		SU 774 304 2307 10
Barn	Rooks Farm, Farnham Road. Used as stables. Timber-clad with timber frame. Tiled roof. Small pane windows, non opening; wooden stable doors.	N.P. Act A.O.N.B.	SU 774 306 2307 12
Ice House	Le Court. On edge of wood. Brick structure with some external ornamental stonework, entrance passage with two large recesses leads to circular brick pit about 40 ft. deep. Plain doorway. Building covered by wooded mound. Ice house belonged to earlier house on site.	N.P. Act A.O.N.B.	SU 763 316 2307 16

Group E — Street Patterns, Street Furniture and Open Spaces

Description and Date	Remarks	Protection	Grid Ref. and Punchcard No.
Green	Greatham Village Green. Site of remains of old church of St. John. Centred on grid reference.	N.P. Act A.O.N.B.	SU 773 303 2307 15

HAWKLEY

The modern parish of Hawkley has included the small parish of Empshott since 1932. Hawkley was not recorded in the Domesday Survey of 1086 as the manor probably formed part of Newton Valence with which Hawkley was closely associated for centuries; lands belonging to Robert de Pont de l'Arche passed to William de Valence in 1249. The hamlet of Hawkley was granted to William de Valence in 1252 and subsequently followed the descent of the manor of Newton Valence. An old cottage at Lower Green was originally mill house of Hawkley mill. The ancient mill belonged to the bishops of Winchester, was seized by Adam Gordon but given back by Edward I in 1280; it was later burnt down, rebuilt in 1774 and used as a cottage from 1882 onwards. The stream behind the house originally drove the overshot wheel of the mill.

A dramatic event occurred at Hawkley in 1774: Gilbert White described how a large part of "the great woody hanger at Hawkley was torn from its place and fell down, leaving a high freestone cliff naked and bare, and resembling the steep cliff of a chalk pit."

The tiny parish of Empshott was distinguished in a survey of 1428 as one of the Hampshire parishes in which there were fewer than ten inhabitants holding houses; in 1931 the population had risen to 171. The manor of Empshott belonged to Edward the Confessor but was leased to Bundi and Saxi; at the time of the Domesday Survey it was held by Geoffrey de Venuz, a marshall to William the Conqueror. The manor remained in the Venuz family during the twelfth and thirteenth centuries but by the reign of Edward II it had passed to Aymer de Valence. Grange Farm was originally the manor house, and the manor courts were always held there.

Description and Date	Remarks	Protection	Grid Ref. and Punchcard No.

Group A — Natural Features

Description and Date	Remarks	Protection	Grid Ref. and Punchcard No.
Area of Ecological Importance	The entire parish of Hawkley. Fine views westward with a skyline of hangers and extensive views north-east towards the Hogs Back. Different types of soils have produced a varied flora and fauna. Most of the species mentioned by Gilbert White are still to be found.	N.P. Act A.O.N.B.	SU 753 303 2308 25
Pond	Jolly Robins Pond. A curiosity as the water level never varies. Not likely to be spring fed as the water table is 120 ft. below. Possibly constructed on dew pond principle to water the horses when the Jolly Robins was a coaching station.	N.P. Act A.O.N.B.	SU 747 294 2308 21
Lake	Near Tulls Cottage. Manmade, but date of origin unknown.	N.P. Act A.O.N.B.	SU 751 307 2308 20
Trees	Hawkley Hurst. Various species standing on land that originally comprised the grounds of Hawkley Hurst house.	T.P.O. No. 50 E.H.D. A.O.N.B.	SU 754 305 2308 27
Trees	Combe Hanger, Farewell Hanger, The Slip. Attractive stretches of trees east of Hawkley Village. Centred on grid reference.	N.P. Act A.O.N.B.	SU 752 292 2308 23
Trees	Church Row. Two large beech, a purple sycamore hybrid and a horse chestnut standing on land fronting the south west side of Church Row.	T.P.O. No. 3 E.H.D. A.O.N.B.	SU 746 292 2308 28

Group B — Archaeological

Post Norman

Description and Date	Remarks	Protection	Grid Ref. and Punchcard No.
Deserted Village (Site)	Empshott. Hundred — Selborne. Less than ten houses in 1428. Ref: 1. V.C.H., Vol. I, p.p. 430, 512. 2. V.C.H., Vol. II, p.p. 17—19. 3. Deserted Mediaeval Villages (Beresford and Hurst).	N.P. Act A.O.N.B.	SU 753 312 2308 26
Brick Kiln (Site)	Very little remains of the original site except the clay pit, which is very deep and is now a tree-lined pond, well stocked with a variety of fish.	N.P. Act A.O.N.B.	SU 756 285 2308 19

Group D — Buildings, Monuments and Engineering Works

Description and Date	Remarks	Protection	Grid Ref. and Punchcard No.
Church C.12/13	Church of the Holy Rood, Empshott. 4-bay arcades with round and octagonal piers. Pointed arches with dogtooth hood moulds. Aisles with small lancet windows. Purbeck marble font. Victorian bell turret with spire. O.S.A. No. SU73 SE1. Ref: Buildings of England; Hants and I.O.W., (Pevsner and Lloyd), p.p. 211—212.	T. & C.P. Act N.P. Act A.O.N.B.	SU 753 312 2308 01

Description and Date	Remarks	Protection	Grid Ref. and Punchcard No.

Group D — (cont.)

Description and Date	Remarks	Protection	Grid Ref. and Punchcard No.
Farmhouse C.16	Mabbotts Farm. 2 storeys. Timber-framed with malmstone filling. Upper storey tile hung. Thatched roof with windows at eaves level. Old central chimney.	T. & C.P. Act N.P. Act A.O.N.B.	SU 751 299 2308 04
Cottage C.16	Walnut Cottage. 2 storeys. Malmstone and brick with malmstone quoins. Tiles replace a thatched roof. Half-timbered wing with brick filling at rear. Old chimney.	N.P. Act A.O.N.B.	SU 749 298 2308 16
House C.17	Hill Place, Empshott. Brick with some malmstone and plaster. Hipped tiled roof. Old central chimney. The porch section is an impressive feature ranging through 2 storeys, brick built with hipped tiled roof, with heavy wooden cornice. The doorway has heavy pediment of moulded and cut brickwork. A wide door is reached up a flight of five steps. The roof extends almost to ground level at rear. The kitchen contains a well with a large wheel.	T. & C.P. Act N.P. Act A.O.N.B.	SU 754 312 2308 02
Cottage C.17	Mill Cottage, Mill Lane. 2 storeys. Malmstone with plinth and raised flat band of malmrock between storeys. Tiled roof with central chimney. Casement windows. Was used as two cottages but now restored to the original single cottage. Over the door is written, '16 M 83 M ◇ E '.	T. & C.P. Act N.P. Act A.O.N.B.	SU 749 306 2308 07
Cottages (2) C.17	Nos. 1 and 2, Gardeners' Cottages, The Grange. 2 storeys. Malmstone with brick dressings. Front refaced at later date, probably in C.18. Wing added to south. Sash and casement windows.	T. & C.P. Act N.P. Act A.O.N.B.	SU 753 312 2308 03
Farmhouse and Stable C.18	Lower Green Farm. Date about 1760. Hipped tiled roof with two dormers. Frontage of brick, east wall malmstone with brick dressings with extension to north. West wall, malmstone, also with extension to north. The stable has been incorporated as part of the house.	T. & C.P. Act N.P. Act A.O.N.B.	SU 747 299 2308 05
House C.18	Parsons Piece. 2 storeys. Galleted malmstone with brick dressings. Tiled roof. Casement windows. Timber porch with thatched gable.	N.P. Act A.O.N.B.	SU 746 293 2308 14
Cottage C.18	Brook Cottage. 2 storeys. Malmrock with brick dressings. Hipped thatched roof. Gable end partly tile hung. Upper storey windows at eaves level.	N.P. Act A.O.N.B.	SU 746 310 2308 13

Group D — (cont.)

Description and Date	Remarks	Protection	Grid Ref. and Punchcard No.
Farmhouse C.18	Cheesecomb Farm. 2 storeys. Brick structure with tiled roof. Brick dentilled cornice and plinth. Brick porch. Casement windows surmounted by cambered arches. The rear of the house is of malmstone construction with brick dressings, and the roof descends to door level. A fireplace discovered during modernisation is thought to be C.14.	N.P. Act A.O.N.B.	SU 747 286 2308 10
House C.18	Mill House, Mill Lane. 2 storeys. Galleted malmstone with brick band and brick dressings. Slate roof. Diamond leaded casements in gable end. Present house dated 'R.W.H. 1774', but considerably altered. An inset stone bears an inscription giving details of the history of 'Hockeleye Mill'.	T. & C.P. Act N.P. Act A.O.N.B.	SU 749 306 2308 06
Cottage C.18	Farewell Cottage. Originally two cottages now converted to one dwelling. 2 storeys. Brick with purple headers, on a plinth of malmrock. Tiled roof. Casement windows with glazing bars, those on ground floor with cambered arches. Lean-to at each end.	N.P. Act A.O.N.B.	SU 751 288 2308 09
Church C.19	St. Peter and St. Paul. Built in 1865 on the site of a C.12 church. Neo-Norman style, with Rhenish Helm type tower. Gabled rose window with tracery. The church contains C.12 Purbeck marble font and a C.15 alabaster panel depicting Christ's betrayal. Some of the bells date from C.15. Architect S. S. Teulon. Ref: Buildings of England; Hants and I.O.W., (Pevsner and Lloyd), p. 280.	T. & C.P. Act N.P. Act A.O.N.B.	SU 745 291 2308 24
House	The Old House, formerly Jolly Robin. Oldest end of C.17 or earlier with some timber-framing. 2 storeys. Mainly malmstone with brick dressings. Upper storey tile hung. Hipped tiled roof. Casement windows. More recent part to north of same structure.	N.P. Act A.O.N.B.	SU 747 294 2308 15
Cottage	Primmers Cottage, Snailing Lane. 1½ storeys. Ironstone with brick dressings. Tiled roof. Some timber work at north end. Recently renovated.	N.P. Act A.O.N.B.	SU 762 292 2308 08
Cottage	Grange Farm Cottage, Empshott Green. Parts date from C.16. Timber-framed rear wing with brick dressings. Tile-hanging on frontage is modern. Tiled roof, central chimney. Some casement windows, leaded lights.	N.P. Act A.O.N.B.	SU 749 310 2308 12
Cottage	West of Lower Green Farm. Converted from a stable in 1976. Malmstone with brick dressings. The original thatched roof has been tiled using old tiles.	N.P. Act A.O.N.B.	SU 746 299 2308 17

Description and Date	Remarks	Protection	Grid Ref. and Punchcard No.

Group F — Historical or Literary Associations

Landslip	Slip Cottage and pond near Scotland Farm. Cottage built 1684 survived a 100 ft. subsidence together with its occupants on 28th March, 1784. 50 acres slipped including the pond and spring, which continued to run afterwards. A collection from over 2,000 sightseers was sufficient to repair and enlarge the cottage. Ref: Natural History of Selborne, (Gilbert White).	N.P. Act A.O.N.B.	SU 754 293 2308 18

HEADLEY

Some eight miles south-east of Alton, between Bordon and Grayshott, Headley is a large village surrounded by heaths and downs with the open heather slopes of Headley Down. The church was rebuilt in 1936 after a fire and has a rugged castellated fifteenth century tower.

Description and Date	Remarks	Protection	Grid Ref. and Punchcard No.
Group A — Natural Features			
Woodland	Hilland Woods. Mixed trees predominantly beech along Fullers Vale.	T.P.O. No. 152	SU 828 357 — 831 360 1610 45
Woodland	Hilland Woods. Mixed trees in north-west part of the estate and Philips Crescent.	T.P.O. No. 288	SU 826 362 1610 47
Woodland	Wishanger Farm and New Farm. Variety of species including many birch and conifer trees.	T.P.O. No. 207	SU 838 391 — 833 382 1610 48
Trees	White Lilacs, Liphook Road. Variety of trees standing in what was once the garden. Now developed and named Pound Close.	T.P.O. No. 383	SU 826 361 1610 49
Trees	Honeysuckle Lane/Wilsons Road. One sweet chestnut and three oaks standing near road junction.	T.P.O. No. 403	SU 837 362 1610 50
Trees	Kirk Knoll, Arford Road. Mainly conifers forming important backdrop to the village green.	T.P.O. No. 492	SU 824 364 1610 51
Trees	Stagsdene, Fairlawn, Birkenholme. Variety of trees standing in the grounds. Centred on grid reference.	T.P.O. No. 776	SU 842 357 1610 53
Tree	High Street. Chestnut, planted 1891 to mark the site of the stocks.	C.A.	SU 821 362 1610 88
Trees	Noar, Mill Lane. Sweet chestnuts and beech, standing on top of hill and forming conspicuous backdrop to the centre of the village.	T.P.O. No. 15 E.H.D.	SU 821 361 1610 54
Trees	The Paddock. Several trees of different species standing in the area centred on grid reference.	T.P.O. No. 569	SU 823 360 1610 104
Trees	Coolgreany Gardens. Various species standing in the area.	T.P.O. No. 46 E.H.D.	SU 819 364 1610 105
Trees	Kirklands, Arford Road. Various species standing in the area.	T.P.O. No. 10 E.H.D.	SU 826 365 1610 106
Trees	Barley Mow Hill. Several trees standing on the north-east side of the junction.	T.P.O. No. 47 E.H.D.	SU 828 369 1610 107
Trees	Headley Hill Road. Various species standing on the land fronting the north east side.	T.P.O. No. 42 E.H.D.	SU 830 364 1610 108
Trees	Windmill Estate, Arford. Various species standing in the area centred on grid reference.	T.P.O. No. 24 E.H.D.	SU 834 367 1610 109
Trees	Archway Cottage, Churt Road. Various species of deciduous and coniferous trees. Centred on grid reference.	T.P.O. No. 11 E.H.D.	SU 834 369 1610 110

Description and Date	Remarks	Protection	Grid Ref. and Punchcard No.
Group A — (cont.)			
Area of Ecological Interest	Broxhead Common. Heathland and developing woodland on Folkestone beds in the western weald area includes spur of mature heath dominated by heather and gorse. Also areas of birch and oak woodland. The whole area supports many characteristic heathland organisms.	N.P. Act S.S.S.I.	SU 804 374 1610 111
Trees	Land adjoining Beech Hill, Coppice Knoll, Headley Down. Two limes and two beech standing in area centred on grid reference.	T.P.O. No. 73 E.H.D.	SU 826 361 1610 112
Trees	Headley Hill Road. Coniferous and deciduous trees consisting of mixed firs, scots pine, silver birch and oaks. Centred on grid reference.	T.P.O. No. 78 E.H.D.	SU 832 364 1610 113
Woodland	Fairlawn, Furze Hill Road, Headley Down. Mixed deciduous and coniferous trees consisting of birch, beech, hornbeam, lawsons cypresses, scots pine and one red oak.	T.P.O. No. 84 E.H.D.	SU 842 357 1610 114
Trees	Headley Fields. Five sequoia standing along the frontage of 'Mayfield House' and one in the garden of 'Leighswood'.	T.P.O. No. 48 E.H.D.	SU 821 359 1610 115
Fossil Beds	Headley Farm Pit, Southwest of Headleywood Farm. The best known section of fossiliferous Puttenham Beds.	N.P. Act S.S.S.I.	SU 814 373 1610 103
Group B — Archaeological			
Stone Age			
Occupation and Flint Working Sites	Group of Mesolithic sites at Trottsford, Sleaford. Finds include narrow-blade cores, microliths, end-scrapers etc. Heathland now overgrown and farmland under cultivation. O.S.A. No. SU83 NW5. Ref: P.H.F.C., Vol. 18, 1951–3, p. 157.		SU 806 380 1610 43
Bronze Age			
Implement	Palstave found in garden near Beech Hill Social Club. Bronze, with well defined stop ridge. Now in Haslemere Educational Museum. O.S.A. No. SU83 NW7.		SU 837 364 1610 93
Bowl Barrow	Broxhead Common. Situated on small hill. Damaged by ploughing before being put over to pasture. O.S.A. No. SU83 NW1. Ref: P.H.F.C., Vol. 14, 1938–40, p. 352.	S.A.M. No. 76	SU 807 381 1610 42
Stone Bowl	Picketts Hill Farm. Old bowl, possibly for grinding corn, used for many years as feeding trough for chickens. Reputed to be of Saxon date. Formerly at Trottsford Farm.		SU 821 382 1610 67

Description and Date	Remarks	Protection	Grid Ref. and Punchcard No.

Group C — Footpaths and Bridleways

Description and Date	Remarks	Protection	Grid Ref. and Punchcard No.
Old Travelway	Cradle Lane. Bridleway going north from the rear gate of Headley Park and across the river. One of eleven bridleways and thirty-eight footpaths in the parish.		SU 813 382 — 816 389 1610 102

Group D — Buildings, Monuments and Engineering Works

Description and Date	Remarks	Protection	Grid Ref. and Punchcard No.
Church C.14	All Saints. Rebuilt 1859. Stone structure with C.14 perpendicular tower. Wide-spanned and massive timbered roof, dating from C.14. Fine C.14 window with elaborate super-tracery in west wall and C.13 lancet incorporated in south wall of chancel. O.S.A. No. SU83 NW4. Ref: 1. Headley — The Story of a Hampshire Parish, 1066—1966. (Canon Tudor Jones, Rector of Headley 1934—1965). 2. V.C.H., Vol. 3, p. 54.	T. & C.P. Act C.A.	SU 821 362 1610 01
Farmhouse C.16	Picketts Hill Farm. Brick structure, restored and modernised. Elizabethan kitchen. 2 storeys, tiled roof. Fine stone wall surrounding the garden. Old wooden hop shovel found during alterations.		SU 821 381 1610 68
Cottage C.16	Appletree Cottage. 2 storeys. Roughly coursed ironstone with red brick dressings. Ridge tiled roof. Square lattice windows. Two simple cottage doors. Originally three cottages. Dated 1590.	C.A.	SU 821 362 1610 09
Farmhouse C.16	Tulls, formerly Chase Farm, Tulls Lane, Standford. 2 storeys. Small coursed stone blocks. Ridge tiled roof. Plainwood casements. Tile hung gable towards road. Formerly two cottages.		SU 820 349 1610 39
Farmhouse and Cottage C.16	Bayfields Farn, Frensham Lane. 2 storeys. Stone structure. Tiled roof. Beams made from ships timbers. Until 1968 water was pumped from well under lounge floor. Former Oast House (with some wattle and daub walls) converted into gardeners cottage.		SU 823 375 1610 82
Cottage C.16	Overton Cottage, Arford. 2 storeys. Timber-framed with brick infilling. Thatched roof. Three dormer windows. Interior walls of wattle and daub. Bread oven and inglenook.	T. & C.P. Act C.A.	SU 826 365 1610 39
Farmhouse and Barn C.16/17	Hatch House Farm. Restored and enlarged. 2 storeys. Timber-framed with coursed and random stone infilling. Old half-hipped tiled roof. Modern lattice casements and french windows. Large stone barn converted into dwelling.		SU 812 363 1610 33

Description and Date	Remarks	Protection	Grid Ref. and Punchcard No.

Group D — (cont.)

Description and Date	Remarks	Protection	Grid Ref. and Punchcard No.
Farmhouse C.16/17	Huntingford Cottage. 2 storeys. Partly exposed timber-framing. High pitched tiled roof. Plain wood casements. Short projecting gabled wing. Small gabled porch.	T. & C.P. Act	SU 823 386 610 03
Cottage C.17	Riverside, Standford. 2 storeys. Coursed stone walls. Tiled roof. Half-hipped gables. Front facade probably of later date, with two bay windows and two casements. Reputed to be formerly the Red Lion inn.	C.A.	SU 816 347 1610 60
Barn C.17	Riverside, Standford. Coursed stone structure. Ridge tiled roof. Square wooden window frames. Remains of thatch visible under tiles. Once a wheelwrights workshop. Thick stone walls at gate are all that remains of smithy.	C.A.	SU 816 347 1610 60A
Cottage C.17	Rooks Cottage, Churt Road. 2 storeys. Stone structure. Tiled roof. Wood-framed diamond paned casements. Long pentice roof at rear.		SU 842 378 1610 84
Cottage C.17	Barford Stream Cottage, Churt Road. 2 storeys. Timber-framed with limewashed brick and plaster infilling. Ridge tiled roof. Square paned sliding casements. Tile hung side gable.	T. & C.P. Act	SU 852 380 1610 06
Farmhouse and Oast Barn C.17/18	Weyhouse, Headley Mill. 2 storeys. Coursed and random stone on ground floor, tile hung above. Tiled roof. Square paned wood casements. Modern gabled additions. Oast barn to south.	C.A.	SU 813 356 1610 35
Farmhouse C.17/18	Curtis Farm. Restored. 2 storeys. Coursed stone structure with galleting decoration. Steep hipped tiled roof. Gabled projecting wing to right, rendered and probably modern. Casement windows.		SU 822 367 1610 16
House C.18	The Rectory. 3 storeys. Stone structure. Steep hipped slate roof. Panelled parapet and narrow cornice band. Sash windows and three pedimented dormers. Side facade of coursed ironstone with brick dressings.	T. & C.P. Act C.A.	SU 821 363 1610 02
Building C.18	Wakefords, High Street. Formerly the Holly Bush Inn. 2 storeys. Creamwashed brick walls. Hipped tiled roof. Sash windows. Ground floor shop windows under flat arched brick lintels.	C.A.	SU 822 361 1610 08
House C.18	The Grange. Built 1795. 2 storeys. Stone structure. Tiled roof. Sash windows. One large bay with tiled pediment. Five pedimented dormers with decorative fascia boards. Long low wing and other adjoining additions. Ref: 1. Headley — The Story of a Hampshire Parish, 1066–1966. (Canon Tudor Jones, Rector of Headley 1934–1965).		SU 826 356 1610 57

18th/19th Century Mill, HEADLEY

Description and Date	Remarks	Protection	Grid Ref. and Punchcard No.
Group D — (cont.)			
House C.18	The Old Bakery, Arford. 2 storeys with single storey extension. Rendered walls. Hipped tiled roof. Modern wooden casement windows. Boarded door.	C.A.	SU 826 365 1610 14
Cottage C.18	Crown Cottage, Arford. 2 storeys. Stone structure. Ridge tiled roof. Boarded door.	C.A.	SU 826 365 1610 62
House C.18	Stores House, Arford. 2 storeys. Roughcast. Hipped tiled roof with moulded eaves. Pentice addition to left. Formerly a general store.	C.A.	SU 826 366 1610 13
House C.18	Bohannas, Arford. 2 storeys. Colourwashed white brick, plinth and band. Ridge tiled roof. Lattice casement windows. Large cellar built into hillside at ground level. Formerly an inn.		SU 827 368 1610 11
Farmhouse C.18	Tignals. 2 storeys. Limewashed brick walls. Ridge tiled roof, half-hipped to right. Triple casement windows, those on ground floor with boarded shutters.		SU 828 374 1610 30
Mill C.18/19	Headley Mill. 2 storeys. Coursed stone blocks and some brickwork. Three small gabled dormers, plain metal casements and loft entrances. Mill powered by steel breast-shot water wheel from a head of 7½ ft. The wheel drives four pairs of millstones measuring 4 ft. in diameter through cast iron gears. Believed to be the only water mill still in active use in Hampshire.	C.A.	SU 811 357 1610 34
Cottage C.18/19	Adjoining Headley Mill. 2 storeys. Random stone walls. Half-hipped ridge tiled roof, with pentice to rear. Sash windows. Formerly two cottages.		SU 811 357 1610 34A
House C.18/19	Yeomans Place, formerly Crabtree. 2 storeys. Roughly coursed ironstone. Half-hipped ridge tiled roof. Victorian gabled brick porch. Adjoining mock Tudor house, vertical mock timber-framing with plaster infilling. Built 1880. Now two dwellings.		SU 821 364 1610 10
House C.19	The Corner House, Arford. 2 storeys. White plaster walls, part to left painted weatherboarding. Ridge slate roof. Sash windows. Trellis porch. Now divided into flats.	C.A.	SU 826 366 1610 12
Inn	The New Inn, Sleaford. Victorian front with old timber-framed wing to the rear. 2 storeys. Limewashed brick with stone and plaster infilling. Hipped tiled roof. Half glazed door with flat projecting hood.		SU 802 382 1610 32

Group D — (cont.)

Description and Date	Remarks	Protection	Grid Ref. and Punchcard No.
Farmhouse and Barn	Trottsford Farm. 2 storeys. Stone and brick structure. Hipped tiled roof. Square-paned casement windows. Barn at right angles to house, now joined to main farmhouse. Modern metal-framed windows and large cellar with interesting niches in the walls. In 1547 this was church property.		SU 808 386 1610 71
Farmbuilding	Trottsford Farm. Large, solid, stone barn, partly weatherboarded at one end. Dated 1815 possibly after a major repair or addition.		SU 808 385 1610 72
Building	Corn Mill Cottage, Standford. Renovated mill and attached cottage now forming one dwelling. Mill of coursed stone with short half-hipped ridge tiled roof. Cottage of random stone, with weatherboarded store/garage at end towards road. O.S.A. No. SU83 NW3.	C.A.	SU 813 353 1610 36
Cottage	Sunnyside, Standford. 2 storeys. Stone and brick structure. Tiled roof. Wood framed lattice windows.	C.A.	SU 815 348 1610 75
Cottage	Standford Cottage. 2 storeys, with single storey extension. Painted stone structure. Tiled roof. Off-centre double chimney.	C.A.	SU 815 349 1610 74
Cottages (4)	Gravel Cottages, Standford. 2 storeys. Stone and brick sturcture. Half-hipped old tiled roof. Central chimney.	C.A.	SU 816 348 1610 76
House	Eveley, Standford. 2 storeys. Stone structure. Gabled tiled roof. Dormer window. 2-storey extension. Surrounded by beautiful landscaped gardens, through which flows the River Wey.	C.A.	SU 815 349 1610 77
Farmhouse	The Old Farm House, Standford. Formerly Standford Farm. Timber-framed structure. Gable to right and left with part pentice ridge in centre containing modern dormer and a half dormer. Old tiled roof. Modern red brick extension.	C.A.	SU 814 350 1610 37
Farm Buildings	The Old Farm House, Standford. Two weather-boarded barns, forming attractive group with farmhouse and nearby house.	C.A.	SU 815 349 1610 38
Farmhouse	Hatch Farm, Standford. 2 storeys. Stone structure with some tile hanging and exposed timbers, believed to be old ship's timber brought from Portsmouth when Pepys was modernising the Navy. Timber roof. Sash and square paned casement windows. C.19 wing. A tributary of the River Wey flows through the cellar. Ref: 1. History and Directory of Hampshire, 1859 (White). 2. P.H.F.C., Vol. 18, (Shorters "Paper Mills in Hampshire").	C.A.	SU 817 347 1610 73

Description and Date	Remarks	Protection	Grid Ref. and Punchcard No.

Group D — (cont.)

Description and Date	Remarks	Protection	Grid Ref. and Punchcard No.
Cottage	Nos. 1, and 2, Peters or Petars Barn, Lindford. Restored and now one dwelling. 2 storeys. Timber-framed with roughly coursed stone infilling. Ridge tiled roof with half pentice addition to left. Square lattice windows. Old chimney with plain coupled stacks. Mud and wattle structure visible internally.		SU 813 368 1610 61
Cottage	No. 3, Peters or Petars Barn Cottage, Lindford. 2 storeys. Timber-framed with brick, stone and plaster infilling. Thatched roof. Modern lattice casements and centre boarded door. Possibly C.16.		SU 813 368 1610 18
Cottages (3)	Headley Park. Unusual group; one a converted oast house and one built in the C.19. The oldest cottage has blocked up church windows on two walls. Traditionally believed to be private chapel of the original Headley Park House, or it could be merely a Victorian Gothic folly.		SU 813 382 1610 70
Farmhouse	Huntingford Farm, Frensham Lane. 2 storeys. Creamwashed brick and coursed stone, with exposed light timberwork on first floor. A modern cement-tiled roof. Replaces the original thatch which was destroyed by fire in 1958. Plain square paned wooden casement windows.		SU 819 368 1610 19
Farmhouse	Linstead Farm, Frensham Lane. 2 storeys. L-shaped with wide stone plinth. Exposed timber-framing with brick infilling on ground floor, fishscale tile hanging above. Old tiled roof.		SU 819 371 1610 20
Farm Building	Tulls, formerly Chase Farm, Tulls Lane. Old stone barn with long ridge tiled roof brought down as continuous pentice in front towards farmyard.		SU 820 349 1610 40
Farm Buildings	Picketts Hill Farm. Large stone built barn with massive internal timbers. Date 'June ye 20th 1769', beautifully carved on one of the beams. Stone built wagon shed with stout supporting beams.		SU 821 381 1610 69
Farmhouse	Mellow Farm. 2 storeys. Exposed timber framing with red brick infilling and wide stone base on ground floor. First floor slightly over-hung. Ridge tiled roof, hipped to left. Casement windows.	T. & C.P. Act	SU 821 388 1610 04
Farm Building	Mellow Farm. Old weatherboarded barn at right angles to farmhouse, with steep hipped tiled roof.		SU 821 388 1610 23

Description and Date	Remarks	Protection	Grid Ref. and Punchcard No.

Group D — (cont.)

Description and Date	Remarks	Protection	Grid Ref. and Punchcard No.
Cottage	Suters, High Street. 2 storeys. Random stone on ground floor, tilehung above. Long ridge tiled roof, hipped at each end. Exposed timber-framing on side gable. Sash and casement windows. Wattle and daub walls revealed during alterations. Originally a row of three cottages. Ref: 1. Highways and Byways in Hampshire, (pencil sketch), 1908, (Read), p. 394.	C.A.	SU 822 361 1610 07
Building	The Stores, High Street. Rambling stone structure with barns incorporated. Modernised and used as a shop. Owned by the Rogers family from 1870–1957.	C.A.	SU 821 361 1610 90
Building	Tithe Barn. Converted into house. Thick stone walls with heavy interior beams. Long steeply pitched ridge tiled roof, hipped at each end. Initials and date on south end of east wall — 'W.M. 1680 and $\overset{S.}{H.S.}$ 1812'. Fine example of farm building converted to residential use.	C.A.	SU 821 363 1610 56
Farm Buildings	Curtis Farm. Picturesque group including two large stone barns and range of outhouses and stabling.		SU 822 367 1610 17
Cottage	Yeomans Cottage. Stone structure. Ridge tiled roof, half-hipped at each end. Modern porch and cement rendered addition at back. May once have been a granary.		SU 824 361 1610 58
Cottage	Holme School House, Headley Green. 2 storeys. Stone structure. Lattice windows. Tiled roof. Large extension. Part of bequest to be used to benefit the children of the parish.		SU 824 362 1610 79
House	The Square House, Headley Green. 2 storeys. Stone structure. Slate roof. Sash windows. Possibly early C.18.		SU 824 363 1610 81
Farmhouse	Longcross Farm, Longcross Hill. Part 2 storeys, part single storey and dormers. Limewashed stonework with exposed timber-framing. Old tiled roof. Lattice windows.		SU 824 365 1610 15
House	Arford House. 2 storeys. Coursed square stone blocks, creamwashed. Slate roof. Casement windows with flat lintels and 'Gothic' tracery. Stable block converted into dwelling.	C.A.	SU 826 365 1610 63
Farm Building	Tignals, Saunders Green. Small weather-boarded barn with short half-hipped ridge tiled roof.		SU 828 374 1610 31
Cottage	Yew Tree Cottage, Arford Common. Long low single storey stone structure. Slate roof.		SU 829 367 1610 91

Description and Date	Remarks	Protection	Grid Ref. and Punchcard No.

Group D — (cont.)

Farmhouse — Moore House Farm. 2 storeys and attic gable window. Timber-framed with red brick nogging and some modern herring-bone nogging. Two fine projecting chimneys at side, of red brick with diamond pattern picked out in blue brick. Coupled stacks. Casement windows. Wing to right of recent date. Two dwellings.
    SU 829 387   1610 24

Farmhouse — Wishanger Oasts, Frensham Lane. Coursed stone structure. Barn incorporated into house. Some sash windows, some modern.
    SU 831 388   1610 85

Cottage — Chatterton Lodge, Fullers Vale. 2 storeys. Stone and brick structure. Tiled roof. Extension to right. Believed to have been a forester's lodge.
    SU 833 358   1610 78

Cottage — The Old Cottage, Hearn. Restored. Timber-framed with red brick infilling on ground floor, tile-hung above. Two large half dormers with eaves, waved over ridge tiled roof. Square paned wooden casement windows.
    SU 835 374   1610 29

Farm Buildings — Lower Hearn. Picturesque group, converted and restored. Barn to south, random stone with weatherboarding above. Modern mullioned and transomed windows. Half-hipped tiled roof. North barn forms two dwellings with modern dormers and modern metal casements below. Ridge tiled roof.
    SU 837 376   1610 28

Farmhouse — Lower Hearn. Restored structure, faced with white plaster. 2 storeys. Hipped tiled roof. Slightly projecting flanking wings. Modern metal casement windows. Small timbered porch.
    SU 838 377   1610 27

House — Field House. One wing, timber-framed with limewashed brick and stone infilling. Single storey and modern hipped dormers. Lattice casements. Old tiled roof. Believed C.16. New wing has mock timberwork and first floor overhang.
    SU 843 394   1610 25

Farmhouse — Plasterhill Farm. 2 storeys. Timber-framed, including closely spaced vertical strutting, with white plaster infilling. Hipped tiled roof. Modern lattice casements. Barns to north, south and west form square with farmhouse. Some parts of farm allegedly date from 1580.
    SU 847 378   1610 26

Cottage — Laurel Cottage, Hammer Lane. Single storey stone structure. Old tiled roof. One of the few remaining squatters cottages, built of local materials, by members of a family, who, if they had a fire burning in the hearth within 24 hours, could claim "squatters rights" over the piece of land. Now considerably modernised.
    SU 852 375   1610 86

Description and Date	Remarks	Protection	Grid Ref. and Punchcard No.

Group D — (cont.)

Description and Date	Remarks	Protection	Grid Ref. and Punchcard No.
Cottage	Holly Cottage, Hammer Lane. Single storey stone structure. Old tiled roof. Lattice windows. Now modernised.		SU 852 375 1610 92
Building	Barford Mill, Churt. Old flock mill and mill house converted into attractive house. Original mill, possibly C.17, timber-framed with random stone infilling. Lattice casement windows. Mill House, C.18. 2 storeys. Colourwashed brick walls. Long ridge tiled roof. Ref: 1. White's History and Directory of Hampshire, 1859. 2. P.H.F.C., Vol. 18. (Shorters "Paper Mills in Hampshire"). 3. Headley Booklet, (Tudor Jones).	T. & C.P. Act	SU 853 377 1610 05
Millhouse	Old Mill, Barford. 3 storeys. Brick walls, with galleting between bricks. Ridge tiled roof, with stacks each end. Sash windows under segmental lintels. Elaborate pedimented porch.		SU 853 380 1610 55
Building	Bulls Hollow. Remains of lime kiln. Brick and stone structure. Believed to be the only one left in the parish.		SU 820 383 1610 65
Bridge	Huntingford Bridge. Plain stone structure consisting of two round arches and parapet, crossing the River Wey northwest of Huntingford Cottage.		SU 823 387 1610 22
Bridge	Northwest of Linstead Farm. Mediaeval packhorse bridge, consisting of single stone arch. Parapets removed and replaced with decorative wrought iron railings of recent origin. Stage coaches once crossed this bridge on the way through Headley Wood to the Toll Gate opposite the New Inn at Sleaford.		SU 818 372 1610 21
Aqueduct	River Wey, Headley Park. Brick and stone structure possibly C.17 or C.18. Part of a complex system which encompasses similar aqueducts in surrounding parishes. Thought either to serve water meadows or possibly used in conjunction with iron works in this area.	S.A.M. No. 469	SU 813 372 1610 66
Memorial	Adjacent All Saints Church. War Memorial (1914—1918). Two pillars linked by concave wall, surmounted by a cross. Contains three bronze tablets bearing ninety-six names.	C.A.	SU 821 362 1610 98
Gravestone	All Saints Churchyard. Designed by sculptor J. Reid in memory of Alida, Lady Brittain and Sir Harry Brittain, founder of The Pilgrims.	C.A.	SU 821 363 1610 101

Description and Date	Remarks	Protection	Grid Ref. and Punchcard No.

Group D — (cont.)

Description and Date	Remarks	Protection	Grid Ref. and Punchcard No.
Memorial Book	All Saints Church. Desk made of Hampshire oak containing book, bound in blue leather, resting on blue Italian velvet. Dedicated to forty-eight men who died in the Second World War.	C.A.	SU 821 362 1610 99
Window	All Saints Church. Magnificent C.13. Stained glass, representing the martyrdom of a saint. Bears marked resemblance to the world famous glass in Chartres Cathedral. Removed for safe keeping during the Second World War and now protected by plate glass.	C.A.	SU 821 362 1610 96

Group E — Street Patterns, Street Furniture and Open Spaces

Description and Date	Remarks	Protection	Grid Ref. and Punchcard No.
Village Pound (Site)	Corner of Crabtree Gardens, Liphook Road. Two sides of walls remain. On them is a plaque which reads, 'This wall was part of the Headley Village Pound, erected probably in the C.17 and demolished in 1929'.		SU 825 362 1610 87
Sheepwash	By the parish boundary at Frensham Pond. Wall by roadside intact, and the ramp over which the animals scrambled can still be traced.		SU 840 402 1610 64
Lychgate	All Saints Church. Oak gate with roof, erected to commemorate the coronation of Queen Elizabeth II and dedicated in May 1954.	C.A.	SU 821 362 1610 100

Group F — Historical or Literary Associations

Description and Date	Remarks	Protection	Grid Ref. and Punchcard No.
House C.18	The Grange. Built by combined parishes of Headley, Bramshott and Kingsley as a Union Workhouse. Attacked in 1830 by gang of labourers led by Robert Holdaway, a wheelwright. Ref: 1. Bramshott, (Canon Cape). 2. Headley — The story of a Hampshire Parish 1066—1966, (Canon Tudor Jones, Rector of Headley 1934—1965).		SU 826 356 1610 57
Building	Standford Mill. Present dwelling modern, but built of old materials. Original mill burnt down in C.19. Turned "shoddy" into paper, and traditionally believed to have been used by Portals of Laverstoke for Bank of England Notes. Ref: It Happened in Hampshire, (Beddington and Christy), p. 75.	C.A.	SU 812 349 1610 95

HORNDEAN

Horndean Parish was formed in 1932 and covered the south-east part of the Hundred of "Ceptune" or Finchdean. Various changes of boundaries have altered the area and it now covers the old Catherington parish and Blendworth village. It is a widespread parish with several interesting associations.

The Church of All Saints dates from the end of the twelfth century and in it is a large monument to Sir Nicholas Hyde, Chief Justice of the King's Bench in 1627, who lived at Hinton Dausney. It is said that here the marriage of the Duke of York (later James II) took place in 1660.

Buried in the churchyard are the wife and son of Edward Keane, the celebrated tragedian who lived at Keydell House. Admiral Sir Charles John Napier, K.C.B., owner of Merchiston House, was also buried here.

Description and Date	Remarks	Protection	Grid Ref. and Punchcard No.

Group A — Natural Features

Description and Date	Remarks	Protection	Grid Ref. and Punchcard No.
Viewpoints	Catherington Down. Fine views northwards to Butser Hill and South to Portsdown Hill. Extensive views from Church Meadows to the Isle of Wight and Solent. Vista stretches from Cowes to the Nab Tower. Attractive downland scenery with some wooded areas. An area of rich chalk grassland flora. Managed as a nature reserve by the Hampshire and I.O.W. Naturalist Trust.	N.P. Act C.O.S.	SU 692 144 2309 35
Viewpoint	Whitedells Copse. Pleasant views over Lone Barn Farm, in the hollow below, to Broad Halfpenny Down.	N.P. Act A.O.N.B.	SU 681 152 2309 41
Pond	In the centre of Old Blendworth, close to a road junction. Habitat for wildlife and flowers.		SU 716 135 2309 50
Wooded Area	Catherington Lith, Southeast of Catherington. Centred on grid reference.	T.P.O. No. 29 E.H.D.	SU 701 140 2309 36
Trees	Keydell Estate. Includes two horse chestnuts, a cedar and others.	T.P.O. No. 200	SU 691 121 2309 43
Trees	An attractive belt of trees along the London Road. Varieties include oak, ash, horse chestnut, plane, beech and sycamore. Centred on grid reference.	T.P.O. No. 129	SU 698 127 2309 42
Trees	Copses and groups of trees at Lovedean Farm and Hinton Manor Farm, Catherington.	T.P.O. No. 287	SU 686 145 2309 45
Trees	No. 216, Portsmouth Road. Many black pine trees.	T.P.O. No. 237	SU 695 122 2309 44
Trees	Catherington House, Catherington. Various species centred on grid reference.	T.P.O. No. 63 E.H.D.	SU 694 139 2309 52
Trees	Crookley Park, Blendworth Lane. Various species both deciduous and coniferous. Centred on grid reference.	T.P.O. No. 8 E.H.D.	SU 707 133 2309 60
Trees	Blendworth Lodge. Various species both deciduous and coniferous standing in the area centred on grid reference.	T.P.O. No. 9 E.H.D.	SU 709 129 2309 61
Trees	Area between Portsmouth Road and Rosemary Way, several trees of various species.	T.P.O. No. 76 E.H.D.	SU 696 123 2309 65
Woodland	Blendworth Down. Mixed Hardwoods including yew, in the area centred on grid reference.	T.P.O. No. 75 E.H.D. N.P. Act A.O.N.B.	SU 712 148 2309 64
Area of Scenic Beauty	The extreme eastern part of the parish is designated as being of particular ecological interest. The grid reference given locates the centre of the area.	N.P. Act A.O.N.B.	SU 684 163 2309 62

Group A — (cont.)

Description and Date	Remarks	Protection	Grid Ref. and Punchcard No.
Area of Scenic Beauty	The extreme western part of the parish is designated as being of particular ecological interest. The grid reference given locates the centre of the area.	N.P. Act A.O.N.B.	SU 718 147 2309 63

Group B — Archaeological

Stone Age

Axe	Neolithic flint axe found. Exact location unknown. Also tanged and barbed white flint arrowhead of bronze age date found at same location. O.S.A. No. SU61 SE3. Ref: Archaeological Journal, No. 20, 1863, p.p. 371—2.		SU 690 140 2309 30

Bronze Age

Disc Barrow (Probable)	Close to London Road. Originally a low mound with shallow ditch, but no trace remains. Excavation revealed a crouched female burial. No grave goods found. O.S.A. No. SU71 NW17. Ref: Field Archaeology as Illustrated in Hampshire, 1915, (Williams-Freeman), p.p. 276—7.	N.P. Act A.O.N.B.	SU 707 154 2309 26

Iron Age/Roman

Occupation Site	Site of farm occupied from C.1—C.3/4. Late Belgic and Roman finds of potsherds, querns and loomweights now in Portsmouth City Museum. O.S.A. No. SU61 SE4. Ref: P.H.F.C., Vol. 22, 1961, (Cunliffe), p.p. 25—29.		SU 696 125 2309 25
Cemetery	Three late Iron Age, six Romano-British and thirty-three Anglo Saxon burials found in 1947 during roadworks. Iron Age burials at a depth of 8 ins. with some pottery sherds. Romano-British graves contained hob nails, a bone comb and C.4 coins. Anglo Saxon graves with iron knives, buckles, beads and pottery. Finds in Cumberland House Museum, Southsea. O.S.A. No. SU71 NW18. Ref: Roman Britain and the English Settlements, 1936, (Myres), p. 399.		SU 707 153 2309 27

Description and Date	Remarks	Protection	Grid Ref. and Punchcard No.
Group B – (cont.)			
Roman			
Coin	Coin of Diocletian found in a garden. Exact location unknown. Struck at Treves, but probably gilded later. O.S.A. No. SU61 SE2.		SU 690 140 2309 29
Building (Site)	Romano-British coarse ware fragments found. Two pieces of Romano-British flat roof tile found in early mediaeval pit, which also contained pottery, a Saxon bone implement, and a C.14 bronze buckle. O.S.A. No. SU61 SE10. Ref: 1. P.H.F.C., 1971, (Pile and Barton), p.p. 49–56. 2. Mediaeval Archaeology, Vol. 16, 1972, (Cunliffe), p.p. 4–12.		SU 695 145 2309 48
Coin and Pottery	Radiate coin and pottery including rims and colour coated ware found 100 yds. east of the Bat and Ball Inn. O.S.A. No. SU61 NE22.	N.P. Act A.O.N.B.	SU 677 166 2309 47
Pottery	Forty-one sherds of Romano-British coarse ware found in the filling of a V-shaped ditch. Exposed during excavation work 1962. O.S.A. No. SU61 NE2.	N.P. Act A.O.N.B.	SU 689 159 2309 28
Building (Possible Site)	Plaster and sherds found in 1961. Rotary quern fragment also found. O.S.A. No. SU71 SW8.	N.P. Act A.O.N.B.	SU 725 142 2309 31
Villa (Site)	North of Blendworth. A dense concentration of Roman brick and flanged tile. O.S.A. No. SU71 SW10.		SU 716 140 2309 32
Post Norman			
Strip Lynchets	Series of cultivation terraces on the east side of Catherington Down. Some well preserved and standing to a height of 4.0 m. Average strip width 45.0–50.0 m. Centred on grid reference. O.S.A. No. SU61 SE1.	C.O.S.	SU 690 142 2309 24
Deserted Mediaeval Village (Site)	Blendworth. Hundred = Finchdean. O.S.A. No. SU71 SW26. Ref: 1. V.C.H., Vol. 3, p.p. 82–84, Vol. I, p. 478. 2. Deserted Mediaeval Villages (Bereford and Hurst). 3. Buildings of England; Hants and I.O.W., (Pevsner and Lloyd), p. 111.		SU 712 136 2309 46

Description and Date	Remarks	Protection	Grid Ref. and Punchcard No.
	Group D — Buildings, Monuments and Engineering Works		
Church C.12	Church of All Saints, Catherington. Mainly dates from late C.12. Southwest tower with small Norman windows on ground and first floors, and plain C.18 battlemented top. C.14 style wall painting of St. Michael weighing souls. Fine monument to Sir Nicholas Hyde and his Lady, 1631. Building restored in 1883. O.S.A. No. SU61 SE8. Ref: Buildings of England; Hants and I.O.W., (Pevsner and Lloyd), p. 158.	T. & C.P. Act	SU 696 145 2309 01
Cottages (2) C.16	Nos. 116 and 117, Blendworth. 2 storeys. Timber-framed with whitewashed brick filling. Tiled roof, once thatched. One flat and two hipped tiled dormers. Casement windows. One hipped tiled porch.		SU 715 136 2309 14
Cottages (2) C.16/17	Nos. 107 and 108, Blendworth. 2 storeys. Timber-framed with brick nogging. South side with external chimney tile hung. Hipped thatched roof. Casement windows with glazing bars.		SU 717 135 2309 12
Cottage C.16/17	No. 109, Blendworth. 1½ storeys. Half-timbered with flint and brick. Brick dressings. Thatched roof with barn end. Central chimney. Casement windows.		SU 717 135 2309 13
Inn C.17	Bird in Hand, Lovedean. 2 storeys. White painted walls. Hipped tiled roof. Casement windows. Two open sided porches with tiled roofs. Single storey extension at rear, with tiled roof.		SU 683 133 2309 33
House C.17	Hinton Manor. 3 storeys. Flint with quoins of thin bricks. Centre part flanked by gabled wings. Tiled roof. Mullion windows in gables blocked with bricks and plastered over. Remnants of brick dripstones. Later addition to northeast Victorian bay windows on south side of ground floor.		SU 689 153 2309 09
Cottages (2) C.17	Tudor Cottages, Catherington. Timber-framed with overhanging upper storey. Brick infilling mainly of herringbone pattern. Central chimney. Thatched roof. Casement windows with glazing bars. Timber-framing visible inside. Well uncovered July 1975, water at a depth of nearly 300 ft.	T. & C.P. Act	SU 694 144 2309 06
Cottages (2) C.17	The Walnuts, Nos. 224—226, Lovedean Lane. Timber-framed with whitewashed brick infilling. Thatched roof with central chimney. Casement windows with glazing bars. Later extensions to side and rear.		SU 684 130 2309 21

Description and Date	Remarks	Protection	Grid Ref. and Punchcard No.
Group D — (cont.)			
Inn C.18	Bat and Ball, Hambledon. C.18 with more recent additions. Brick with tile hung upper storey. Tiled roof with projecting chimney to north. Brick porch. Casement windows.	T. & C.P. Act N.P. Act A.O.N.B.	SU 676 166 2309 02
House C.18	Catherington Retreat House. Western part 3 storeys of brick with grey headers and red brick dressings. Cornice and parapet, sash windows. Classical doorway with columns. Eastern part of 2 storeys, brick with dentilled cornice and pediment. Tiled roof. Single storey addition, and service quarters of later date. Regency verandah on garden front. Detached single storey room used as chapel.	T. & C.P. Act	SU 694 140 2309 05
Farmhouse C.18	Lovedean Farm. 2 storeys. Flint and brick structure. Double hipped tiled roof. West front with sash windows and door with flat hood. South side with casement windows.		SU 684 131 2309 22
Farmhouse C.18	Pyle Farm, Blendworth. Banded grey brick with red brick dressings. Brick dentilled cornice. 2 storeys. Tiled roof with coping on gable ends. Sash windows. Lower 2-storey wing to east.	T. & C.P. Act	SU 713 124 2309 04
Inn C.18	The Red Lion, London Road. Building of two different dates. South end of flint with flat band between 2 storeys. Two gabled dormers and casement windows. North end built a little later, of brick with sash windows. Whole building colourwashed with tiled roof.	C.A.	SU 706 131 2309 19
Inn C.18	The Ship and Bell, London Road. 2 storeys and attics. Creamwashed, plaster faced front. Tiled roof with five hipped tiled dormers. Upper storey windows sash with bay at south end. Victorian addition at rear.	C.A.	SU 706 132 2309 20
Cottage C.19	Catherington Cottage. 2 storeys and attics. Colourwashed brick with brick dentil cornice. Tiled roof with two gabled tile hung dormers. Sash windows, those on ground floor with louvred shutters. Brick porch with gabled roof. Single storey extension. A sealed well is located under sitting room floor.		SU 694 142 2309 16
Farmhouse C.19	Five Heads Farm. 2 storeys. Plaster-faced structure. Tiled roof. Sash windows with glazing bars and sliding slatted shutters. Two gables at north end with bargeboards.		SU 700 135 2309 18
Building C.19	Hinton Daubnay, Lovedean. Rebuilt 1868. 2 storeys. Flint and brick structure. Plain sash windows, and two massive ground floor windows. Low pitched slate roof. Former house of the Hyde family. Originally a crown grant to the Daubnay family from Henry III. Ref: Buildings of England; Hants and I.O.W., (Pevsner and Lloyd), p. 160.		SU 680 140 2309 40

Group D — (cont.)

Description and Date	Remarks	Protection	Grid Ref. and Punchcard No.
Church C.19	Holy Trinity, Blendworth. Built 1851—2 by Habershon. Prominent spire with sharp gables where it rises from the tower. Ref: Buildings of England; Hants and I.O.W., (Pevsner and Lloyd), p. 111.		SU 711 135 2309 49
Cottage C.19	Hook Cottage, Blendworth. 2 storeys. Flint with brick dressings. Yellow brick centre portion and porch. Slate roof gabled over porch with hexagonal finial and fox weathervane. South windows with C.18 glazing. Western extension in character with original part.		SU 714 129 2309 15
Farmhouse C.19	Packhurst Farm. 2 storeys. Plaster faced flint structure. Low pitched slate roof. Sash windows. Door with semi-circular head.	N.P. Act A.O.N.B.	SU 694 172 2309 11
Cottage	No. 203, Lovedean Lane, Lovedean. 2 storeys. Hipped slate roof. Flint structure with brick quoins and window dressings. Casement windows. Porch of flint and brick. Central window over porch blocked.		SU 684 128 2309 34
Granary	Parsonage Farm, Catherington Lane. Brick built structure on substantial oak beams resting on staddle stones 3ft. high. Approximately 18ft. by 10ft. Hipped roof covered with plain clay tiles. One door in long wall and two small shuttered windows in the shorter walls.		SU 693 139 2309 66
Brewery	Gales Brewery. Last independent brewery in the county. Gales family started brewing in C.17. An early boiler house and hop store survive, but most of buildings built 1869. Brick brewhouse tower and chimney. Well with two steam engines once used for pumping water. Modern bottling plant. Ref: 1. A Gazetteer of Hampshire Breweries (Tighe). 2. Buildings of England; Hants and I.O.W., (Pevsner and Lloyd), p. 297.	C.A..	SU 706 132 2309 51

Group E — Street Patterns, Street Furniture and Open Spaces

Description and Date	Remarks	Protection	Grid Ref. and Punchcard No.
Open Space	Catheringdon Down. 31 acres of downland east of the Lovedean-Clanfield Road. Managed by the Hants and I.O.W. Naturalists Trust to preserve the downland habitat. Fine views over surrounding countryside. Crossed by footpaths.	N.P. Act C.O.S.	SU 690 143 2309 23

Group F — Historical or Literary Associations

Description and Date	Remarks	Protection	Grid Ref. and Punchcard No.
Church (Site)	St. Giles, Blendworth. Demolished in recent times. Churchyard has been made into an attractive garden. Yew tree and gravestones remain.		SU 716 135 2309 08

19th Century Brewery Building, HORNDEAN

Description and Date	Remarks	Protection	Grid Ref. and Punchcard No.

Group F. — (cont.)

Description and Date	Remarks	Protection	Grid Ref. and Punchcard No.
Treadwheel (Site)	Kinches Farm, Catherington. A donkey or treadwell. Built circa. 1600 to serve a well 300ft. in depth. Removed from site in 1970 and re-erected in the Weald and Downland Museum, Singleton, Chichester.		SU 693 140 2309 39
House C.17	Hinton Manor. Parts are reputed to date back to 1296. Charles II sheltered here during his flight to France. Also it is said to be where James II secretly married Anne Hyde, daughter of the Earl of Clarendon.		SU 689 153 2309 09
Inn C.18	The Bat and Ball. Hambledon. Associated with early cricket and formerly called 'Broadhalfpenny Hut'. Hambledon Cricket Club played on Broadhalfpenny Down in the C.18. The inn sign shows an early cricket match and a portrait of John Nyren of Hambledon, 1764—1837.	T. & C.P. Act N.P. Act A.O.N.B.	SU 676 166 2309 02
House C.18	Catherington Retreat House. The country house of Admiral Hood, Master of H.M. Dockyard and friend of Nelson. Originally called Catherington House. Nelson danced here. Queen Caroline lived here before her trial in 1820.	T. & C.P. Act	SU 694 140 2309 05

KINGSLEY

Five miles south-east of Alton, the village was once a clearing between the forests of Alice Holt to the north and Woolmer to the south. The present church dates from 1875, but not far away is the old church largely rebuilt in 1778 which contains an 800 year old tub font, a fifteenth century parish chest and a thirteenth century window. Mediaeval kings maintained a hunting lodge at Lode Farm.

Description and Date	Remarks	Protection	Grid Ref. and Punchcard No.
Group A — Natural Features			
Geological Feature	South of the village on the parish boundary. Erosion and deposition with wide flood plain.		SU 787 376 1611 45
Geological Feature	Sand pit, Kingsley Common. One of a number in the parish where sand is extracted mainly for use in the building industry.		SU 791 382 1611 38
Trees	Ockham Hall. Several different species standing in an area southwest of Kingsley Pond. Centred on grid reference.	T.P.O. No. 35 E.H.D.	SU 788 380 1611 50
Area of Ecological Importance	Shortheath Common. The most northern part of this area comes into the parish. An area of acid grassland, bracken and heather. The common centres on a substantial valley bog of outstanding structural and biological interest. The site as a whole embraces a wide range of acid habitats.	N.P. Act S.S.S.I.	SU 778 371 1611 51
Group B — Archaeological			
Stone Age			
Mesolithic Flint-Working Site	Kingsley Common. Finds include microliths, and indicate flint working over a large area. Typical artifacts displayed and stored in Alton Museum. O.S.A. No. SU73 NE14. Ref: P.H.F.C., Vol. 18, 1951—3, p. 169.		SU 795 380 1611 06
Mesolithic Implement	Tranchet axe found in field south of Bakers Farm.		SU 780 375 1611 47
Mesolithic Implement	Tranchet axe found in Potters Field, Malthouse Lane. Now in Alton Museum. O.S.A. No. SU73 NE15. Ref: P.H.F.C., Vol. 18, 1951—3, p. 169.		SU 797 387 1611 07
Mesolithic Flint-Working Site	Fir Hill. Finds include a tranchet axe, sub-triangular microliths and other flints. Large chipping floor obliterated by vehicle training. O.S.A. No. SU73 NE16. Ref: P.H.F.C., Vol. 18, 1951—3, p. 169.		SU 790 377 1611 08
Iron Age/Roman			
Occupation Site	Woodfield. Pottery, fragments of quern, fragments of burnt earth and Iron Age potsherds found during building work. Finds stored in Alton Museum. O.S.A. No. SU73 NE5.		SU 788 383 1611 03

Description and Date	Remarks	Protection	Grid Ref. and Punchcard No.

Group B — (cont.)

Roman

Description and Date	Remarks	Protection	Grid Ref. and Punchcard No.
Pottery Kiln	Malthouse Farm. Large quantity of C.3/4 pottery found, including jars, flagon necks and handles. Finds in Godalming and Alton Museums. O.S.A. No. SU73 NE20. Ref: Survey of the Prehistory of Farnham District, (Lowther), p.p. 224–249.		SU 797 387 1611 10
Building (Possible Site of)	West of Bakers Farm. Pottery and fragments of brick and tile found in face of sandpit. Stored in Alton Museum. O.S.A. No. SU73 NE21. Ref: Hampshire Observer, 26.8.39, p. 11.		SU 778 377 1611 11
Coin	Sickles House. C.3 coin found in the garden. O.S.A. No. SU73 NE26. Ref: Alton Museum: Accession Diary.		SU 790 384 1611 12

Group D — Buildings, Monuments and Engineering Works

Description and Date	Remarks	Protection	Grid Ref. and Punchcard No.
Church C.14	St. Nicholas. Mainly rebuilt 1778 but retaining C.14 east wall and window. Brick structure with plaster vaulted barrel ceiling. Contains mortuary crib, church warden's chest and leper door. On supposed site of ancient chapel of King John. O.S.A. No. SU73 NE9. Ref: 1. V.C.H., Vol. 2, p. 516. 2. Buildings of England; Hants and I.O.W., (Pevsner & Lloyd), p. 311.	T. & C.P. Act	SU 778 378 1611 05
Mill C.17/18	Kingsley Mill. 2 storeys. Walls of coursed stone blocks. Tiled roof brought down as part pentice to rear. Now a dwelling house but part of mill mechanism in situ. Damaged by fire October 1976.		SU 784 376 1611 19
Farmhouse C.18	Lode Farm. Part Tudor. 2 storeys. Brick on ground floor, tilehung above. Half-hipped ridge tiled roof. Older wing projects to rear. On supposed site of mediaeval hunting lodge. O.S.A. No. SU73 NE8. Ref: V.C.H., Vol. 2, p. 514.		SU 776 377 1611 04
Cottages (2) C.18	Bakers Corner Cottages. Red brick walls. Ridge tiled roof. Tilehung gable to right with coursed stonework on ground floor. Plain wooden casements.		SU 779 377 1611 13
Farmhouse C.18	Malthouse Farm. 2 storeys. Red brick with some blue headers. Half-hipped ridge tiled roof. Centre glazed porch.		SU 799 385 1611 49
House C.18	Westakirk. 2 storeys. Red brick with blue headers. Half-hipped ridge tiled roof. Centre columned porch. Single storey coach house projection.		SU 786 381 1611 15

Description and Date	Remarks	Protection	Grid Ref. and Punchcard No.

Group D — (cont.)

Description and Date	Remarks	Grid Ref. and Punchcard No.
Inn C.18	The Cricketers. 2 storeys. Front elevation covered with grey cement roughcast in C.19. Ridge tiled roof. Columned porch. Scolds bridle found in chimney during renovations.	SU 787 381 1611 16
Farmhouse C.18	Old Park Farm. 2 storeys. Colourwashed brick. Old ridge tiled roof. Casement windows. Wattle and daub wall. Exposed interior beams. Modern additions.	SU 792 385 1611 17
House C.18/19	Cold Harbour. Built circa 1800. 2 storeys, slate and tile hung walls. Bay windows. Slate and tiled roof. Six chimneys. Verandah.	SU 797 383 1611 34
Church C.19	All Saints. Built by the Dutton family in 1876. Nave, chancel and bellcote. Exterior, chalk with crazy paving pattern. Interior has red brickwork exposed, with yellow brick patterns. Ref: Buildings of England; Hants and I.O.W., (Pevsner and Lloyd), p. 311.	SU 788 382 1611 01
House C.19	Foundry House. Limewashed brick structure. 2-storey gabled porch with ornamental barge boards. Sash windows.	SU 791 384 1611 18
Building C.19	Kingsley School and School House. Built 1851. School house, 2 storeys, brick walls, cement covered and pebble dashed. Slate roof. School consists of old and new buildings.	SU 787 383 1611 26
House	Grooms Farm, Frith End. 3 storeys. Brick, roughcast walls. Tiled roof. Three chimneys.	SU 810 392 1611 48
House	Rose Cottage. 2 storeys. Brick, cement covered walls. Slate roof. Three chimneys. Formerly a chapel.	SU 788 379 1611 33
Farmhouse	Dean Farm. Georgian structure with two bricked-in windows. Large bread oven.	SU 784 381 1611 23
House	Frith End Cottage. Limewashed brick walls with exposed timberwork on upper floor. Ridge tiled roof.	SU 808 398 1611 20
Cottage	The Spindle. 2 storeys and basement. Two gabled dormers. Brick walls partly tile-hung. Tiled roof. Restored, retaining bread oven.	SU 786 381 1611 14
House	Meadowside Farm. Partly Tudor. 2 storeys. Brick walls. Tiled roof. Three chimneys.	SU 788 378 1611 22
Farm Building	Bakers Corner Farm. Stone walled and sandstone with slate roof.	SU 780 377 1611 42
Farmhouse	Sickles Farm. Part Tudor. 2 storeys. Brick, cement covered walls. Tiled roof.	SU 790 384 1611 21
Farmhouse	Rookery Farm. Part Tudor. 2 storeys. Brick walls, tiled roof. Five chimneys.	SU 774 371 1611 24

Group D — (cont.)

Description and Date	Remarks	Protection	Grid Ref. and Punchcard No.
House	Ockham House. 2 storeys. Brick, cement covered walls. Tiled roof with ornamental ridging tiles. Clock tower. Formerly a school.		SU 788 381 1611 25
House	Spring Cottage. 2 storeys. Brick and stone walls. Slate roof. Three chimneys.		SU 778 384 1611 27
House	Foxes, Green Street. Old barn converted into dwelling. 2 storeys. Brick and stone walls. Tiled roof. Two chimneys.		SU 768 379 1611 28
House	Birch Cottage. 2 storeys. Brick, cement covered walls. Slate roof. Three chimneys. Formerly a chapel.		SU 788 378 1611 32
House	Old Rectory. 2 storeys. Brick construction with cement rendering. Tiled roof. Two pairs of brick chimneys. Glass porch. Formerly the vicarage.		SU 786 382 1611 30
House	Burningham Cottage. 3 storeys, two of which are in the roof. Lower half of walls brick with cement rendering, the upper half being tile-hung. Tiled roof. Formerly a Hop kiln.		SU 778 379 1611 29

Group E — Street Patterns, Street Furniture and Open Spaces

Description and Date	Remarks	Protection	Grid Ref. and Punchcard No.
Pound	Malthouse Barn. Brick-walled former village pound.		SU 799 385 1611 44

Group F — Historical or Literary Associations

Description and Date	Remarks	Protection	Grid Ref. and Punchcard No.
Farmhouse	Lode Farm. Includes remains of manor house and alleged site of mediaeval hunting lodge. Frequently visited by Henry VIII when Prince of Wales, and for this reason he was nick-named "Harry of Lode". O.S.A. No. SU73 NE8. Ref: V.C.H., Vol. 2, p. 514.		SU 776 377 1611 04

LANGRISH

The parish of Langrish was formed in 1894 and included the tithings of Bordean, Langrish, Ramsdean and part of Stroud Common, all these having been in the parish of East Meon. In 1932 part of the civil parish was transferred to Petersfield urban district.

Langrish was a sub-manor dependent upon the manor of East Meon, and was held by John Langrish in 1419. The property continued in the Langrish family until the seventeenth century when it was sold to the Long family. In 1719 the manor was sold to Thomas Ridge of Portsmouth but his son Thomas was declared bankrupt in 1764 and the estate was auctioned to William Joliffe of Petersfield in 1771.

The tithing of Bordean occupies high ground in the parish and contained lime-works for many years; in 1649 William Musgrave was fined sixpence for offending his neighbours by emptying his lime-pits and throwing his skins into the water. The village of Ramsdean once had a pond but this was filled in in the early 1930s, the place is now known as Ramsdean Green but the pond is commemorated by the nearby Pond Cottages.

The relatively low-lying land of Stroud Common yielded clay for making bricks, tiles and pipes. In 1571 John Robynnet obtained a licence to dig clay on some waste land for the purposes of making bricks and tiles, and the industry continued into the present century.

Description and Date	Remarks	Protection	Grid Ref. and Punchcard No.
Group A — Natural Features			
Area of Scenic Beauty	The entire parish is included in the East Hampshire A.O.N.B. Butser Hill and Ramsdean Down in the south are part of a County Open Space. Dairy farming predominates although formerly hops and corn were grown. It is a regular resting place for swallows and warblers on migration, and supports many varieties of plant life. Centred on grid reference.	N.P. Act A.O.N.B. C.O.S.	SU 710 230 2310 26
Area of Ecological Interest	Butser Hill. Part of the 505 acre site falls within the parish. It is an area of chalk grassland with yew woods in southwest facing combes. Scientific recordings have been made since the 1930s. It commands fine views to Petersfield and Portsmouth. The area is also part of the Queen Elizabeth Country Park. Including information centre and ancient farms project. Centred on grid reference.	N.P. Act S.S.S.I. A.O.N.B. C.O.S.	SU 713 206 2310 30
Geological Features	A narrow fold of Green Sandstone runs from northeast of the parish to Barrow Hill, and then turns east. West of the fold are chalk downs. V.C.H. locates a lime-kiln at Bordean. Gault or blue clay lies east of the fold, and was dug for brick making. The southern tip of the parish reverts to chalk downlands. Centred on grid reference.	N.P. Act A.O.N.B.	SU 710 230 2310 26
Grounds	Langrish House. A fine collection of specimen trees including cedar and coniferous varieties A flint wall on the road boundary is surmounted by a beech and yew hedge. Behind the house is Wool Pond, formerly two ponds connected by a sluice controlling the flow of water.	N.P. Act A.O.N.B.	SU 701 231 2310 11
Group B — Archaeological			
Stone Age			
Axe	Polished flint axe of Neolithic date found on surface of Butser Hill in 1967. O.S.A. No. SU72 SW17. Ref: Portsmouth City Museum Card Index.	N.P. Act A.O.N.B. C.O.S.	SU 715 203 2310 20
Mesolithic Finds	Microliths, axes and sharpening flakes found in fields close to Wireless Station on Butser Hill. Neolithic implement also found. Some finds in Portsmouth City Museum. O.S.A. No. SU72 SW20.	N.P. Act S.S.S.I. A.O.N.B. C.O.S.	SU 715 203 2310 19
Bronze Age			
Bowl Barrow	Butser Hill. Mutilated by O.S. pillar and water tank. Subject to annual ploughing. Within curtilage of S.A.M. O.S.A. No. SU72 SW6.	S.A.M. No. 15 N.P. Act A.O.N.B. C.O.S.	SU 716 203 2310 15

Description and Date	Remarks	Protection	Grid Ref. and Punchcard No.

Group B — (cont.)

Description and Date	Remarks	Protection	Grid Ref. and Punchcard No.
Bell Barrow	Bordean crossroads. Tall barrow surmounted by bushes.	N.P. Act A.O.N.B.	SU 691 247 2310 23
Bowl Barrows (3)	North side of Ramsdean Down. All have large central excavation hollows and no trace of ditches. O.S.A. No. SU72 SW2.	S.A.M. No. 137 N.P. Act S.S.S.I. A.O.N.B. C.O.S.	SU 713 208 2310 14
Bowl Barrows (3)	Close to Lower Bordean Farm. In a Saxon charter Bordean is called "Barrow Dean". Two barrows are under pasture, the third affected by roadworks is otherwise in good condition. O.S.A. No. SU62 SE4.	N.P. Act A.O.N.B.	SU 693 247 2310 21
Bowl Barrow	South of Barrowhill Copse. Low mound in poor condition approximately 38 m. across. Under pasture. O.S.A. No. SU72 SW14.	N.P. Act A.O.N.B.	SU 700 223 2310 18
Bowl Barrow (Probable)	North of Bordean House. Mound 19 m. x 1 m. overgrown by trees. O.S.A. No. SU62 SE5. Ref: P.H.F.C., Vol. 14, 1938–40, (Grinsell), p. 355.	N.P. Act A.O.N.B.	SU 698 245 2310 22
Barrows (2)	Bell barrow 27 m. in diameter close to Butser Hill wireless station. Faint traces of ditch. Site of bowl barrow to south. O.S.A. No. SU72 SW9. Ref: P.H.F.C., Vol. 14, 1940, p. 210.	S.A.M. No. 15 N.P. Act A.O.N.B. C.O.S.	SU 714 202 2310 17

Period Unknown

Description and Date	Remarks	Protection	Grid Ref. and Punchcard No.
Earthworks	On summit of Butser Hill. A large area with several sites which are recorded separately. Partly scrub covered.	S.A.M. No. 15 N.P. Act A.O.N.B. C.O.S.	SU 711 201 2310 27
Entrenchment	Two parallel bank and ditch earthworks on a spur of Butser Hill. Each spur dyke is a single bank with uphill ditch. At southwest end both earthworks rest on an old terraceway. O.S.A. No. SU72 SW7. Ref: Aspects of Archaeology, 1951, Cross Ridge Dykes in Sussex. (Curwen), p.p. 93–107.	S.A.M. No. 15 N.P. Act S.S.S.I. A.O.N.B. C.O.S.	SU 711 203 2310 16
Entrenchment	Part of the Froxfield Entrenchments, close to Bordean House. Defensive works possibly of Dark Age date, with a rampart and ditch on the west side. Stretch along Bordean Lane may only be terracing. Centred on grid reference. O.S.A. No. SU72 NW4. Ref: Field Archaeology as Illustrated by Hampshire, 1915, (Williams-Freeman), p.p. 33, 286–92, 374–6.	S.A.M. No. 33 N.P. Act A.O.N.B.	SU 700 246 2310 28

Description and Date	Remarks	Protection	Grid Ref. and Punchcard No.

Group D — Buildings Monuments and Engineering Works

Description and Date	Remarks	Protection	Grid Ref. and Punchcard No.
Dovecote C.16	Manor Farm. Square plan of malmstone rubble with Tudor brick dressings. Weather boarded central lantern with pyramidal tiled roof. Nesting holes in inner skin of double walls. Converted from dovecote to hop store in C.18 with insertion of floor and Gothic windows. Recently renovated.	T. & C.P. Act S.A.M. No. 470 N.P. Act A.O.N.B.	SU 710 240 2310 25
House C.17	Bordean House. Mansion of 2 storeys and attics built in 1611. Malmstone with brick quoins, plinth and dressings. Slate roof with early dormer windows. Sash windows with glazing bars. Later additions.	N.P. Act A.O.N.B.	SU 698 244 2310 06
Cottage C.17	Underwood Cottage. Timber-framed with brick and plaster filling. Upstairs casement windows cut into the thatched roof. Gable at south end with bedroom window.	T. & C.P. Act N.P. Act A.O.N.B.	SU 702 238 2310 01
Farmhouse C.17/18	Upper House Farm. 2 storeys. Malmstone with a brick plinth, quoins and dressings. Tiled roof hipped at south gable end. Porch. Casement windows with a modern bay.	T. & C.P. Act N.P. Act A.O.N.B.	SU 705 223 2310 03
House C.18	The White House, Langrish Hill, 2 storeys. Plaster faced. Double hipped slate roof. Sash windows with glazing bars. Regency porch. Front flanked by walls curving up to level of first floor window cill.	N.P. Act A.O.N.B.	SU 709 239 2310 07
Farmhouse C.18	Pitts Farm. 2 storeys of brick with purple headers. East side of malmstone with brick dressings. Tiled roof hipped at east end. Casement windows. Modern porch.	T. & C.P. Act N.P. Act A.O.N.B.	SU 704 236 2310 02
Farmhouse C.18	Church Farm. Malmstone with brick dressings. Thatched roof. Two eaves windows cut into thatch. Lean-to at west end.	N.P. Act A.O.N.B.	SU 703 236 2310 08
House C.18	Home Farm. 2 storeys. Malmstone with malmstone quoins and brick dressings to windows. Casement windows with cambered arches. Tiled roof. Wing to south west.	N.P. Act A.O.N.B.	SU 701 233 2310 04
Farmhouse C.18	Lower Bordean Farm. 2 storeys. Brick with plaster faced front. West side of original brick with flat band. Brick cornice. Hipped tiled roof. Casement windows. Interior with some panelling and original fireplace.	N.P. Act A.O.N.B.	SU 693 246 2310 05
Farmhouse C.18	Homelands Farm, Ramsdean. Possibly of earlier date. Stone with brick dressings and brick band between storeys. West side plaster faced. Hipped tiled roof. North wall of white-washed flint. South wing of a later date.	N.P. Act A.O.N.B.	SU 705 223 2310 09

Description and Date	Remarks	Protection	Grid Ref. and Punchcard No.

Group D — (cont.)

Description and Date	Remarks	Protection	Grid Ref. and Punchcard No.
House	Langrish House. Built of Malmstone blocks. Formerly a farmhouse, but wings added in 1842 when the property changed hands. Fine oak floors. Large cellar traditionally made by Royalist prisoners in 1642, during the Civil War.	N.P. Act A.O.N.B.	SU 701 231 2310 11

Group F — Historical or Literary Associations

Description and Date	Remarks	Protection	Grid Ref. and Punchcard No.
Natural Spring	The large spring of water behind Ramsdean End is traditionally thought to have been a holy well. It was known until recently as God's Pool.	N.P. Act A.O.N.B.	SU 705 219 2310 29

LASHAM

Situated four miles to the north west of Alton, just off the Alton to Basingstoke road, Lasham was once famous as a wartime airfield and is now a well-known gliding centre. The village was once served by the Basingstoke and Alton Light Railway which ran from 1901—1932. Modern development has brought new life to the area, but the centre of the village still retains much of its original character.

17th Century Timber-Framed Thatched Cottage, LASHAM

Description and Date	Remarks	Protection	Grid Ref. and Punchcard No.

Group A — Natural Features

Description and Date	Remarks	Protection	Grid Ref. and Punchcard No.
View	East of the village. Attractive views across open farmland through to Selbourne Hanger.	C.A.	SU 677 425 1612 12
Village Pond	Located almost opposite St. Mary's Church and bounded by road on one side. Surrounded by trees and reeds. Contains fish and wildlife. Typical example of English village pond.	C.A.	SU 675 424 1612 16

Group B — Archaeological

Bronze Age

Description and Date	Remarks	Protection	Grid Ref. and Punchcard No.
Inhumed Cremation and Urn	Parallel to A339 on western boundary of parish. Tripartite cinerary urn, inverted over cremation, found 1955. On view in Alton Museum. O.S.A. No. SU64 SE8.		SU 663 421 1612 13

Period Unknown

Description and Date	Remarks	Protection	Grid Ref. and Punchcard No.
Inhumation Burials	Located on north face of old chalkpit on Lasham Hill. Rough grave containing two skeletons, possibly of the Civil War period. Stored at Basingstoke Museum. O.S.A. No. SU64 SE3.		SU 659 429 1612 14

Group D — Buildings, Monuments and Engineering Works

Description and Date	Remarks	Protection	Grid Ref. and Punchcard No.
Cottage C.17	Pepper Box Cottage. Exposed timber-framing with brick infilling. Thatched roof, brought down as pentice to right and left. Brick and thatched extension to rear.	C.A.	SU 676 425 1612 07
Farmhouse C.17/18	Manor Farm. L-shaped. 2-storey brick structure. Gabled wing to rear, tile-hung on first floor. Stepped ridge tiled roof. Core probably C.17. Timber-framed.		SU 674 426 1612 05
Granary C.18	Manor Farm. Small square weatherboard building on staddle stones. Thatched roof.		SU 674 427 1612 06
House C.18	Lasham House. 2 storeys. Red brick, plinth and band. High pitched slate mansard roof. Sash windows. 2-storey wing to left with sash windows and ridge slate roof.	T. & C.P. Act C.A.	SU 675 423 1612 08
Barn C.18	Church Farm. Old timber-frame with weather-boarding on red brick base. Central entrance. Hipped tiled roof. Forms part of an interesting group around stockyard.	C.A.	SU 676 425 1612 11
Cottage C.18/19	Post Office. Red brick exterior wall probably masking earlier timber-framed structure. Thatched roof, brought down as pentice to right. Boarded door.	C.A.	SU 675 424 1612 04

Description and Date	Remarks	Protection	Grid Ref. and Punchcard No.

Group D — (cont.)

Description and Date	Remarks	Protection	Grid Ref. and Punchcard No.
Cottages (2) C.18/19	The Barracks. Red brick exterior walls possibly mask earlier timber-framed structure. Thatched roof. Ground floor has three square paned casement windows with old lattice glazing.		SU 673 424 1612 01
Cottages (2) C.18/19	Badgers Cottage. Walls of red brick in panels. Five brick pilasters, plinth and band. Thatched roof. Plain wood casement windows.		SU 673 424 1612 02
Church C.19	St. Mary's. Erected 1868 on site of earlier church. Coursed square flint structure. Nave and lower chancel. Tall east window. Bell turret with shingled broach-spire. Slab dated 1698 in floor of nave. Register dates from 1560. O.S.A. No. SU64 SE7. Ref: 1. V.C.H., Vol. 4, p. 83. 2. Buildings of England; Hants and I.O.W., (Pevsner & Lloyd), p. 315.		SU 676 425 1612 09
Farmhouse C.19	Church Farm. L-shaped. 2 storeys. Red brick structure. Tiled roof, originally thatched. Surrounded by farm buildings.	C.A.	SU 676 425 1612 10
Traction Engine Shed C.19	Adjacent Pepper Box Cottage. Red brick structure. Hipped tiled roof. High double doors each end. Three windows. Ash pit in floor.	C.A.	SU 676 425 1612 15
Cottages (2)	Malt Cottages. Standing at right angles to road. Thatched with tiled roof addition to rear. Thatched eaves square cut around upper windows. Square paned metal casement windows.	C.A.	SU 674 424 1612 03

LISS

In 1086, at the time of the Domesday Survey, the manor of Liss probably formed part of the original endowment of the abbey of St. Mary at Winchester. The manor was later known as Liss Abbess, and the Abbess and nuns of Winchester kept the land until the dissolution of the monasteries in 1538. Liss remained crown property until about 1610, and was subsequently held by the Cole, Fitzpatrick, Taylor and Hawkshaw families.

The Church of St. Mary is late Victorian, while the Church of St. Peter at West Liss is largely thirteenth century with only a few later additions.

Liss was primarily an agricultural village but became famous locally during the nineteenth century for the production of peppermint. The mint was grown, distilled and sold at fourpence a pint by the Money family.

A local Liss tradition concerns the ceremony of beating the bounds of the parish. A small boy was traditionally put in the oven of the Flying Bull Inn as the parish boundary was believed to pass through the kitchen of the inn.

Description and Date	Remarks	Protection	Grid Ref. and Punchcard No.
Group A — Natural Features			
Scenic Beauty	The entire parish is within the East Hampshire Area of Outstanding Natural Beauty. Centred on grid reference.	N.P. Act A.O.N.B.	SU 781 274 2311 40
Tree	An oak tree on a small green near Plestor House, West Liss. Known locally as Stocks or Tara Oak from associations with local justice and the annual fair.	C.A. N.P. Act A.O.N.B.	SU 771 284 2311 39
Trees	Warren Hill, Warren Road. Various groups of trees. Centred on grid reference.	T.P.O. No. 297 N.P. Act A.O.N.B.	SU 785 292 2311 33
Trees	Forest Lodge, Liss Forest. Centred on grid reference.	T.P.O. No. 661 N.P. Act A.O.N.B.	SU 783 289 2311 36
Trees	Highfield House, Hatch Lane, and the south-west boundary of O.S. parcel of land 279.	T.P.O. No. 668 N.P. Act A.O.N.B.	SU 787 276 2311 37
Trees	Hatchlands, Huntsbottom Lane. Various species.	T.P.O. No. 701 N.P. Act A.O.N.B.	SU 785 275 2311 38
Trees	Stodham Park. Several trees of different species. Centred on grid reference.	T.P.O. No. 250 E.H.D. N.P. Act A.O.N.B.	SU 771 261 2311 41
Trees	East Hill Hotel, Hillbrow Road. Several trees of various species standing in the area centred on grid reference.	T.P.O. No. 33 E.H.D. A.O.N.B.	SU 782 273 2311 44
Tree	Old London, Rake Road. A single yew standing in the grounds of the above property.	T.P.O. No. 22 E.H.D. A.O.N.B.	SU 787 279 2311 45
Trees	Pidgeon Copse, Rake Common. Several trees of various species standing in the area centred on grid reference.	T.P.O. No. 62 E.H.D. A.O.N.B.	SU 783 268 2311 46
Group B — Archaeological			
Bronze Age			
Axe and Bracelets	Irish decorated axe and two bracelets engraved with parallel lines and chevrons. Finds now in British Museum. O.S.A. No. SU78 NE8.	N.P. Act A.O.N.B.	SU 776 278 2311 28
Arrowhead	Barbed and tanged flint arrowhead found in a garden at Liss Forest. Find in Winchester City Museum. O.S.A. No. SU72 NE1.	N.P. Act A.O.N.B.	SU 787 289 2311 29

Description and Date	Remarks	Protection	Grid Ref. and Punchcard No.

Group B — (cont.)

Description and Date	Remarks	Protection	Grid Ref. and Punchcard No.
Bowl Barrow	23.0 m. in diameter, and 2.0 m. high. Surrounded by tree ring of dry stone walling, and planted with fir trees. Traces of human and animal hair found in tree trunk coffin burial. O.S.A. No. SU82 NW4.	N.P. Act A.O.N.B.	SU 801 299 2311 23
Bowl Barrow (Probable)	Berry Grove. Located in the garden, 12 m. in diameter and 1.5 m. high. Has two large oaks growing on it. O.S.A. No. SU72 NE3.	N.P. Act A.O.N.B.	SU 769 286 2311 27

Period Unknown

Description and Date	Remarks	Protection	Grid Ref. and Punchcard No.
Implements	Flint spearheads, arrowheads, scrapers, flakes and cores found on surface. O.S.A. No. SU72 NE7.	N.P. Act A.O.N.B.	SU 787 277 2311 32
Earthwork	Farther Common. An almost circular enclosure on a slight northern slope. Enclosure contains trees. O.S.A. No. SU72 NE6.	S.A.M. No. 172 N.P. Act A.O.N.B.	SU 783 265 2311 22

Group C — Footpaths and Bridleways

Description and Date	Remarks	Protection	Grid Ref. and Punchcard No.
Old Travel Way	Course of Roman road in northeast corner of parish.	N.P. Act A.O.N.B.	SU 804 300 2311 24

Group D — Buildings, Monuments and Engineering Works

Description and Date	Remarks	Protection	Grid Ref. and Punchcard No.
Church C.13	St. Peter, West Liss. Chancel, parts of tower, and octagonal piers of arcade date from C.13. Octagonal font. Mullioned and transomed window in south aisle. Top stage of tower weatherboard with pyramid roof. O.S.A. No. SU72 NE4. Ref: Buildings of England; Hants and I.O.W., (Pevsner and Lloyd), p.p. 319—320.	T. & C.P. Act C.A. N.P. Act A.O.N.B.	SU 770 286 2311 01
Building C.14	Liss Place Farm, West Liss. Part dates from the C.14 with an addition of C.19 date. Remains of monastic manorhouse and fishponds. Reputed to have priest's escape tunnel to Wheatham Hill Farm. Malmstone with sandstone quoins and buttresses, patched with brick. Blocked mullion window. Tiled roof. C.18 sash windows. C.19 house of 2 storeys. Brick with double hipped slate roof. Porch of classical style with columns. O.S.A. No. SU72 NE5. Ref: 1. V.C.H., Vol. 4, p. 84. 2. All About Lyss, 1922, (Bashford).	T. & C.P. Act N.P. Act A.O.N.B.	SU 764 282 2311 05

Description and Date	Remarks	Protection	Grid Ref. and Punchcard No.

Group D — (cont.)

Description and Date	Remarks	Protection	Grid Ref. and Punchcard No.
Farmhouse C.15/16	Wheatham Farm. C.18 additions and alterations. 2 storeys. Malmrock with sandstone quoins, and partly roughcast plinth. Tiled roof. Two mullioned sandstone windows on east wall. Single storey wing to northeast. Recent brick porch with slate roof. Ref: Buildings of England; Hants and I.O.W., (Pevsner and Lloyd), p. 320.	T. & C.P. Act N.P. Act A.O.N.B.	SU 751 273 2311 04
Farmhouse C.16	Mangers Farm. Two cottages. Timber-framed with brick and ironstone infilling, some in herring-bone pattern. 2 storeys. Part of back galleted ironstone with brick dressings. Upper storey tile-hung. Tiled roof with central chimney.	N.P. Act A.O.N.B.	SU 795 287 2311 09
House C.16	Ciddy Hall. Back partly timber-framed with ironstone infilling. Rest of building ironstone with narrow brick dressings. C.16 date or later. Tiled roof with hipped dormers. Tile hung gable to west front restored. Ironstone and brick garden wall.	T. & C.P. Act N.P. Act A.O.N.B.	SU 790 281 2311 03
Building C.17	Barn Place, East Liss. Tiled roof. Gables with bargeboards. Partly timber-framed but altered in the C.19. Ground floor restored with modern windows.	N.P. Act A.O.N.B.	SU 786 277 2311 13
Farmhouse C.17	Brewells Farm. 2 storeys. Timber-framed with brick and rubble filling. C.18 extension to west of ironstone with north wall of roughcast. Double hipped tiled roof. New single-storey extension to east.	T. & C.P. Act N.P. Act A.O.N.B.	SU 802 287 2311 02
Cottage C.17	Knights Cottage, East Liss. 2 storeys. Timber-framed with whitewashed brick infilling. Single storey lean-to each end. Double hipped tiled roof. Casement windows. Gabled tiled porch.	N.P. Act A.O.N.B.	SU 787 279 2311 07
Farmhouse C.17	Pophole Farm. East Liss. 2 storeys. Timber-framed with some ironstone, and brick dressings. Tiled roof with central chimney. Small modern wings to north.	N.P. Act A.O.N.B.	SU 779 273 2311 15
Cottage C.17	Old London Gardens, formerly Yew Tree Cottage. Single storey. Tiled roof with three dormers at eaves. Rubble with brick dressings, partly plaster faced. Some timber work at rear.	N.P. Act A.O.N.B.	SU 787 279 2311 12
Cottages (3) C.17	Potwell Cottages, West Liss. 2 storeys. Colour-washed brick and ironstone. Central portion the oldest. Double hipped tiled roof with central chimney. Casement windows, sash windows to northern cottage.	N.P. Act A.O.N.B.	SU 772 282 2311 19
House C.18	Bishearne House, West Liss. 2 storeys. Brick. Tiled roof with wooden cornice on tiled brackets. Sash windows with glazing bars. Extensions to north and east. Later brick porch.	N.P. Act A.O.N.B.	SU 773 280 2311 17

Description and Date	Remarks	Protection	Grid Ref. and Punchcard No.
Group D — (cont.)			
Building C.18	Bluebell Inn, West Liss. 2 storeys. Brick with cement faced front. Double hipped tiled roof. Sash windows. Door with flat hood. Single storey extension to south.	N.P. Act A.O.N.B.	SU 772 282 2311 18
Cottages (4) C.18	Church Street Cottages, West Liss. 2 storeys. Brick with some ironstone. Tiled roof. No. 3 has 2-gabled dormers. No. 4 with bay windows.	C.A. N.P. Act A.O.N.B.	SU 771 286 2311 21
Building C.18	Clarks, Hunt Bottom Lane, East Liss. 2 storeys. Rubble with brick dressings, colourwashed. Double hipped slate roof. Upper storey tile hung. Sash windows, flat hood on brackets.	N.P. Act A.O.N.B.	SU 785 274 2311 14
Cottages (2) C.18	Little Brewells. 2 storeys. Galleted ironstone with brick dressings. Plinth with double course of brick. Double hipped tiled roof. Date over door 'G.T.A. 1770'. Casement windows, those on ground floor with cambered arches.	N.P. Act A.O.N.B.	SU 802 286 2311 08
House C.18	Plestor House, West Liss. 2 storeys. Colour-washed brick with brick dentil cornice. Tiled roof. Sash windows with glazing bars. Doorcase with reeded surround and flat hood. Wing to rear.	T. & C.P. Act C.A. N.P. Act A.O.N.B.	SU 771 284 2311 06
Building C.18	The Spread Eagle, West Liss. 2 storeys. L-shaped plan. Whitewashed brick structure. Southern part with slate roof and sash windows. Rest with rubble extensions, has tiled roof and casement windows.	C.A. N.P. Act A.O.N.B.	SU 771 284 2311 20
Building C.18	Upper Adhurst. 2 storeys. Brick with flat band between storeys. Tiled roof. Sash windows with glazing bars. Trellised wooden porch. Wing to southwest with casement windows.	N.P. Act A.O.N.B.	SU 773 252 2311 11
Building C.19	The Railway Hotel, East Liss. 2 storeys. Cement faced brick, with double hipped slate roof. Sash windows. Verandah, porch at front, stone porch to west. Single storey extension to rear.	N.P. Act A.O.N.B.	SU 778 276 2311 16
Church C.19	St. Mary, East Liss. Built 1891–2 by Sir A. Blomfield. Stone structure with brick interior. Lancet windows. West tower and south porch added 1930. Square bell openings. Sculpture by Eric Gill in porch. Ref: Buildings of England; Hants and I.O.W., (Pevsner and Lloyd), p. 319.	N.P. Act A.O.N.B.	SU 775 279 2311 34
House C.19	Stodham Park House. Built circa. 1820. 3 storeys and basement. Projecting wing of 2 storeys. Rendered structure. Slate roof. Sash windows, small panes in wing, single panes in main block. Imposing 4-pillared porch with steps to main door. Pillared verandah along length of south front.	A.O.N.B.	SU 770 261 2311 43

13th Century St. Peter's Church, LISS

Description and Date	Remarks	Protection	Grid Ref. and Punchcard No.
Group D — (cont.)			
House	Cumbers. 2 storeys. Brick structure one side tile-hung. Two painted walls. Part slate, part tile roof, with two gables at rear. Mixed windows, some C.18 sash. Two brick chimneys. Modern porch.	A.O.N.B.	SU 776 272 2311 35
Farmhouse	Flexcombe Old Farmhouse. 2 storeys and cellar. Rendered structure. Tiled hipped roof. Three brick chimneys. Twentyone windows of various dates. Late C.19 closed gabled porch with steps.	A.O.N.B.	SU 766 270 2311 42
House	Palmers. Brick structure with tiled roof. Possibly of C.17 date. Associations with the Pilgrims Way.	N.P. Act A.O.N.B.	SU 794 285 2311 25
Building	Pruetts. Formerly two cottages of C.17 or earlier date. 2 storeys. Cement rendered. Tiled roof with hipped gable ends. Queen Anne doorway with flat hood. Interior shows timber framing.	N.P. Act A.O.N.B.	SU 774 262 2311 10
Cottage	Old Forge Cottage, Mill Road. 2 storeys, with a single storey lean-to extension. Rendered brick and stone structure which has been whitewashed. Tiled roof with gable ends. Two chimneys. Wooden casement windows. Extensively renovated in 1978.	A.O.N.B.	SU 778 276 2311 47
Cottages (2)	Bridge Cottages, Station Road. 2 storeys, brick structure. Hipped and gabled, tiled roof, with three tiled dormers. One gable tile-hung. Three chimneys. Wooden casement windows. Two porches.	A.O.N.B.	SU 775 277 2311 48

MEDSTEAD

Four miles west of Alton, Medstead is some 700 feet above sea level. It has a very attractive little church with a small wooden bell turret capping a shingle roof. Two of the original Norman arches can be seen, as can an interesting window showing St. Joan of Arc, erected some years before she was canonised. Medstead Manor was recently acquired by an American Roman Catholic Order, and the Convent of St. Lucy has been established there.

Description and Date	Remarks	Protection	Grid Ref. and Punchcard No.

Group A — Natural Features

Description and Date	Remarks	Protection	Grid Ref. and Punchcard No.
Trees	Medstead House, Meld Road. On land fronting the former stables and the adjoining plot to the east. Three groups comprised of lime, ash and sycamore, and a single yew.	T.P.O. No. 60 E.H.D.	SU 654 371 1613 16

Group B — Archaeological

Bronze Age

Description and Date	Remarks	Protection	Grid Ref. and Punchcard No.
Barrow	Domboshawa adjacent to Kingsmead on south - west side of Wield Road. Mutilated bowl barrow, 27.0 m. by 17.0 m. in diameter, with no visible ditch. O.S.A. No. SU63 NW11. Ref: 1. P.H.F.C., Vol. 14, 1938—40, p. 352. 2. Field Archaeology as Illustrated in Hampshire, 1915, (Williams-Freeman), p. 384.	S.A.M. No. 255	SU 649 373 1613 04
Barrow	West of Trinity Lane. Mutilated bowl barrow, 26.0 m. average diameter, 1.6 m. high, with no visible ditch. O.S.A. No. SU63 NE10. Ref: P.H.F.C., Vol. 14, 1938—40, p. 352.	S.A.M. No. 210	SU 652 377 1613 10
Palstave	Fine example of bronze axe head found 1932 in gravel bed at West End. Photograph in Alton Museum. O.S.A. No. SU63 NW17. Ref: A Short History of Medstead, 1932, (Moody), p. 8.		SU 642 357 1613 08

Roman

Description and Date	Remarks	Protection	Grid Ref. and Punchcard No.
Pottery and Tiles	Pullingers Farm. Amphora top and other potsherds found 1925. Centred on grid reference. O.S.A. No. SU63 NW10.		SU 644 372 1613 06
Coins and Nail	East of Pullingers Farm. Finds include coins the size of halfpennies and farthings and a large triangular nail. Present location not known. O.S.A. No. SU63 NW1.		SU 647 373 1613 05
Coin	Field View, Homestead Road. Bronze coin of Antoninus Pius, found August 1949. O.S.A. No. SU63 NW16. Ref: Accessions Book, Alton Museum.		SU 648 362 1613 07
Coin	Larchwood, Paice Lane. Coin of Constantine The Great, found May 1943. O.S.A. No. SU63 NW18. Ref: Accessions Book, Alton Museum.		SU 649 358 1613 09
Coin	Lymington Bottom Road. Coin of Constantius II presented to Alton Museum, September 1963. Exact site of find not known. O.S.A. No. SU63 NE14. Ref: Accession Book, Alton Museum.		SU 662 354 1613 11

Group B — (cont.)

Period Unknown

Description and Date	Remarks	Protection	Grid Ref. and Punchcard No.
Earthwork	North-west of Medstead Manor. Strong, sub-rectangular defensive enclosure, now part of copse. One entrance on south east side. Possibly Iron Age, but could be mediaeval. O.S.A. No. SU63 NE11. Ref: Field Archaeology as Illustrated in Hampshire, (Williams-Freeman), p.p. 300, 384.	S.A.M. No. 49	SU 656 373 1613 03

Group D — Buildings, Monuments and Engineering Works

Description and Date	Remarks	Protection	Grid Ref. and Punchcard No.
Church C.12	St. Andrew. Modernised and enlarged 1833. Stone structure. Well preserved Norman arcade of two arches between nave and north aisle. Weatherboarded bell turret. Fine C.13 tripartite corbel with leaf decoration. O.S.A. No. SU63 NE12. Ref: 1. V.C.H., Vol. 3, p. 329. 2. Buildings of England; Hants and I.O.W., (Pevsner & Lloyd), p. 332.	T. & C.P. Act	SU 654 371 1613 01
Cottage	Three Ways, Common Hill. 2 storeys. Part timber-framed, part whitewashed brick and stone. Thatched roof. Casement windows. One thatched roof porch and one tiled roof porch. Modern brick garden wall with wrought iron gates.		SU 654 363 1613 14
Cottage	Green Hedges, Grosvenor Road, Soldridge. Single storey. Whitewashed brick walls. Thatched roof. Brick chimney. Possibly 300—400 years old.		SU 652 349 1613 15
Cottage	The Old Rectory Cottage, Castle Street. 2 storeys. Colourwashed brick. Ridge tiled roof. Lattice casements. Light-columned porch with C.16 panelled door. Possibly C.17.		SU 655 372 1613 02
Cottage	Fir Tree Cottage, Hussell Lane. 2 storeys. White-washed brick walls. Thatched roof. A thatched 2-storey extension has recently been added.		SU 659 371 1613 12
Building	Convent of St. Lucy, formerly Medstead Manor. Part 2 storeys, part 3 storeys. The old sections of the building are of flint construction, with ornamental tile-hung gable. The main facade built 1904—5. In recent years a residential wing has been added to the main range of buildings, and a chapel built in the grounds.		SU 685 373 1613 13

NEWTON VALENCE

Situated between East Tisted and Selborne, some five and a half miles south of Alton. The village is recorded in the Domesday Book as Newentone, while the place derives its name from Aylmerde Valence, who was given it as a grant of land. Alongside the impressive Manor House is the centuries old church. Much thirteenth century work is displayed as well as a massive 700 year old font. Beside the huge yew tree in the churchyard is the grave of Colonel Phayve, one of the signatories to the death warrant of Charles I.

Description and Date	Remarks	Protection	Grid Ref. and Punchcard No.
Group A — Natural Features			
Dene Hole	East northeast of Headmoor Farm. 45 ft. deep shaft, opening into dome shaped chamber 18 ft. high, 20 ft. in diameter. Ref: P.H.F.C., Vol. 16, Part 2, p. 193.	N.P. Act A.O.N.B.	SU 689 341 1614 12
Site of Ecological Interest	Noar Hill. Area of chalk grassland rich in flora on former chalk workings, and structurally diverse beech hanger on westerly facing scarp. Nature reserve managed by Hampshire and I.O.W. Naturalist Trust.	N.P. Act S.S.S.I. A.O.N.B.	SU 744 317 1614 13
Sarsen Stone No. 49A	At junction leading to St. Marys Church.	N.P. Act A.O.N.B.	SU 723 327 1614 14
Trees	On land adjoining the Manor House. A group of three horse chestnut, a group of three sycamore, and a single horse chestnut.	T.P.O. No. 68 E.H.D. N.P. Act. A.O.N.B.	SU 724 328 1614 15
Group B — Archaeological			
Bronze Age			
Bowl Barrow	North-east of Lodge Farm. 36.0 m. in diameter and 1.8 m. high. No visual ditch. Damaged by ploughing. O.S.A. No. SU73 SW2. Ref: P.H.F.C., Vol. 14, 1938—40, p. 354.	N.P. Act A.O.N.B.	SU 704 333 1614 09
Iron Age			
Field System	Southern edge of Goldridge Plantation. Series of three contour lynchets extending for nearly a mile. Probable Celtic fields. O.S.A. No. SU73 SW5.	N.P. Act A.O.N.B.	SU 722 339 1614 10
Field System	South-west of village. Series of parallel lynchets extending for over half a mile. Probable Celtic fields. O.S.A. No. SU73 SW7.	N.P. Act A.O.N.B.	SU 720 325 1614 11
Group D — Buildings, Monuments and Engineering Works			
Church C.13/14	St. Mary. Restored 1871. Nave and chancel early English, west tower, early English with C.19 brick top. Large Norman font and two piscinas. O.S.A. No. SU73 SW9. Ref: Buildings of England; Hants and I.O.W., (Pevsner & Lloyd), p. 353.	T. & C.P. Act N.P. Act A.O.N.B.	SU 724 328 1614 08
House C.17/18	The Manor House. Long irregular building. Oldest portion, 2 storeys, coursed stone blocks with brick dressings, plinth and band and long ridge slate roof. Red brick Georgian portion with parapet and hipped tiled roof. Victorian wing, 2 storeys, yellow brick, low pitched slate roof and sash windows.	T. & C.P. Act N.P. Act A.O.N.B.	SU 724 328 1614 07

Description and Date	Remarks	Protection	Grid Ref. and Punchcard No.
Group D — (cont.)			
House C.18	Kitcombe House. 2 storeys. Main elevation, blue brick with red brick dressings. Hipped slate roof. Stone string course at first floor level and dwarf parapet. Gabled Victorian additions to rear.	T. & C.P. Act N.P. Act A.O.N.B.	SU 704 342 1614 05
House C.18/19	Longhope. Formerly The Vicarage. Red brick walls. Tiled roof. Parapet. Sash windows to principal facades. Modern 2-storey brick porch with classical doorway. Stands in landscaped park.	T. & C.P. Act N.P. Act A.O.N.B.	SU 727 326 1614 06
House C.19	Pelham Place. Romantic Gothic mansion in landscaped park. Grey cement rendered walls. Three gables. Splayed oriel windows. Battlemented verandah with pointed arches. Lofty porte-cochere. O.S.A. No. SU73 SW(M).	N.P. Act A.O.N.B.	SU 700 334 1614 03
Lodge C.19	Lower Lodge. Stands at the entrance to Rotherfield Park. Single storey, octagonal shaped structure. Cement rendered walls. Flat roof renewed in asphalt. Pointed Gothic windows.	N.P. Act A.O.N.B.	SU 703 332 1614 02
Farmhouse	Charity Farm. 2 storeys. Exposed timber-framing on first floor with modern herringbone infilling. Hipped tiled roof. Single storey wing in coursed stone with brick quoins. Interior contains some plain Elizabethan panelling.	N.P. Act A.O.N.B.	SU 737 319 1614 04

The parish of Petersfield was enlarged in 1894 by the inclusion of parts of Buriton and Sheet parishes. Petersfield is not mentioned by name in the Domesday Book as it was probably included with Mapledurham.

The town received a charter in the reign of Henry II whereby William, Earl of Gloucester, granted the burgesses of Petersfield all the liberties and customs enjoyed by the citizens of Winchester, including the right to have a merchant guild. Petersfield prospered as a market town and first sent members to Parliament in 1306—7 when two members were returned. The representation lapsed, however, but was restored in 1552—3: the Reform Act of 1832 reduced the number of members to one and in 1885 the representation of Petersfield was merged in that of the county.

The cattle market at Petersfield gave rise to industries such as cloth manufacture and leather working in Tudor times. The town became prosperous and in 1428 at least one corn-grinding mill had been converted to a fulling-mill for the preparation of cloth. Tanning and other leather industries also flourished but the manufacture of cloth was the principal occupation in the Stuart period, employing over 1000 people in the reign of James I. Both industries gradually waned towards the end of the seventeenth century, but Petersfield was still important as a market town and administrative centre. Situated strategically at the junction of the London to Portsmouth and Winchester to Midhurst roads, Petersfield enjoyed a brisk trade in the coaching days: no fewer than nine inns are listed in a rent roll of 1696—7, namely the White Hart, the Anchor, the Lion, the Half Moon, the Crown, the Swan, the Dragon, the Ship and the George. The importance of Petersfield was enhanced with the building of the railway in the nineteenth century, and today the town is the principal shopping and administrative centre for the surrounding countryside.

Description and Date	Remarks	Protection	Grid Ref. and Punchcard No.
Group A — Natural Features			
Trees	West of the Tilmore Road. A single birch and clump of smaller trees and furze bushes.	N.P. Act A.O.N.B.	SU 744 240 1301 215
Trees	Groups of oaks on Bell Hill recreation ground, off the Winchester Road.	N.P. Act A.O.N.B.	SU 739 238 1301 222
Trees	Corner of Tilmore Gardens and Tilmore Road.	T.P.O. No. 17 E.H. N.P. Act A.O.N.B.	SU 745 242 1302 244
Tree	Cedarcote, College St. One large cedar of Lebanon in view from road.	T.P.O. No. 7 E.H. N.P. Act A.O.N.B.	SU 749 233 1302 197
Tree	Starcross, Love Lane. A single oak, within the boundary of the property.	T.P.O. No. 43 E.H. N.P. Act A.O.N.B.	SU 756 237 1302 245
Trees	Durford Road. Oak, chestnut, silver birch, willow and pine trees, now surrounded by houses.	T.P.O. No. 286 N.P. Act A.O.N.B.	SU 763 231 1305 225A
Trees	The Avenue. An avenue of chestnut trees.	N.P. Act A.O.N.B.	SU 750 230 1303 201
Trees	Sussex Road, and Russell Way. Single specimens, and groups of copper beech, horse chestnut, Scots pine, sycamore, and oak within the area.	T.P.O. No. 61 E.H. N.P. Act A.O.N.B.	SU 753 225 1303 246
Trees	Winchester Road, south of Rushes Farm and along the track to Buckmoore Farm. Mainly oak, ash and elm.	T.P.O. No. 142 N.P. Act A.O.N.B.	SU 739 238 1301 223
Trees	St. Peter's Churchyard, near The Square. A group of trees which includes chestnuts and limes.	C.A. N.P. Act A.O.N.B.	SU 746 231 1301 199
Trees	A fine group of silver birches at the entrance of Oaklands Road.	N.P. Act A.O.N.B.	SU 742 237 1301 193
Tree	Sheet Green, chestnut tree planted to commemorate the Diamond Jubilee of Queen Victoria.	C.A. N.P. Act A.O.N.B.	SU 758 245 1302 230
Trees	Land behind Clare Gardens. Centred on grid reference.	T.P.O. No. 58 N.P. Act A.O.N.B.	SU 763 233 1302 225A
Trees	Groups of trees in an area behind College Street properties, and including that to the north of the garden centre, bounded to north and east by the stream. Centred on grid reference.	T.P.O. No. 725 N.P. Act A.O.N.B.	SU 749 235 1302 196

Description and Date	Remarks	Protection	Grid Ref. and Punchcard No.
Group A — (cont.)			
Trees	Monks Barn, The Purrocks, Reservoir Lane. Tree types protected include Scots pine, cherry, beech, pine, ash, oak and a red chestnut. Centred on grid reference	T.P.O. No. 317 N.P. Act A.O.N.B.	SU 745 244 1302 233
Trees	Tilmore Road, up to and including The Purrocks. Centred on grid reference.	N.P. Act A.O.N.B.	SU 746 243 1302 214
Trees	Ramshill. A line of beech and other trees around the perimeter to the north of Silverlands and an avenue of limes and conifers to the cemetery. Centred on grid reference.	N.P. Act A.O.N.B.	SU 751 238 1302 411
Woodland	Behind 12, High Street. A strip of woodland and overgrown garden which forms an attractive natural landscape in an increasingly built up area.	C.A. N.P. Act A.O.N.B.	SU 747 233 1302 198
Scenic Beauty	River Rother at Old Sheet Mill, Old Mill Lane. Attractive landscape with river and pond.	N.P. Act A.O.N.B.	SU 760 241 1302 240
Scenic Beauty	Kettlebrook. Meandering stretch of the Ashford Stream with bridge. A ford can be traced back to the C.10. On ward boundary. Ref: Meon Charters.	N.P. Act A.O.N.B.	SU 752 252 1302 236
Scenic Beauty	Area surrounding Sheet Bridge Mill, Mill Lane. River Rother, River banks and trees make this an extremely attractive spot.	C.A. N.P. Act A.O.N.B.	SU 760 246 1302 301A
Viewpoints	From the Durford Road near Clare Gardens. Fine views of the South Downs.	N.P. Act A.O.N.B.	SU 763 231 1303 234
Viewpoint	From the end of the Avenue. Views of Heath Pond and the South Downs.	N.P. Act A.O.N.B.	SU 750 230 1303 201
Viewpoint	Ramshill Cemetery. Fine views of Wheatham Hill and the Hangers.	N.P. Act A.O.N.B.	SU 749 239 1302 190
Viewpoint	Near sports ground, Love Lane. Views of the Downs.	N.P. Act A.O.N.B.	SU 752 236 1302 184
Viewpoint	Heath Road. Looking south, views of the Downs including Butser Hill	N.P. Act A.O.N.B.	SU 754 231 1303 400
Viewpoint	Hazelbank Close, off Pulens Lane, Sheet. Excellent view of the Weald to the east.	N.P. Act A.O.N.B.	SU 758 239 1302 401
Viewpoint	Love Lane. Excellent vantage point for views of The Downs. Centred on grid reference.	N.P. Act A.O.N.B.	SU 756 238 1302 410
Viewpoint	Fine views of the South Downs from the public seat on the top of Bell Hill.	N.P. Act A.O.N.B.	SU 740 241 1301 216
Viewpoint	From Bell Hill Ridge. Pleasant views north to the Hangers.	N.P. Act A.O.N.B.	SU 743 242 1301 217
Viewpoint	View east from the Jolly Sailor, The Causeway, to Nursted and the South Downs.	N.P. Act A.O.N.B.	SU 742 223 1301 209

Description and Date	Remarks	Protection	Grid Ref. and Punchcard No.

Group A — (cont.)

Description and Date	Remarks	Protection	Grid Ref. and Punchcard No.
Viewpoint	Fine views of Butser Hill and the Downs from Ramsdean Road, Stroud.	N.P. Act A.O.N.B.	SU 720 230 1301 210
Viewpoint	Along the Winchester Road from Berelands Farm to the district boundary there are pleasant views of the Hangers and Downs.	N.P. Act A.O.N.B.	SU 730 236 1301 211
Viewpoint	Kimbers, Tilmore. An area of new housing. Extensive views of Butser, Wardown and the intervening countryside, also eastwards to the Sussex Downs.	N.P. Act A.O.N.B.	SU 744 239 1301 188
Viewpoint	Fine views of Butser Hill, from Oaklands Road.	N.P. Act A.O.N.B.	SU 743 239 1301 189
Viewpoint	Borough Hill open space. Pleasant views of the South Downs, and north to the Hangers.	N.P. Act A.O.N.B.	SU 740 231 1301 183
Landscape Feature	Sheet Bridge. An area of alder with a rich ground flora.	N.P. Act A.O.N.B.	SU 761 245 1302 309
Sarsen Stone No. 55A	On the corner of "The Spain".	C.A. N.P. Act A.O.N.B.	SU 745 233 1301 235

Group B — Archaeological

Stone Age

Description and Date	Remarks	Protection	Grid Ref. and Punchcard No.
Mesolithic Working Floor	Heath Common. Arrowheads, axehead and flakes found in 1907. The working floor and flakes were uncovered in 1962 during mains-trench excavation. Finds now in Portsmouth City Museum. O.S.A. No. SU72 SE15. Ref: 1. P.H.F.C., Vol. 9, Part 3, 1924, p. 41. 2. Portsmouth City Museum Daybook; Entry No. H/63/38.	N.P. Act A.O.N.B.	SU 754 231 1303 203
Neolithic Flint Impliments	Many worked flints, including a polished axe found on the surface of the field. O.S.A. No. SU72 SE17.	N.P. Act A.O.N.B.	SU 762 230 1303 229
Axe	Palaeolithic hand axe found in 1889 near Churchers College. Flint fabricator also found. O.S.A. No. SU72 SE19. Ref: 1. Archaeological Journal, Vol. 8, p.p. 412, 413. 2. Alton Museum Accession Register.	N.P. Act A.O.N.B.	SU 753 238 1302 204
Barrows (21)	Heath Common. A group of different types, the majority of which are bowl barrows, but there are also examples of the bell, disc and saucer types, though most of them are tree covered. Nine of the barrows are scheduled as ancient monuments. O.S.A. No. SU72 SE18. Ref: 1. P.H.F.C., Vol. 14, 1940, p. 356. 2. Archaeology of Wessex, (Grinsell), p. 358.	S.A.M. No. 60 N.P. Act A.O.N.B.	SU 756 231 1303 202

Description and Date	Remarks	Protection	Grid Ref. and Punchcard No.

Group B — (cont.)

Roman

Description and Date	Remarks	Protection	Grid Ref. and Punchcard No.
Coffin	Lead coffin found in a gravel pit immediately north of the Roman villa in 1898. O.S.A. No. SU72 SW1.	N.P. Act A.O.N.B.	SU 725 236 1301 213
Villa (Site)	South of Finchmead Lane, Stroud. A large villa with baths excavated 1907—8. Basilican house measuring 140 ft. x 52 ft. of rectangular plan with projecting wings. At first divided by two rows of wooden columns, later divided into rooms with front corridor. Concrete posts mark site which has been turfed. O.S.A. No. SU72 SW1. Ref: Archaeological Journal, Vol. 65, (Moray Williams), p.p. 57—60.	S.A.M. No. 112 N.P. Act A.O.N.B.	SU 725 235 1301 212

Post Mediaeval

Description and Date	Remarks	Protection	Grid Ref. and Punchcard No.
Pottery	Excavations on site of 11, Sheep Street revealed pieces of mediaeval pottery and the foundations of two ancient wells.	C.A. N.P. Act A.O.N.B.	SU 745 232 1301 241

Group C — Footpaths and Bridleways

Description and Date	Remarks	Protection	Grid Ref. and Punchcard No.
Travelway	Joins A3 to A272 at Sheet. Old travelway, part sunken up to about 15 ft. in places. Leads from Sheet Bridge round the edge of Sheet Common to the A272.	N.P. Act A.O.N.B.	SU 762 245 — 767 242 1302 221
Footpath	Folly Lane. Formerly known as White Hart Passage, when it was a track for horse-drawn coaches travelling to the Old White Hart Inn, now Nos. 18 and 20 High Street. The path runs from between these two properties, through a brick passageway out to the footpath by the stream in the present car park. Originally it continued over a bridge and on to College Street.	C.A. N.P. Act A.O.N.B.	SU 748 233 1302 206
Travelway	Old route between The Harrow Inn and Kettlebrook Cottages. Centred on grid reference.	N.P. Act A.O.N.B.	SU 752 251 1302 237
Travelway	Brook Lane, The Spain. One of the old lanes connecting The Spain with the stream to the south. Formed old boundary between the borough of Petersfield and the tithing of Weston. Flanked by walls.	C.A. N.P. Act A.O.N.B.	SU 744 231 1301 205
Travelway	Old Bell Hill sunken track. The old road over Bell Hill which lies west of the present road. Runs through a belt of trees in grounds of private houses.	N.P. Act A.O.N.B.	SU 739 241 — 740 243 1301 224
Trackway	Boundary Lane. Ancient pack horse route avoiding steep gradients. At northern end meets Dark Hollow and Bell Hill Ridge, other trackways, and continues to Tilmore Road. Ref: 1. Boundary Commission Map 1831. 2. Tithe Map 1841. (Named Fennell Lane).	N.P. Act A.O.N.B.	SU 743 236 — 744 240 1301 195

Description and Date	Remarks	Protection	Grid Ref. and Punchcard No.

Group C — (cont.)

Description and Date	Remarks	Protection	Grid Ref. and Punchcard No.
Trackway	Dark Hollow. An ancient pack horse route now used as a footpath. It runs between Bell Hill and Tilmore Road.	N.P. Act A.O.N.B.	SU 741 238 — 745 242 1301 194
Old Road	Harrow Lane, Steep. At one time a highway from the Petersfield area to Liss, Liphook and beyond.	N.P. Act A.O.N.B.	SU 745 243 — 753 253 1302 208
Footpath	From the Borough to Weston. An ancient route to Petersfield from Weston.	N.P. Act A.O.N.B.	SU 733 221 — 739 227 1301 227
Footpath	From Borough Road by the hospital over Borough Hill to Stroud and on to Langrish. Mainly straight with traces of banks in parts. At times forms a boundary.	N.P. Act A.O.N.B.	SU 721 233 — 744 232 1301 228
Track	Track and footpath from The Causeway at Landpits to Weston. Formerly a boundary between Petersfield and Buriton.	N.P. Act A.O.N.B.	SU 730 218 — 738 221 1301 226

Group D — Buildings, Monuments and Engineering Works

Bell Hill

Description and Date	Remarks	Protection	Grid Ref. and Punchcard No.
Farmhouse C.17/18	No. 2. Rushes Farmhouse. 2 storeys. Double fronted with tiled roof. Painted brick ground floor, tile hung above. Sash windows. Door with reeded architrave and hood. Interior has massive beams.	T. & C.P. Act N.P. Act A.O.N.B.	SU 740 238 1301 03
House C.19	No. 24. Brick structure with some tile hanging. Tiled hipped roof with dormer window. Three modern leaded casement windows on ground floor.	N.P. Act A.O.N.B.	SU 740 244 1301 02
Cottage C.19	No. 26. 2 storeys. Brick walls. Tiled roof with hipped gable at southern end. One chimney. Iron cross bands. Outshot on western side. First floor windows partly dormer.	N.P. Act A.O.N.B.	SU 740 244 1301 161
Cottage C.19	No. 28. Bell Hill Cottage. 2 storeys. Slate roof with end chimneys. Malmstone structure galleted with ironstone. Brick dressings. Sash windows with glazing bars. Hood on curved brackets over door.	T. & C.P. Act N.P. Act A.O.N.B.	SU 740 244 1301 162

Borough Hill

Description and Date	Remarks	Protection	Grid Ref. and Punchcard No.
House C.18	Borough Hill House. Shallow pitched roof with two chimneys at gable ends. Rendered walls. Stone window arches. Modern metal windows. Small brick and tile stable with loft over.	N.P. Act A.O.N.B.	SU 741 232 1301 05

Description and Date	Remarks	Protection	Grid Ref. and Punchcard No.

Group D — (cont.)

Description and Date	Remarks	Protection	Grid Ref. and Punchcard No.
House C.18	Sumachs, formerly Borough Farmhouse. 2 storeys. Hipped slate roof with end chimneys. Yellow brick with brick cornice. Sash windows with low segmental arches. Semi-circular classical porch with two columns. Fanlight and projecting lampholder.	T. & C.P. Act N.P. Act A.O.N.B.	SU 739 230 1301 147
Cottages	Nos. 5—29. Group of artisan cottages. Built in a variety of materials, brick, stone, flint and fish-scale tile hanging. Cottages of various dates from C.18 to C.20.	N.P. Act A.O.N.B.	SU 741 232 1301 242
Wall	Borough Road. Between the hospital garden and 36, Borough Road. Old wall showing many periods of construction and repair, using iron-stone, malmstone, sandstone, flint and brick.	N.P. Act A.O.N.B.	SU 743 231 1301 04

The Causeway

Description and Date	Remarks	Protection	Grid Ref. and Punchcard No.
House C.18	Nos. 1—6. The Grange. L-shaped plan. 2 storeys. Hipped, tiled roof. Walls of galleted malmstone with heavy dressed quoins. Sash windows in stone surrounds with keystones on front. Pedimented classical doorway with fanlight. West front has blocked carriage entrance. Originally built as stables and coachman's house by John Joliffe.	T. & C.P. Act N.P. Act A.O.N.B.	SU 746 229 1303 131
Stables C.19	Jolly Sailor. Brick structure with tiled roof. Brickwork includes bull nosed headers. Ironstone cobbles are remains of old Portsmouth road. Terra Cotta dog each side of ridge; once kennels for hounds.	N.P. Act A.O.N.B.	SU 741 224 1301 132
House C.18/19	No. 127. 2 storeys. Hipped slate roof with two chimneys. Flemish bond brickwork with blue headers. Windows with splayed brick lintels. One blocked window over front door. Lattice work porch.	N.P. Act A.O.N.B.	SU 741 224 1301 133
House C.17/18	No. 211. Landpits. High pitched hipped, tiled roof. 2 storeys. Malmstone front with red brick dressings. South end tile hung. Casement windows under brick arches. Two doors with tiled, gabled hoods.	T. & C.P. Act N.P. Act A.O.N.B.	SU 738 221 1301 157
Barn C.17	Causeway Farm Dairy. Walls of galleted malmstone with dressings of narrow brick. Limewashed front. Barn of three bays, with aisles on four sides formed by low sweep of hipped tiled roof. Hipped gabled porch. Interior has four arch braced corner posts. Door at either end.	T. & C.P. Act N.P. Act A.O.N.B.	SU 746 225 1303 130

Description and Date	Remarks	Protection	Grid Ref. and Punchcard No.
Group D — (cont.)			
Farmhouse C.18	No. 158. Causeway Farmhouse. 2 storeys and attic. Brick central section projects with gabled parapet and three stone ball finials. Tiled roof with two hipped tiled dormers, descends to first floor level at rear. Central section has rustic Venetian window partly painted in 'Trompe L'oeil'. Central door with bracketed hood. South wall tile hung.	T. & C.P. Act N.P. Act A.O.N.B.	SU 741 223 1303 129
Chapel Street			
Building C.16	No. 1, continuous with 1, The Square. High pitched tiled roof with tile hung gable end. Close set timbers with flint infilling on first floor. Ground floor modern shop front.	T. & C.P. Act C.A. N.P. Act A.O.N.B.	SU 746 233 1302 06
Cottage C.17	No. 57. Tiny cottage of 2 storeys. Tiled roof with tile hung gable to road. Plastered front. Massive rebuilt chimney. Sash, and early C.19 casement, windows.	T. & C.P. Act N.P. Act A.O.N.B.	SU 745 234 1302 08
Building C.17/18	Nos. 63 and 65. Range of single storey and attic. Hipped tiled roof. Roughcast front with high plinth. Large hipped gabled dormers breaking eaves. Sash windows, most with glazing bars. Large chimney stack at right end, two on ridge. 6-panel doors in plain frames.	T. & C.P. Act N.P. Act A.O.N.B.	SU 745 235 1302 165
Building C.18	Old Drum Inn. Plaster-faced, 2-storey building. Tiled roof, half-hipped at northern end. Two chimneys. Front has off-centre gable with main entrance door beneath.	C.A. N.P. Act A.O.N.B.	SU 745 233 1301 07
Church Path			
Building C.17	Church Art Studio. Single storey and basement. High pitched, tiled roof with off-centre chimney. Three sash and one oriel window. Entrance up steps. Modern extensions. Once a Malt House.	T. & C.P. Act C.A. N.P. Act A.O.N.B.	SU 746 231 1301 09
Building C.18	Nos. 22 and 23. Former vicarage, now two dwellings. Hipped tiled roof with end chimneys. Painted brick front with dentil cornice. Casement windows. Central double door under cornice hood, leads to a brick arched barrel-vaulted cellar. Later extension at right.	T. & C.P. Act C.A. N.P. Act A.O.N.B.	SU 746 231 1301 10
College Street			
Building C.18	Nos. 4—8. 2 storeys. Hipped tiled roof. Painted brick front with brick dentil cornice. Sash windows. Two blocked windows. Three mid C.19 shop fronts on ground floor. Some exposed beams inside. No. 6 has 6-panel door with rectangular fanlight.	T. & C.P. Act C.A. N.P. Act A.O.N.B.	SU 748 232 1302 11

Group D — (cont.)

Description and Date	Remarks	Protection	Grid Ref. and Punchcard No.
House C.17	No. 18. Antrobus House. 2 storeys. Refronted in C.19 and later pebbledashed. Later hipped slate roof. Sash windows with glazing bars. Interior has some C.17 and C.18 panelling on first floor. Modern shop front. Door with fanlight over.	T. & C.P. Act N.P. Act A.O.N.B.	SU 748 233 1302 13
House C.17	Nos. 36 and 36A. 3-bay timber-framed building. C.18 brick ground floor. Fishscale tile hung first floor. Hipped roof of clay tiles. Central brick chimney. C.19 and modern windows. Three gabled dormers. Internally the post, beams and tiles are still visible. Roof ceiled at Purlin level with relatively complete side purlin roof, with triple Queen-post and collar beam trusses.	T. & C.P. Act N.P. Act A.O.N.B.	SU 748 235 1302 300
Inn C.16	Nos. 40—44. The Good Intent. Range of 1½ storeys with high pitched, tiled roof. C.18 brick addition to left of 2 storeys. Tiled roof, hipped at left. Timber-framed central section with brick infilling. Modern casement windows. Projecting wing at right is of a later date.	T. & C.P. Act N.P. Act A.O.N.B.	SU 748 235 1302 163
Building C.17/18	No. 48. Early C.18 front to C.17 or earlier building. Tiled roof hipped at right. Stuccoed cornice and parapet. Red brick and blue headers on galleted plinth. Brick angle pilasters to projecting centre section. Sash windows. Large chimney on south wall.	T. & C.P. Act N.P. Act A.O.N.B.	SU 748 236 1302 18
Cottages C.16	Nos. 50, 52, formerly The Black Horse Inn. 2 storeys. Timber-framed but refronted in C.18. Steeply pitched tiled roof with massive chimney. Limewashed brick front with leaded casements on first floor. Ground floor sash windows. Gabled rear extension.	T. & C.P. Act N.P. Act A.O.N.B.	SU 748 236 1302 19
Building C.18	No. 1. Red Lion Hotel. 2 storeys. Tiled roof, hipped at right. Central gable over projecting 2-bay section. Plaster faced brick walls. Doric porch supported on fluted columns flanked by two round bay windows. 2-storey C.19 addition at left with hipped slate roof. C.16 Building at rear used as public bar 'The Tap' until recently. Refer to separate entry under Heath Road.	T. & C.P. Act C.A. N.P. Act A.O.N.B.	SU 748 232 1303 15
Building C.19	Old Masonic Hall, in grounds of Red Lion Hotel. Slate roof carried forward at gable ends to give pediment effect. Brick structure with recessed bays on ground and first floor level. Windows have stone dressed 4-centred heads. Double doors on west front with fanlight. Used as storeroom.	T. & C.P. Act C.A. N.P. Act A.O.N.B.	SU 748 232 1303 159

Description and Date	Remarks	Protection	Grid Ref. and Punchcard No.

Group D — (cont.)

Description and Date	Remarks	Protection	Grid Ref. and Punchcard No.
House C.19	No. 5. Cedar Cote. Red brick front. 3 storeys. Hipped slate roof. Side wall of malmstone galleted with ironstone. Gauged brick arches to sash windows. Doorway with patterned fanlight and cornice on large brackets. Modern extensions to right and rear.	T. & C.P. Act N.P. Act A.O.N.B.	SU 749 233 1302 12
Cottage C.18	No. 17. Fir Cottage. Dated 1742. 2 storeys. Double span tiled roof, the front half-hipped, the rear hipped. Central chimney. Mathematical tiles to front, the sides tile-hung at first floor level. Sash windows. Door with cornice hood on brackets.	T. & C.P. Act N.P. Act A.O.N.B.	SU 749 235 1302 164
Building C.16	No. 19. Timber-framed with brick infilling. Rendered walls to road and south elevation. Shallow slate roof of later date. 2 storeys. Interior reveals C.16 origins with paired rafters in roof. Quaker meetings once held in this house.	N.P. Act A.O.N.B.	SU 749 235 1302 14
Buildings C.19	Nos. 25—31. 2 storeys. Slate roof. Two large shared chimneys. Each dwelling with one window and a door at ground floor level. Two windows above. Replaced windows, but No. 25 retains original small apertures. Walls rendered. Terrace fits in well with a group of eight listed buildings and a church at north end of College Street.	N.P. Act A.O.N.B.	SU 749 235 1302 16
Church C.18	United Reform, formerly the Congregational, dated 1749. Random stone walls. Slate roof. Gothic style doorways and windows. Cross at apex of gable. Front extended in 1872 to provide stair and gallery with new front wall.	N.P. Act A.O.N.B.	SU 749 236 1302 403
Building C.18	The Old College. Now council offices. 3 storeys. Red brick with purple headers. Projecting central section with pilasters. Stone cornice and brick parapet. Sash windows with brick arches. Three steps to door with rectangular fanlight and cornice hood. Inscription on frieze 'Churchers College, 1729'. Leaded casement windows to rear. Single storey attic wings at either side.	T. & C.P. Act N.P. Act A.O.N.B.	SU 749 236 1302 17

Dragon Street

Description and Date	Remarks	Protection	Grid Ref. and Punchcard No.
Building C.18	Nos. 2 and 4, incorporating Nos. 1 and 3, Heath Road. 3 storeys. Hipped slate roof with off-centre chimney. Painted brick structure. Sash windows with glazing bars. Later shop fronts. No. 4 has Doric doorcase with fluted pilasters and frieze, and patterned fanlight.	T. & C.P. Act C.A. N.P. Act A.O.N.B.	SU 748 232 1303 20
Building C.17	Nos. 14—18. 2 storeys. Painted brick structure. Tiled roof. Wide gable over three central bays, with blocked lunette. Sash windows with glazing bars and some shutters. Modern shop windows on ground floor. Facade dates from C.18.	T. & C.P. Act C.A. N.P. Act A.O.N.B.	SU 748 231 1303 23

Description and Date	Remarks	Protection	Grid Ref. and Punchcard No.

Group D — (cont.)

Description and Date	Remarks	Protection	Grid Ref. and Punchcard No.
Inn C.16	No. 20. The Green Dragon. Formerly The Sun Inn. C.16 with early C.19 stuccoed front of 2 storeys. Hipped slate roof. Behind, to south, an C.18 brick wing with tiled roof and gabled dormers. To north a C.16/17 section of painted brick with tiled roof and gabled end. Front has sash windows. Door with flat hood flanked by canted bay windows.	T. & C.P. Act C.A. N.P. Act A.O.N.B.	SU 748 231 1303 24
Building C.16	Nos. 22–26. 2 storeys. C.18 brick facade to earlier timber-framed building. Half-hipped tiled roof with massive off-centre chimney. Canted bay window on ground floor. Two early C.19 doors under hood. Two half-hipped gabled extensions at rear.	T. & C.P. Act C.A. N.P. Act A.O.N.B.	SU 748 230 1303 27
House C.16	No. 28. Dragon House. 2 storeys and attic. Refronted early C.18. Steeply pitched tiled roof with large chimney, and four hipped gabled dormers. Grey brick walls with red brick dressings. Sash windows with glazing bars. Sun insurance sign. East elevation timber-framed. Two tile-hung gables contain mullion windows with diamond-shaped leaded lights. Interior with massive beams, old oak floors. C.16 fireplaces and some panelling.	T. & C.P. Act C.A. N.P. Act A.O.N.B.	SU 748 230 1303 28
Garden Walls and Gazebo C.18	Dragon House. Old brick walls to north and east of back garden. C.18 brick gazebo of 2 storeys on east wall. Hipped tiled roof. Interior has narrow stair case, some wainscoting, and tiny window seats.	T. & C.P. Act C.A. N.P. Act A.O.N.B.	SU 748 230 1303 26
House C.18	No. 32. 2 storeys. Stuccoed malmstone and brick. Hipped tiled roof. South wall tile hung. Central door with square bay window on right.	C.A. N.P. Act A.O.N.B.	SU 748 230 1303 29
Building C.17	Nos. 34 and 36. Refronted in red brick in mid C.18. Uneven tiled roof. Dentilled cornice and brick parapet. Sash windows. Three steps to doors, which have flat hoods on cut brackets.	T. & C.P. Act C.A. N.P. Act A.O.N.B.	SU 747 230 1303 30
Cottage C.17	No. 38. Refronted in C.18. 2 storeys. Hipped tiled roof, sweeping low at back. Plaster faced with rendered plinth. Sash windows with glazing bars. Modern shop front.	T. & C.P. Act C.A.. N.P. Act	SU 748 230 1303 31
Building C.18	Nos. 9 and 11. 2 storeys and attic. Uneven tiled roof with two flat dormers. Deep moulded eaves cornice. Painted slate hung front. Central oriel bay window with sash window either side, on first floor. Central bowed shop front with double door.	T. & C.P. Act C.A. N.P. Act A.O.N.B.	SU 748 230 1302 21
House C.18	No. 13. 2 storeys. High pitched tiled roof, hipped at left. Modillioned eaves cornice. Brick front. Sash windows with glazing bars on first floor. C.19 shop fronts converted to office windows and doors. Modern 2-storey extension.	T. & C.P. Act C.A. N.P. Act A.O.N.B.	SU 748 230 1302 22

Description and Date	Remarks	Protection	Grid Ref. and Punchcard No.

Group D — (cont.)

Farnham Road, Sheet

Description and Date	Remarks	Protection	Grid Ref. and Punchcard No.
Church C.19	Church of St. Mary. Built 1868/9 by Sir Arthur Blomfield. Early English Transitional style. Coursed rubble with pitched tiled roof. Tower of three stages with stepped angle buttresses and shingled broach spire with clock.	T. & C.P. Act C.A. N.P. Act A.O.N.B.	SU 757 245 1302 171
Terrace C.19	Nos. 1—6, The Vale. Originally Tan Yard Cottages, close to stream used for tanning. 2 storeys. Walls of painted greensand. Flint at sides and outshot. Sliding sash windows, some altered.	C.A. N.P. Act A.O.N.B.	SU 757 247 1302 172
Cottage C.18	Bridge Cottage. Greensand structure, rendered on front and right side. 2 storeys. Slate roof. Leaded windows of Gothic style. Door with curved panels in diamond patterned frame.	C.A. N.P. Act A.O.N.B.	SU 757 247 1302 170

Harrow Lane, Sheet

Description and Date	Remarks	Protection	Grid Ref. and Punchcard No.
Farmhouse C.19	Tilmore Farm. 2 storeys. Red and blue brick front. Slate roof with two chimneys. Righthand wall of flint with brick chimney and quoins. Blocked window over door. Segmental arches to upper casement windows.	N.P. Act A.O.N.B.	SU 747 245 1302 174
Cottage C.19	Hillside. Small cottage of whitewashed greensand and brick dressings. 1 storey. Modern tiled roof. Casement window with glazing bars. Blocked up well.	N.P. Act A.O.N.B.	SU 748 247 1302 175
Inn C.17/18	The Harrow. 1½ and 2 storeys. Old tiled roof with four chimneys. Painted stone ground floor, tile-hung above. Casement windows. Doorway with tiled hood. 3-bay verandah with wooden supports. Left hand wing timber-framed. Interior has some panelling.	T. & C.P. Act N.P. Act A.O.N.B.	SU 751 251 1302 239

Heath Road

Description and Date	Remarks	Protection	Grid Ref. and Punchcard No.
House C.17	Hatton's Mead. Partly converted from a malthouse. 3 storeys. Brick with tile roof. Original timbers in roof. Sash windows at the front, sash and casements at the side and original casements at rear on second floor. Upper 2 storeys tile-hung. Restored this century.	C.A. N.P. Act A.O.N.B.	SU 749 232 1303 33
Cottages C.17	Nos. 4 and 6. Dated 1611. 2 storeys. Steeply pitched tiled roof with gables, hipped at left, half, hipped at right. Ground floor rendered, with overhanging tile-hung first floor. Square bay windows on ground floor, casement windows with glazing bars above. Timber-frame visible at east end. No. 4 jettied. Former coachman's and groom's cottages.	T. & C.P. Act C.A. N.P. Act A.O.N.B.	SU 749 232 1303 34

Description and Date	Remarks	Protection	Grid Ref. and Punchcard No.
Group D — (cont.)			
Barn C.18	No. 26. 5-bay with aisle on western side. Substantial timbers, some replaced in southern bay. At right angles to the barn, and lying along the road-side is a 2-storey brick building of similar size with "J.G. 1899" in blue headers set in the red brick wall.	N.P. Act A.O.N.B.	SU 750 232 1303 454
Building C.16	The Tap. Part of original buildings of Red Lion Hotel, College Street. 2 low storeys. Hipped tiled roof. Casement and horizontal sliding windows with glazing bars. Rendered, painted walls. Door with flat canopy on curved brackets, part glazed door. Sun Fire Insurance plaque in blocked window recess.	T. & C.P. Act C.A. N.P. Act A.O.N.B.	SU 749 232 1303 15A
House C.16	Herne House. Originally C.16 farmhouse with C.17 extension, enlarged to 3 storeys in C.19. Wing added. Stuccoed with slate roof. Glass roofed verandah with iron pillars on west side. Sash windows.	N.P. Act A.O.N.B.	SU 750 232 1303 32
High Street			
House C.18	No. 15. 3 storeys. Hipped slate roof with deep eaves cornice. Colourwashed brick front. Sash windows under brick arches. Partially glazed panelled door. Doorway with panelled pilasters and dentilled cornice hood on brackets.	T. & C.P. Act C.A. N.P. Act A.O.N.B.	SU 747 232 1302 36
Building C.17	No. 17 and 19. 2 storeys and attic. Timber-framed and plaster faced. Tiled roof of high pitch. Each storey slightly overhangs. Three pendants under gable carved '1613 NP'. Sash windows. Ground floor shop fronts. No. 19 has semi-circular hood over door.	T. & C.P. Act C.A. N.P. Act A.O.N.B.	SU 747 232 1302 39
House C.17	No. 6. C.19 brick front and parapet. Tiled roof partly hidden. 2 storeys. West side shows timber framing and roughcast infilling. Sash and casement windows. Regency room to north with semi-circular end, rounded slate roof and domed ceiling.	T. & C.P. Act C.A. N.P. Act A.O.N.B.	SU 747 232 1302 35
House C.17	No. 12. Lyndum House. 2 storeys. Painted brick with rendered left hand bay. Hipped slate roof. Bay windows on both floors alternate with smaller windows. Bays have pilasters and modillioned cornice. Doorcase with fanlight, pilasters and open pediment. East wall timber framed with brick and malmstone infilling. Core of building probably C.17.	T. & C.P. Act C.A. N.P. Act A.O.N.B.	SU 747 232 1302 37
House C.18	No. 16. 2 storeys. Tiled roof, hipped at left. Curved rafter ends visible. Plastered front. Late C.19 sash windows. At right 2-storey canted bay. Doorway with reeded pilasters and cornice hood on carved consoles.	T. & C.P. Act C.A. N.P. Act A.O.N.B.	SU 747 232 1302 38

18th Century Cottages, Sheep Street, PETERSFIELD

Description and Date	Remarks	Protection	Grid Ref. and Punchcard No.

Group D — (cont.)

Description and Date	Remarks	Protection	Grid Ref. and Punchcard No.
House C.18	No. 18. Winton House, formerly part of the Old White Hart. 3 storeys. Plaster faced. Brick with parapet. Hidden slate roof. Sash windows with glazing bars. Central 6-panel door with diamond-patterned fanlight. Massive doric porch with fluted columns. C.16 rear section.	T. & C.P. Act C.A. N.P. Act A.O.N.B.	SU 747 232 1302 40
Walls	Garden walls north of High Street, on boundaries of No. 16. Brick and stone wall ramped high up the side of rear extension to Winton House.	T. & C.P. Act C.A. N.P. Act A.O.N.B.	SU 748 232 1302 179
Shop C.16/17	No. 20. 2 storeys C.18. Front of brick with stone cornice and parapet. Double span tiled roof. Sash windows and modern shop front. Late C.17 gabled rear extension. Tall brick chimney. Beams and Tudor arch fireplace inside. Formerly part of The Old White Hart. Plaque inscribed "Old White Hart, 1590'.	T. & C.P. Act C.A. N.P. Act A.O.N.B.	SU 747 232 1302 41
Building C.16/17	No. 22. Brick front with dentilled cornice and parapet. Tiled roof u-shaped at rear suggesting C.16/17 date. Sash windows with stuccoed lintels. 6-panel door with fanlight and later cornice hood. Doorcase at back with lion masks. Window extension to east with jettied tile-hung first floor.	T. & C.P. Act C.A. N.P. Act A.O.N.B.	SU 747 232 1302 42
House C.17/18	No. 24. Narrow front of 3 storeys in painted brick. Hipped tiled roof of six roof ridges. Sash window in bay on all three floors. Doorway with flat pilasters, entablature, and open pediment. Tile-hung west wall with early C.19 door.	T. & C.P. Act C.A. N.P. Act A.O.N.B.	SU 748 232 1302 43
Building C.16	Nos. 26, 28 and 28A. Long building of 2 storeys and attic. High pitched tiled roof with two chimneys and three dormers. C.18 brick front with segmental brick arches to first floor windows. Sash windows. Sun Insurance signs on first floor of Nos. 26 and 28.	T. & C.P, Act C.A. N.P. Act A.O.N.B.	SU 748 232 1302 44
Building C.18	No. 32. 2 storeys. Plaster faced brick, with slate roof. Sash windows. Two ground floor shop fronts.	C.A. N.P. Act A.O.N.B.	SU 748 232 1302 45
Building C.19	No. 34. 2 storeys. Hipped slate roof with parapet to centre section. Curved corner with four windows. Plaster faced. Sash windows with glazing bars. Ground floor shop front. Important corner site, High Street/College Street.	T. & C.P. Act C.A. N.P. Act A.O.N.B.	SU 748 232 1302 46
Building C.19	No. 36. Important site closing vista of the High Street. 3 storeys. Stuccoed front. Hipped slate roof with deep eaves soffit. Centre windows on first and second floor blocked. Sash windows. Modern shop front. Extensions at back.	T. & C.P. Act C.A. N.P. Act A.O.N.B.	SU 748 232 1303 47

Description and Date	Remarks	Protection	Grid Ref. and Punchcard No.

Group D — (cont.)

Hylton Road

Description and Date	Remarks	Protection	Grid Ref. and Punchcard No.
House C.17	No. 17. Painted brick front of 2 storeys. Tiled roof with massive chimney and two later gabled dormers. Sash windows. Door with rectangular fanlight and margin lights. Later tiled hood. Later extension with lower roof line.	T. & C.P. Act C.A. N.P. Act A.O.N.B.	SU 746 231 1301 48
House C.17	No. 19. 2 storeys. High pitched, tiled roof. Painted brick front with large sash windows. Doorway with fanlight, reeded architrave and small hood on brackets. Hipped gable with attic window. Modern extension.	T. & C.P. Act C.A. N.P. Act A.O.N.B.	SU 746 231 1301 49
House C.16	No. 21. 2 storeys. C.18 brick front probably to earlier building. Pilasters at sides of front. Slate roof of steep pitch at back. Tile-hung west end. Sash windows. Some timber-framing inside.	T. & C.P. Act C.A. N.P. Act A.O.N.B.	SU 745 231 1301 50
Walls	Flint and ironstone walls close to the infant school and Gas Board properties. All have brick capping. Part is within a conservation area.	C.A. N.P. Act A.O.N.B.	SU 746 230 1301 51

Lavant Street

Description and Date	Remarks	Protection	Grid Ref. and Punchcard No.
House C.19	Railway station house. 3 storeys. Entrance on station approach and access to down platform. Ornamental bargeboards gable. Central brick chimney with stone mouldings. Station and station house cement rendered, colourwashed white with square headed windows. Drip stones over windows and door. Station building is single storey.	N.P. Act A.O.N.B.	SU 743 235 1301 111

London Road, Sheet

Description and Date	Remarks	Protection	Grid Ref. and Punchcard No.
House and Wall C.18	Old Sheet House. High pitched hipped, tiled roof. 2 storeys. Centre gable with stone coping and urns at sides. Lunette in gable. Sash windows. Door with cornice hood on cut brackets. Gabled extension of brick and stone. Garden wall to northwest, of stone with brick dressings and flint band.	T. & C.P. Act C.A. N.P. Act A.O.N.B.	SU 760 244 1302 166
House C.16	No. 21. White Cottage. Now two dwellings. C.17 and C.18 additions. 2 storeys. Tiled roof. Brick ground floor with coursed rubble above, all limewashed. Half glazed doors under segmental arches, casement windows. C.19 rear extensions.	T. & C.P. Act N.P. Act A.O.N.B.	SU 758 241 1302 173
Building C.16/17	Nos. 25 and 27. Barnside and Farm End Cottage. Timber-framed but refronted with brick in C.19. Single storey and attic. Tiled roof, formerly thatched with three dormers. Massive crow-stepped chimney. Casement windows.	T. & C.P. Act N.P. Act A.O.N.B.	SU 759 242 1302 52
Barn	At rear of Farm End Cottage and Barnside. Timber-framed. Queen-post truss, windbrace and purlin construction. Corrugated iron roof.	N.P. Act A.O.N.B.	SU 759 242 1302 53

Description and Date	Remarks	Protection	Grid Ref. and Punchcard No.
Group D — (cont.)			
House C.18	No. 10. Built 1792. 2 storeys. Shallow slate roof with two chimneys. Red and blue brick front. Side walls of stone. Sash windows. Central door with rectangular patterned fanlight. Small bay window to left. Modern extension.	N.P. Act A.O.N.B.	SU 758 242 1302 55
Stable C.19	No. 10. Greensand ground floor, red brick first floor. Half glazed door with gabled hood. Two windows flank loft door. Dovecote in gable. Built 1897.	N.P. Act A.O.N.B.	SU 758 242 1302 55A
Long Lane, Sheet			
Farmhouse C.19	Lords Farm. 2 storeys. Tiled roof with two chimneys. First floor red brick with dentil cornice, ground floor red and blue brick. Steps to front door with open porch. Single storey extension.	N.P. Act A.O.N.B.	SU 753 246 1302 54
Love Lane			
Building C.19	Health Centre, formerly The Workhouse. 2 storeys. Red brick with blue headers to first floor. Building dated 1843. Outer wings of E-shaped building have flint walls with two brick string courses to ground floor. Central wing all brick, but malmstone on end wall, showing above lean-to. Slate roof. Sash windows with glazing bars. Small separate single storey chapel. Red brick with two diamonds and a cross in blue headers on walls of semi-octagonal chancel. Decorative wooden window frames and bargeboards. Tiled roof. Now used as Petersfield Evangelical Church.	N.P. Act A.O.N.B.	SU 751 237 1302 405
Mill Lane, Sheet			
Building C.17/18	No. 13. Brook Rising and Mallards Reach. 2 storeys and attic. Tiled roof with catslide to rear. Two hipped dormers at front one at rear. Malmstone with brick dressings. Casement windows. Inner walls timber-framed.	C.A. N.P. Act A.O.N.B.	SU 760 246 1302 167
House	No. 33. 2 storeys. Timber-framed with tile-hung front. Four small windows. Timber-framing visible inside.	C.A. N.P. Act A.O.N.B.	SU 760 246 1302 168
House C.19	Sheet Bridge Mill. Formerly part of mill, now converted to a residence. 2-storey with loft. Brick structure, slate roof. Three bays. Sash windows with glazing bars, bay windows either side of door, which has a flat canopy on moulded brackets. No machinery remains. Water turbine used when wheel was working. Ref: A Gazetteer of the Water, Wind and Tide Mills of Hampshire, (Ellis), p. 135.	C.A. N.P. Act A.O.N.B.	SU 759 247 1302 243

Group D — (cont.)

Old Mill Lane, Sheet

Description and Date	Remarks	Protection	Grid Ref. and Punchcard No.
Cottages (3) C.16	Nos. 10, 14 and 16. Old Mill Cottages. L-shaped group. Dated 1606 but of earlier appearance. 2 storeys and basement. Timber-framed with brick infilling on stone foundations. Jettied first floor with oriel window on side facing Old Mill Lane. West two bays much restored with modern casements. Malmstone walling at right over brick basement storey. Casement windows. At rear one storey and attic. Tile-hung upper part, brick and stone with some visible timber below. Interior has very large beams of early date.	T. & C.P. Act N.P. Act A.O.N.B.	SU 760 241 1302 33
Cottage C.17	Old Mill Cottage. 2 storeys. Timber-framed with roughcast infilling. High pitched tiled roof hipped at left with gable. Tudor chimney of stone and brick. Extension at left. Sash windows with glazing bars. Outshot at rear.	T. & C.P. Act N.P. Act A.O.N.B.	SU 760 241 1302 34
Mill C.18	The Old Mill. Building dated 1742, on older brick foundations. Brick with tile-hung upper storey and tiled roof. Hipped tile-hung gable. Converted to house 1937. Mill wheel removed. Sun Fire mark on front. Traces of mediaeval stone foundations.	N.P. Act A.O.N.B.	SU 760 241 1302 35

Osborne Road

Description and Date	Remarks	Protection	Grid Ref. and Punchcard No.
Terrace C.20	South side of road. Twenty 2-storey houses. Slate roofed with shared chimneys. Square bay windows with sloping slate roofs. Paired long sash windows above with smaller window over front door. Front doors with slated canopies.	N.P. Act A.O.N.B.	SU 746 236 — 747 236 1302 56

Pulens Lane, Sheet

Description and Date	Remarks	Protection	Grid Ref. and Punchcard No.
House C.16	Mill House. C.16 house with C.17 west wing. Refronted C.18. 2 storeys. Hipped tiled roof. Tile-hung first floor, ground floor of malmstone with brick dressings. Sash windows. Door with fanlight under small hood. Earlier wing has roof of higher pitch, casement windows and some interior panelling. C.19 kitchen wing.	T. & C.P. Act N.P. Act A.O.N.B.	SU 759 241 1302 32

Ramsdean Road, Stroud

Description and Date	Remarks	Protection	Grid Ref. and Punchcard No.
Farmhouse C.16	Stroudbridge Farmhouse. 2 storeys and attic. Timber-framed. Steeply pitched half-hipped tiled roof, with square dormer. Close studded first floor with flint infilling at right, brick at left with square framing. Ground floor of bulging C.18 brick with C.19 brick buttresses. South wall tile-hung. Interior has long, chamfered beams.	T. & C.P. Act N.P. Act A.O.N.B.	SU 720 229 1301 158
Cottage	Vine Cottage. Brick structure with hipped tiled roof.	N.P. Act A.O.N.B.	SU 721 233 1301 150

Description and Date	Remarks	Protection	Grid Ref. and Punchcard No.
Group D — (cont.)			
House C.18/19	Holmwood Cottage, off Ramsdean Road, Stroud Common. 2 storeys. Western section C.18 farmhouse fronted by narrow bricks irregularly coloured in flemish bond. Eastern section in standard brickwork. One chimney stack in central position. Modern casements, those on upper storey narrow and under eaves. Plain door to right of centre. Slate roof of low pitch with one chimney stack in central position and one at east end.	N.P. Act A.O.N.B.	SU 723 233 1301 151
Cottage C.18	No. 7 Primrose Cottage. 2 storeys. Tiled hipped roof. First floor brick rat trap bond now colour-washed. Second floor tile-hung. Simple door on north side. Two casement windows on each storey. Outshot at rear. Recent modern wing at right angles.	N.P. Act A.O.N.B.	SU 721 234 1301 450
Ramshill			
House C.19	The Gables. In tree lined lane off Ramshill. 1½ storeys. Knapped flints with brick dressings. Gothic style windows. Multi-gabled roof with fishscale tiles.	N.P. Act A.O.N.B.	SU 750 239 1302 61
Building C.19	Cliff Cottage. 2 storeys. Hipped slate roof with deep eaves soffit. Stuccoed walls. Sash windows with glazing bars. French doors lead to 5-column verandah. 6-panel door with fanlight and reeded architrave. Additions to rear.	T. & C.P. Act N.P. Act A.O.N.B.	SU 750 237 1302 60
Terrace C.18	Nos. 24—28. (even). Timber-framed with infilling of brick nogging. Modern brick ground floor. Steeply pitched roof. Central pediment with small window. Cottages in terrace of seven bays.	N.P. Act A.O.N.B.	SU 751 238 1302 59
Building C.19	Ramshill House, formerly White Readons. 2 storeys. Flint walls with ashlar dressings. Tiled roof.	N.P. Act A.O.N.B.	SU 752 238 1302 402
House C.19	Beechlands. 2 storeys. Shallow pitched roof. Three windows. Regency verandah of wrought iron. Central pediment above contains coloured glass.	N.P. Act A.O.N.B.	SU 753 240 1302 176
Building C.18	Broadlands. 2 storeys. Malmstone with brick dressings. Front and side faced with slates and whitewashed. Slate roof with wide eaves. Sash windows. Centre of front recessed, with classical porch on Doric columns. Doorcase with egg and dart moulding and decorated frieze. Three stone steps. Tile-hung additions.	T. & C.P. Act N.P. Act A.O.N.B.	SU 755 241 1302 58

Group D — (cont.)

Description and Date	Remarks	Protection	Grid Ref. and Punchcard No.
Building C.19	Churchers College. Built 1881. 3-storey gabled centre section with 2-storey wings. Walls of Godalming Bargate stone with ashlar dressings. Tiled roof with zig-zag pattern in blue tiles on red. Many chimneys. Square headed sash windows. Hall with rose window. Clock tower with spire to left. Modern additions. Gate posts and wrought iron gate erected by past and present scholars in memory of J. Bonham-Carter in 1907. Centre top of gate has representation of a sailing ship (the college badge) to note connection of founder with East India Company. Architect: Crickmay.	N.P. Act A.O.N.B.	SU 753 239 1302 57
House C.19	Heath Harrison House (Headmasters House Churchers College). 2 storeys. Slate roof with two chimneys. North side flint with brick dressings, other walls rendered. Door at west, with fanlight, and porch with two plain columns. Verandah on east side with plain columns.	N.P. Act A.O.N.B.	SU 753 239 1302 62

Reservoir Lane, Sheet

Description and Date	Remarks	Protection	Grid Ref. and Punchcard No.
Farmhouse C.18	Tilmore House, formerly Shirtles. Rubble walls galleted with ironstone. Brick quoins and window dressings. Tiled roof, formerly thatched. Road front of 2 storeys with two small windows. Single storey extension formerly the dairy. Garden side has rounded bay of 2 storeys. Leaded casement windows. 2-storey stone extension partly tile-hung.	T. & C.P. Act N.P. Act A.O.N.B.	SU 747 244 1302 63

Rothercombe Lane, Stroud

Description and Date	Remarks	Protection	Grid Ref. and Punchcard No.
Farmhouse C.16	Rothercombe Farmhouse. Tiled roof with two chimneys. Red brick walls with diaper of blue-grey headers. Casement windows alternate with blank window panels. Door with hood. South and west walls tile-hung.	T. & C.P. Act N.P. Act A.O.N.B.	SU 721 240 1301 160

Russell Way

Description and Date	Remarks	Protection	Grid Ref. and Punchcard No.
Cottage C.16	No. 1. Chapel Cottage. 2 storeys and attic. Tiled roof with dormer at rear. Malmstone structure with brick dressings. Casement windows under segmental brick arches. Brick porch at rear. High curved, old brick wall to southeast with moulded coping, which formerly connected the cottage to Heath House.	T. & C.P. Act N.P. Act A.O.N.B.	SU 753 225 1303 135
House C.18	No. 16. Wealh Lodge. 2 storeys. Steeply pitched tiled roof descends to door level at rear. Three gabled dormers of later date. Red brick facade with diaper pattern of blue headers. Other walls of malmstone construction. Casement windows under brick arches, some with shutters. Brick porch with tiled gable.	T. & C.P. Act N.P. Act A.O.N.B.	SU 754 224 1305 136

Description and Date	Remarks	Protection	Grid Ref. and Punchcard No.

Group D — (cont.)

St. Peter's Road

Description and Date	Remarks	Protection	Grid Ref. and Punchcard No.
Building C.17	No. 2A. Small building of 2 storeys. High pitched tiled roof. Timber-framed with brick infilling. Casement windows on first floor. Shop front below.	T. & C.P. Act C.A. N.P. Act A.O.N.B.	SU 746 231 1302 97
Cottages C.17/18	Nos. 2 and 4. 2 storeys. Red brick front with blue headers. Tiled roof, half hipped at left. Windows over doors are blocked. Casement and sash windows. Plain plank doors.	T. & C.P. Act C.A. N.P. Act A.O.N.B.	SU 746 231 1302 120
House C.18	No. 12. Hipped tiled roof. 2 storeys. Red brick structure. Renewed sash windows. Door at left with gabled hood. Main door has doorcase with round attached columns.	T. & C.P. Act C.A. N.P. Act A.O.N.B.	SU 747 231 1302 119

Sheep Street

Description and Date	Remarks	Protection	Grid Ref. and Punchcard No.
Cottage C.18	No. 2. 2 storeys. Basement and attic. Tiled roof with two hipped dormers. Ground floor oriel bow window. Sash windows with glazing bars. Four steps to door under flat hood with curved brackets.	T. & C.P. Act C.A. N.P. Act A.O.N.B.	SU 746 232 1301 64
Cottages (3) C.18	Nos. 4, 6 and 8. Range of 2 storeys with tiled roof. Moulded wooden eaves cornice. Red brick with blue headers. Sash windows. Nos. 4 and 6 have bow windows on ground floor. 6-panel doors under flat hoods.	T. & C.P. Act C.A. N.P. Act A.O.N.B.	SU 745 231 1301 65
Cottages C.18	Nos. 10 and 12. 2 storeys. Tiled roof. One hipped dormer with leaded casement window. Limewashed brick front. Oriel bow windows on ground floor, casements above. Projecting hood over doors and windows. No. 10 has keystone bearing date '1789'.	T. & C.P. Act C.A. N.P. Act A.O.N.B.	SU 745 231 1301 66
Cottages (2) C.18/19	Nos. 14 and 16. Hipped slate roof, fairly low pitch. Plastered front of 2 storeys. Sash windows with glazing bars. Doors in reeded architrave with fanlight and flat hood over.	T. & C.P. Act C.A. N.P. Act A.O.N.B.	SU 745 231 1301 67
Cottage C.18	No. 18. C.18 2-storey facade to earlier cottage. Uneven tiled roof of high pitch. Brick structure with plinth. Restored windows. 6-panel door with hood over.	T. & C.P. Act N.P. Act A.O.N.B.	SU 745 231 1301 70
Cottages (3) C.16	Nos. 20—24. 2 storeys. Uneven steeply pitched tiled roof. Overhanging eaves. Three chimneys. Jettied first floor mostly of close studded timbers. Brick ground floor. Metal casements with diamond leading on first floor. Plain plank doors.	T. & C.P. Act C.A. N.P. Act A.O.N.B.	SU 745 231 1301 71
Cottage C.16/17	No. 26. Continuous with 2A, The Spain. 2 storeys. High pitched, tiled roof. Pebbledashed with mock timbers, some signs of jettied front. Casement and sash windows.	T. & C.P. Act C.A. N.P. Act A.O.N.B.	SU 745 231 1301 72

Group D — (cont.)

Description and Date	Remarks	Protection	Grid Ref. and Punchcard No.
Outbuilding	To rear of No. 15. Small structure of brick with timber-framing. Loft over. Hipped tiled roof.	C.A. N.P. Act A.O.N.B.	SU 745 232 1301 68
Building C.18/19	No. 17. Brick structure with tiled roof. Rectangular sash window on first floor. Interior beams. Shop premises.	C.A. N.P. Act A.O.N.B.	SU 745 231 1301 69

Sheet Green, Sheet

Description and Date	Remarks	Protection	Grid Ref. and Punchcard No.
Building C.16	Nos. 4 and 5. Old Post Office. 2 storeys. Tiled roof. Massive chimney of narrow bricks with several shafts. Plastered front. Front extension with trellis porch and G.P.O. letterbox. C.19 door under hood at left. Sash windows with glazing bars and two small modern bay windows.	T. & C.P. Act C.A. N.P. Act A.O.N.B.	SU 758 245 1302 73
Building C.19	Mount Pleasant. Formerly a school with two cottages attached, now one dwelling. Single storey and attic. Casement windows with glazing bars and chamfered brick surrounds. Plain wooden door. Walls, brick in Dearne bond. Schoolroom has gable to front with 8-light window and stone tablet. Building dated 1898.	N.P. Act A.O.N.B.	SU 757 245 1302 404
Building C.16	Nos. 5 and 6 Broadlands Cottages. Single storey and attic. Three dormers. Hipped tiled roof with large chimney of thin bricks. Square timber-framing with brick infilling, colourwashed. Casement windows. Modern gabled porch.	T. & C.P. Act C.A. N.P. Act A.O.N.B.	SU 758 245 1302 74

The Spain

Description and Date	Remarks	Protection	Grid Ref. and Punchcard No.
Cottage C.19	No. 1. 2 storeys. Hipped slate roof. Stuccoed front. Sash windows. Oriel bay window on ground floor. Door with rectangular fanlight, reeded architrave and cornice hood over.	T. & C.P. Act C.A. N.P. Act A.O.N.B.	SU 745 231 1301 75
House C.18	No. 3. 2 storeys. Plastered front. Modern bay windows on ground floor. Rear of first floor has semi-circular lunette.	C.A. N.P. Act A.O.N.B.	SU 745 231 1301 77
House C.19	No. 5. Spain House. Hipped slate roof. 3 storeys. Brick walls with stuccoed front and rendered plinth. Sash windows. Three steps to door. Tuscan doorcase with columns and cornice.	T. & C.P. Act C.A. N.P. Act A.O.N.B.	SU 745 232 1301 81
Coach House	East of Spain House, adjoining No. 3 and wall to carriage gate. Brick walls with brick dentil cornice. Two blocked segment headed windows. Hipped, tiled roof.	T. & C.P. Act C.A. N.P. Act A.O.N.B.	SU 745 231 1301 80
House C.18	No. 7. 2 storeys. Tiled roof with brick dentil cornice. Front of grey brick with red brick dressings. Rendered plinth. Sash windows. Doorway with moulded architrave and flat hood.	T. & C.P. Act C.A. N.P. Act A.O.N.B.	SU 745 232 1301 84

Description and Date	Remarks	Protection	Grid Ref. and Punchcard No.

Group D — (cont.)

Description and Date	Remarks	Protection	Grid Ref. and Punchcard No.
House C.16/17	No. 9. Painted brick early C.18 front. High pitched half-hipped tiled roof with gablets. Two chimneys. Recessed sash windows with glazing bars. Ground floor windows with segmental brick arches. Timber-framing visible on west wall. Formerly known as the Bricklayers Arms.	T. & C.P. Act C.A. N.P. Act A.O.N.B.	SU 744 232 1301 86
Cottage	No. 13. Painted brick. 2 storeys. Tiled roof. Two windows. Front wall of flint with brick capping and dressings. Ancient wall to rear.	C.A. N.P. Act A.O.N.B.	SU 744 232 1301 87
House C.17	No. 15. Altered timber-framed house of 2 storeys. Tiled roof with large chimney. Tile-hung first floor. Brick and ironstone ground floor supported by two large brick buttresses. Casement windows. New door.	T. & C.P. Act C.A. N.P. Act A.O.N.B.	SU 744 232 1301 88
Building C.18	No. 2. 2 storeys. High pitched tiled roof with end chimney. Pebbledashed front with flat band between floors. Sash and casement windows. Plain door with cornice hood on cut brackets above.	C.A. N.P. Act A.O.N.B.	SU 745 231 1301 76A
Building C.16/17	No. 2A. 2 storeys. High pitched tiled roof. Pebbledashed with signs of jettied front. Rendered plinth. Sash windows. Plain plank door.	T. & C.P. Act C.A. N.P. Act A.O.N.B.	SU 745 231 1301 76
House C.19	No. 4. 2 storeys. Hipped slated roof with tiled ridges. Plastered walls. Sash windows with glazing bars. Doorcase with reeded pilasters and rectangular fanlight. Single-storey extension.	T. & C.P. Act C.A.. N.P. Act A.O.N.B.	SU 745 231 1301 79
House C.19	No. 6. Moreton House. 2 storeys. Renewed hipped pantile roof with deep eaves soffit. Flint and brick walls with stuccoed front. Pilasters with panels of rustication between. Sash windows. Porch with square columns. Stone balconies to some upstairs windows. Carriage entrance to west. Inside has curved staircase. Now a school.	T. & C.P. Act C.A. N.P. Act A.O.N.B.	SU 745 231 1301 82
House C.18	Nos. 8 and 10. 2 storeys. Tiled roof, with three parallel roof ridges behind. No. 8 red brick, No. 10 red brick with blue headers. Sash windows, No. 8 with ground floor oriel window. 6-panel doors. House may be older than facade.	T. & C.P. Act C.A. N.P. Act A.O.N.B.	SU 745 231 1301 85

Description and Date	Remarks	Protection	Grid Ref. and Punchcard No.

Group D — (cont.)

Description and Date	Remarks	Protection	Grid Ref. and Punchcard No.
House C.15/16	No. 22. Goodyers. Stone construction. Hipped tiled roof. Left hand bay of 2 storeys. Plastered with jettied first floor. C.18 brick front of 2 storeys and attic to most of house. Lunettes with keystones in gables. Sash windows with segmental brick arches and keystones. Rendered plinth. South and west walls of galleted sandstone and ironstone with some flint and red brick dressings. Tile-hung first floor to rear. Interior has six stone fireplaces with Tudor arches. Plaque on wall states "John Goodyer, Botanist and Royalist 1592—1664" lived here. Stone built vice in small courtyard. Ref: Early English Botanists, (Gunther).	T. & C.P. Act C.A. N.P. Act A.O.N.B.	SU 744 231 1301 89
House C.15	No. 26. Tullys. Formerly Nos. 26 and 28, The Spain. The two remaining bays of a Wealden halled house, now modernised. 2 storeys, tile-hung first floor with brick below at the front, north wall timber-framed with brick infilling. New casement windows with leaded lights. Steeply pitched tiled roof, new chimney. Interior of roof has sooted rafters with purlins and wind-braces, and two arched braced collar trusses, one with superior moulding. Built over stone cellar of mediaeval house. Later extensions at left and rear.	T. & C.P. Act C.A. N.P. Act A.O.N.B.	SU 744 231 1301 90
Cottage C.16	No. 24. Formerly Goodyers Cottage. 2 low storeys and tile-hung attic. Half-hipped tiled roof. Recessed casement windows with glazing bars. Timber-framing visible at back. Roof is framed with staggered butt purlins and windbraces. Large chimney.	T. & C.P. Act C.A. N.P. Act A.O.N.B.	SU 744 231 1301 89A
Walls	Brook Lane. Flanked by walls. To east, flint with brick capping and dressing. To west, wall of malmstone and sandstone with tile ridge capping. Four old brick doorways with 4-centred arches open on to the lane. Forms east boundary wall of No. 22, The Spain.	C.A. N.P. Act A.O.N.B.	SU 744 231 1301 205
Building	No. 28. Extended and converted from barn to offices. Hipped, tiled roof. Structure of flint and malmstone with brick dressings. Barn originally connected with No. 22, The Spain.	N.P. Act A.O.N.B.	SU 744 232 1301 91
Cottage C.18	No. 30. Crumbles. Tiled roof with renewed chimney. 2 storeys. Limewashed brick walls with casement windows. Ground floor windows with segmental brick arches and modern louvred shutters.	T. & C.P. Act N.P. Act A.O.N.B.	SU 744 232 1301 92

Description and Date	Remarks	Protection	Grid Ref. and Punchcard No.

Group D — (cont.)

The Square

Description and Date	Remarks	Protection	Grid Ref. and Punchcard No.
Building C.16	No. 1. 2 storeys. Tiled roof with gabled dormers and chimney. Overhanging first floor, close studded with knapped flint infilling. Exposed beam ends. Rendered ground floor with modern shop fronts. Leaded casement windows above.	T. & C.P. Act C.A. N.P. Act A.O.N.B.	SU 747 233 1302 95
Building C.18	Nos. 3 and 4. 2 storeys and attic. Tiled roof with rebuilt brick chimney. Two hipped tiled dormers. Colourwashed brick walls. Sash windows. Centre window on first floor blocked. Sun Insurance plaque dated 1798. Entrance to 4A contains stone wall circa. 1600. Flat above contains oak panelling circa. 1580—1600.	T. & C.P. Act C.A. N.P. Act A.O.N.B.	SU 746 233 1302 96
Building C.19	No. 5. 3 storeys. Hipped slate roof. Brick structure. Slightly projecting centre section, with reproduction classical work. Sash windows with glazing bars. Deep modillion cornice. 2-storey extension with classical doorcase. Lead rainwater heads and pipes decorated with roses.	T. & C.P. Act C.A. N.P. Act A.O.N.B.	SU 746 233 1302 98
Shop C.17/18	No. 9. Tiled roof with brick dentilled cornice. Plaster front. 2 storeys. Bay on first floor. Timber work visible at west side. Ground floor shop front.	C.A. N.P. Act A.O.N.B.	SU 746 232 1302 99
Building C.18	Nos. 11 and 12. 3 storeys. Hipped tiled roof. Front of red brick with blue headers, and red brick dressings. Arches to windows. Seven second floor windows blocked. Modern shop fronts on ground floor. Rebuilt behind facade.	T. & C.P. Act C.A. N.P. Act A.O.N.B.	SU 746 232 1302 100
Shop C.18	No. 13. 3 storeys. Tiled roof. Brick structure. Ground floor shop front. Upper 2 storeys with modern bay windows.	C.A. N.P. Act A.O.N.B.	SU 746 232 1302 101
Shop C.18	No. 18. 3 storeys. Hipped tiled roof partly hidden behind tile-hung parapet. Red brick with blue headers and red brick dressings. Sash windows with glazing bars. Early C.20 shop front. C.17 gabled part at rear.	T. & C.P. Act C.A. N.P. Act A.O.N.B.	SU 746 232 1302 102
Building C.17	No. 19. 2 storeys. High pitched tiled roof with projecting chimney stack. Deep eaves. Plastered front. Casement windows. Ground floor shop front. Gabled rear extension with Gothic style window.	T. & C.P. Act C.A. N.P. Act A.O.N.B.	SU 746 232 1302 103
Inn C.18/19	Market Inn. Altered early C.19. 2 storeys. Tiled roof. Plastered front with diagonal brick cornice. Sash windows. Bow window on two floors. Two half glazed doors under bracketed hoods.	T. & C.P. Act C.A. N.P. Act A.O.N.B.	SU 746 232 1301 104

Group D — (cont.)

Description and Date	Remarks	Protection	Grid Ref. and Punchcard No.
Church C.12	St. Peter's. Begun in 1120 with cruciform plan and crossing tower of which east wall remains. Late C.12 aisles and central west tower. Chancel, nave roof, clerestory, vestry and north porch by Blomfield in C.19. Octagonal, perpendicular, panelled front. Weathervane of wrought iron. Clock. The flight of steps from the east side of churchyard into St. Peter's Road was built by the Jolliffe family for their own use. O.S.A. No. SU72 SW15. Ref: Buildings of England; Hants and I.O.W., (Pevsner and Lloyd), p. 371.	T. & C.P. Act C.A. N.P. Act A.O.N.B.	SU 746 231 1301 110
Tombstone	St. Peter's Churchyard. Tombstone of John Small, the famous Hambledon cricketer who died in 1826.	C.A. N.P. Act A.O.N.B.	SU 746 232 1301 106
House C.18	No. 24. 3 storeys. Red brick cornice and walls with blue headers. Sash, oriel, and bay windows. Three steps to doorway with brick pilasters, cornice and pediment in cut brick-work.	T. & C.P. Act C.A. N.P. Act A.O.N.B.	SU 746 232 1301 105
Building C.18	No. 25. 3 storeys with tiled roof. Formerly 2 storeys with dormer in roof. Plastered front. Bay window on lower 2 storeys. C.20 Gothic window inserted. Modern large window on second floor at back. Many alterations.	T. & C.P. Act C.A. N.P. Act A.O.N.B.	SU 746 232 1301 107
Statue C.18	Fine equestrian statue of William III dressed as a Roman Senator. Lead statue standing on stone pedestal, with Latin inscription. Cast in 1753, and restored in 1913 by public subscription. The statue is a focal point of the Square, and the town in general.	T. & C.P. Act S.A.M. No. 84 C.A. N.P. Act A.O.N.B.	SU 746 232 1301 108
Inn C.16/17	The George Inn. Timber-framed with Victorian front. Tiled roof with gable ends. Decorative bargeboards. 2 storeys. Colourwashed and rendered front. Sash windows. Gable over two windows at left.	C.A. N.P. Act A.O.N.B.	SU 746 232 1301 180

Station Road

Description and Date	Remarks	Protection	Grid Ref. and Punchcard No.
Church C.19	Roman Catholic Church of St. Lawrence, 1890—91 by Kelly. Cruciform plan. Red brick in Italian style. Copper dome. Round arched first floor windows. One bay chancel with apse to east. Segmental vault to nave.	T. & C.P. Act N.P. Act A.O.N.B.	SU 745 236 1301 113

Group D — (cont.)

Description and Date	Remarks	Protection	Grid Ref. and Punchcard No.
House C.17	No. 16. Formerly known as Chapel House. 2 storeys. Front elevation has ground floor plastered, tile-hung above, other walls flint with brick quoins. Originally timber-framed, still partly visible, tiled roof, half-hipped at right, sweeps down over outshot at rear. West end chimney of narrow bricks, ridge chimney renewed. Casement windows, three leaded light windows first floor, three below. Door in open porch. Modern single storey extension at left with two windows and a door.	N.P. Act A.O.N.B.	SU 745 235 1301 115
Coach House	No. 16. Flint structure with brick quoins. Gable over front door. Two brick buttresses. Three rows of fishscale tiles on roof.	N.P. Act A.O.N.B.	SU 745 235 1301 115A
House C.18	No. 18. 2 storeys. Brick with tile-hung first floor at front and back. Timber-framing visible in east facing wall. Three windows at front. Half-hipped tiled roof. Large central chimney.	N.P. Act A.O.N.B.	SU 745 235 1302 116
Notable Group C.20	Nos. 64—70. Detached houses of brick with stone dressings and porticos. 3 storeys. Each with ground floor stone bay window. Three sash windows on first floor. Slate roof with attic dormer.	N.P. Act A.O.N.B.	SU 747 236 1302 112
House C.17	No. 84. 3 storeys. Hipped tiled roof. Refronted with red brick and blue headers. Brick dentil cornice. Sash windows on second floor only. Early C.19 door under new bracketed hood.	T. & C.P. Act N.P. Act A.O.N.B.	SU 749 236 1302 117
House C.18	No. 86. 2 storeys and basement. Tiled roof with end chimneys, one on left stuccoed. Stuccoed walls. Sash windows with glazing bars. Doorway with reeded architrave and cornice hood on curved brackets. Four stone steps. Back and east walls of malmstone with brick dressings.	T. & C.P. Act N.P. Act A.O.N.B.	SU 750 236 1302 118
Gate Piers and Railings C.18	No. 86. Railings on low brick wall to front garden. C.18 cast iron with standards of spear-head and palmette pattern. Square piers with quatrefoil and Gothic patterns, and heavy urn finials. Gate combines patterns of railings and piers.	T. & C.P. Act N.P. Act A.O.N.B.	SU 750 236 1302 118A
Outbuilding C.18	Northwest of No. 86. Malmstone with brick dressings. High pitched tiled roof.	T. & C.P. Act N.P. Act A.O.N.B.	SU 749 236 1302 118B
Church C.20	Methodist. Built 1903. Flint structure with brick dressings. Tower with spire buttressed at corners. Nave. Rose window over door. Other windows, tall and arched with tracery. Situated on the west side of the church is a church hall built of similar materials and in similar style.	N.P. Act A.O.N.B.	SU 745 235 1301 114

Description and Date	Remarks	Protection	Grid Ref. and Punchcard No.
Group D — (cont.)			
Sussex Road			
Cottages C.17/18	Nos. 4 and 6. High pitched, tiled roof. Chimney removed. Brick structure of 2 storeys. Wooden casement windows. Those on ground floor of No. 6, under segmental brick arches. Plain plank doors. C.17 brick vault with stables over at rear of No. 4.	T. & C.P. Act C.A. N.P. Act A.O.N.B.	SU 747 229 1303 138
Cottages C.18	Nos. 8, 10 and 12. Tiled roofs. 2 storeys. Malmstone galleted with ironstone and dressed with red brick. Segmental brick arches to ground floor casement windows. No. 10 has old door with hood on cut brackets.	T. & C.P. Act C.A. N.P. Act A.O.N.B.	SU 747 229 1303 137
Building C.16	No. 14. 2 storeys. Side walls flint and random brick. Front wall slate hung. Hipped tiled roof. Large chimney. One casement window on first floor. One horizontal sliding window on ground floor. Side entrance.	C.A. N.P. Act A.O.N.B.	SU 748 229 1303 401
Cottage C.16/17	No. 18. Formerly L-shaped plan, but projecting wing removed. High pitched tiled roof, with Tudor brick chimney. 2 storeys. Structure of brick, and timber frame with malmstone and brick infilling. Door under heavy bracketed hood. Dormer window. Later oriel window below.	T. & C.P. Act C.A. N.P. Act A.O.N.B.	SU 748 229 1303 139
Cottage C.17	No. 20. Formerly Nos. 20 and 22, Sussex Road. 2 storeys. Steeply pitched tiled roof, hipped at right side. Rendered front. Sash and casement windows with glazing bars. Door with bracketed hood, another sharing segmental arch with windows.	T. & C.P. Act C.A. N.P. Act A.O.N.B.	SU 748 229 1303 140
Terrace C.16/17	Nos. 22, 24 and 26. Timber-framed but refronted in early C.18. 2 storeys. Highpitched tiled roof sweeping to door level at rear of No. 24. Timber framing with malmstone and brick infilling visible at left and at rear. Later casement windows.	T. & C.P. Act C.A. N.P. Act A.O.N.B.	SU 748 228 1303 142
House C.18	No. 32. Heath Lodge. Hipped tiled roof. 3 storeys. Painted brick structure. Sash windows with glazing bars, under brick arches. Door with semi-circular fanlight in moulded architrave. Five curved steps and wrought iron handrail to semi-circular porch, supported on four columns. Kitchen wing at back in similar style.	T. & C.P. Act N.P. Act A.O.N.B.	SU 749 228 1303 143
Garden Wall and Railings	Heath Lodge. Wrought iron railings on low brick plinth in front of house. Brick pier with ball finial either side. The walls facing the road are of brick construction, whilst those to the garden are of galleted ironstone surmounted by malmstone. Remains of brick gazebo in back wall. Centred on grid reference.	T. & C.P. Act C.A. N.P. Act A.O.N.B.	SU 749 228 1303 145

Description and Date	Remarks	Protection	Grid Ref. and Punchcard No.
Group D — (cont.)			
Building C.18	Heath Cottage & Wych Elm Cottage, formerly No. 34. Long range of single storey with attic buildings over cellars. Part was a malthouse. Tiled roof. Malmstone with brick facings. Back has windows with segmental brick arches. Dated 1789.	T. & C.P. Act N.P. Act A.O.N.B.	SU 749 228 1303 144
Garden Walls	To Wych Elm Cottage and Heath Cottage. High brick wall continuous with wall of No. 32, which sweeps round corner to Heath Pond Road. Also a dividing wall across the garden.	T. & C.P. Act N.P. Act A.O.N.B.	SU 750 228 1303 145A
Cottage C.18	No. 113. Malmstone and brick. Tiled roof descending to door level at back. Casement windows with leaded panes. Brick porch with tiled gable roof. Door approached by steps.	N.P. Act A.O.N.B.	SU 753 225 1303 146
Farmhouse C.19	Heath Farmhoush. 2 storeys. Hipped slate roof. Stuccoed walls, except north wall which is malmstone galleted with ironstone and red brick dressings. Sash windows with glazing bars. Front has glass roofed loggia on twisted iron columns .	T. & C.P. Act N.P. Act A.O.N.B.	SU 757 224 1303 141
Almhouses C.19	Nos. 141—145. Roof of fishscale tiles with bands of plain tiles. Spearheaded ridge tiles. 2 storeys. Walls of large knapped flints with black mortar and red brick dressings. Three gables to road, with two tall chimneys in gullies. Casement windows. Plaque now illegible.	T. & C.P. Act N.P. Act A.O.N.B.	SU 755 219 1303 169
Swan Street			
Walls	Swan Street, Frenchmans Road and west of The Spain. Flint walls capped with half round brick. Brick dressings at intervals.	N.P. Act A.O.N.B.	SU 741 232 — 744 233 1301 83
Cottages (4) C.17/18	Nos. 36—42. 2 storeys. Hipped, tiled roof. Timber-framed faced with brick, on a foundation of flint, malmstone and ironstone. Northern extension added in C.18 when building became a poor-house. Red brick with diaper of blue headers. Inscribed stone on north side with date 1771. Sash and modern bay windows. West wing possibly C.16.	T. & C.P. Act N.P. Act A.O.N.B.	SU 744 233 1301 121
Tilmore Road			
Houses C.19	Nos. 10—20. Crescent shaped terrace of 2-storey houses. Plaster faced with tiled roofs. Bay windows on ground floor.	N.P. Act A.O.N.B.	SU 744 237 1301 122
Village Street, Sheet			
House C.18	Sheet House. 2 storeys. Originally three bays, two bays added at later date. Hipped, double span tiled roof. Brick dentil cornice. Red brick with random blue headers in outer bays. Sash windows. Doorcase of slender columns and cornice hood. Rear extensions.	T. & C.P. Act C.A. N.P. Act A.O.N.B.	SU 759 245 1302 123

Description and Date	Remarks	Protection	Grid Ref. and Punchcard No.

Group D — (cont.)

Description and Date	Remarks	Protection	Grid Ref. and Punchcard No.
Building C.18	In grounds of Sheet House. Tiled roof with two chimneys. 2 storeys. Flint with brick dressings. Windows and stable doors at side. Loading door at first floor level. Used as store when house belonged to woolstapler.	C.A. N.P. Act A.O.N.B.	SU 758 245 1302 177
Cottages C.17	Nos. 1—5. Single-storey and attic. High pitched tiled roofs with gabled dormers. Pebbledashed walls. Casement windows with glazing bars.	T. & C.P. Act C.A. N.P. Act A.O.N.B.	SU 758 245 1302 125
House C.16/17	Nos. 6 and 7. 2 storeys, high pitched tiled roof with chimney. Pebbledashed. Timber-framing and brick infilling visible on west wall. Replaced casement windows and doors.	T. & C.P. Act C.A. N.P. Act A.O.N.B.	SU 758 245 1302 126
Cottages (2) C.18	Nos. 19 and 20. 2 storeys. Slate roof with eaves soffit. Colourwashed brick walls. Sash windows with glazing bars. No. 20 has panelled door surmounted by a flat hood.	T. & C.P. Act C.A. N.P. Act A.O.N.B.	SU 759 245 1302 127
Inn	Queen's Head. C.19 structure with C.16/17 timber-framing visible at left side. 2 storeys. Shallow slate hipped roof. Central chimney. Central modern door on west side with flat canopy over. Sash windows. North side central large oriel window. Sash windows with glazing bars. Single storey extension at rear, of red and blue brick structure with slate roof and chimney.	C.A. N.P. Act A.O.N.B.	SU 758 245 1302 400

Waterworks Road, Sheet

Description and Date	Remarks	Protection	Grid Ref. and Punchcard No.
Farm Buildings C.19	Johnson's Farm. Farmhouse of 2 storeys with slate roof. Front part tile-hung, part white-washed. Outshot each side of red and blue brick. Two chimneys. Three farm buildings. (1) Flint with five horizontal brick band dressings, and slate roof. (2) Flint with brick dressings and slate roof. (3) Greensand with brick dressings and corrugated iron roof.	N.P. Act A.O.N.B.	SU 753 248 1302 232

Winchester Road, Stroud

Description and Date	Remarks	Protection	Grid Ref. and Punchcard No.
Building C.19	No. 10. 2 storeys. Hipped roof, renewed in pantiles. Galleted flint walls with brick quoins, door jambs and window arches. Sash windows. Two steps to door. Doorway with reeded architrave, fanlight, and cornice hood with acorn pattern.	T. & C.P. Act N.P. Act A.O.N.B.	SU 741 237 1301 128
Farmhouse and Barn C.17	Buckmore Farmhouse. Kitchen wing of house timber-framed with brick infilling. Tiled hipped roof. Victorian extension of brick with tile-hanging. Brick barn with timber-framing and corrugated iron roof.	N.P. Act A.O.N.B.	SU 736 238 1301 156

Description and Date	Remarks	Protection	Grid Ref. and Punchcard No.

Group D — (cont.)

Description and Date	Remarks	Protection	Grid Ref. and Punchcard No.
Farmhouse C.19	Myrtle Farmhouse. 2 storeys. Low pitched hipped slate roof. Stuccoed walls. Recessed sash windows. Central doorcase in Tuscan style with detached columns.	T. & C.P. Act N.P. Act A.O.N.B.	SU 726 237 1301 155
Inn C.18	Seven Stars. Coursed flint structure with brick quoins. Colourwashed. Square plan with slate roof. Slate hung at rear. Tiled outshots of later date.	N.P. Act A.O.N.B.	SU 723 236 1301 153
Barn	Seven Stars. Hipped, tiled roof. Flint with brick quoins. Loft doorway with brick surround. Outshot on south side.	N.P. Act A.O.N.B.	SU 723 236 1301 154
House C.17/18	Freshwater House. Hipped slate roof. Refronted in C.19 with grey brick and red brick dressings. Stuccoed lintels to sash windows. Shutters to lower windows. Early brickwork and casement windows at rear.	T. & C.P. Act N.P. Act A.O.N.B.	SU 720 237 1301 152
Barn C.18/19	Ash Barn. Brick structure, possibly rejects. Hipped tiled roof. Wall ties on south wall. Now in use as an art gallery.	N.P. Act A.O.N.B.	SU 719 237 1301 238

Group E — Street Patterns, Street Furniture and Open Spaces

Description and Date	Remarks	Protection	Grid Ref. and Punchcard No.
Boundary Stones (3)	For preservation purposes moved from original position as borough boundary markers to form a group in the precinct of the Town Hall. Two are Portland stone the other a sarsen.	N.P. Act A.O.N.B.	SU 749 232 1303 187
Boundary Stone	Near 26, The Spain. Large ironstone boulder marking change of direction of boundary between old Borough of Petersfield and Tithing of Weston. Position of stone altered in 1964 for road widening.	C.A. N.P. Act A.O.N.B.	SU 744 231 1301 181
Boundary Marker	Adjacent to 2, Swan Street. Metal post marked 'W.P.J.' indicating northwest boundary of land formerly owned by Jacob and Hunt for the poultry market.	C.A. N.P. Act A.O.N.B.	SU 745 232 1301 182
Boundary Stone (Site)	Tilmore Road. Removed to environs of Petersfield Town Hall for safekeeping.	N.P. Act A.O.N.B.	SU 745 242 1301 219
Inscribed Stone	In wall of 21, Dragon Street. Inscribed 'I rebuilt these two ancient dwelling houses on the old foundation and exactly of the size they were before. Alexander Outridge — Mason'.	C.A. N.P. Act A.O.N.B.	SU 747 230 1302 25
Open Space	The Heath. An area of 90 acres which serves as a recreation ground. Situated east of the main London-Portsmouth Road. It includes a large man made pond. Fine views of the Downs.	N.P. Act A.O.N.B.	SU 751 230 1303 191

Description and Date	Remarks	Protection	Grid Ref. and Punchcard No.

Group E — (cont.)

Description and Date	Remarks	Protection	Grid Ref. and Punchcard No.
Open Space	Borough Hill. Formerly part of Borough Hill Common. Part taken for a sandpit, but now grassed over. Fine views.	N.P. Act A.O.N.B.	SU 740 231 1301 183
Open Space	Bell Common. Grassland with some trees.	N.P. Act A.O.N.B.	SU 740 243 1301 218
Open Space	Bell Hill recreation ground, near the A272 Winchester Road. Groups of oak trees.	N.P. Act A.O.N.B.	SU 739 238 1301 222
Open Space	Love Lane sports ground, north east of Petersfield. Fine views of The Downs. Centred on grid reference.	N.P. Act A.O.N.B.	SU 752 236 1302 200
Village Green	Sheet Green, Sheet. Small triangular green, with chestnut tree, bounded by roads. Groups of old cottages and buildings face on to the green.	N.P. Act A.O.N.B.	SU 758 245 1302 230
Common	Sheet Common, Sheet. An open space surrounded on all sides by mixed woodland. Situated on high ground to east of Sheet Village. Bounded by River Rother to west, the A3 to north, and the A272 to east. Centred on grid reference.	N.P. Act A.O.N.B.	SU 763 244 1302 220
The Square	Ancient market place and focal point of town. Railings on the east, south and west came from the old cattle market. Fine equestrian statue of William III stands in the middle.	C.A. N.P. Act A.O.N.B.	SU 746 232 1301 185
The Spain	Rectangular group of old houses fronting a green. Prior to the C.16 it was known as The Green.	C.A. N.P. Act A.O.N.B.	SU 745 231 1301 78
Fountain	Situated in main car park to the rear of Fine Fare on the bridge over the stream. Presented by Richard Barlow Kennett, Esq. in 1882.	C.A. N.P. Act A.O.N.B.	SU 747 233 1301 94
Horse Trough	The Square. Presented in 1882 by S. D. Money-Coutts, Esq.	C.A. N.P. Act A.O.N.B.	SU 746 232 1301 93
Milestone	Cast iron plate in wall of 15, Dragon Street. Reading '52 miles from London, 17 to Portsmouth'.	C.A. N.P. Act A.O.N.B.	SU 748 230 1302 207
Milestone	West side of A.3. to the east of Bolinge Hill Copse. Large white stone with cast iron plate, the distances have been removed. Inscription should read 'London 53 . Portsmouth 15'.	N.P. Act A.O.N.B.	SU 737 218 1301 453
Milestone	London Road, Sheet. Halfway between junctions with A325 and Inmans Lane. Original plate replaced inscribed '51 miles to London, 18 miles to Portsmouth'.	N.P. Act A.O.N.B.	SU 758 241 1302 408

Description and Date	Remarks	Protection	Grid Ref. and Punchcard No.
Group E — (cont.)			
Cast Iron Canopy Frame C.20	Nos. 7 and 11, Sandringham Road. Decorative cast iron door canopy frame and brackets, circa. 1911, with sloping glass top. This is a worth-while example of a style of decorative iron work which is becoming rare.	N.P. Act A.O.N.B.	SU 747 237 1302 409
Cast Iron Brackets C.20	Nos. 4—10 (even), King George Avenue. Decora-tive cast iron brackets and posts, circa. 1911, to sloping canopy over the front doors and windows of the above property. This ironwork is worthy of note.	N.P. Act A.O.N.B.	SU 747 235 1301 452
Group F — Historical or Literary Associations			
Brickworks. (Site)	Causeway or Larcombes, The Causeway. The brickworks produced red bricks and tiles. The pit was on the opposite side of the road but can hardly be seen because of the undergrowth. There are two Scotch kilns but these have been converted to a barn. There are also two drying sheds. Local housing contains examples of this firms bricks. Ref: A Gazetteer of Brick and Tile Works in Hampshire, (White), p. 92.	N.P. Act A.O.N.B.	SU 742 224 1303 300
Buildings (7) C.19	Nos. 11—21, Chapel Street (upper storeys). Although there are modern shop fronts at ground floor level, the gables show pargetting and other decorative work including dates. At the rear of No. 9, a terra cotta bull's head adorns a former slaughter house, on the south gable.	C.A. N.P. Act A.O.N.B.	SU 746 233 1302 406
Brewery (Site ony)	Lukers, College Street. The brewery was to the north of the hotel, but it was badly damaged during World War II, and little but the founda-tions survive. Ref: A Gazetteer of Hampshire Breweries, (Tighe), p. 98.	N.P. Act A.O.N.B.	SU 748 233 1301 401
Brewery Buildings	Ameys, Frenchmans Road. Site is now occupied by a firm of building contractors, original red brick buildings survive, although greatly altered, as is the ventilated loading shed for steam lorries. There is evidence of a private siding to the railway, and it is interesting that Ameys owned a public house opposite Waterloo Station. Brewing con-tinued until Ameys were acquired by Strongs and the machinery and vats were removed in the late 1940s. Ref: A Gazetteer of Hampshire Breweries, (Tighe), p. 98.	N.P. Act A.O.N.B.	SU 742 232 1301 400

Description and Date	Remarks	Protection	Grid Ref. and Punchcard No.

Group F — (cont.)

Description and Date	Remarks	Protection	Grid Ref. and Punchcard No.
Open Space	The Heath. Site of the annual "Taro" Horse Fair on October 6th. The Fair has been held there since the early C.19. In the C.12 Petersfield was granted two Fairs on St. Andrew's and St. Peter's day, held in the Square and the Spain until the C.19.	N.P. Act A.O.N.B.	SU 751 230 1303 186
Pest House C.18	The Pest House formerly Mount Pleasant, 5 Ramsdean Road, Stroud. At one time the East Meon pest house. Plaque on north wall gives name of building and date 1703.	N.P. Act A.O.N.B.	SU 721 235 1301 148
Buildings C.19	St. Peters Road. The two schools, police station, Church hall, and houses Nos. 8, 10 and 12, form a good group of period buildings. Built between 1854 and 1893. Except No. 12 which is C.18 and also listed.	T. & C.P. Act C.A. N.P. Act A.O.N.B.	SU 747 231 1302 407
Building	The Square Brewery, The Square. The inn of this name survives, but the buildings at the rear have not been used for brewing in living memory. Presumably acquired by Gales of Horndean. Ref: A Gazetteer of Hampshire Breweries, (Tighe), p. 98.	C.A. N.P. Act A.O.N.B.	SU 745 233 1301 402
Building C.19	No. 15, The Square. Built 1866 as the Corn Exchange, and subsequently used for public entertainment. Slate roof with raised centre attic over front section only, with circular lunette. Formerly this attic extended the full length of building. The long side faces the High Street and contains four shops. Walls of stone, rendered. Replacement windows are casement with leaded lights. Modern shop fronts at ground floor. Originally the building had two tall arched windows with a matching doorway between, there being no upper storey inserted at that time.	C.A. N.P. Act A.O.N.B.	SU 746 232 1302 404

ROPLEY

Ropley lies some eight miles south west of Alton; it is the home of the Hampshire Hunt. Tradition has it that Ropley supplied the honey for William the Conqueror's mead. The church has been much restored but still shows the work of six or seven centuries ago. Of interest are the old aumbry and piscina, the fifteenth century font and an Elizabethan chalice. It seems likely that the Pilgrims Way from Winchester to Canterbury passed through the parish via the present Gascoigne Lane and Brislands Lane.

Description and Date	Remarks	Protection	Grid Ref. and Punchcard No.

Group A — Natural Features

Description and Date	Remarks	Protection	Grid Ref. and Punchcard No.
Trees	Rockwood and Monksmead, formerly The Vicarage. Belt of beeches in grounds of several houses.	T.P.O. No. 93	SU 639 318 1615 46
Trees	Old Coalyard, Petersfield Road. Two horse chestnut whithin the curtilage of the above property.	T.P.O. No. 639	SU 630 318 1615 57
Trees	Gascoine Lane. Several oak and a group of beech on land adjoining Gascoine Lane.	T.P.O. No. 80 E.H.D.	SU 644 326 1615 58

Group B — Archaeological

Bronze Age

Description and Date	Remarks	Protection	Grid Ref. and Punchcard No.
Barrow (Site)	Near Old Down Wood. Destroyed by ploughing. O.S.A. No. SU63 SE15. Ref: P.H.F.C., Vol. 14, (1938—40), p. 353.		SU 653 330 1615 50
Necklace	Northeast of Lyewood House. Gold torque of circa 1,000—800 B.C., found 1843. Now in Cornwall County Museum (replica in Alton Museum). O.S.A. No. SU63 SE13. Ref: 1. Annals of Old Ropley, 1929, p. 45 illustrated. 2. Gentlemans Magazine, vol. 19, 1843, p. 420. 3. Journal Royal Institute, Cornwall, vol. 22, 1926, p. 38. 4. P.H.F.C., Vol. 4, 1898—1903, p. 147.		SU 657 316 1615 49

Iron Age

Description and Date	Remarks	Protection	Grid Ref. and Punchcard No.
Enclosure (Site)	Field behind Harcombe House. Enclosure complex visible as soil marks. Site under pasture. O.S.A. No. SU63 SW2.		SU 637 304 1615 52
Farmstead (Site)	South of The Kennels. Crop or soil mark of enclosure. O.S.A. No. SU63 SW16.		SU 632 313 1615 55

Roman

Description and Date	Remarks	Protection	Grid Ref. and Punchcard No.
Coin and Ring	Near Little Down. Third brass of Constantine I or II and bronze ring found in old stone pit. Coin in Alton Museum. O.S.A. No. SU63 SE6. Ref: Alton Museum, Accession, No. 401 33/68.		SU 657 315 1615 48

Description and Date	Remarks	Protection	Grid Ref. and Punchcard No.

Group D — Buildings, Monuments and Engineering Works

Description and Date	Remarks	Protection	Grid Ref. and Punchcard No.
Church C.12	St. Peter. Extensively restored 1847 and 1897. Mainly flint structure with shingled tower. C.13 door. C.17 brick porch. Octangonal font. O.S.A. No. 63 SW6. Ref: 1. V.C.H., Vol. 3, p. 57. 2. Buildings of England; Hants and I.O.W., (Pevsner and Lloyd), p.p. 488—9.	T. & C.P. Act C.A.	SU 645 319 1615 01
House C.18	Ropley House, Berry Hill. Restored Georgian house. 2 storeys. Red brick with blue brick bands. Sash windows. Parapet, ridge tiled roof with hipped dormers. Central door. 2-storey modern wing to side, with a ridge tiled roof. O.S.A. No. SU63 SW(M). Ref: Buildings of England; Hants and I.O.W., (Pevsner and Lloyd), p. 489.	T. & C.P. Act	SU 636 319 1615 06
House C.18	Hall Place, Petersfield Road. 2 storeys. Colour-washed brick walls. High pitched mansard slate roof. Sash windows. Centre panelled door with Doric pilasters.	T. & C.P. Act C.A.	SU 642 316 1615 03
House C.18	The Old Forge, Church Street. 2 storeys. Brown brick with occasional blue headers. Old ridge tiled roof. Single-storey red brick forge building to left. Used as forge until circa 1965.	C.A.	SU 643 319 1615 24
Farmhouse C.18	North Street Farm, North Street. 2 storeys. Red brick with blue headers. Steep hipped tiled roof. Stone over door dated '1730', restored 1925.		SU 643 333 1615 42
House C.18	The Old Post House, Church Street. 2 storeys. Red brick with old patches of dark brick. Attractive bow windows. Name probably derives from previous use as shop or public house.	C.A.	SU 646 319 1615 12
House C.18	Exeter House, Church Street. 2 storeys. Blue brick with red brick dressings. Hipped tiled roof.	C.A.	SU 647 319 1615 16
House C.18/19	Fordes, Church Street. 2 storeys. Limewashed plaster walls. Half-hipped tiled roof. Large fireplace. Attractive cottage-type house.	C.A.	SU 649 319 1615 13
House C.19	Ropley Lodge, Winchester Road. 2 storeys. Stuccoed walls. Slate roof. Attractive Regency windows on garden side.		SU 618 319 1615 36
House C.19	Ropley Manor, known as Ropley Cottage until 1920. Long limewashed brick structure. Slate roof. Columned porch. Columned verandah towards garden. Restored and recast.		SU 638 317 1615 31
Houses (2) C.19	Monksmead and Rockwood. Formerly The Vicarage. Grey cement rendered. High pitched slate roof with moulded coved stone eaves. Georgian casement windows.		SU 639 318 1615 30

12th Century St. Hubert's Church, Idsworth, ROWLANDS CASTLE

Description and Date	Remarks	Protection	Grid Ref. and Punchcard No.

Group D — (cont.)

Description and Date	Remarks	Protection	Grid Ref. and Punchcard No.
Building C.19	Meadowside, Church Street. 2 storeys. M-shaped tiled roof. Flint and brick structure, with colourwashed facade. Wooden casement windows surmounted by cambered brick arches. Small colourwashed porch with arched entrance. Built circa 1883 by a Miss Hagen who erected a plaque dedicated to her parents which reads 'In Memoriam T.H. M.H.'	C.A.	SU 645 319 1615 61
Building C.19	Coffee Rooms, Church Street. Adjoining Meadowside and of the same construction, but of only one storey. Built in 1883 by Miss Hagen, as a working men's club.	C.A.	SU 645 319 1615 65
Farmhouse C.19	Manor Farm, North Street. Flint and brick structure. Built on site of older house, of which the cellars remain. Owned by Winchester College to whom it was deeded in the C.14 by William of Wykeham, when he founded the College.		SU 645 335 1615 43
House C.20	Andross Manor, Chapel Lane. Built 1925 using old materials. Timber-framed with brick infilling. Tiled roof. Named after Greek island of Andros.		SU 655 324 1615 38
Cottage	Little Barton, Petersfield Road. Brick and flint structure. Ridge thatched roof. Rustic thatched porch. Formerly two cottages.		SU 629 318 1615 35
Farmhouse	New Barn Farm, Park Lane. 2 storeys. Flint structure with brick surrounds to the arched windows. Flat tiled roof with square brick chimneys. Two later extensions, one pebble-dashed, one brick.		SU 636 309 1615 64
Cottage	Kennel Cottages, (east), Petersfield Road. Single storey. Brick structure, one wing timber-framed. Thatched roof.		SU 633 316 1615 32
Cottage	Kennel Cottage (west), Petersfield Road. 2 storeys. Flint with brick dressings. Steep conical thatched roof with centre brick stack. Extended in keeping with original structure over the years.		SU 633 316 1615 33
Cottages (2)	Rosa Cottage and Elm Cottage, South Street. Flint and brick walls with panels of tile-hanging below windows. Thatched roofs.		SU 640 317 1615 29
Cottage	Fairways, Petersfield Road. 2 storeys. Cream-washed flint on ground floor, exposed timber-framing above. Thatched roof. Possibly C.17	C.A.	SU 641 316 1615 53

Description and Date	Remarks	Protection	Grid Ref. and Punchcard No.
Group D — (cont.)			
House	Ropley Grove, Petersfield Road. Enlarged Georgian house standing in walled grounds. 2 storeys, red brick with blue headers. Sash windows, several blocked windows and a modern casement over door. Panelled door set in rusticated brick surround. Modern hipped tiled roof with dormers. The side to the right has a parapet with moulded cornice. Projection at corner has bow windows facing the garden. A reputed 'smugglers' cellar, was found during restoration in the 1920s.	T. & C.P. Act C.A.	SU 643 315 1615 02
Cottage	Gardeners Cottage, Ropley Grove, Petersfield Road. Creamwashed flint walls. Thatched roof with eaves squarecut around two upper windows. Centre brick porch. Attractive setting.	C.A.	SU 643 315 1615 27
Cottages (2)	Little Grove Farm, Petersfield Road. Flint and brick walls. Thatched roof. Casement windows on ground floor.		SU 644 314 1615 26
House and Barn	100 yards northeast of North Street Farmhouse. 2 storeys. Exposed light timber-framing with limewashed brick and plaster infilling. Thatched roof, eaves square cut around small upper window. Odd casement windows. Thatched roof brought down as pentice to right and in front over boarded store. Formerly two cottages. Weatherboarded barn adjoins to left under continuous ridge thatched roof.	T. & C.P. Act	SU 644 334 1615 56
House	The Old Manor House, Petersfield Road. Red brick mixed with some blue brick. Core probably timber-framed. Thatched roof. Tiled gable porch. Originally several cottages.	T. & C.P. Act C.A.	SU 646 372 1615 05
Cottage	Carpenters, Gilbert Street. Flint and brick structure. Thatched roof, partly replaced. Modern centre porch.		SU 646 324 1615 37
Cottage	Sparrow Thatch, Church Street. Plain brick exterior walls with timber-framed core. Thatched roof.	C.A.	SU 646 319 1615 14
Cottage	Yew Tree Cottage, Hammonds Lane. Single storey limewashed brick. Thatched roof.		SU 642 318 1615 25
Cottage	Turn Pike Cottage, North Street. 2 storeys. Flint and timber-framed, part colourwashed brick. Thatched roof. Well restored circa 1970.	T. & C.P. Act	SU 643 332 1615 09
Cottage	Ropelia Cottage, formerly Arnolds Cottage, North Street. Brick structure. Thatched roof. Almost completely rebuilt circa 1968.	T. & C.P. Act	SU 644 334 1615 10
Cottage	East Winds, Church Street. Flint and brick rubble walls. Thatched roof with eaves raised over upper windows.	C.A.	SU 645 319 1615 21

Description and Date	Remarks	Protection	Grid Ref. and Punchcard No.
Group D — (cont.)			
Cottages (3)	Dover Cottages and Old Post Office, Church Street. Dover Cottage, thatched, brick patched with plaster. Old Post Office, tiled roof, creamwashed brick. Used as Post Office until 1930s.	C.A.	SU 645 319 1615 20
House	The Old Parsonage, Church Street. Colour-washed brick and cement structure. Old hipped tiled roof. Triple lattice casements. No record of use as Parsonage. Possibly C.18.	C.A.	SU 649 319 1615 22
Barn	The Old Parsonage, Church Street. Thatched and weatherboarded on wide base of flint with brick dressings.	C.A.	SU 649 319 1615 23
Cottage	Cromwell Cottage, Church Street. Brick structure, patched in places with flint and plaster. Thatched roof. Name derived from Cromwellian coins found in cellar.	C.A.	SU 646 319 1615 15
House	Bounty House, Gilbert Street. Blue brick with red dressings. Moulded string course between ground and first floor. Re-fronted 1757. Originally several cottages, one room being the Telephone Exchange. Formerly known as The Alberts or Great Alberts. (Grete Alberts mentioned in Court Roll of 1628).	T. & C.P. Act	SU 647 314 1615 07
Farmhouse	The Old Farmhouse, Gilbert Street. Limewashed brick and flint structure with exposed light timber-work. Short single storey wing. Interesting open staircase, many low beams.	T. & C.P. Act	SU 647 319 1615 08
House	Town Street Farm, Dunsells Lane. 2 storeys. Good herringbone brickwork. Hipped tiled roof. Contains 'priest's hole'. Formerly a farmhouse.	C.A.	SU 647 319 1615 17
Cottages (3)	Laurel Cottage, Pond Cottage and Appletree Cottage, Lyeway Lane. Single storeys. Lime-washed brick walls. Ridge thatched roof.	C.A.	SU 647 319 1615 19
Cottage	Archibishop's Cottage, Lyeway Lane. Brick structure with flint panels below window. Steep thatched roof.	C.A.	SU 647 319 1615 18
Cottage	Lyewood Cottage, Petersfield Road. Colour-washed, flint walls. Ridge thatched roof. C.19 double sash windows. Rustic thatched roof.		SU 653 312 1615 44
House	Soames Place, Soames Lane. 2 storeys. Timber-framed with red brick infilling. Thatched roof and centre ridge chimney. Originally part of the Tichborne Estate at West Tisted.	T. & C.P. Act	SU 654 306 1615 11
Cottage	Little Reeds, Chapel Lane. Limewashed brick structure. Thatched roof replaced by modern tiles. Lattice casement windows.		SU 654 324 1615 39

Description and Date	Remarks	Protection	Grid Ref. and Punchcard No.

Group D — (cont.)

Description and Date	Remarks	Protection	Grid Ref. and Punchcard No.
House and Barn	The Malthouse. Swelling Hill. Part C.16, part C.18, with late C.19 extension. Timber-framed walls revealed in recent restoration. Attractive Regency windows. Tiled roof. Large barn with good roof timbers.		SU 656 326 1615 40
Cottage	Smugglers Cottage, Smugglers Lane. Colour-washed brick structure. Thatched roof.		SU 659 310 1615 45
Cottage	Old Down Cottage, Swelling Hill. Red brick with blue headers on first floor, flint panels on ground floor. Ridge thatched roof. Modern extension, also thatched.		SU 660 328 1615 41
Cottages (5)	Nos. 1–5, Church Cottages, Church Street. An uneven-terrace row of 2-storey cottages. No. 1, probably rebuilt, flint structure with brick dressings, and slate roof. Nos. 2 and 3, lower construction than No. 1, flint structure with brick surrounds to lattice paned windows. No. 4, brick structure with higher slate roof. No. 5, is of brick structure of more recent construction.	C.A.	SU 645 319 1615 62
Cottages (3)	Nos. 1, 2 and 3, Sunnyside Cottages, Lyeway Lane. Three non-terraced cottages of 2 storeys. Tiled roof, half-hipped at No. 1 and hipped at No. 3. Modern additions to the rear of all cottages and to the side of No. 3. All have modern porches in different styles. No. 1 is partly tile-hung, partly colourwashed. 6-paned casement windows with wooden glazing bars. No. 2, Five Bells, colourwashed with windows matching No. 1. No. 3, brick structure. One square lattice window in upper storey, other windows of the vertical sash type.	C.A.	SU 647 319 1615 60

Group F — Historical or Literary Associations

Description and Date	Remarks	Protection	Grid Ref. and Punchcard No.
House C.18	Ropley House. Home of John Duthy, author of "Sketches of Hampshire" (1839). Reputed smugglers' passage in grounds, used in C.18 when Ropley Woods and various houses were used as hiding places for goods brought up from Portsmouth. O.S.A. No. SU63 SW(M). Ref: Buildings of England; Hants and I.O.W., (Pevsner and Lloyd), p. 489.	T. & C.P. Act	SU 636 319 1615 06
Cottage	Archibishops Cottage, Lyeway Lane. Name derived from Archbishop Howley, son of a rector of Ropley who was fostered by a woman living in the cottage. Howley succeeded his father as Vicar of Bishop Sutton and Ropley from 1796–1813. Later he became Bishop of London and from 1828–48 was Archbishop of Caterbury.	C.A.	SU 647 319 1615 18

272

ROWLANDS CASTLE

The Castle once stood to the east of the present-day centre of the village. Its towers and battlements are known to have been in good repair in the twelfth century, when Henry II spent several days there in hunting and amusement. The Castle is thought to have lasted until the mid-fourteenth century, and in the nineteenth century a report states "the remains of Rowlands Castle consists of two masses of wall which are about 10 feet thick with a fosse of considerable depth."

The parish of Rowlands Castle was formed in 1932 consisting of Blendworth parish, Idsworth parish (which had been attached to Chalton at one time) and parts of five other parishes. One of these, Havant (Redhill), provided Rowlands Castle with a church, the Church of St. John, built about 1840 (registers date from 1841).

The 'Castle Inn' was in the possession of the Outen family for 200 years, and was said to have been the headquarters of a notorious gang of smugglers.

Idsworth House was erected in 1852, in the Elizabethan style, and was the property of Lorna, Countess Howe.

The ancient chapel of St. Hubert stands in the middle of a field, thought to be the site of a mediaeval village, on what was part of Idsworth Park. Parts of the chapel date from the twelfth century.

Description and Date	Remarks	Protection	Grid Ref. and Punchcard No.
Group A — Natural Features			
Tree	No. 13, Redhill Road. Yew tree in the garden of the above property.	T.P.O. No. 525	SU 730 105 2312 42
Trees	Idsworth House. Mixed coniferous and deciduous trees.	T.P.O. No. 79 E.H.D. N.P. Act A.O.N.B.	SU 728 130 2312 52
Trees	Red Hill, Manor Lodge Road. Several trees of differing species standing in the area centred on grid reference.	T.P.O. No. 85 E.H.D.	SU 725 103 2312 53
Area of Scenic Beauty	The Northern half of the parish comes within the East Hampshire Area of Outstanding Natural Beauty, an area rich in flora and fauna and with viewpoints of the whole area.	N.P. Act A.O.N.B.	SU 735 138 2312 51
Woodland	Land of Durrants Road. Known as Hammonds Land Copse and Thicket Bottom. Mixed hazel coppice with hardwood mainly oak and spruce.	T.P.O. No. 67 E.H.D.	SU 721 095 2312 50
Trees	On land adjacent to 20, Redhill Road, two groups mainly oak, and one single oak.	T.P.O. No. 88 E.H.D.	SU 730 105 2312 58
Trees	Situated at Wick Hanger, Idsworth, an area containing oak trees.	T.P.O. No. 97 E.H.D. N.P. Act A.O.N.B.	SU 728 133 2312 56
Trees	On land situated to the east of, and adjoining Meadowlands, one acer, one silver birch and one larch.	T.P.O. No. 92 E.H.D.	SU 733 111 2312 57
Group B — Archaeological			
Bronze Age			
Round Barrow (Site)	On Chalton Down. Now ploughed out. O.S.A. No. SU71 NW21. Ref: P.H.F.C., Vol. 14, (Grinsell), p. 359.	N.P. Act A.O.N.B.	SU 733 152 2312 18
Round Barrows (9)	On Chalton Down. Much reduced by ploughing. Centred on grid reference. O.S.A. No. SU71 SW4.	S.A.M. No. 426 N.P. Act A.O.N.B.	SU 734 147 2312 19
Iron Age			
Celtic Field System	Traces of field system almost completely ploughed out. Two lynchets remain measuring up to 1.2 m in height. Centred on grid reference. O.S.A. No. SU71 SW6.	N.P. Act A.O.N.B.	SU 732 145 2312 20
Settlement (Site)	North of Huckswood Lane. Sub-circular ditch enclosure 185 ft. from east to west and 150 ft. from north to south. Signs of continuous occupation for 400 years. Finds include an Iron Age quarter slater, a bronze pin and a green bead/spindle whorl. Evidence of later Roman occupation. O.S.A. No. SU71 NW19.	N.P. Act A.O.N.B.	SU 750 155 2312 16

Description and Date	Remarks	Protection	Grid Ref. and Punchcard No.

Group B — (cont.)

Romano-British

Description and Date	Remarks	Protection	Grid Ref. and Punchcard No.
Pottery Kiln	South east of Rowlands Castle. Ref: South Hampshire Archaeological Rescue Group Records.		SU 735 103 2312 44
Pottery	Found close to motte and bailey in Motley's Copse. Possibly mediaeval in view of proximity to this site. O.S.A. No. SU71 SW12.		SU 724 122 2312 24

Roman

Field System	Lynchet field system. Pieces of Romano-British greyware have also been found. Site mostly in gardens. O.S.A. No. SU71 SW15.		SU 730 115 2312 28
Building (Site)	Footings of wall uncovered by plough on the corner of Wellsworth Lane. Complete pot and coins found in 1961. O.S.A. No. SU71 SW16.		SU 732 113 2312 29
Building (Site)	Partly under lawn in gardens of Nos. 42/44, Bowes Hill. Traces of Romano-British coarseware also found. O.S.A. No. SU71 SW18.		SU 732 109 2312 31
Occupation Site	Villa found north of Mays Coppice Farm, before 1817. Apartment 18 ft. x 14 ft. with entire ornamented pavement. Pieces of painted stucco found. Traces of adjoining bath houses (possibly), and larger buildings to east. Site strewn with charcoal and pottery. Foundations now destroyed. A variety of coins have been found including a pot of Roman copper coins, in 1850. Ash, charcoal and kiln wasters indicate site of pottery kilns. A tumulus close by contained charcoal and a pottery sherd marked with crescents. O.S.A. No. SU71 SW21. Ref: 1. V.C.H., (Haverfield), p. 310. 2. Hundred of Bosmere, 1817, (Bingley), p.p. 56—62.		SU 734 098 2312 35

Post Norman

Earthwork	Small motte with no recognisable remains of bailey, 250 m. southwest of motte in Motley's Copse. 45 m. in diameter overall. Holt pond encroaches on the earthwork, and the top of the motte is dug into. O.S.A. No. SU71 SW13.	S.A.M. No. 129	SU 722 120 2312 26

Description and Date	Remarks	Protection	Grid Ref. and Punchcard No.

Group B — (cont.)

Description and Date	Remarks	Protection	Grid Ref. and Punchcard No.
Castle Ring and Bailey	Motley's Castle, Motley's Copse. Circular motte with divided bailey extending westwards. In centre of keep is depression of well. Old iron, wooden buckets, crockery and bones found when cleaned out. Complex of small castle ring and bailey overlaid by a larger one. Damaged by quarrying, and traversed by old banks and ditches. O.S.A. No. SU71 SW14.	S.A.M. No. 129	SU 725 122 2312 27
Motte and Bailey (Remains)	Rowland's Castle. North of brick works. Partly dug away on east side. Entrance appears to have been in centre of western bank opposite mound. Prior to construction of railway a deep gorge existed east of the mound. Ditch 80 yds. east remains. This suggests plan of rectangular bailey with central mound. Large piece of masonry said to be part of keep. O.S.A. No. SU71 SW20. Ref: Field Archaeology as Illustrated by Hampshire, 1915. (Williams-Freeman), p.p. 400—1.	S.A.M. No. 128 C.A.	SU 733 105 2312 34
Village Site (Supposed)	South of St. Huberts Church, Idsworth. Flint and stone footings of buildings found when lane ploughed. May be site of mediaeval settlement, or more recent cottages. Surface irregularities in field suggest former occupation. Isolated church and name, Old Idsworth, may be significant. Hundred=Finchdean. O.S.A. No. SU71 SW7. Ref: 1. V.C.H., Vol. 1, p. 478. 2. V.C.H., Vol. 3, p.p. 102—3, 109. 3. Mediaeval Village Research Group List, 1966.	N.P. Act A.O.N.B.	SU 743 139 2312 38

Period Unknown

Description and Date	Remarks	Protection	Grid Ref. and Punchcard No.
Pottery	Pieces of British pottery and fragments of black ancient pottery found. O.S.A. No. SU71 SW19.		SU 735 105 2312 33
Bank and Ditch	Once formed the boundary between the ancient parish of Havant and its neighbours. Sections still traceable. Ref: The Hundred of Bosmere, (Longcroft).		SU 715 110 — 720 115 2312 46

Group C — Footpaths and Bridleways

Description and Date	Remarks	Protection	Grid Ref. and Punchcard No.
Bridleway (B.W.24)	Has served as parish and manorial boundary for almost 1,000 years, AD935—1902. Described as the ridgeway or straight way. Ref: 1. The Early Charters of Wessex, (Finberg). 2. Hants. Place Names and Charters, (Grundy).		SU 730 103 — 730 095 2312 45

Description and Date	Remarks	Protection	Grid Ref. and Punchcard No.
Group D — Buildings, Monuments and Engineering Works			
Church C.12	St. Hubert's Church, Idsworth. Originally dedicated to St. Peter and St. Paul. Simple plan of nave and chancel, with boarded bell turret over east end of nave. Fine C.13 wall paintings of St. Peter, St. Paul, a feast, and scenes of a hunt. Jacobean pulpit. Restored in 1912. O.S.A. No. SU71 SW31. Ref: Buildings of England; Hants and I.O.W., (Pevsner and Lloyd), p.p. 305—6.	T. & C.P. Act N.P. Act A.O.N.B.	SU 742 140 2312 01
House C.17	Great Wellsworth, Wellsworth Lane. 2 storeys. Brick and flint structure. Thatched roof descends to door lintel at rear. Old chimney. Simple porch. Casement windows with cambered arches, some with leaded lights.	T. & C.P. Act	SU 733 114 2312 03
Coach House C.18	Old Idsworth House. 2 storeys. Tiled roof. Brick walls with timber work in gable. Converted to living quarters. Some windows now blocked. Interior has some carved door surrounds from the old house.	N.P. Act A.O.N.B.	SU 742 137 2312 09
Farmhouse C.18	Heberdens Farm, Idsworth. 2-storey brick building. Flat band between storeys. Tiled roof. Two wings to north. Mainly casement windows with glazing bars. Georgian addition has sash windows and glazing bars.	N.P. Act A.O.N.B.	SU 739 140 2312 08
Building C.18	Little Woodhouse, Woodhouse Lane. Two cottages, nos. 19 and 20. Flint with brick dressings and a simple tiled roof. 2 storeys. 2-storey wing to rear with some timberwork. Casement windows. Lean-to at each end with corrugated roof.		SU 730 112 2312 14
Farmhouse C.18	Mays Coppice Farm. 2 storeys with attics. Knapped flint, galleted and with brick dressings. Double hipped tiled roof, with central dormer. Sash and casement windows. Later trellised porch with tiled roof.		SU 735 095 2312 04
Cottages (3) C.18	Nos. 10, 11 and 12, The Green. 2 storeys. Plaster faced. Brick dentilled cornice. Tiled roof. Sash windows with glazing bars. Doors with small simple hoods.	C.A.	SU 732 107 2312 10
House C.18	No. 13, The Green. Double fronted. Plaster faced. Brick dentilled cornice. Tiled roof. Sash windows with glazing bars. Recessed panelled doorcase with small flat hood.	C.A.	SU 732 107 2312 11
House C.18	Woodhouse Ashes, Woodhouse Lane. 2 storeys. Brick with band between storeys, and tiled roof. Formerly two cottages. Cambered arches to ground floor windows. Dairy to west of flint with brick dressings, and tiled roof.		SU 730 116 2312 13

Description and Date	Remarks	Protection	Grid Ref. and Punchcard No.

Group D — (cont.)

Description and Date	Remarks	Protection	Grid Ref. and Punchcard No.
House C.18/19	Finchdean House, Finchdean. 2 storeys. Plaster faced and colourwashed brick with slate roof. Sash windows and bay windows on ground floor. Door has flat hood on brackets. Single-storey wing to northeast.	N.P. Act A.O.N.B.	SU 738 127 2312 15
Cottage C.19	No. 9, Dean Lane End Cottages. 2 storeys. Whitened brick with flat pitched hipped slate roof. Small paned casement windows.	T. & C.P. Act N.P. Act A.O.N.B.	SU 730 121 2312 41
House C.19	Idsworth House. Built in 1852, with additions 1912–14 by Goodhurst-Rendel. 2 storeys and attics. Neo-Jacobean style. Front of seven bays with tower to left. Brick structure with stone quoins and dressings. Steeply pitched coped gables with small finials and half dormers. Double pitched slate roof with many chimneys. Jacobean style porte cochere and entrance hall. Sash windows with glazing bars. Mullioned and transomed windows to entrance hall. Large single storey library at rear, with canted bay.	T. & C.P. Act N.P. Act A.O.N.B.	SU 729 130 2312 40
House C.19	The Limes, Finchdean. 2 storeys. Front of plaster faced flint. Rear of flint with brick dressings. Double hipped slate roof. Sash and casement windows with glazing bars. Later porch with slate roof.	N.P. Act A.O.N.B.	SU 738 127 2312 05
House C.19	Redhill House, Manor Lodge Road. 2 storeys. Red brick structure incorporating blue-grey headers. Hipped tiled roof with brick chimneys. Full height square window bay to right of entrance. Later C.19 sash windows. Glazed central door.	T. & C.P. Act	SU 725 101 2312 54
Coach House C.19	Situated to the west of Redhill House. 2 storeys. Brick with flint panels. Tiled roof. Two windows one sash and one casement. Boarded double door surmounted by segmental arch.	T. & C.P. Act	SU 725 101 2312 55
Granary C.19	Situated to the east of Redhill House. 2 storeys. Brick structure. Base rests on brick arches. Low pitched pyramidal tiled roof. One wide bay. Wooden steps to boarded double door. Similar loading door above.	T. & C.P. Act	SU 725 101 2312 55A
Church C.19	St. John. Originally a cruciform church of about 1838. Aisles added and chancel rebuilt 1853. Intricate pattern of pine roof timbers with slate roof. Carved heads in spandrels of arcades. The church was extended by two arches towards the west end, and completed in 1929. Choir and vestry placed on northwest corner. Ref: Buildings of England; Hants and I.O.W., (Pevsner and Lloyd), p. 490.		SU 725 100 2312 47

Group D — (cont.)

Description and Date	Remarks	Protection	Grid Ref. and Punchcard No.
Building C.19	Staunton Arms, Redhill Road. 2 storeys. Plaster faced brick and rubble. Double hipped slate roof. Sash windows with glazing bars. Wing to west. Carriage entrance under upper storey at east end.		SU 726 098 2312 12
Commemoration Stone C.20	Manor Lodge Road, Redhill. Rectangular stone on moulded plinth with capping of Portland stone. Inscription. 'Here on 22nd May 1944 His Majesty King George VI reviewed and bade Godspeed to his troops about to embark for the invasion and liberation of Europe. Deo Gratias'.	T. & C.P. Act	SU 724 101 2312 02
Chapel	Congregational Chapel, Finchdean. Formerly a barn used as a church for about 50 years. Brick structure with some timber at gable ends. Double hipped tiled roof. Some quatrefoil windows, others with diamond and Gothic glazing.	N.P. Act A.O.N.B.	SU 730 128 2312 07
Cottage	The Cottage, Finchdean. 2 storeys. Plaster faced. Slate roof with brick chimneys. Casement windows with glazing bars and small panes. Cambered arches to ground floor windows.	N.P. Act A.O.N.B.	SU 738 127 2312 06
Icehouse	Old Idsworth, near Finchdean. Roofless ruins in the grounds.	N.P. Act A.O.N.B.	SU 742 138 2312 43

SELBORNE

Selborne is forever associated with Gilbert White, author of the National History of Selborne, whose house The Wakes is now open to the public. A recent addition to the Wakes is a museum to Captain Oates and a Field Centre for nature study. The church contains much thirteenth century work, the font is 800 years old, the chancel arch is Norman and there is a fine sixteenth century Flemish triptych.

Description and Date	Remarks	Protection	Grid Ref. and Punchcard No.
Group A — Natural Features			
Tree	Cupressus adjacent Maltbys Engineering Works, The Street.	T.P.O. No. 196 C.A. N.P. Act A.O.N.B.	SU 743 335 1616 65
Tree	Adjacent to Maltbys Engineering Works. A Chile pine or monkey puzzle tree.	T.P.O. No. 196 C.A. N.P. Act A.O.N.B.	SU 743 335 1616 64
Trees	Near Old Butchers Shop and opposite The Wakes. Two limes planted by Gilbert White in 1756, "to shield him from the blood and filth of the butchers shop".	C.A. N.P. Act A.O.N.B.	SU 741 336 1616 66
Tree	Yew tree standing in St. Mary's churchyard estimated to be over 1,000 years old. Trunk measures 27 ft. in circumference.	C.A. N.P. Act A.O.N.B.	SU 741 337 1616 76
Area of Scenic Beauty	Kings Field. One of the old common fields. Breeding ground of several species of butterfly and moth.	N.P. Act A.O.N.B.	SU 743 334 1616 78
Area of Scenic Beauty	The Ewell. Old park-like field leading up to the Hanger and Beech woods. Crossed by a footpath.	N.P. Act A.O.N.B.	SU 737 336 1616 77
Area of Scenic Beauty	Dorton Common, Dorton Wood, New Barn Valley. Ref: Gilbert White and his Selborne, (Rye).	N.P. Act S.S.S.I. A.O.N.B.	SU 743 341 1616 73
Area of Scenic Beauty	Glebe Lands surrounding St. Mary's Church. Public footpath across Church meadow.	C.A. N.P. Act A.O.N.B.	SU 742 338 1616 69
Site of Ecological Interest	Long Lythe and Short Lythe. 16½ acres of woodland, mainly hanging beech woods, over-looking Selborne stream. Presented to the National Trust in 1961 by R. R. Edgar.	N.P. Act S.S.S.I. A.O.N.B.	SU 744 341 1616 71
Site Ecological Interest	Selborne Hanger and Common. Large area of common and freehold land where Gilbert White made many observations recorded in The Natural History of Selborne. Given to The National Trust by Magdalen College Oxford in 1932.	N.P. Act S.S.S.I. A.O.N.B.	SU 735 333 1616 84
Site of Ecological Interest	Milking Hanger, Coombe Wood. Area of scenic beauty. Includes a series of Hanger woods, and supporting a relatively rich calcareous ground flora.	N.P. Act S.S.S.I. A.O.N.B.	SU 748 350 1616 72
Garden	Selborne Vicarage Garden. Lawn and terrace laid out by Gilbert White's grandfather (of the same name). Ref: Gilbert White and His Selborne, (Rye).	C.A. N.P. Act A.O.N.B.	SU 750 338 1616 68

Description and Date	Remarks	Protection	Grid Ref. and Punchcard No.

Group A — (cont.)

Description and Date	Remarks	Protection	Grid Ref. and Punchcard No.
Streams	Selborne Streams. Seale stream rises in Knights pond, the millstream from a spring on Noar Hill. They converge at Dorton Cottage. Cast iron facade with lions head, from which water from the wellshead gushes all the year round.	· C.A. N.P. Act A.O.N.B.	SU 743 327 — 738 337 1616 74
Garden	Wakes Museum. Attractive feature which includes a brick path leading to Gilbert White's birdwatching arbour. Short length of brick wall built by the naturalist and bearing stone plaque inscribed 'G. W. 1761'.	C.A. N.P. Act A.O.N.B.	SU 740 336 161604A
Site Ecological Interest	Shortheath Common. 148 acres of mainly grassland and bracken with many oak and birch trees. The common centres on substantial valley bog, of outstanding structural and biological interest.	N.P. Act S.S.S.I.	SU 775 366 1616 98

Group B — Archaeological

Stone Age

Description and Date	Remarks	Protection	Grid Ref. and Punchcard No.
Mesolithic Occupation Site	Shortheath Common. Large hearth containing flints revealed when gun pit was sunk, in area covered with dunes or hummocks of blown sand. No trace now remains. O.S.A. No. SU73 NE7. Ref: 1. P.H.F.C., Vol. 18, (1951—3), p. 170. 　　　2. Mesolithic Sites in East Hampshire, (Rankine).	N.P. Act S.S.S.I.	SU 774 365 1616 46
Mesolithic Remains	Opposite The White House, Oakhanger. Hearth or floor with flakes and cores, also Iron Age sherds, one Romano-British sherd and mediaeval sherds found 1967 during road widening operations. Majority of finds in Portsmouth Museum. O.S.A. No. SU73 NE27.		SU 769 358 1616 50
Mesolithic Flints	Small blades and large flint graver found north-west of Regency house. O.S.A. No. SU73 SE18. Ref: P.H.F.C., Vol. 18, 1931—4, p. 170.	N.P. Act A.O.N.B.	SU 782 324 1616 62
Mesolithic Site	The Warren and the Slab, Oakhanger. Chipping floor and flints found 1950. Area overgrown and used as heavy vehicle practice ground. O.S.A. No. SU73 NE6. Ref: P.H.F.C., Vol. 18, 1951—4, p.p. 157—172.		SU 778 354 1616 45
Implement	The Warren, Oakhanger. Half of a sarcen mace-head found south of Warren VII, a mesolithic site. O.S.A. No. SU73 NE18.		SU 773 353 1616 47

Description and Date	Remarks	Protection	Grid Ref. and Punchcard No.
Group B — (cont.)			
Bronze Age			
Bowl Barrow	East of St. Matthews Church, Blackmoor and close to parish boundary. Averaging 30.0 m. in diameter with maximum height of 1.8 m. Contains remains of wartime gunpit, but otherwise fairly well preserved. O.S.A. No. SU73 SE11. Ref: P.H.F.C., Vol. 14, 1938—40, p. 354.	S.A.M. No. 75	SU 784 335 1616 58
Bowl Barrow	The Warren. Averaging 24.0 m. in diameter and 1.4 m. high, with no visible ditch. Covered in heather, bracken and gorse. O.S.A. No. SU73 NE23. Ref: P.H.F.C., Vol. 14, 1938—40, p. 354.		SU 774 351 1616 49
Roman			
Cremation Burial	South of Blackmoor House. Large sepulchral earthenware vase containing small bronze cup, remains of bronze patera, brass coin and bones, found 1867. O.S.A. No. SU73 SE13. Ref: The Natural History and Antiquities of Selborne, (White).	N.P. Act A.O.N.B.	SU 779 330 1616 59
Coin and Flints	Coneycroft. In 1923 small bronze coin dated 320—350 A.D. found in the garden. Also a number of flint flakes. O.S.A. No. SU73 SW11. Ref: P.H.F.C., Vol. 9, 1920—4, p.p. 409—10.	C.A. N.P. Act A.O.N.B.	SU 735 339 1616 53
Coin	Bronze coin of Augustus found 1958 during excavations of foundations of Grange Farm. In Basingstoke Museum. O.S.A. No. SU73 SW15. Ref: P.H.F.C., Vol. 21, 1959, p.p. 111—2.	C.A. N.P. Act A.O.N.B.	SU 737 338 1616 91
Coins (2)	Jasmine Cottage. Coins of Carausius and Allectus found a number of years ago in the garden. O.S.A. No. SU73 SW16. Ref: P.H.F.C., Vol. 21, 1959, p. 112.	C.A. N.P. Act A.O.N.B.	SU 737 338 1616 92
Occupation Site	Tiles, potsherds etc. found 1875 in grounds of Blackmoor House. Collection in the British Museum. O.S.A. No. SU73 SE14. Ref: The Natural History and Antiquities of Selborne, (White).	N.P. Act A.O.N.B.	SU 778 335 1616 60
Potsherds	Near Temple Manor. Fragments of pottery found 1869—70 during construction of reservoir. Now in British Museum. O.S.A. No. SU73 SE15. Ref: 1. The Natural History and Antiquities of Selborne, (White). 2. V.C.H., Vol. 1, p. 341.	N.P. Act A.O.N.B.	SU 762 335 1616 61

Description and Date	Remarks	Protection	Grid Ref. and Punchcard No.

Group B — (cont.)

Description and Date	Remarks	Protection	Grid Ref. and Punchcard No.
Coin Hoard	Grounds of Blackmoor House. Large collection of C.3 A.D. coins found 1873. Suggested the hoard represented army pay chest of the Army of Allectus (296 A.D.) now in British Museum. O.S.A. No. SU73 SE22. Ref: 1. The Natural History and Antiquities of Selborne, (White). 2. V.C.H., Vol. 1, p. 341. 3. Coinage and Currency of Roman Britain, (Sutherland), p. 62.	N.P. Act A.O.N.B.	SU 779 322 1616 63

Post Norman

Description and Date	Remarks	Protection	Grid Ref. and Punchcard No.
Manor House and Preceptory (Site)	Temple Manor. The Knights Templars had a preceptory at Southerington and held the Manor as early as 1240. Present house modern, except for fragments of uncoursed rubble masonry incorporated into walling at the back. O.S.A. No. SU73 SE8. Ref: 1. V.C.H., Vol. 3, p.p. 5—7. 2. Mediaeval Religious Houses of England and Wales, (Knowles and Hadcock), p. 237.	N.P. Act A.O.N.B.	SU 761 333 1616 55
Priory (Site)	Priory Farm. St. Mary's Augustinian Priory founded 1233, dissolved 1484. Excavated from 1953—1969/70. Finds include skeletons of former priors in shallow stone coffins, mediaeval coins, iron and bronze utensils, pottery, tiles etc. Finds in the Wakes Museum, Selborne, and Curtis Museum, Alton. O.S.A. No. SU73 SE7. Ref: 1. Mediaeval Religious Houses in England and Wales, (Knowles and Hadcock), p. 153. 2. Selborne Priory, Hants (issued by Excavation Committee). 3. Natural History and Antiquities of Selborne, (White).	S.A.M. No. 434 N.P. Act A.O.N.B.	SU 755 344 1616 54
Chapel (Possible Site)	Blackmoor. Chapel existed here as early as 1254 and mentioned in account of repairs to property of Selborne Priory in 1462. Exact site not known but probably in area named on 1860 map as Great Chapel Field. O.S.A. No. SU73 SE12. Ref: V.C.H., Vol. 3, p. 15.	N.P. Act A.O.N.B.	SU 780 330 1616 93
Homestead Moat	Grounds of Blackmoor House. Finds include pottery, tiles and iron objects. Probable site of mediaeval Manor House. O.S.A. No. SU73 SE9. Ref: 1. V.C.H., Vol. 3, p. 10. 2. The Natural History and Antiquities of Selborne, (White).	N.P. Act A.O.N.B.	SU 778 328 1616 56

Description and Date	Remarks	Protection	Grid Ref. and Punchcard No.
Group B — (cont.)			
Wayside Cross (Site)	Crouchers Field. Priory Cross mentioned in grants and deeds of Selborne Priory. Disappeared many years ago. O.S.A. No. SU73 SE10.	N.P. Act A.O.N.B.	SU 758 340 1616 57

Chapel (Probable Site)	North of Chapel Farm. St. Mary of Oakhanger Chapel, mentioned 1254 in Selborne Priory Charters. Many tiles and large stones found under raised area in field. Traditional site of chapel.
	O.S.A. No. SU73 NE22.
	Ref: 1. V.C.H., Vol. 3, p.p. 12—15.
	       2. Selborne Priory Charters, Vol. 1, (Hants Record Society), p. 46.
	       3. Natural History and Antiquities of Selborne, (White).
			SU 767 353
			1616 48

Monastic Grange (Site)	Grange Farm. The farm is situated on the original site of The Grange belonging to Selborne Priory. The possible foundations of the original grange building were discovered in 1957. The site is now the lawn of Grange Farm. Mediaeval sherds and oyster sherds were also found. Two small holding ponds for fish are situated in the garden of Coneycroft. These were the 'fish-stews' belonging to The Grange.
	O.S.A. No. SU73 SW12.
	Ref: 1. V.C.H., Vol. 3, p. 6.
	       2. Natural History and Antiquities of Selborne, (White).
	       3. P.H.F.C., Vol. 9, 1920—4, p. 409.
	       4. P.H.F.C., Vol. 21, 1958, p. 111.
		C.A.
		N.P. Act
		A.O.N.B.
			SU 737 338
			1616 15A

Ancient Remains	Norton. Site of deserted mediaeval village. Hundred=Selborne.
	Ref: 1. V.C.H., Vol. 1, p. 485.
	       2. V.C.H., Vol. 2, p. 471.
	       3. V.C.H., Vol. 3, p.p. 5, 8.
			SU 738 350
			1616 95

Period Unknown			
Cultivation Terraces	"The Linchets". Series of terraces. May have been used for cultivation of grapes in C.17/18. Probable celtic fields, now used for cattle grazing. O.S.A. No. SU73 SW6.	N.P. Act A.O.N.B.	SU 732 340 1616 52
Group C — Footpaths and Bridleways			
Ancient Lane	Honey Lane. Here the greensand rock has been deeply eroded by many years of use, to produce one of the best examples of a sunken lane or holloway to be found in Hampshire. Ref: Ancient Lanes and Tracks, 1981, (H.C.C.).	N.P. Act A.O.N.B.	SU 747 335 1616 79
Old Travelway	Via Canonorum or Monks Way. Metalled way built by monks in the C.14 between Selborne Village and the Priory. Now public bridleway.	N.P. Act S.S.S.I. A.O.N.B.	SU 745 340 1616 88

Description and Date	Remarks	Protection	Grid Ref. and Punchcard No.

Group D — Buildings, Monuments and Engineering Works

Description and Date	Remarks	Protection	Grid Ref. and Punchcard No.
Church C.12	St. Mary the Virgin. Built circa 1180 on site of Saxon church. Restored in C.19. Early C.14 work in north transept. Tiles C.13 in chantry, probably from Selborne Priory. Triptych over communion table given by Benjamin White, (brother of Gilbert) in 1793. Stained glass window in memory of Gilbert White shows St. Francis of Assisi surrounded by fifty species of birds. O.S.A. No. SU73 SW13. Ref: 1. Selborne Handbook, (Scott). 2. Gilbert White and his Selborne, (Rye). 3. V.C.H., Vol. 3, p.p. 13—16. 4. Buildings of England; Hants and I.O.W., (Pevsner & Lloyd), p.p. 495—6.	T. & C.P. Act C.A. N.P. Act A.O.N.B.	SU 741 337 1616 01
Cottage C.17	Wheelwrights Cottage. Single storey colour-washed stone blocks. Modern shingled roof. Old brick stack. Dated 1697 with initials 'A.S.' and 'T.R.A.' Adjacent to the wheelwrights shop and in continuous use as smithy from C.13 until 1943.	T. & C.P. Act C.A. N.P. Act A.O.N.B.	SU 737 336 1616 20
Barn C.17	West Barn at Grange Farm, Gracious Street. Timber-framed with thatched hipped roof. Two through cartways. Weatherboarded walls.	T. & C.P. Act C.A. N.P. Act A.O.N.B.	SU 737 339 1616 101
Cottage C.17	Trimmings, Gracious Street. 2 storeys. Lime-washed coursed stone walls. Thatched roof. Lattice casement windows.	T. & C.P. Act C.A. N.P. Act A.O.N.B.	SU 737 338 1616 17
Building C.17/18	Wakes Museum. Original house built of free-stone with brick facing and rounded doors, windows, and corners. Tiled roof and half-hipped gable. Great parlour built 1777 and wing completed 1794. Two cottages terminate main range either end. Garden with brick wall, brick path, sun-dial and Ha-Ha. Ref: 1. Guide of the Wakes, 1971. 2. Gilbert White and his Selborne, (Rye). 3. Buildings of England; Hants and I.O.W., (Pevsner & Lloyd), p. 496.	T. & C.P. Act C.A. N.P. Act A.O.N.B.	SU 740 336 1616 04
House C.18	Plestor House. 2 storeys. Large square stone blocks with red brick quoins and dressings to windows, random stone plinth and brick band. Square centre chimney. Ridge tiled roof. Sash windows. Ref: The use of Hearth Tax Returns, (Meirion-Jones).	T. & C.P. Act C.A. N.P. Act A.O.N.B.	SU 741 337 1616 03
Cottages (2) C.18	Nos. 1 and 2, Plestor Cottages. 2 storeys. Lime-washed pink with stone plinth and brick band. Long ridge tiled roof, half-hipped to right. Side gable of coursed stonework. Formerly three cottages, three front doors remaining.	T. & C.P. Act C.A. N.P. Act A.O.N.B.	SU 741 337 1616 02

Memorial Stone, Ashford Chace, STEEP

17th/18th Century Wakes Museum, SELBORNE

Description and Date	Remarks	Protection	Grid Ref. and Punchcard No.
Group D — (cont.)			
Barn C.18	Small barn at Grange Farm, Gracious Street. Weatherboarded cartshed open on east side. Hipped thatched roof.	T. & C.P. Act C.A. N.P. Act A.O.N.B.	SU 737 339 1616 102
House C.18	White House, High Street. Built circa 1700. Extended at rear mid C.19 and altered C.20. Single storey and attic. 2 storeys at rear. Rubble and brick structure. Slate roofs, half-hipped at front, hipped at rear. Partly timber-framed, visible in north gable. Casement windows. Plain doors. Brick stack.	T. & C.P. Act C.A. N.P. Act A.O.N.B.	SU 744 334 1616 103
Cottage C.18	Peasants Cottage, Honey Lane. 2 storeys. Coursed square rubble structure. Tile-hung first floor at front. 3-light casement windows. Tiled roof with brick end stacks, catslide at rear. Some evidence of timber-framing on rear wall. Gabled porch.	T. & C.P. Act C.A. N.P. Act A.O.N.B.	SU 744 333 1616 104
House C.18	Nuthatch, Under-the-Hill. Single storey and attic. Brick and stone structure, part rendered and tile-hung. Casement and gabled half-dormer windows. Tiled roof. Lean-to at end wing and also at rear.	T. & C.P. Act N.P. Act A.O.N.B.	SU 742 332 1616 105
Inn C.18	The Selborne Arms. 2 storeys. Brick rendered walls. Black tarred plinth. Half-hipped ridge tiled roof. Casement windows. Parts of structure date from C.16. Originally a private house.	T. & C.P. Act C.A. N.P. Act A.O.N.B.	SU 742 335 1616 11
Cottage C.18	No. 3, Wakes Cottage. (Cobbler Cottage). Coursed stone blocks with rusticated brick quoins and surrounds to windows. Thatched roof with eaves square cut around three large upper lattice casement windows. Plain panelled door.	T. & C.P. Act C.A. N.P. Act A.O.N.B.	SU 741 336 1616 05
Building C.18	Old Butchers Shop. Single storey. Colour-washed brick with shutters. Hipped old tiled roof. Pentice roof in front supported on three wooden posts. Central dutch door. Used as butchers shop until 1911.	T. & C.P. Act C.A. N.P. Act A.O.N.B.	SU 741 336 1616 26
Houses (2) C.18	Seale View Cottage and Seale Cottage. Nos. 1 and 2, Gracious Street. 2 storeys. Coursed stone blocks with red brick rusticated quoins and dressings. Thatched roof. Modern thatched extension.	T. & C.P. Act C.A. N.P. Act A.O.N.B.	SU 737 337 1616 18
Farmhouse C.18	Priory Farm, on site of C.13 Selborne Priory. 2 storeys. Grey cement rendered. Hipped tiled roof. Sash windows. Incorporates masonry from the Priory. O.S.A. No. SU73 SE8. Ref: 1. Medieval Religious Houses of England and Wales, (Knowles and Hadcock). 2. Selborne Priory, Hants., (issued by Excavation Committee).	T. & C.P. Act N.P. Act A.O.N.B.	SU 755 344 1616 32

Group D — (cont.)

Description and Date	Remarks	Protection	Grid Ref. and Punchcard No.
House C.18	Temple Manor. On site of Preceptory of Knights Templars and later Manor House. 2 storeys. White cement rendered. Hipped tiled roof. Large sash windows. Victorian additions. Beautifully sited on wooded hillside. O.S.A. No. SU73 SE8.	T. & C.P. Act N.P. Act A.O.N.B.	SU 761 333 1616 30
Farmhouse C.18	Galley Hill Farm. 2 storeys. Coursed stone blocks with rusticated red brick quoins and dressings. Hipped tiled roof.	N.P. Act A.O.N.B.	SU 743 326 1616 33
Farmhouse C.18	Oakhanger Farm, Oakhanger. 2 storeys. Red brick walls. Tiled roof. Sash windows. Centre panelled door.		SU 769 353 1616 42
Farmhouse C.18	Chapel Farm, Oakhanger. 2 storeys. Stuccoed facade. Wing to rear of coursed ironstone. Ridge tiled roof.		SU 769 352 1616 43
Farmhouse C.18	Norton Farm. 2 storeys. Coursed stone blocks. Hipped tiled roof. Ground floor has Victorian splayed bays either side of doorways.		SU 738 349 1616 34
House C.18/19	Forge House. 2 storeys. Limewashed brick walls. Hipped tiled roof. Modernised 1971.	T. & C.P. Act C.A. N.P. Act A.O.N.B.	SU 741 336 1616 07
House C.19	The Old Vicarage. Built 1845 on site of Tudor House, of which the cellars remain. 2½ storeys. Stone structure. Slate roof. Old sash type windows. Three gabled dormer windows. Tall ornate chimneys. Decorated bargeboards. Small red brick extension with tiled roof.	C.A. N.P. Act A.O.N.B.	SU 740 337 1616 67
House C.19	Blackmoor House, Blackmoor. 2/3 storeys. Local stone with bath stone dressings. Tiled roof. Gabled entrance porch. Mullion, transom and sash windows. Service court with Gothic gateway. Clock tower with pyramid tile roof and weather-vane. Built 1869—1872 by Waterhouse. Additions by original builder in 1882.	T. & C.P. Act N.P. Act A.O.N.B.	SU 779 329 1616 90
House C.19	South Lodge at Blackmoor House. 2 storeys. Ground floor local stone with Bath stone dressings. Upper floor tile-hung. Casement windows. 2-storey porch with oriel projecting towards the drive.	T. & C.P. Act N.P. Act A.O.N.B.	SU 778 331 1616 96
Church C.19	St. Matthew, Blackmoor. Built 1868 by Waterhouse. Nave and chancel and large west tower with steep pyramid roof. Plaques by Sir Charles Wheeler. Cloistered war memorial by Sir Herbert Baker at gate. Ref: Buildings of England; Hants and I.O.W., (Pevsner and Lloyd), p. 110.	T. & C.P. Act	SU 780 335 1616 28

Description and Date	Remarks	Protection	Grid Ref. and Punchcard No.
Group D — (cont.)			
Barn C.19	East Barn at Grange Farm, Gracious Street. Stone barn with hipped pantile roof.	T. & C.P. Act C.A. N.P. Act A.O.N.B.	SU 737 339 1616 100
Cottage C.19	Bell Cottage. 2 storeys. Coursed stone with red brick dressings. Hipped tiled roof. Three metal casements. Modernised and extended.	T. & C.P. Act C.A. N.P. Act A.O.N.B.	SU 739 336 1616 12
House	Bush House. C.19 White cement front masking timber-framed structure. Long ridge tiled roof. half-hipped either end. Old centre brick chimney. End gable has exposed timber-framing and brick nogging.	C.A. N.P. Act A.O.N.B.	SU 741 335 1616 10
Farmhouse	Benhams Farm, Blackmoor. 2 storeys. Timber-framed with cement infilling. Short ridge tiled roof. Simple cottage doorway.	N.P. Act A.O.N.B.	SU 776 316 1616 37
Cottages (2)	Albury Farm Cottages, Blackmoor. 2 storeys. Limewashed stone with portion of brickwork at one end. Thatched roof. Probably a C.19 reconstruction of earlier building.		SU 773 339 1616 44
House	Brockbridge House, Blackmoor. Exposed timber work, colourwashed plaster, roughcast brick and stone infilling. Thatched roof. Modern thatched porch.	N.P. Act A.O.N.B.	SU 770 324 1616 31
Cottage	The Thatched Cottage, Blackmoor. 2 storeys. Timber-framed with colourwashed brick and coursed stone infilling. Portion to left of stone blocks painted in imitation of exposed timber-framing. Thatched roof. Formerly two dwellings.	T. & C.P. Act	SU 778 331 1616 29
Cottage	April Cottage, Oakhanger. Limewashed stone with red painted brick dressings to ground floor windows. Thatched roof. Exposed timber-framing in side gable. Modern extension in 1976.	N.P. Act A.O.N.B.	SU 770 362 1616 38
Cottage	Yew Tree Cottage, Oakhanger. Timber-framed with exposed stone rubble infilling. Recently modernised and extended.	T. & C.P. Act	SU 768 356 1616 39
Cottage	Tudor Thatch, Oakhanger. Timber-framed structure. Thatched roof. Now mostly reconstructed.		SU 768 355 1616 40
Cottage	Tunford Cottage, Oakhanger. Gable with exposed timber framing and brick infilling. Thatched roof. Single storey addition of coursed stone. Fire Insurance plaque on side of house.		SU 768 355 1616 41

Description and Date	Remarks	Protection	Grid Ref. and Punchcard No.

Group D — (cont.)

Description and Date	Remarks	Protection	Grid Ref. and Punchcard No.
Cottages (2)	Lower Wick Hill Cottages. Timber-framed with brick infilling, one end coursed stone blocks. Long ridge thatched roof, with eaves square cut around three upper windows.		SU 749 354 1616 36
Cottages (6)	Fishers Buildings, Gracious Street. Range of old stone cottages, formerly village poorhouse. 2 storeys. Tiled roofs. Ref: 1. A. Selborne Handbook, (Scott). 2. Gilbert White and his Selborne, (Rye).	T. & C.P. Act C.A. N.P. Act A.O.N.B.	SU 736 338 1616 16
Building	The Grange, Gracious Street. 2 storeys. Coursed stone blocks. Long tiled roof with stepped ridge in centre, hipped to left, half-hipped to right. Modern windows.	T. & C.P. Act C.A. N.P. Act A.O.N.B.	SU 737 338 1616 15
Cottages (2)	Winkleigh Cottage and Jasmine Cottage. Nos. 1, 2 and 3, Gracious Street. 2 storeys. Coursed stone blocks with rusticated brick quoins and dressings. Old ridge tiled roofs.	T. & C.P. Act C.A. N.P. Act A.O.N.B.	SU 737 337 1616 19
Cottage	Deep Thatch, Gracious Street. Limewashed brick, black tarred plinth. Thatched roof. Modern lattice casement. Interior has exposed beams and large open fireplace. Barrel ceiling. Once the home of the village maltster.	T. & C.P. Act C.A. N.P. Act A.O.N.B.	SU 739 337 1616 14
Cottage	Old Thatch, Gracious Street. Red brick with blue headers, coursed stone plinth. Thatched roof. Timberwork exposed in gable end. Formerly two cottages.	T. & C.P. Act C.A. N.P. Act A.O.N.B.	SU 739 337 1616 13
Cottage	Dortons Cottage, Dortons Lane. Single storey and four half dormers. Coursed stone and red brick structure. Old uneven ridge tiled roof. Possibly once a resthouse of Selborne Priory. Ref: 1. Gilbert White and his Selborne, (Rye). 2. Natural History and Antiquities of Selborne, (White).	T. & C.P. Act C.A. N.P. Act A.O.N.B.	SU 743 338 1616 23
Farmhouse	Dowlings, Huckers Lane. 2 storeys. Cement rendered with small portion of exposed timber-framing. Long ridge tiled roof, half-hipped to left. Old stone retaining wall bordering road.	T. & C.P. Act C.A. N.P. Act A.O.N.B.	SU 742 336 1616 21
Barn	Dowlings, Huckers Lane. Small weatherboarded structure with thatched roof.	T. & C.P. Act C.A. N.P. Act A.O.N.B.	SU 742 336 1616 22
Cottage	No. 4, Wakes Cottage. Timber-framed with plaster and colourwashed brick infilling. Wide random stone plinth. Thatched roof.	T. & C.P. Act C.A. N.P. Act A.O.N.B.	SU 741 336 1616 06
Building	The Forge. Single storey. Weatherboarded structure. Half-hipped tiled roof. Side gable of coursed stone.	C.A. N.P. Act A.O.N.B.	SU 742 336 1616 08

Description and Date	Remarks	Protection	Grid Ref. and Punchcard No.
Group D — (cont.)			
Cottages (2)	Rose Cottages. Single storey and attic. Colour-washed brick walls. Probably C.17 altered. Later extension.	C.A. N.P. Act A.O.N.B.	SU 742 335 1616 27
Cottage and Shop	Yew Tree Cottage and adjoining shop. Yellow colourwashed brick. Exposed timber-framing in side gable. Plain centre door. Two dwellings. Projecting gabled shop adjoining has pleasant display windows.	T. & C.P. Act C.A. N.P. Act A.O.N.B.	SU 741 335 1616 09
Cottage	Lassams. Single storey and four hipped tiled dormers. Timber-framed with red herringbone nogging. Half-hipped ridge tiled roof. Has deepest well in the village.	T. & C.P. Act C.A. N.P. Act A.O.N.B.	SU 743 334 1616 24
Cottage	Box Cottage. Light timber-framing. Limewashed brick and stone infilling. Old uneven ridge tiled roof.	T. & C.P. Act C.A. N.P. Act A.O.N.B.	SU 744 333 1616 25
Barn	Norton Farm. Large weatherboarded structure. Long half-hipped ridge tiled roof. Centre hipped wagon entrance.		SU 738 350 1616 35
Tombstones	St. Marys Churchyard. (1) Gilbert White's grave against north east corner of church, simple stone inscribed 'G.W. 26th June 1793'. (2) Trumpeters grave under old yew tree commemorates John Newland who led Selborne Tithe Riots in 1830.	C.A. N.P. Act A.O.N.B.	SU 742 338 1616 75
Tomb	St. Marys Church. Adam De Gurdon, renowned warrior, who died at Selborne in C.14.	C.A. N.P. Act A.O.N.B.	SU 741 337 1616 01A
Building	Queens Hotel. Formerly The Compasses and then The Queens Head. 2½ storeys. Colour-washed brick structure. Tiled roof. Dormer windows and sash type windows. Two double chimney stacks. Modern extensions. Scene of wedding party described by Gilbert White.	C.A. N.P. Act A.O.N.B.	SU 741 336 1616 87
Building	Village Store, The Plestor. 2 storeys. Dressed stone structure with cement block extension. Slate roof. 2-bay shop front with central door. Sash windows each side.	C.A. N.P. Act A.O.N.B.	SU 740 337 1616 80
Building	Old Bakehouse, formerly part of Village Store. 2 storeys. Dressed stone structure. Slate roof. Modern windows. Extensions to side and rear. No longer used as a bakery.	C.A. N.P. Act A.O.N.B.	SU 740 337 1616 83

Description and Date	Remarks	Protection	Grid Ref. and Punchcard No.

Group E — Street Patterns, Street Furniture and Open Spaces

Description and Date	Remarks	Protection	Grid Ref. and Punchcard No.
Local Open Space	The Plestor. Situated between St. Mary's Church and The Street. Ground given to villagers in 1270 by Sir Adam De Gurdon a former Lord of the Manor. Scene of yearly Summer Fair until end of the C.18.	C.A. N.P. Act A.O.N.B.	SU 740 337 1616 70
Village Pound (Site)	Grange Farm Cottage. No trace remains.	N.P. Act A.O.N.B.	SU 736 339 1616 82

Group F — Historical or Literary Associations

Description and Date	Remarks	Protection	Grid Ref. and Punchcard No.
Tithe Barn	Grange Farm. The Court Leet and Court Baron of Selborne held here from mediaeval times until 1925 when copyhold tenure was abolished. President and Bursar of Magdalen College, Oxford, came once a year to hold Manorial Courts in Great Tithe Barn.	T. & C.P. Act C.A. N.P. Act A.O.N.B.	SU 737 339 1616 81
Cottages (6)	Fishers Buildings, Gracious Street. Former poor-house, famous in economic history when sacked by the 'Selborne Mob' in 1830. Ref: 1. A Selborne Handbook, (Scott). 2. Gilbert White and his Selborne, (Rye). 3. Trouble at Selborne, (Sunderland).	T. & C.P. Act C.A. N.P. Act A.O.N.B.	SU 736 338 1616 16
Building	The Wakes Museum. Famous as the home of Gilbert White and now endowed as a memorial to the Father of English Natural History. Also houses the Oates Memorial Library, formed in memory of Captain Oates, who gave his life for his fellow members of Captain Scott's Antarctic Expedition.	T. & C.P. Act C.A. N.P. Act A.O.N.B.	SU 740 336 1616 04

SHALDEN

Shalden is a small village, reached by pleasant footpaths across the fields from Alton three miles away to the south-east. Its old Saxon church has gone and the present one dates from the nineteenth century, built of flint with Bath stone dressing in the Early English style. It also possesses a fifteenth century font of considerable merit.

Group B — Archaeological

Iron Age

Celtic Fields — Shalden Park Wood and Gregorys Wood. Rectangular fields occupying eastern slope, bounded by lynchets and field banks.
O.S.A. No. SU74 SW7.
SU 706 424
1617 25

Roman

Coin — Large brass of Commodus found 1905 near Shalden school. Now in Alton Museum.
O.S.A. No. SU64 SE9.
SU 697 421
1617 22

Coin and Tile — Bronze coin and fragment of tile found east of the church of St. Peter and St. Paul. Now in Alton Museum.
O.S.A. No. SU64 SE14.
SU 695 416
1617 24

Building (Site) — Manor Farm. Local tradition states building with tessellated pavement uncovered here. Finds include coins, tile fragments and flints.
O.S.A. No. SU64 SE4.
Ref: 1. V.C.H., Vol. 1, p. 346.
    2. P.H.F.C., Vol. 15, 1941–3, p. 246.
    3. P.H.F.C., Vol. 18, 1951–3, p. 137.
    4. P.H.F.C., Vol. 13, 1935–7, p. 294.
SU 692 419
1617 21

Post Norman

Church (Site) — The old church of Shalden which stood a few feet to the south of present Church of St. Peter and St. Paul. Now part of the graveyard.
O.S.A. No. SU64 SE13.
Ref: V.C.H., Vol. 4, p. 103.
SU 693 416
1617 23

Group C — Footpaths and Bridleways

Old Travelway — Green Lane. Crossing the eastern boundary of the parish into Froyle and formerly part of Holybourne parish.
SU 713 423
1617 20

Old Travelway — Stancombe Lane. With Green Lane forms part of old road described in the C.18 as from Stancombe to Shoreditch'. Neither place can now be identified.
SU 697 420
— 707 424
1617 19

Group D — Buildings, Monuments and Engineering Works

Farmhouse C.17 — Aylesfield Farm, Froyle Road. 2 storeys. Brickwork in English bond, with plinth and band. Half-hipped clay tile roof with centre chimney. Iron lattice casement windows.
SU 712 432
1617 09

House C.17 — Greenmount Cottage. 2 storeys. Timber-framed with plinth and painted brick infilling. Half-hipped clay tile roof. Casement windows. Restored.
SU 695 419
1617 05

Description and Date	Remarks	Protection	Grid Ref. and Punchcard No.

Group D — (cont.)

Description and Date	Remarks	Protection	Grid Ref. and Punchcard No.
Farmhouse C.17	Manor Farm, formerly Gregory's Farm. 2 storeys. Timber-framed with flint and brick extensions, tile-hung at upper level. Clay tiled gabled roof. Iron lattice windows. Modern additions.		SU 696 420 1617 07
House C.17	The Old Cottage. 3 storeys. Brick of Flemish bond with plinth. Half-hipped clay tiled roof. Wooden casement windows. Later extensions.		SU 694 417 1617 03
House C.18	Shalden Lodge. 2 storeys. White plaster rendering. Low-pitch hipped clay tiled roof. Sash windows. Centre columned porch.		SU 695 418 1617 04
Cottage C.18	Honeycomb Cottage. 1½ storeys. Brick with exposed timber-framing in gable wall. Clay tiled half-hipped roof. Variety of windows with brick segmental arches. Modern additions.		SU 696 420 1617 06
House C.18	The Old Forge. 2 storeys. Red brick with blue headers in Flemish bond with breaking joint. Clay tiled gabled roof. Iron lattice casement windows. Forge in front of house. Square single storey brick building with hipped roof. Modern extensions.		SU 696 421 1617 08
House C.18	Jordans, Old Odiham Road. 2 storeys. Selborne stone blocks faced with plaster and painted pink with black painted plinth. Square pitched slate roof, rising to large square central chimney stack. Originally a pair of farm cottages.		SU 714 415 1617 13
Church C.19	St. Peter and St. Paul. Built 1865 in style of the C.13. Flint with ashlar dressings. Gable roof in two sections, nave and chancel, and covered with clay tiles. Small timbered bell turret with shingle spire. C.15 octagonal font. Ref: Buildings of England; Hants and I.O.W., (Pevsner & Lloyd), p. 496.	T. & C.P. Act	SU 693 416 1617 01
House C.19	Old School House, Southwood Road. Flint with brick coursing, quoins and window jambs, and brick plinth. Slate gabled roof. Formerly the village school.		SU 697 420 1617 10
House C.19	Glebe Cottage. Flint and brick structure, built by the Rev. C. H. White according to tablet "C.H.W. 1844". Formerly the stables of the Rectory.		SU 693 417 1617 15
House	The Thatched Cottage. 1½ storeys. Timber-framed with brick infilling. Thatched roof.		SU 693 417 1617 02
House	Waverley Cottage, Southwood Road. Brick with some timber-framing. Thatched half-hipped roof. Modern wooden-framed windows. Possibly C.18.		SU 698 419 1617 11

Group D — (cont.)

Description and Date	Remarks	Protection	Grid Ref. and Punchcard No.
Cottage	Shalden Green Cottage. 1½ storeys. Front elevation brick with plinth. Slate roof with chimney on each gable end and long rear slope. Wooden casement windows. Internal exposed timber-framing.		SU 698 434 1617 12
House	May Cottage, Southwood Road. 1½ storeys. Front elevation C.17. Painted brick with plinth. Slate roof, half-hipped to left, hipped to right.		SU 697 419 1617 16
Farm Buildings	Jordans Farm, Old Odiham Road. U-shaped complex. Large timber-framed barn with half-hipped roof and wagon entrance. Other buildings, flint with brick courses, quoins and jambs. Now converted into houses.		SU 714 415 1617 14
House	Shalden Manor. Outward appearance suggests mid C.19 but plan conforms closely with house on site in 1769. Probably re-roofed and refaced with plaster.		SU 694 419 1617 17

Group E — Street Patterns, Street Furniture and Open Spaces

Description and Date	Remarks	Protection	Grid Ref. and Punchcard No.
Open Space	Shalden Green Common. Was once part of the manor of Shalden. Registered with Commons Commissioners.		SU 698 434 1617 18

STEEP

Steep is not mentioned in the Domesday Book as it was probably included in the entry for the Meons. After the Norman Conquest it was almost certainly part of the great episcopal manor of East Meon. Until 1916 the parish also included a strip of land ten miles away in Sussex at Ambersham; links between the two places were strong until the mid-nineteenth century.

The Church of St. Nicholas is essentially thirteenth century and contains the tombs of some members of the Austen family. There are also the remains of a wall-painting and a ninth century Saxon cross-shaft. The principal occupations of the inhabitants of Steep were agricultural, but a prosperous cloth-making industry flourished in the early seventeenth century.

Steep has become famous both nationally and internationally as the home of the innovatory public school, Bedales. Founded by John Haden Badley at Lindfield, Sussex in 1893, Bedales moved to its present site at the turn of the century and the children of many famous people, including Princess Margaret, have been educated there. The poet, Edward Thomas, made his home in Steep; his children attended Bedales and his wife taught there for a while. Edward Thomas met an untimely death in 1917 at the Battle of Arras, and on top of Shoulder of Mutton, Hill overlooking the village, is a sarsen stone simply dedicated to his memory.

Description and Date	Remarks	Protection	Grid Ref. and Punchcard No.

Group A — Natural Features

Description and Date	Remarks	Protection	Grid Ref. and Punchcard No.
Parkland	Coldhayes. Lies on rising ground with both coniferous and deciduous specimen trees. Also impressive clumps of trees and shelter belts. Fine views over surrounding countryside.	N.P. Act A.O.N.B.	SU 756 269 2313 50
Area of Scenic Beauty	Ashford Chace Hangers. Known locally as Steep Hangers or Ashford Hangers. The dramatically formed Hangers, clad with mature beech and yew trees, have earned the name of 'Little Switzerland'. There are many fine views over the surrounding area. The woodlands originally belonged to the sub-Manor of Ashford.	N.P. Act A.O.N.B. C.O.S.	SU 727 255 — 749 270 2313 24
Area of Scenic Beauty	Lythe Hanger. Tree clad scenery with fine views to the south. Old road to Soal Pond runs between high banks and now used as a footpath. Centred on grid reference.	N.P. Act A.O.N.B.	SU 722 251 2313 31
Trees	Ryder Poultry Farm, Steep Marsh. Several species of trees planted to help screen the buildings of the poultry farm.	T.P.O. No. 66 E.H.D. N.P. Act A.O.N.B.	SU 752 262 2313 52
Trees	The Lodge, Stoner House. Three individual limes standing along the side of the road in the grounds of the property.	T.P.O. No. 87 E.H.D. N.P. Act A.O.N.B.	SU 735 254 2313 55
Spring	St. Mary's Well. A remarkable spring that rises only a few yards from the River Rother, yet it is completely separate. It has never failed in living memory. It has no known history, an unsupported idea from the Victorian era designates the spring as a 'Holy Well' visited by mediaeval pilgrims. The spring flows into a stone basin contained in a modern brick wall.	N.P. Act A.O.N.B.	SU 762 246 2313 23

Group B — Archaeological

Description and Date	Remarks	Protection	Grid Ref. and Punchcard No.
Pottery C.13	Found in a pit, close to Cold Hayes Hanger. Now held in Winchester Museum.	N.P. Act A.O.N.B.	SU 752 269 2313 25

Period Unknown

Description and Date	Remarks	Protection	Grid Ref. and Punchcard No.
Enclosure (Site)	Crop mark of sub-rectangular enclosure. Site under pasture. O.S.A. No. SU72 SW22.	N.P. Act A.O.N.B.	SU 735 249 2313 49
Earthwork	Bank and ditch, unnamed and unrecorded, along northern boundary of parish. It coincides with the present parish boundary. Probably an early estate boundary.	N.P. Act A.O.N.B. C.O.S.	SU 739 271 — 747 270 2313 32

Description and Date	Remarks	Protection	Grid Ref. and Punchcard No.

Group C — Footpaths and Bridleways

Description and Date	Remarks	Protection	Grid Ref. and Punchcard No.
Footpath	Shoulder of Mutton footpath. Part of the Petersfield to Alton Footpath No. 17. Magnificent views towards the South Downs. It passes the Edward Thomas Memorial Stone.	N.P. Act A.O.N.B. C.O.S.	SU 740 265 — 737 270 2313 36
Bridleway	Ancient bridleway from Ashford to Week Green. Part of old road to Alton. Steep Bridleway 16. Known locally as the Woodcutter's Path. Part runs through County Open Space. Ref: Field Archaeology as Illustrated in Hampshire, 1915, (Williams-Freeman).	N.P. Act A.O.N.B. C.O.S.	SU 737 263 — 729 266 2313 35
Footpath	Steep Footpath No. 20. Part of the Petersfield to Alton footpath, and formerly an old road. Road marked on 1839 tithe map.	N.P. Act A.O.N.B.	SU 745 253 — 742 257 2313 46
Old Road (Disused)	Old Stoner Hill Road up escarpment to Alton. Steep Bridleway No. 33. Turnpiked under a local act of 1772. An important route to Winchester via Ropley in C.18, as the alternative across Stroud Common was often marshy.	N.P. Act A.O.N.B. C.O.S.	SU 729 258 — 735 258 2313 33
Road	Stoner Hill Road. A zigzag from the Island Steep, to Week Green, Froxfield. Constructed under Turnpike Act of 1825 to avoid steep climb up Stoner Hill, the area known as Little Switzerland. Scenic route through steep wooded hangers with many viewpoints.	N.P. Act A.O.N.B. C.O.S.	SU 735 258 — 729 266 2313 34

Group D — Buildings, Monuments and Engineering Works

Description and Date	Remarks	Protection	Grid Ref. and Punchcard No.
Church C.12	All Saints. C.12 south aisle and arcade of of circular piers and trumpet capitals. North aisle and chancel with lancet windows dates from early C.13. Font with pointed trefoil arches. Restored 1876. Bell turret of this date partly tile-hung. Carved oak organ screen by Edward Barnsley. O.S.A. No. SU72 SW14. Ref: 1. V.C.H., Vol. 3, p.p. 79–80. 2. Buildings of England; Hants and the I.O.W., (Pevsner and Lloyd).	T. & C.P. Act N.P. Act A.O.N.B.	SU 745 253 2313 01
Farmhouse C.16	Sole or Scal Farm. L-shaped plan. 2 storeys and attics. Tiled hipped roof. Timber framing, exposed in places, with brick infilling and tile-hanging. Basically C.16 with many later alterations. Wooden casement windows. Interior has three Tudor brick fireplaces.	N.P. Act A.O.N.B.	SU 728 246 2313 20
Farmhouse C.16	Steep Farm. 2 storeys. Originally box-framed, but now clad with brick and some flint. Tiled roof with modern dormers. Old chimney. Modern casement windows. One stone mullion window possibly from another building. Interior has massive ceiling beams. Extensively modernised.	N.P. Act A.O.N.B.	SU 749 255 2313 21

Description and Date	Remarks	Protection	Grid Ref. and Punchcard No.
Group D — (cont.)			
Farmhouse C.16	Tankerdale. 2 storeys and attics. Tiled roof with old chimney. Timber-framed. Southwest and southeast elevations stuccoed with tile-hanging on upper storey. Northwest face timber-famed with brick infilling. A gable-topped, timber-framed tower, projecting on two faces, houses a wide spiral staircase. Sash casement and mullioned windows. Large cellar.	T. & C.P. Act N.P. Act A.O.N.B.	SU 766 258 2313 09
House C.16/17	Restalls, formerly Church House. L-shaped plan. 2 storeys. Tiled roof with gabled dormers and tile-hung gables. Old chimneys. Leaded light casement windows. Interior has massive timbers, old fireplaces and much oak panelling. The original name 'Church House' probably described its function, that of a 'Parish Hall', rather than its position close to the Church. The house was reconstructed by Unsworth about 1905. Ref: 1. V.C.H., Vol. 3, p.p. 70 and 80. 2. Small Country Houses of Today, (Weaver). 3. Old English Country Cottages, 1906—7, (Studio Winter).	T. & C.P. Act N.P. Act A.O.N.B.	SU 746 253 2313 08
Farmhouse C.16/17	Steep Marsh Farm. 2 storeys. Mainly brick structure with some timber-framing on east side. Double hipped tiled roof. T-shaped plan. Modern casement windows. Extensively modernised.	N.P. Act A.O.N.B.	SU 754 263 2313 14
Cottage C.16/17	Vine Cottage, formerly Dunannie Cottage. Thatched and tiled roof. Half-timbered with brick infilling, some herringbone work. Leaded diamond casement windows. Two later gabled dormers. Large modern addition to rear.	T. & C.P. Act N.P. Act A.O.N.B.	SU 739 248 2313 04
Farmhouse C.16/17	Gardner's Farm, Steep Marsh. 2 storeys. Timber-framed with brick infilling, some herringbone ironstone work. Double hipped slated roof. Tile-hung upper storey on southeast front. Wooden casement windows with glazing bars. Large cellar.	N.P. Act A.O.N.B.	SU 761 263 2313 17
Farmhouse C.17	Ashford Farm. Formerly two cottages possibly incorporating older building. Oldest part of ironstone with brick quoins and ironstone galleting. Other portions refaced with brick. Tiled roof with gable ends. Wooden casement windows. Some timber-framing visible inside.	N.P. Act A.O.N.B.	SU 743 266 2313 13
Cottage C.17	Bees Cottage. 2 storeys. Formerly two cottages. Malmstone with brick dressings. Tile-hung on upper storey. Timber-faming visible on north side. Most windows modern. Remnants of iron framed casement windows survive. Tiled roof. Old central chimney.	N.P. Act A.O.N.B.	SU 738 263 2313 11

Description and Date	Remarks	Protection	Grid Ref. and Punchcard No.

Group D — (cont.)

Description and Date	Remarks	Protection	Grid Ref. and Punchcard No.
Farmhouse C.17	The Old Farm, formerly Dunhill Farm. Timber-framed with brick infilling, some herringbone pattern. Enlarged in C.18. Tiled roof. Sash windows with Gothic glazing and moulded drip-stones. Old chimney at east end. Classical doorway, pedimented hood on fluted columns.	T. & C.P. Act N.P. Act A.O.N.B.	SU 738 249 2313 05
Farmhouse C.17	Burnt Ash Farm. 2 storeys. Malmstone, iron-stone and brick dressings. Timber-framing visible in north wall. Double hipped tiled roof with old chimney. Wooden casement windows. Small upper window has brick dripstone mould-ing. Inscription in stone over door 'I.T.M. 1656'. Large cellar partly above ground.	N.P. Act A.O.N.B.	SU 757 251 2313 15
Cottage C.17	Greenlands, Park Lane. Single storey with attics. Brick structure, little timber-framing visible. Tiled roof with three hipped dormers at eaves level. Modern leaded casement windows. Extensively restored.	N.P. Act A.O.N.B.	SU 736 253 2313 18
Cottages C.17	Kettlebrook Cottages. Two dwellings but originally a small farmhouse. Timber-framed with brick infilling, north end upper storey jettied on four carved brackets. Tiled roof hipped at north end, gabled at south. Gabled tiled dormers. Casement windows with glazing bars. Interior with large ceiling beams.	T. & C.P. Act N.P. Act A.O.N.B.	SU 753 252 2313 06
House C.17	Ackmals. Formerly a farmhouse. Originally box framed, now brick clad, but timber-framing survives on front and back walls. Double hipped roof, formerly thatch, now slated. Old central chimney stack. Old ceiling joists. Much altered at various periods.	N.P. Act A.O.N.B.	SU 756 262 2313 53
Farmhouse C.18	Lythe Farm, Stroud Common. 2 storeys. South front, brick with central pediment and porch with Gothic ogee arch moulding. Windows ogee arched and one round. North face galleted malm-stone with brick dressings. Gable in roof with ogee arch window. Tiled roof. Some good C.18 doors.	T. & C.P. Act N.P. Act A.O.N.B.	SU 724 247 2313 07
Former Stable Block and Coach-house	Old Ashford Manor. Now converted to accomo-dation and garage. Double-hipped tiled roof with gable to south. Wall facing lane of malmstone with brick dressings. South wall of brick with some malmstone. Small square dovecote in centre of roof with wind vane of running fox, probably of later date. On north side roof descends to first storey floor level. 8 ft. garden wall of malmstone topped by coping and tiles.	N.P. Act A.O.N.B.	SU 737 263 2313 12

Description and Date	Remarks	Protection	Grid Ref. and Punchcard No.
Group D — (cont.)			
Cottage C.18	Downgate Cottage, Steep Marsh. Now one dwelling though formerly two. Galleted malmstone with brick dressings and ironstone between storeys. Tiled roof descends to door level at rear. Iron casement windows with square leaded panes.	N.P. Act A.O.N.B.	SU 756 255 2313 16
Farmhouse C.19	Aldersnapp Farm. 2 storeys. Double hipped tiled roof, once slate. Building rendered with stucco, grooved to imitate stone. French door with reeded surround. Sash windows with glazing bars. Door with simple hood. Barns with flint walls and slate roofs.	N.P. Act A.O.N.B.	SU 729 242 2313 10
Cottage C.19	Berryfield Cottage. Formerly New Farm or New House Farm. Dated '1820' on the west front. Double hipped tiled roof. Malmstone with brick dressing. Wooden casement windows. Projecting centre section with porch. Round headed doorway surmounted by a window. Bronze tablet over the door records it as the home of the poet Edward Thomas from 1906–1909.	T. & C.P. Act N.P. Act A.O.N.B.	SU 739 264 2313 03
Irrigation System C.19	System of conduits and sluices used to flood meadows and improve hay crops, using water from Ashford Stream. At least six sluices set in masonry of brick and sandstone released water into fields. Sharp bends also reinforced with masonry. System in use until 1947. Best preserved section centred on grid reference.	N.P. Act A.O.N.B.	SU 753 250 2313 45
Mansion C.19	Adhurst St. Mary. Large building in a mixture of Jacobean and Gothic styles. Stone structure with gables. Tower at southwest front. Mullioned windows and carved tracery balconies. Built of stone from East Meon area. Designed by P. C. Hardwick for John Bonham-Carter II. The grounds contain fine specimen trees. Ref: The Buildings of England; Hants and the I.O.W., (Pevsner and Lloyd), p. 500.	N.P. Act A.O.N.B.	SU 763 248 2313 44
Mansion C.19	Coldhayes. Built 1869 by Waterhouse. Mixture of styles including Jacobean and Gothic. Mullioned windows, round arches, half-hipped dormers. Decorated Tudor brick chimney. Tiled pitched roof. Mediaeval style porch and Elizabethan bay window. Inside a fine hall staircase, the walls lined with fretted panels of grasses, vines etc., in the manner of Charles Eastlake. Interior also has a classical arcade with rounded arches and Tuscan columns. Ref: Buildings of England; Hants and I.O.W., (Pevsner and Lloyd), p. 610.	N.P. Act A.O.N.B.	SU 756 269 2313 27

Description and Date	Remarks	Protection	Grid Ref. and Punchcard No.
Group D — (cont.)			
Hall and Library C.20	Bedales New Hall and Memorial Library. Designed by Ernest Gimson in the William Morris tradition. Walls of handmade bricks and roof of handmade tiles. Woodwork of English oak. Wrought iron casement windows. The Lupton Hall similar in style to a mediaeval tithe barn with a 31 ft. span timber roof built in 1913. The library is flanked by aisles and divided into bays and has a gallery. Built 1921, by Geoffrey Lupton. Ref: The Buildings of England; Hants and I.O.W., (Pevsner and Lloyd).	T. & C.P. Act N.P. Act A.O.N.B.	SU 743 251 2313 02
Cottage C.20	Row Cottage, Church Road. Built to low price limit in William Morris craftsman tradition, by Geoffrey Lupton. Mansard roof descends in places to 3 ft. off the ground. Brick walls. Central chimney with back to back hearths. Handmade doors and door nails. Floor boards consist of 15 in. elm.	N.P. Act A.O.N.B.	SU 742 253 2313 41
Farmhouse	The Red House, Stroud. 2-storey timber-framed section probably dates from C.17. East wing, a Georgian addition. Older part has tiled roof, east wing slated.	N.P. Act A.O.N.B.	SU 727 237 2313 39
Cottage	Church Cottage, Church Road. Originally timber-framed tithe barn converted to four cottages. Two cottages remain, occupied as one. Tiled roof. Some weatherboarding.	N.P. Act A.O.N.B.	SU 745 253 2313 43
Barn	Steep Marsh Farm. Weatherboarded barn of three bays. Aisles on all four sides. Old tiled roof formerly thatched.	N.P. Act A.O.N.B.	SU 754 263 2313 14A
Barn	Gardner's Farm. One wall of brick, the rest weatherboarded. Stone plinth. Tiled roof probably once thatched.	N.P. Act A.O.N.B.	SU 761 263 2313 40
Outbuildings	Westmark Farm. Brick barn of four bays with double hipped tiled roof. Aisles on both sides and doors to east and west. Mostly original piers and roof timbers. Range of cowhouses to the west. Semi-circular duckpond filled in, but malmstone retaining wall with brick capping remains.	N.P. Act A.O.N.B.	SU 769 241 2313 22
Group F — Historical or Literary Associations			
Cottage	No. 2, Yew Tree Cottages. A semi-detached cottage built in 1913, home of the poet Edward Thomas from 1913—16. Identifiable as the setting of his poem 'Old Man'.	N.P. Act A.O.N.B.	SU 738 253 2313 54

Description and Date	Remarks	Protection	Grid Ref. and Punchcard No.

Group F. — (cont.)

Description and Date	Remarks	Protection	Grid Ref. and Punchcard No.
Memorial Stone	Dedicated to Edward Thomas the poet, situated on Shoulder of Mutton Hill. The memorial marks a superb viewpoint much favoured by the poet when he lived at Berryfield Cottage. The original location of the sarsen stone is not sure, but a contemporary report of the unveiling says Wiltshire, this is likely as the poet had special links with the county. Ref: P.H.F.C., Vol. 17, Part 3, Hampshire Writers, (Wilkinson).	T. & C.P. Act N.P. Act A.O.N.B. C.O.S.	SU 739 269 2313 37
House	Hillcroft, Church Road. Occupied by T. Sturge Moore, poet, critic, and wood engraver, between 1919 and 1927. Commemorative plaque on front wall, though wrongly dated.	N.P. Act A.O.N.B.	SU 739 253 2313 30
House C.20	Ashford Chace. Built 1912 for A. B. R. Trevor-Battye, explorer and naturalist, later occupied by First Lord Horder. Early C.20 romantic. Gatehouse to courtyard converted from 1820 barn. Important gardens, originally incorporating those of Old Ashford Manor and Berryfield Cottage, laid out by Triggs, Author of formal Gardens in England and Scotland' 1901—2, Architects W. F. Unsworth and H. Inigo Jones. Ref: The Edward Thomas Country, 1978, (Whiteman), p.p. 24, 26.	N.P. Act A.O.N.B.	SU 740 264 2313 51
Mill Ponds	Ashford Mill Ponds. Probably of mediaeval date. Buildings demolished early C.20. The fall of water from the lower pond is still visible. Centred on grid reference. Ref: 1. V.C.H., Vol. 3, p. 78. 2. Steep Rates List from 1707.	N.P. Act A.O.N.B.	SU 741 260 2313 29
Fulling Mill (Site of)	Oakhurst Farm, Steep. Site identified by remains of dam, and field names. Ref: 1. V.C.H., Vol. 3, p. 78. 2. Survey of Manor of East Meon, 1647.	N.P. Act A.O.N.B.	SU 744 258 2313 42
Old Toll House	Bowyers Cottage. On the Sheet — Farnham Road, turnpiked in 1825. The toll gate was sited to catch traffic on old road from Petersfield via Harrow Lane and the ford at Kettlebrook, and on the highway from Sheet.	N.P. Act A.O.N.B.	SU 762 260 2313 48

WEST TISTED

West Tisted is a very pleasant village, and its church and manor house form an attractive group typical of the small villages in this part of Hampshire. The church is Saxon in origin and has a Norman font and a roof whose beams are 700 years old.

There is a large Jacobean altar table and a delightful tablet to Sir Benjamin Tichborne and his wife. Not far from the church is a large ancient oak tree, in whose welcoming foliage Sir Benjamin hid from Cromwell's forces in the Civil War.

Old Travelway (possibly Pilgrims' Way), WEST TISTED

Description and Date	Remarks	Protection	Grid Ref. and Punchcard No.

Group A — Natural Features

Viewing Point	North of the village. Good scenic views.		SU 647 297 1618 08
Area of Scenic Beauty	Good scenic views of whole area. Includes Hathman Wood and Plantation. Abundant fauna and flora. Centred on grid reference.	N.P. Act A.O.N.B.	SU 641 286 — 637 296 1618 12

Group B — Archaeological

Bronze Age

Flints	Manor Farm. Finds include barbed and tanged arrowhead, waste flakes and a Mesolithic worked point. In Alton Museum. O.S.A. No. SU62 NE13.		SU 650 292 1618 06
Barrows (4)	The Devils Jump. Fine barrows situated in straight line within roadside copse. Traditional site of battle between Danes and Saxons and also Civil War Cemetery. O.S.A. No. SU62 NE8. Ref: 1. P.H.F.C., Vol. 14, 1938—40, p.p. 28—9, 355. 　　2. Field Archaeology as Illustrated in Hampshire, 1915, (Williams-Freeman), p. 293.	S.A.M. No. 41	SU 667 281 1618 07

Post Norman

Manor House (Site)	North of St. Mary Magdalene Church. The Manor of West Tisted was held by the Tichborne family from the C.14 to recent times. The Manor House was demolished 1955—6. Modern dwelling now on site. O.S.A. No. SU62 NE1. Ref: 1. V.C.H., Vol. 3, p. 59. 　　2. Field Archaeology as Illustrated in Hampshire, 1915, (Williams-Freeman), p.p. 43, 296—7, 331.		SU 650 292 1618 04
Ancient Site	Site of Deserted Mediaeval Village. Ref: 1. V.C.H., Vol. 1, p. 463. 　　2. V.C.H., Vol. 3, p. 37, 58—62. 　　3. Deserted Mediaeval Villages, (Beresford and Hurst).		SU 650 290 1618 10

Group C — Footpaths and Bridleways

Bridleway	North of the village. Reputed to be part of the old Pilgrims' Way from Winchester to Canterbury. Centred on grid reference.		SU 652 302 1618 09

Description and Date	Remarks	Protection	Grid Ref. and Punchcard No.

Group D — Buildings, Monuments and Engineering Works

Description and Date	Remarks	Protection	Grid Ref. and Punchcard No.
Church C.12	St. Mary Magdalene. Flint structure with wooden bell turret. Blocked window, possibly 1,000 years old. Font and Holy Water Stoup date from C.19. Jacobean altar. O.S.A. No. SU62 NE3. Ref: 1. V.C.H., Vol. 3, p. 61. 2. Buildings of England; Hants and I.O.W., (Pevsner and Lloyd), p. 648. 3. Parish Church Leaflet.	T. & C.P. Act	SU 650 292 1618 01
Lodge C.19	To Basing Park. Single storey classical structure. Stuccoed walls. Slate roof. Recessed columned porch. Sash windows. Low balustraded parapet.		SU 684 299 1618 03

Group E — Street Patterns, Street Furniture and Open Spaces

Description and Date	Remarks	Protection	Grid Ref. and Punchcard No.
Chalk Well	West side of Fawley Lane. Shaft approximately 2.0 m. in diameter opening out into bell-shaped chamber. This type of feature is generally considered to be merely a well of comparatively recent date and should not be confused with a Dene Hole. O.S.A. No. SU62 NE9.		SU 668 282 1618 05

314

WHITEHILL

The parish of Whitehill includes the military camps of Bordon and Longmoor, which form one of the most important military establishments in the south of England. Longmoor Camp is of interest for it was here that officers and men were trained in the operation of railway transport. The Longmoor Military Railway, which closed in 1969, had an extensive mileage of line in regular use for goods and military passenger traffic. The line used to connect with the British Rail network at Bordon to the north and at Liss to the south.

Description and Date	Remarks	Protection	Grid Ref. and Punchcard No.
Group A — Natural Features			
Area of Ecological Importance	Woolmer Pond. A shallow peat stained base, poor lake with peripheral wet and dry heath on Lower Greensand. Herpetologically and ornithologically an important site.	N.P. Act S.S.S.I.	SU 790 320 1619 25
Area of Ecological Importance	Woolmer Forest. Extensive stretch of dry heath dominated by heather and extensively but not densely colonised by birch. Thought to be best remaining example of dry heath in the western Weald and is of special herpetological importance.	N.P. Act S.S.S.I.	SU 805 324 1619 32
Area of Ecological Importance	Blackmoor. An area of Folkestone Beds at the western extremity of the Weald. Dominated by heather and moor-grass. The site contrasts with the much drier heathland elsewhere.	N.P. Act S.S.S.I.	SU 787 335 1619 36
Geological Feature	South side of Oxney Stream. Peat bog.		SU 794 377 1619 33
Trees	Dormy, Hogmoor Road, Bordon. Many groups of trees of different species standing in the grounds of houses on the above estate. The area is centred on the grid reference given.	T.P.O. No. 13 E.H.D.	SU 786 342 1619 37
Tree	Queen Anne's Tree. Opposite Regency House on A325. Place where royal deer, driven by Verderers, were inspected by Queen Anne.	N.P. Act S.S.S.I.	SU 787 321 1619 27
Trees	To the north of New Road and west of Forest Road. Differing species standing in the area centred on grid reference.	T.P.O. No. 780	SU 794 344 1619 34
Trees	Area of former Whitehill House. Now known as Oak View Estate.	T.P.O. No. 419	SU 795 340 1619 21
Trees	Pinewood House and Whitehill Chase, Petersfield Road. Several trees of various species, both deciduous and coniferous, standing on land to the east of the A325 at Whitehill, centred on grid reference given.	T.P.O. No. 89 E.H.D.	SU 795 345 1619 38
Trees	Links House, Firgrove Road, Blackmoor. A sweet gum inside the northern boundary of the garden, and a group consisting of one Scots pine, one lawson cypress, nine holly and a sweet gum on the frontage of the garden of the above property.	T.P.O. No. 14 E.H.D.	SU 796 341 1619 35
Trees	Beaulieu, New Road. Part of curtilage now developed, most of the trees retained.	T.P.O. No. 516	SU 797 342 1619 22
Trees	Waterside, Mill Chase Road, Bordon. Formerly Deadwater.	T.P.O. No. 568	SU 804 356 1619 20
Springs	Camp Springs. In existence for hundreds of years and served military camping units prior to World War I.		SU 793 339 1619 26

Description and Date	Remarks	Protection	Grid Ref. and Punchcard No.

Group B — Archaeological

Stone Age

Description and Date	Remarks	Protection	Grid Ref. and Punchcard No.
Implements	Woolmer Forest. Polished Neolithic axe found on military range. Scandinavian style with flat sides and ablong section. In Willmer House Museum, Farnham. O.S.A. No. SU73 SE29.		SU 792 331 1619 29
Microliths and Flakes	Longmoor Inclosure. Found when land was bull-dozed for military purposes. Probably a temporary camping area of comparatively short duration. O.S.A. No. SU73 SE19. Ref: P.H.F.C., Vol. 18, 1951–3, p. 170.		SU 790 303 1619 08

Bronze Age

Description and Date	Remarks	Protection	Grid Ref. and Punchcard No.
Bowl Barrow (Remains)	West of Hogmoor Lodge. Mutilated by heavy vehicles. O.S.A. No. SU73 SE4. Ref: P.H.F.C., Vol. 14, 1938–40, p. 354.		SU 789 343 1619 06
Bowl Barrows (9)	South of Regency House. Extending along the crest of low northeast to southwest ridge, with section of Roman road nearby. Centred on grid reference. O.S.A. No. SU73 SE23. Ref: 1. P.H.F.C., Vol. 14, 1938–40, p. 354. 2. The Natural History and Antiquities of Selborne, (White).	S.A.M. No. 38	SU 784 321 1619 10
Bowl Barrow	Northwest of Brimstone Lodge. Average diameter 25.0 m. and 1.9 m. high. Mutilated by army trenches. O.S.A. No. SU73 SE27. Ref: P.H.F.C., Vol. 14, 1938–49, p. 354.		SU 799 313 1619 14
Bowl Barrows (2)	South of Hogmoor Lodge. 1.20 m. in average diameter with no indications of ditch and mutilated in northern quadrant. 2.24 m. in average diameter with slight depression of surrounding ditch visible. O.S.A. No. SU73 SE5. Ref: P.H.F.C., Vol. 14, 1938–40, p. 354.	S.A.M. No. 106	SU 792 343 1619 07
Bowl Barrow (Site)	Southwest of Bordon Station. Tank training area. O.S.A. No. SU73 NE11.		SU 781 359 1619 03
Bowl Barrows (2)	Southeast of Bordon Station. Covered in heather and small trees. Primary inurned crema-tion found during excavations. Barrows mutilated by army activity. O.S.A. No. SU73 NE12.	S.A.M. No. 324	SU 785 357 1619 04
Bowl Barrow (Site)	Quebec Barracks, Bordon Camp. No trace remains. O.S.A. No. SU73 NE13.		SU 799 359 1619 19

Description and Date	Remarks	Protection	Grid Ref. and Punchcard No.

Group B — (cont.)

Description and Date	Remarks	Protection	Grid Ref. and Punchcard No.
Bowl Barrows (3)	East of Bordon Station. Heavily mutilated by army activity.	S.A.M. No. 259	SU 787 362 1619 02
Bowl Barrow	Broxhead Common. Barrow 18.5 m. in diameter and 1.6 m. high, with ditch partly mutilated by old army dugout and army bearing point. Grass covered with some gorse and bracken. O.S.A. No. SU83 NW2. Ref: P.H.F.C., Vol. 14, 1938—40, p. 352.		SU 803 374 1619 01
Bowl Barrow	North of Brimstone Lodge. Barrow 22.5 m. in diameter and 1.52 m. high, no visible ditch, mutilated by rabbit burrows. O.S.A. No. SU83 SW3. Ref: P.H.F.C., Vol. 14, 1938—40, p. 354.		SU 800 313 1619 16
Bowl Barrows (3)	Brimstone Inclosure. Covered in heather and bracken, mutilated by rabbit burrows and vehicle tracks. O.S.A. No. SU73 SE25. Ref: P.H.F.C., Vol. 14, 1938—40, p. 354.	N.P. Act S.S.S.I.	SU 799 321 1619 12
Bowl Barrow	Brimstone Inclosure. 7.60 m. in diameter and 1.82 m. high. O.S.A. No. SU73 SE24. Ref: P.H.F.C., Vol. 14, 1938—40, p. 354.	N.P. Act S.S.S.I.	SU 797 320 1619 11
Bowl Barrows (6)	Situated upon Woolmer Down, a bracken and heather covered sand ridge, mutilated by old army dugouts, tracks etc. O.S.A. No. SU73 SE26. Ref: P.H.F.C., Vol. 14, 1938—40, p. 354.	N.P. Act S.S.S.I.	SU 790 317 1619 13
Bowl Barrows (Possible)	Southeast corner of the parish. Group of mounds may be simple tree rings. Situated in prominent position upon sandy heathland. O.S.A. No. SU83 SW4.		SU 810 305 1619 17
Round Barrow (Remains)	West of Heifers Down. Northwest half completely destroyed during construction of military road. O.S.A. No. SU83 SW6.	N.P. Act S.S.S.I.	SU 805 317 1619 18

Bronze Age/Roman

Description and Date	Remarks	Protection	Grid Ref. and Punchcard No.
Weapon Hoard and Coin Hoard	Hogmoor Lane. Number of bronze weapons including complete swords, fragments of sword blades and sheaths, etc. found 1870 in garden of cottage. Fragment of eathenware pot with nearly one hundred Roman coins later discovered in same area. Majority of finds now in British Museum and Alton Museum. O.S.A. No. SU73 S3 Ref: The Natural History and Antiquities of Selborne, (White).		SU 785 347 1619 05

Group B — (cont.)

Roman

Description and Date	Remarks	Protection	Grid Ref. and Punchcard No.
Coin Hoards (2)	Woolmer Pond. Hundreds of coins and some medallions found 1740. Large pot of coins or medals found circa 1774. Finds in the British Museum. O.S.A. No. SU73 SE21. Ref: The Natural History and Antiquities of Selbourne, (White).	N.P. Act S.S.S.I.	SU 787 319 1619 09
Coin	North corner of Hollywater Clump. Bronze Antoninianus of Tetricus I found. In private ownership. O.S.A. No. SU83 SW1.		SU 804 336 1619 15

Post Norman

Description and Date	Remarks	Protection	Grid Ref. and Punchcard No.
Ancient Site	Broxhead. Site of deserted mediaeval village. Originally part of Woolmer Forest. Hundred of Bishop's Sutton. Ref: V.C.H., Vol. 3, p.p. 52—3.		SU 779 369 1619 30

Period Unknown

Description and Date	Remarks	Protection	Grid Ref. and Punchcard No.
Camp	Wall Down. Off Forest Road and Wall Down. Outer ditch, bank and inner ditch. Apparent entrance in south east corner. Overgrown with fern. O.S.A. No. SU73 SE6.	S.A.M. No. 123	SU 798 342 1619 23

Group D — Buildings, Monuments and Engineering Works

Description and Date	Remarks	Protection	Grid Ref. and Punchcard No.
Farmhouse C.16/17	Watermeadow Farm or Lower House Farm. 2 storeys. Timber-framed with colourwashed brick, stone and plaster infilling. Steep hipped tiled roof. Mock half-timber porch.	T. & C.P. Act	SU 810 358 1619 24

Situated about six miles west of Alton, the scattered village is divided into Upper and Lower Wield. The numerous thatched cottages in the village and its situation away from main roads in the midst of much woodland makes this one of the most attractive areas in the district. There is a fine Norman church with traces of many old paintings on its walls. The church has a finely carved Norman doorway over which there is a runes dial. There is also an arcade font and a sixteenth century chalice. The church contains a splendid alabaster monument incorporating the figures of Sir William Wallop and his third wife, he in Tudor armour and she in a simple dress with lace cuffs on the sleeves. Sir William was High Sheriff of the county and three times Mayor of Southampton.

Group B — Archaeological

Post Norman

Description and Date	Remarks	Protection	Grid Ref. and Punchcard No.
Alleged Castle (Site)	Barton Castle Barton Copse. Motte and bailey type earthwork close to right of way between Wield Church and Godsfield. Well defined walls of tooled clunch remain, suggesting date coeval with church. O.S.A. No. SU63 NW9. Ref: 1. Field Archaeology as Illustrated in Hampshire, 1915, p.p. 229, 422.		SU 622 382 1620 23

Group D — Buildings, Monuments and Engineering Works

Description and Date	Remarks	Protection	Grid Ref. and Punchcard No.

Church C.12	St. James. Restored 1884—5 and 1931. Stone structure. Norman shell with north and south doorways and chancel arch of that period. Two consecration crosses of especial interest. Royal Arms of Queen Anne over chancel arch. Fine C.17 alabaster monument to William Wallop and his wife.
	Ref: 1. V.C.H., Vol. 3, p. 347.
	    2. Wield Parish History, 1965, (Mills).
	    3. Buildings of England; Hants and I.O.W., (Pevsner and Lloyd), p. 656.
		T. & C.P. Act	SU 628 387
			1620 01

Cottages (2) C.16/17	Rose Cottage and Corner House. Timber-framed with brick and plaster infilling. Lime-washed flint addition to right, probably C.18. Thatched roofs, with corrugated iron to the rear of Rose Cottage.	T. & C.P. Act	SU 629 387 1620 04
Cottage C.17	Church Cottage. Red brick with exposed timber-framing on rear facade. Thatched roof. Modern lattice casement windows. Small modern single storey extension.		SU 628 387 1620 05
Cottage C.17	Church Farm. Rendered walls. Thatched roof with eaves square cut around two upper windows. Centre boarded door. Small modern porch.		SU 629 387 1620 09
Farmhouse C.17/18	Nicholas Farm. 2 storeys. Red brick with blue headers. Earlier portion with exposed timber-framing and brick infilling. C.19 fishscale tile hanging above. Long ridge thatched roof. Recently restored and modernised.		SU 635 403 1620 21
House C.18	The Manor. Built on site of older structure. 2 storeys. Brick walls. Modern ridge tiled roof. Sash windows. Half-glazed and panelled double doors. C.19 canopied porch. Large modern addition.	T. & C.P. Act	SU 672 389 1620 02
Cottage C.18	Pond Cottage. Coursed flint with red brick dressings. Thatched roof with eaves square cut around two upper windows. Thatched pentice to rear.		SU 629 387 1620 07

Description and Date	Remarks	Protection	Grid Ref. and Punchcard No.

Group D — (cont.)

Description and Date	Remarks	Protection	Grid Ref. and Punchcard No.
Farmhouse C.18	Wield Farm. Stands on site of earlier building, of which the cellars remain. 2 storeys. Red brick walls. Ridge tiled roof. Remains of Wallop coat-of-arms over porch. Surrounded by good tile-capped flint wall.		SU 629 388 1620 11
Cottage C.18	Old Rectory Cottage. 2 storeys. Limewashed brick walls. Ridge tiled roof. Large plain windows. Formerly a shoe-makers premises.		SU 633 387 1620 14
House C.18	Yew Tree Inn. Brick structure partly tile-hung, with slate roof. The building is partly an C.18 inn.		SU 636 89 1620 32
Farm Building C.18	Cart shed at Wield Manor Farm. Five bays. Steeply pitched thatched roof strutted purlin framework. Weatherboarded on three sides with open front.		SU 628 388 1620 35
House C.18	Whites Farm. 2 storeys. Brick construction with slate roof, recently partly modernised. Farm buildings include a thatched barn and an open-sided cart shed. There is also a disused well.		SU 636 403 1620 34
Farmhouse C.18	Pitters Farm. Red brick structure. Thatched roof. Plain casements. Centre panelled door with thatched porch.		SU 636 403 1620 20
Cottage C.18	Hut Cottage. Flint with brick bands and dressings. Thatched roof. Two lattice casement windows. Central boarded door.		SU 635 397 1620 16
Cottage C.18	Sparrows. 2 storeys. Part timber-framed, part white colourwashed brick. Thatched roof. Small latticed upper windows.		SU 636 402 1620 28
Building C.19	Wield School and School House. Red brick structure, with slate roof and three brick built chimneys. The school house is the eastern half of the building. The single school room, with windows facing south, west and north, is on the western side. There is a small bell cope, with bell, over the large southern schoolroom window. A stone inscribed 'W.B.S. 1876' is set in an ornamental brickwork surround beneath the bell-cope. There is a small brickwork porch, with a slate roof on the west side, which leads to the small playground.		SU 631 387 1620 33
Building C.19	Wield Chapel. Situated so close to Church Cottage that it appears to be in the garden, but it does have a narrow frontage with a low railed fence. Brick construction in simple style, just a very small rectangular building with a slate roof and white painted walls. The date 1848 is carved above the south facing door. Two windows in east wall and one in the west wall.		SU 628 387 1620 31

Description and Date	Remarks	Protection	Grid Ref. and Punchcard No.

Group D — (cont.)

Description and Date	Remarks	Protection	Grid Ref. and Punchcard No.
Farmhouse C.19	Lower Wield Farm. 2 storeys. Red brick structure. Hipped tiled roof. Sash windows. Plain projecting brick porch.		SU 635 405 1620 22
Cottage	Pound Cottage. Creamwashed flint and brick dressings. Ridge thatched roof. Modern glazed porch. Part thatched pentice to rear. Recently restored. Formerly two cottages.	T. & C.P. Act	SU 629 387 1620 03
Building	Sherwood Cottage. Red brick with blue headers. Thatched roof. Large modern shop at right angles to house. Now the Post Office and Village Shop.		SU 628 387 1620 08
Cottage	Box Cottage. Limewashed brick walls. Thatched roof. Plain casement windows. So named because letter box was formerly let into roadside wall of house.		SU 629 387 1620 10
Cottage	The Old Post Office. Brick structure, mainly rendered. Thatched roof. Recently extended and extensively modernised.		SU 672 389 1620 12
Cottages (2)	The Yews. Timber-framed with cement infilling and partly flint with brick quoins. Thatched roof. Gable towards road cement rendered.		SU 633 387 1620 13
Cottage	Harrow Cottage. Flint and brick structure. Thatched roof. Three upper windows. Sympathetically restored and modernised. Formerly two cottages.		SU 634 387 1620 15
Cottages (3)	Windmill Cottages. Partly timber-framed with red brick infilling and some stone-work. Sympathetically restored and modernised.		SU 631 401 1620 17
Cottage	The Cottage. Brick structure. Thatched roof with eaves splayed over two upper windows. Plain casement windows. Rear extension.		SU 631 401 1620 19
Cottage	Windmill Cottage. Brick structure. Thatched roof with eaves splayed over upper windows. Plain casement windows. Thatched porch.		SU 636 401 1620 18

Group E — Street Patterns, Street Furniture and Open Spaces

Description and Date	Remarks	Protection	Grid Ref. and Punchcard No.
Pound (Site)	Corner of Village Green and Wield Farm garden. Surrounded on two sides with knapped flint wall.		SU 629 387 1620 26
Stocks (Site)	Corner of Village Green close to the Pound along knapped flint wall. Ref: Wield Parish History, (Mills).		SU 629 387 1620 27
Well (Site)	Kings Farm. Well no longer there, the winding gear is now in Alton Museum. Ref: Wield Parish History, (Mills).		SU 636 398 1620 29

Description and Date	Remarks	Protection	Grid Ref. and Punchcard No.

Group E — (cont.)

Description and Date	Remarks	Protection	Grid Ref. and Punchcard No.
Village Well	Wield Manor garden. 300 ft. deep and protected by shelter roof. Early C.20 wheels and winding gear. Ref: Wield Parish History, (Mills).		SU 628 388 1620 25
Village Pond	Upper Wield. Until about 150 years ago was the sole source of water in the village, except for rainwater, for both villagers and their cattle.		SU 629 388 1620 30
Boundary Marker	Pug Dell, Wield Wood Estate. Chalkpit, mentioned in Saxon Land Charter of Edward the Elder as the "Twin bottomed pits". Ref: Wessex Charters (Finberg).		SU 624 395 1620 24

WORLDHAM

The parish of Worldham lies about two and a half miles south east of Alton. Its lofty situation gives it fine views both to Alton, towards the Surrey hills, and the Sussex Downs.

East Worldham church dates from the twelfth century, though it was restored in 1865. Inside the church on the south wall there is an effigy thought to represent Philippa, wife of Geoffrey Chaucer, whose son Thomas was Lord of the Manor from 1418 to 1434. To the south-east of the village is the isolated King John's Hill on whose summit King John had one of his hunting lodges.

The small church of West Worldham also dates back to Norman times. The east window is in the perpendicular style and the timber porch is fifteenth century.

Also included in the parish is the lost village of Hartley Mauditt. The church has a beautiful south doorway constructed about 1190. The chancel was built in the early thirteenth century and contains a number of memorials with interesting heraldry. The font is fifteenth century.

12th Century Church and Hartley Pond, Hartley Mauditt, WORLDHAM

Description and Date	Remarks	Protection	Grid Ref. and Punchcard No.

Group A — Natural Features

Description and Date	Remarks	Protection	Grid Ref. and Punchcard No.
View	Public Footpath No. 25 on 1975 diverted route along top of Worldham/Warners Hanger.		SU 749 372 — 750 375 1621 26
Site of Ecological Interest	Candovers Farm Pit. Rare exposure of the fossiliferous malmstone, Upper Greensand, Lower Cretaceous.	N.P. Act S.S.S.I.	SU 752 359 1621 30
Trees	Binswood Common. Several different species standing in the area centred on grid reference.	T.P.O. No. 1 E.H.D.C.	SU 765 371 1621 31
Area of Scenic Beauty	Part of the East Hants area of natural beauty. Includes the Wick Hill Hanger which is an attractive wooded area.	N.P. Act A.O.N.B.	SU 757 355 1621 32

Group B — Archaeological

Bronze Age

Description and Date	Remarks	Protection	Grid Ref. and Punchcard No.
Bowl Barrow (Remains)	Littlewood Copse. Heavily overgrown. Ploughed out on south side. O.S.A. No. SU73 NW19.		SU 737 367 1621 23

Roman

Description and Date	Remarks	Protection	Grid Ref. and Punchcard No.
Building (Site)	St. Marys Churchyard. Square hypocaust tiles and fragments of flue tiles found 1945. O.S.A. No. SU73 NE24. Ref: 1. Farnham Herald 14.9.45 2. Annual Report Curtis Museum, Alton, 1945. 3. Alice Holt Forest; its history and Romano-British Potteries, (Wade).		SU 750 381 1621 25

Post Norman

Description and Date	Remarks	Protection	Grid Ref. and Punchcard No.
Occupation Site	King Johns Hill. Flat-topped, with steep slopes, heavily wooded and in thick undergrowth. Iron Age settlement site and traditional site of mediaeval hunting lodge and later buildings. O.S.A. No. SU73 NE4. Ref: P.H.F.C., Vol. 14, 1938—40, p. 398.	S.A.M. No. 322	SU 755 377 1621 22
Mediaeval Village (Site)	West or Little Worldham. Belonged to Hamble Priory, bought 1414 by Winchester College. In 1428 had less than 10 tenants. Hundred = Alton. Ref: V.C.H., Vol. 2, p.p. 471, 508, 521—3.		SU 743 370 1621 29
Mediaeval Village Site	Hartley Mauditt. Classed as village in 1316 and from the late C.14 property of the Duchy of Lancaster. Village street, now minor metalled road, ran from Jeffries Farm to Hartley Pond. Sites of about ten cottages indicated by slight platforms. O.S.A. No. SU73 NW30. Ref: 1. Lost villages of England, 1954, (Beresford), p.p. 274, 353. 2. V.C.H., Vol. 2, p.p. 508—10.	S.A.M. No. 167	SU 742 362 1621 24

Description and Date	Remarks	Protection	Grid Ref. and Punchcard No.

Group C — Footpaths and Bridleways

Ancient Trackway	Section of Roman road, Fishbourne/Silchester crossing northern boundary of parish near Pookles Lane and eastern boundary at Hartleywood Farm.		SU 755 385 — 766 360 1621 27
Ancient Lane	Water Lane. Part of pre-turnpike route between Selborne and Alton, via West Worldham. Characteristic deeply sunken ancient lane on the greensand.		SU 740 369 1621 33

Group D — Buildings, Monuments and Engineering Works

Church C.12	Hartley Mauditt. Norman nave with plain chancel arch. Octagon font of C.15 date, carved with horshoe badge. Interesting C.17 monuments to the Stuart family. O.S.A. No. SU73 NW31. Ref: Buildings of England; Hants and I.O.W., (Pevsner and Lloyd), p. 273.	T. & C.P. Act	SU 743 361 1621 06
Church C.12	St. Mary. Originally small Transitional Church. Nave rebuilt 1865 using old material. Apse replaced by modern east wall. O.S.A. No. SU73 NE25. Ref: V.C.H., Vol. 2, p.p. 520—1.	T. & C.P. Act	SU 750 381 1621 20
Church C.13	St. Nicholas. Rebuilt 1888 on the old foundations. C.15 porch protects Norman south doorway. Jambs of former lancets in the east wall. O.S.A. No. SU73 NW6. Ref: Buildings of England; Hants and I.O.W., (Pevsner and Lloyd), p. 649.	T. & C.P. Act	SU 741 370 1621 09
Farmhouse C.17	Old House. 2 storeys. Stuccoed facade. Tiled roof. Timber-framed with brick infilling at the back. Sash windows.		SU 748 381 1621 13
Farmhouse C.17	Pullens. Formerly West Worldham Farm. Single storey with four Victorian flat roofed half dormers. Red brick walls. Steep pitched ridge tiled roof. Stone walled garden. Dated 1652.		SU 742 368 1621 07
Farmhouse C.17/18	Candovers Farm. Restored. Red brick, partly coursed stone blocks. Exposed timberwork in attics of half hipped gables. Plain casement windows.	N.P. Act A.O.N.B.	SU 755 358 1621 21
House C.18	Round House, Hartley Mauditt. Octagonal brick structure. Modern conical tiled roof. Single storey additions to rear. Originally a lodge or toll house.		SU 734 366 1621 03
Farmhouse C.18	Hartley Park Farm, Hartley Mauditt. 2 storeys. Coursed stone blocks. Ridge tiled roof. Sash windows.		SU 738 358 1621 02

Description and Date	Remarks	Protection	Grid Ref. and Punchcard No.
Group D — (cont.)			
Farmhouse and Dovecot C.18	Truncheaunts Farm. 2 storeys. Red brick walls. Hipped tiled roof. Sash windows. Probably site of mediaeval manor house. Dovecot, probably C.17. Rectangular stone structure with brick dressings. O.S.A. No. 73 NW16. Ref: V.C.H., Vol. 2, p.p. 478—9.		SU 727 379 1621 01
Farmhouse C.18	Manor Farm, West Worldham. 2 storeys. Red brick with occasional blue headers. Steep hipped tiled roof. Sash windows. Panelled door with rectangular fanlight and projecting hood.		SU 740 370 1621 08
House C.18	East Worldham House. Formerly the Vicarage. Altered in C.19. Rectangular building of coursed stone blocks. Hipped slate roof with spreading eaves. Sash windows.		SU 750 380 1621 19
House C.19	Hartley Mauditt. Formerly the Rectory. 2 storeys. Stuccoed walls. Steep hipped slate roof. Porch with fluted columns. Limewashed brick wing to rear.		SU 742 365 1621 05
Farmhouse	Jeffries Farm. Timber-framing exposed in places, with brick infilling. Partly coursed stone blocks at one end and to rear. Thatched roof. Pentice at back towards road.		SU 742 364 1621 04
Cottage	Heather Cottage. 2 storeys. Exposed timber-work with plaster infilling. Thatched roof. Modern extension at rear. Semi dormers.		SU 752 380 1621 18
Cottage	Marshalls. 2 storeys. Timber-framed with brick infilling. Tiled roof. Modernised.	T. & C.P. Act	SU 754 380 1621 17
Cottages (2)	Manor Farm Cottages. 2 storeys to left, one storey to right. Red brick with timber-framing exposed in places. Thatched roof.		SU 749 370 1621 12
Cottages (3)	Sandles Farm. 2 storeys. Brick with random stonework, tile-hung to left. Stepped tiled roof with half-hipped gable at corner. Modern casements.		SU 749 380 1621 11
Cottage	Nos. 5 and 6, Blanket Street. 2 storeys. Timber-framed with red brick infilling to left. Coursed stone blocks with brick dressings to right. Thatched roof. Now one dwelling.	T. & C.P. Act	SU 747 380 1621 10